SUBSTANTIVE DUE PROCESS OF LAW

A Dichotomy of Sense and Nonsense

SUBSTANTIVE DUE PROCESS OF LAW

A Dichotomy of Sense and Nonsense

Frank R. Strong
Cary C. Boshamer University
Distinguished Professor, Emeritus
University of North Carolina
at Chapel Hill

Carolina Academic Press
Durham, North Carolina

Carolina Academic Press
P.O. Box 8795
Forest Hills Station
Durham, North Carolina 27707

Contents

Preface

This study results from my conviction that, much as has been taught and written on Substantive Due Process of Law, the level of scholarship has been disappointing. I include my own contributions in this criticism; it is disquieting to look back on the occasional misunderstandings and misperceptions that crop up on rereading. With notable exception, other scholars of the Constitution have outdone me in their misjudgments, as subsequent analysis will demonstrate. As a group we constitutionalists cannot take pride in the quality of our scholarly product respecting the topic of substantive due process. Deficiencies include errors of commission and omission within the ambit of genuine constitutional interpretation, of disregard for historic meaning to the opposite extreme of indulgence in spurious noninterpretivism, of failure to comprehend the office of due process as constitutional sword as well as constitutional shield. The present project seeks to "set the record" straight on this central feature in American Constitutional Law before a doctrinal *res judicata* protects inaccuracy beyond recall.

The early version of this work to 1900 was designed for inclusion in a volume of essays honoring Eugene Victor Rostow, to which eighteen friends and admirers contributed. The entire project, revised and extended to the present, is dedicated to the memory of (William) Underhill Moore and Charles Clifford Callahan.* These two remarkable men of the law, possessed of the keen-

---

* Eugene Rostow has had a distinguished career as legal educator and public servant. A contemporary of his, with unusual parallels in our early and mid careers—Yale College, Yale Law School, Editors-in-Chief of the Yale Law Journal, extended public law teaching, and law school deanships—I accepted with appreciation the invitation to join others in tribute to his accomplishments. The essays in his honor, edited by colleagues Myres McDougal and Michael Reisman, are published by Martinus Nijhoff of The Hague in a volume entitled POWER AND POLICY IN QUEST OF LAW (1985).

Enticement of Underhill Moore to the Yale law faculty was one of Robert Hutchins' major achievements during his short yet momentous tenure as Dean of the Yale Law School. Professor Moore's unique teaching method through "supposititious cases" created a stimulating learning experience for those of us who struggled to follow him in his brilliant leadership into four-dimensional analysis of commercial transactions. One left his classes mentally exhausted but emotionally charged with a growing sense of reflective intellectual power. It was an enduring influence to have been a student of this great preceptor.

After receiving his first degree in law with high honors at Ohio State, Charles Callahan

est of legal minds, shaped my thinking about legal concerns. To them I owe much of whatever skills of insight and overview will be found in this effort to leave a faithful appraisal of an ancient theme bloodied and battered by the vicissitudes of time and change.

To the Wettach Library of the University of North Carolina School of Law my indebtedness is great. With occasional "assists" from the university's Davis Library, the collection has met the demands made upon it. Library staff personnel have been unfailing in their professional assistance. I also express gratitude to the School of Law for its generous policy of providing office space and secretarial services to faculty emeriti who desire to remain in the academic environment following retirement. Without such a base, ready access to needed source materials, and the proficiency of reference specialists my objective could not have been attained. Yet even with these essential aids my greatest debt is to Gertrude Way Strong, my partner in all undertakings, who sacrificed endless hours of companionship over a period of five years to allow me to carry to fruition this challenge to conventional scholarship respecting one of the crucial inheritances at the heart of Constitutional Law.

---

went East to pursue graduate law study. At Yale he earned the J. S.D. degree, attained faculty status, and became closely associated with Underhill Moore in fundamental legal research. The product of this collaboration was the celebrated New Haven traffic study, reported in the Yale Law Journal for December, 1943, as Moore and Callahan, *Law and Learning Theory: A Study in Legal Control.* Ridiculed by many who could not grasp the ingenuity of the endeavor, this undertaking was the pioneer venture in investigation *about* law, in inquiry into the efficacy of law as a mechanism of social control. After seven years at Yale, Charles Callahan returned to Ohio State as a member of the faculty of the College of Law. Fortunately for me, we were assigned adjoining offices where for a decade I profited from continuing contact with his brilliant mind. His major academic interests were in private law; students admired his uncanny ability to "unwind" for them the technical law of Property. Yet he was equally remarkable for his grasp of the instability of public law. In my many appeals to him for critical assistance in search for first principles of constitutional design, he never failed to respond with flashes of insight that illumined the way. One of many "findings" thus made possible, first seen but dimly through clouded vision, was the multi-dimensional nature of the historic guaranty from Magna Carta on which the present study is based.

ACKNOWLEDGEMENT

In the processing of this volume for publication, the personnel of Carolina Academic Press have been technically most skillful and professionally ever accommodating. Especially to be commended is Mr. Andrew Wilson who, as editorial assistant on the project, has been painstaking and responsive at every stage in production from manuscript to index.

PART I

ENGLISH ORIGINS OF SUBSTANTIVE DUE PROCESS OF LAW

1. Seedtime in the Mother Country

Magna Carta: Limitations on Crown Prerogative

Only in a technical sense can an adequate account of substantive due process commence with concentration on chapter 39 of Magna Carta, the language of which reads thusly in a recent translation:

> No freeman shall be arrested, or detained in prison, or deprived of his freehold, or in any way molested; and we will not set forth against him, nor send against him, unless by the lawful judgment of his peers and by the law of the land.[1]

The fact Magna Carta was wrung from John by virtue of superior baronial military might makes clear that its chapters represented relief from the excesses of the reigning King and his two immediate predecessors. It is therefore necessary for perspective to go back in time to the Coronation Charter of Henry I.[2] Also known as a Charter of Liberties it was granted by him on acceding to the throne in 1100, but 34 years after the Norman Conquest. In fourteen clauses this first charter ever granted by an English monarch enumerated specific feudal rights of the King's tenants *in capite* and possibly as well of further tenants in the chain of subinfeudation.[3] The nature of the re-

---

1. F. BOSSELMAN, D. CALLIES & J. BANTON, THE TAKING ISSUE 56 (1973). This study was made for the Council on Environmental Quality and published by the U.S. Printing Office. Differences in other translations are noted *infra* note 8.

The last three Latin words—per legem terrae—translated into English as "law of the land" became shorthand for the full text of Chapter 39. In his SECOND INSTITUTE ON THE LAWS OF ENGLAND 50 (published posthumously in 1642 by order of the House of Commons) Sir Edward Coke treated "law of the land" and "due process of law" as interchangeable in meaning. Use of "law of the land" was extensive in early America and continues to this day in eleven State constitutions in preference to "due process of law." First appearing in the wording of the Fifth Amendment to the Constitution of the United States in 1791, the term Due Process has become dominant. Note, however, the title Sir Arthur Goodhart gave to his article on Magna Carta, cited *infra* note 15. The original wording is also used by Berger, *"Law of the Land" Reconsidered,* 74 NW. U. L. REV. 1 (1979).

2. 1 STATUTES OF THE REALM 1-2, with engraving (reprint of 1963).

3. Under feudalism land was not *owned* as in the alloidial concept that obtains in mod-

lational interests that made up the body of feudal law lent substantive caste to many of these recognized rights.

> The charter begins with an admission that the kingdom has been oppressed by unjust exactions and ends on a note of warning that unjustly acquired property must be returned to its legitimate owner. Within this framework statements favoring the protection of property abound.[4]

It was the increasing intrusions upon these rights by Henry II and his sons Richard and John that fueled the revolt of the barons in 1214-15. Joined by those merchants and burgesses of London who opened the gates of the city to them, the barons forced the capitulation of John at Runnymede in 1215. What the barons demanded was in great part restoration of the feudal rights vouchsafed to them by the Coronation Charter. Magna Carta responded to the demand with both specific and broad guarantees. Of the latter, that on which attention has been forever riveted is chapter 39.

However, as recognized by an outstanding scholar on Magna Carta, chapter 39, "in so far as it relates to illegal disseisins," was "supplemented" by chapter 52 which provided remedy for those dispossessed by the Crown.[5] As translated by McKechnie, the first sentence reads:

> If any one has been dispossessed or removed by us, without the legal judgment of his peers, from his lands, castles, franchises, or from his right, we will immediately restore them to him; and if a dispute arise over this, then let it be decided by the five-and-twenty barons of whom mention is made below in the clause for securing the peace.[6]

A second sentence makes essentially the same guarantee to those dispossessed "by our father, King Henry, or by our brother, King Richard, and which we retain in our hand (or which are possessed by others, to whom we are bound to warrant them). . . ."[7]

---

ern times; it was *possessed* on the basis of relational interests held in it. Thus the "first line" of barons owed fealty, military service, and other obligations to the King, who in turn owed them protection from enemies. By subinfeudation these chief tenants would make similar arrangements with others below them in the chain. All land was held by virtue of some form of tenure; the main tenures were military and socage. Chattels, however, were not the subject of tenure capable of carving into estates. A concise explanation of feudal laws is to be found in F. MAITLAND, CONSTITUTIONAL HISTORY OF ENGLAND 23-39 (1955) (The Land-System).

4. G. DIETZE, MAGNA CARTA AND PROPERTY 10 (1965) (The Magna Carta Commission of Virginia).

5. W. MCKECHNIE, MAGNA CARTA 449 (1958).

6. *Id.* at 448.

7. *Ibid.* The same distinction between unlawful disseisins by John and those by his brother and father is made by Chapters 56 and 57 with respect to "lands or liberties, or other things" of Welshmen. Contrast Chapter 55, which makes no such distinction in promising remission of all fines and amercements made or imposed "unjustly and against the law of the land." This commitment is limited to "us," *i.e.,* John.

The presence of chapter 52 in the Great Charter would seem to resolve in the affirmative the question whether chapter 39 was intended to protect substantive property rights. Despite this, the view persists among many constitutional lawyers that the original intendment of chapter 39 was to provide procedural protection. Support for this position has largely derived from the excepting clause that closes the chapter: except/unless by the lawful judgment of his peers and/or by the law of the land.[8] To many of a later time the reference seems clearly to have been to jury trials[9] or to the writ of habeas corpus.[10] But the assumption is too quickly made, even without reference to chapter 52. Holdsworth is authority for the judgment that

> It is not difficult to show that taken literally, these interpretations are false. Trial by jury was as yet in its infancy. The writ of Habeas Corpus was not yet invented; and ... it was long after it was invented that it was applied to protect the liberty of the subject.[11]

Rather, the clauses of the chapter

> do embody a protest against arbitrary punishment, and against arbitrary infringements of personal liberty and rights of property; they do assert a right to a free trial, to a pure and unbought measure of justice.[12]

This view is elaborated by Charles McIlwain, eminent constitutional historian. In his original analysis he reasoned that if his conclusions were correct,

> we must give up the view that the original intent of Magna Carta was to guarantee trial by jury to anyone or to guarantee anything to all Englishmen. We must accept a feudal interpretation of the document as the only one possible in 1215; but we may still hold, as our fathers did, that the law of the land is there, *lex pro tyrannica voluntate,* to invert the words of the Waverley annalist, and we shall still mean by

---

8. There is disagreement respecting translation of all parts of the Chapter. Thus Holt renders it:

> No free man shall be taken or imprisoned or disseised or outlawed or exiled or in any way ruined, nor will we go or send against him, except by the lawful judgment of his peers or by the law of the land.

J. HOLT, MAGNA CARTA 327 (1965). Compare G. DAVIS, MAGNA CARTA 21 (1963) (published by the Trustees of the British Museum):

> No free man shall be seized or imprisoned, or stripped of his rights or possessions, or outlawed or exiled, or deprived of his standing in any other way, nor will we proceed with force against him, or send others to do so, except by the lawful judgement of his equals or by the law of the land.

9. *E.g.* B. BARRINGTON, MAGNA CARTA 321 (1900); E. DUMBAULD, THE BILL OF RIGHTS 90 (1965).

10. *E.g.* 1 W. CHURCH, A TREATISE ON THE WRIT OF HABEAS CORPUS § 2 (1893); E. INGERSOLL, THE HISTORY AND LAW OF THE WRIT OF HABEAS CORPUS 1 (1849).

11. 2 W. HOLDSWORTH, A HISTORY OF ENGLISH LAW 215 (4th ed. 1936, reprinted 1966). Accord on habeas corpus: Crawford, *The Writ of Habeas Corpus,* 42 AMER. L. REV. 481, at 482 (1908).

12. *Ibid.*

the law of the land substantially what old Roger Twysden meant,—"nothing else but those immunities the subject hath ever enjoyed as his owne right, perteyning either to his person or his goods; and the grownd that hee doth so is, that they are allowed him by the law of the land, which the king alone can not at his owne will alter, and therefore can not take them from him, they beeing as auntient as the kingdom itselfe, which the king is to protect."[13]

When permission was later sought to reprint the analysis, Professor McIlwain consented provided an Additional Note were added. In this he observed by way of closing summary, after consideration of intervening published scholarship supportive of a procedural interpretation, that

the conclusions set forth in the original article still hold good, I think, for the interpretation of Magna Carta as a whole, and for all the events and documents which led up to it. What I would now add merely is, that the words per legale judicium parium suorum vel per legem terrae at the end of chapter 39 are not *in themselves* a reference to this broader principle, but to a narrower and more specific safeguard for it in securing a judgment by proper arbiters, either by the fellow tenants of the barons themselves, or by competent royal judges from among those "qui sciant legem terrae et eam bene velint observare," as the barons demanded in section 42 of their Articles.[14]

Strong support for the Holdsworth-McIlwain position has lately come from two recognized constitutional historians writing for the *Magna Carta Essays.* Sir Arthur Goodhart quotes approvingly[15] the conclusion of Powicke

that the thirty-ninth clause was intended to lay stress not so much on any particular form of trial as on the necessity for protection against the arbitrary acts of imprisonment, disseisin, and outlawry in which King John had indulged.[16]

Appeals were not cast in procedural terms alone; other contentions respecting English liberties were either clearly substantive or procedurally oriented to substantive ends. In the words of Professor Goodhart following his above quotation,

It was because the words "law of the land" were given this broad interpretation that Magna Carta became one of the greatest constitutional documents in all history.[17]

---

13. McIlwain, *Due Process of Law in Magna Carta,* 14 Col. L. Rev. 27, at 51 (1914).

14. McIlwain, *supra* note 13, reprinted with Additional Note, 1 Sel. Essays on Constitutional Law 174, at 203 (1938).

15. A. L. Goodhart, *Law of the Land* 3, at 23, in Magna Carta Essays (Howard, ed.) (1966).

16. F. M. Powicke, *Par Judicium Parium vel per Legem Terrae* 96, at 103, in Magna Carta Essays (Howard, ed.) (1966). Published for the Magna Carta Commission of Virginia.

17. Goodhart, *supra* note 15.

Taken in historical perspective, the thrust of chapter 39 was substantive—the ban on invasion of "ancient" rights of personal liberty and feudal property as understood by a select group of equals knowledgeable in the law of the land. As between the two types of rights, a recent study insists that "the protection of property is probably the outstanding feature of Magna Carta."[18] This conclusion is based on the "overwhelming number" of chapters relating to "property" as contrasted with "liberty."[19] The same was true of the Coronation Charter; and the intervening struggle was largely in terms of continuing baronial complaint over encroachments of feudal rights sounding basically in "property."

The protections of property sought by Magna Carta and its early confirmations[20] were normally from royal invasion. However, there also were instances of taking from one individual for the benefit of another. One authority makes general reference to this occurrence.[21] Particularization is found in two other sources. Faith Thompson, one of the most reliable commentators on Magna Carta, states that:

> In the reign of Edward III [Chap.29] was made the basis for a petition against arrest or disseisin simply on petition or suggestion to the king or his counsel [sic] by powerful individuals. Procedure must be according to the law of the land, and to this age the law of the land meant the use of the presenting jury.[22]

She cites[23] to a constitutional history of England in which this instance of 1352 and "similar cases" are reported.[24] The specific case is there described as an "appeal to the thirty-ninth article of the charter" [sic] insisting

> that except on indictment or presentment of a jury no man shall be ousted of his freehold by petition to the king or council; the king grants the request.[25]

A clear instance of lawless transfer of property among subjects of the Crown occurred in 1399 at the close of the reign of Richard II. To resolve a bitter antagonism between Thomas Mowbray, duke of Norfolk, and Henry Bolingbroke, earl of Hereford, the King banished each for life. Upon the banishment of Henry, who was of the House of Lancaster, Richard divided the bulk of Lancastrian lands among his favorites. In comment on this action, a historian of the English Fourteenth Century has observed that

---

18. F. BOSSELMAN, D. CALLIES & J. BANTON, *op. cit. supra* note 1, at 33.

19. *Id.* at 33-38.

20. In the reissue of 1225, consolidation and omission resulted in renumbering Cap. 39 as Cap. 29. Chapters 52, 55, 56, and 57 disappeared.

21. G. DIETZE, *op. cit. supra* note 4, at 38, n. 78.

22. F. THOMPSON, THE FIRST CENTURY OF MAGNA CARTA 63 (1925, reissued 1967).

23. *Id.* at 63, n. 117.

24. 2 W. STUBBS, CONSTITUTIONAL HISTORY OF ENGLAND 637 (1896, reprinted 1967).

25. *Id.* at 637–38. Although no instance has been found of record, it seems reasonable to believe that in turn barons emulated the Crown in unlawfully seizing incidents of land tenure or non-feudal chattels from those below them in the system of subinfeudation.

the sentence on Hereford made it plain to every property owner in the country that here was a king in whose hands the most indefeasible of all rights, the right of inheritance, was no longer safe.[26]

The lands were restored to their former owners when Henry took advantage of Richard's second foray into Ireland to reenter England, force the abdication of Richard, and take the throne as Henry IV, the first of the Lancaster line. History appears to record no appeal to Magna Carta either to condemn the taking or to justify the retaking. Yet the actions involved would seem clearly to fall within the protective mantle of chapter 29.

Whether or not a matter of cause and effect, the instance of 1352 was followed in 1354 by a major confirmation[27] on the part of Edward III. Henry IV, in an effort to restore order in the kingdom, confirmed six times in his fifteen years. From 1415 to Elizabeth's accession to the throne in 1558, further confirmations abounded. Coke estimated that in all there had been thirty since 1215. Thompson is certain there were more.[28] Their explanation cannot wholly lie in anticipation of violation of Magna Carta, especially chapter 29; more realistic is the view that many of them were attempts at deterrence after repeated violation. The principle against arbitrary takings by the sovereign remained steadfast. In practice, on the other hand, it was difficult with strong monarchs to establish that principle as the fundamental law of the land.

Meantime, English monarchs had long exercised the prerogative of issuing patents and franchises granting privileges of various kinds. Initially these letters-patent as they were first known in England served constructive purposes; illustrations were liberalization of trade and encouragement of introductions of new arts from the Continent.[29] But with Elizabeth abuses developed culminating in her use of them as reward to her favorites. Grants of this type fast became known as monopolies. Among the monopoly grants of disadvantage to all save the favored patentee were those in leather, yarn, paper, playing cards, salt, vinegar, starch, tin, horns, bags, stone pots, currants, saltpeter, and wines.[30] Catherine Bowen in her volume on the life of Coke[31] reports that

---

26. M. McKisack, *The Fourteenth Century*, in 5 Oxford History of England 490 (1959).

27. The major confirmation between that of Henry III in 1225 and of Edward III was in 1297 by Edward I.

28. F. Thompson, Magna Carta chap. 1 (1948).

29. Outstanding was the patent for improvement in the making of glass granted in 1567. Although glass had been produced in England throughout the Middle Ages, Europe now had the better technology. S. Jack, Trade and Industry in Tudor and Stuart History 91 (1977).

30. Most items are listed in W. Price, The English Patents of Monopoly chap. 1 (1906). H. Fox, Monopolies and Patents 314-15 (1947), sets out two lists in Appendices II and III. Two patents for the taking of saltpeter were granted by Elizabeth in 1589, a third shortly after her death by James I. There is an account of these in 8 Viners Abridgement 567-568 (1748).

31. C. D. Bowen, The Lion and The Throne (1956).

toward the end of Elizabeth's reign "Abuse had grown beyond all bounds," depriving artisans of employment to the point of serious economic distress.[32] Thompson[33] notes that "Opposition to monopolies was voiced in parliament in 1597 and again in 1601 when a bill was introduced and extensively debated."[34] Indeed, the second of these parliamentary sessions was dubbed the "Parliament of the Monopolies," because "Commons moved to block the royal right of granting to private persons monopolies or patents such as Essex had enjoyed in wines, and Ralegh in playing-cards."[35]

Several of the disliked Elizabethan grants led to litigation challenging the Queen's prerogative. *Matter of Cavendish*[36] concerned the exclusive patent to Richard Cavendish of writing all writs of *supersedeas* in the Court of Common Pleas. The Judges refused to admit the patentee to this office, whereupon of course the Queen remonstrated. The Judges' defense was that "they could not lawfully act" as Her Majesty had ordered because "it might be that by such sequestration others alleging the right to make these writs, might be disseised of their freehold, claimed by them in the making of these writs and fees thereupon."[37] In their rejoinder to the Queen's second remonstrance they predicated their refusal to act on the ground the royal orders were contrary to *le ley de terre.* Cited in support were chapter 29 of the reissue of the Great Charter in 1225 and the Confirmation of 1354.[38]

Matter of Cavendish was shortly followed by *Davenant v. Hurdis.*[39] Davenant, a member of the Merchant Tailors Company chartered in 1502, had violated a by-law of the guild for which he had been fined. Upon his refusal to pay the fine the Company had instructed Hurdis to seize from him goods equal in value to the fine. Davenant thereupon brought an action of trespass in King's Bench. Report of the case largely in Norman French makes comment hazardous. It is clear that Coke, at the time Attorney General, supported Davenant, declaring that while some by-laws are in the public good, by-laws that establish monopolies are against common law and void.[40] The immediately preceding sentence makes reference to "le liberty del grand charter" but in what respect is not certain. Of possible bearing is the fact that Moore, who defended Hurdis, conceded that the by-law would be void if it created a monopoly but denied this was its consequence. Coke appears to be thinking of a type of imprisonment that arguably is contrary to chapter 29 of Magna Carta.

---

32. *Id.* at 172.
33. F. Thompson, *op. cit. supra* note 28.
34. *Id.* at 228.
35. C. D. Bowen, *op. cit. supra* note 31, at 172.
36. 1 Anderson 152, 123 Eng. Rep. 403 (Common Bench 1587), translated in 1 J. B. Thayer, Cases on Constitutional Law 12 (1895).
37. *Id.* at 12-13 (Thayer).
38. *Id.* at 14-15 (Thayer).
39. Moore 576, 72 Eng. Rep. 769 (K. B. 1599).
40. *Id.* at 580, 72 Eng. Rep. at 772.

If so, any connection with by-laws establishing monopolies is remote. However, the reference may mark the faint beginnings of his later assertion that in two respects monopoly grants constituted a violation of the Great Charter. Whatever the intendment of Coke's argument, Davenant took judgment *per touts les Justices* that "a rule of such nature as to bring all trade or traffic into the hands of one company, or one person, and to exclude all others, is illegal."[41]

Far better known in English constitutional history is the *Case of Monopolies*[42] wherein King's Bench, shortly after Elizabeth's death, rejected as void her exclusive grant to Edward Darcy of the importation and manufacture of playing cards. In support of the monopoly, effort was made to show it to be meritorious as a measure to curtail "idle games with cards" but the fact Darcy had been a favorite of the Queen overrode this rationalization. It was

> resolved by Popham, Chief Justice, *et per totam curiam* that the said grant to [Darcy] of the sole making of cards within the realm was utterly void, and that for two reasons: —
> 1. That it is a monopoly, and against the common law.
> 2. That it is against divers Acts of Parliament.[43]

In Coke's extensive reporting of the Court's reasoning, there appears no reference to chapter 29. Nevertheless, both civil and English common law are declared to be opposed to monopoly, while statutes of Elizabeth's reign are cited as having been enacted "for advancement of freedom of trade." On this view the momentous decision is grounded on anti-monopoly's reciprocal; "Darcy's patent was held void on the argument that it violated the rights of others to carry on their trade."[44] Noy's report of the case,[45] which purports to give the complete argument of Fuller, stresses Fuller's contention of a liberty of recreation for all subjects. Thompson is of the view that this argument was bottomed on chapter 29. For support she points out that Fuller's contention is subheaded, significantly, "Nicholas Fuller and 'Liberty of the Subject' *versus* Monopolies." The emphasis is hers.[46]

Some years after the *Case of Monopolies* King's Bench, of which Lord Coke was now Chief Justice, decided the *Case of the Taylors, &c of Ipswich*.[47] A King's grant had given them exclusive right to "work cloth" in the town; no one else could engage in this occupation except after seven years of apprenticeship. Defendant had violated the exclusionary provision, yet prevailed on

---

41. Translation of Letwin, *The English Common Law Concerning Monopolies*, 21 U. CHI. L. REV. 355, 362 (1954).
42. Darcy v. Allein (Allen), 11 Co. 84b, 77 Eng. Rep. 1260 (K. B. 1603) (action on the case, Darcy seeking £2,000 for defendant's infringement on his monopoly).
43. *Id.* at 86a, 77 Eng. Rep. at 1262.
44. Letwin, *supra* note 41, at 363.
45. Darcy v. Allin, Noy 173, 74 Eng. Rep. 1131 (K. B. 1603).
46. F. THOMPSON, *op. cit. supra* note 28, at 228-30.
47. 11 Co. 53a, 77 Eng. Rep. 1218 (K. B. 1615).

the trial because it was against the common law. Again there was no cited dependence on chapter 29. However, in his commentaries on Magna Carta, Cap. 29, in the *Second Institute* Coke wrote:[48]

> So likewise, and for the same reason, if a graunt be made to any man, to have the sole making of cards, or the sole dealing with any other trade, that graunt is against the liberty and freedome of the subject, that before did, or lawfully might have used that trade, and consequently against this great charter.
>
> Generally all monopolies are against this great charter, because they are against the liberty and freedome of the subject, and against the law of the land.[49]

An Elizabethan grant litigated shortly after *Ipswich* cited that decision in a judgment for the defendant. There had been brought against him, by "the fellowship of the weavers of Newbury," an action of debt for violation of an ordinance adopted on the authorization included in letters-patent from the Queen." The grant from Elizabeth ordained "that none should exercise the trade of weaving within the said town, except he were first admitted thereto" by the fellowship. The ordinance provided that unless so admitted "no person should use the said art of weaving within the said town, except he had been an apprentice to the art within the said town, and had used it there by the space of five years before the ordinance." The defendant could not meet either of these restrictions, although an experienced artisan from elsewhere; thus the ordinance gave the fellowship a stranglehold on entry by either foreigners or even apprentices "brought up in the town it self, after the ordinance made, which is absurd." The court observed "that the law (as it now stands) forbids no man to exercise a trade publicly, that hath been an apprentice to it wheresoever. See the case of *The Taylor of Ipswich*, Co. lib. 11. 53."[50]

Agitation over monopoly by patents was intense under James I.[51] The period was marked by added or reissued grants to courtiers, among them hawking, coal, leather, gold and silver thread, cloth, glass, and ale houses. Several developments added insult to injury. Patentees would dispatch spies into the countryside to search out and report infringers. Some patents empowered patentees to arrest and imprison infringers.[52] It is reported there were suits in Star Chamber and Privy Council, where exercises of royal prerogative were likely

---

48. COKE, *op. cit. supra* note 1, at 47.

49. Relying on W. MCKECHNIE, *op. cit. supra* note 5, J. COMMONS, LEGAL FOUNDATIONS OF CAPITALISM 51 (1924), challenged the second paragraph of Coke's statement in the course of criticism of Coke's reliance on the Great Charter as the basis of the liberty and freedom of English subjects. *Id.* at 47-51. Nevertheless, "the error was made in a good cause," that of major contributions to constitutional progress. *Id.* at 51.

50. Norris v. Staps, Hobart 210-13, 80 Eng. Rep. 357-59 (K. B. 1627), citing also "*Darcye's Case* called the Monopolies . . . and in that case *Davenant's case* cited; and *Chamberlain of London's case*, Co. lib. 5, fo. 26.62."

51. H. FOX, *op. cit. supra* note 30, chap. 8, recounts Parliament's growing frustration with James' monopoly grants.

52. C. D. BOWEN, *op. cit. supra* note 31, at 300.

more favorably treated as exertions of the King's authority.[53] Coke's biographer, in opening her chapters on the Parliament of 1621, remarks:

> The monster *monopoly* was strangling trade, reaching its fingers to remote hamlets and affecting the lives of thousands. Nothing less than the concerted voice of the realm could remedy this evil.[54]

A recent study of Coke in Parliament[55] is convincing that he was a major contributor to the development of that "concerted voice." "Coke's attacks on monopolies were so numerous and blunt that his hostility towards monopolistic trading practices is not in doubt."[56] Illustrative is his attack in the House, March 21, 1621, on Sir Robert Flood's patent for the sole engrossing of wills. He declared that

> it was ever the liberty of the subject to engross [his will] himself if he would and bring it to be examined, and so to have the seal put to it. But now by this patent he may neither engross [it] himself nor go to whom he will [to have it engrossed]. He must come to Sir Robert Flood [who] must have his sole engrossing. . . . Here is liberty taken away, an heavy thing. If this be lawful, men may as well be confined to scriveners that none shall make bonds but such a scrivener, and to butchers that we shall buy flesh of none but such an one, which were a miserable servitude.[57]

In support of his attack Coke referred to *Davenant v. Hurdis*[58] of Elizabeth's time. And to Flood's attempt to defend the patent as granted for the purpose of reforming the engrossing of wills, he answered that

> the king's belief that Flood's patent would have beneficial effects did not constitute the ground for a conclusive argument for its legality, because the king had been misinformed about the law and had not known that patent was against Magna Charta and therefore illegal."[59]

That chapter 29 of Magna Carta continued to be considered the bedrock against monopoly grants of no public justification is the conviction of another

---

53. Letwin, *supra* note 41, at 362, citing to H. Fox, *op. cit. supra* 30, at 119.

54. C. D. BOWEN, *op. cit. supra* note 31, at 412-13. Accord: F. THOMPSON, *op. cit. supra* note 28, at 304.

55. S.D. WHITE, SIR EDWARD COKE AND "THE GRIEVANCES OF THE COMMONWEALTH," 1621-1628 (1979).

56. *Id.* at 117 and passim. Coke's opposition extended to grants to boroughs and other corporate bodies as well as to monopoly privileges to private individuals. *Id.* at 119.

57. *Id.* at 122.

58. Considered in the text accompanying note 39, *supra*.

59. S.D. WHITE, *op. cit. supra* note 55, at 122. White, however, finds Coke "softening" in the Parliament of 1628. "Where he had argued against the legality of numerous monopolies in 1621 and 1624, including several not created by royal grant, and had promoted a bill to ban them, in 1628 he merely attacked five of them . . . ." *Id.* at 220. The "most convincing explanation" of Coke's change in attitude White finds in Coke's growing fear of royal power and distrust of the court [of King's Bench]. *Ibid.*

recent commentator. Summarizing the years under the first Stuart, the statement is made that

> [a]nother long-standing grievance in the Commons was monopolies and patents. Magna Carta had been quoted against them even in the reign of Queen Elizabeth I. Once again it was chapter 29 of Henry's Charter that was cited because it was argued that monopolists or patentees, in order to maintain their exclusive privileges, forcibly prevented men from carrying on their legitimate trades, thus depriving free men of their liberties. When in James's third Parliament a Bill was introduced into the Commons for "renewing" Magna Carta or "for the better securing of subjects from wrongful imprisonment and deprivation of trades and occupations contrary to the twenty-ninth chapter," it was aimed at monopolists like Sir Giles Mompesson, who was actually impeached with the King's approval.[60]

So outspoken was Parliamentary opposition that James by Proclamation revoked some of the many monopolies outstanding, among them those regarding pipes, playing cards, stone jugs and pots, and tobacco.[61] These developments were followed three years later by enactment of the Statute of Monopolies.[62] "This was not only the last, it was the most important law passed under King James. Its significance was not so much due to radical innovation as to the emphatic parliamentary sanction which it gave to principles already accepted at common law."[63]

The Statute's primary provisions were two: One was that all monopolies should be determined for validity according to the common law practice. Secondly, monopolies for "new manufacture" were sanctioned for fourteen years, while all other monopolies (*e.g.*, allome, glass, saltpeter) in the form of grants, licenses, and patents for the sole buying, making, working, or using of any commodities within the realm were declared contrary to law. One commentator insists that the Statute "soon put an end to the arbitrary granting of private monopolies."[64] Others, however, are correct in declaring that monopoly grants continued rife under Charles I, who succeeded his father in 1625.[65] Much of this was the result of the Statute's fifteen exceptions to the general prohibition and of an expansion of the jurisdiction of Star Chamber where infringers were subjected to severe penalties for daring to challenge the favored patentees. But more it was the range of exclusive rights sold after Charles had

---

60. M. Ashley, *Magna Carta in the Seventeenth Century* 3, at 16, in Magna Carta Essays (Howard, ed.) (1965). *Cf.* note 16. To like effect is a passage in F. Relf, The Petition of Right 20 (1917) (University of Minnesota Studies in the Social Sciences 8).

61. H. Fox, *op. cit. supra* note 30, Appendix VIII. Monopolies in beer and soap were especially irksome.

62. 21 Jac. I, cap. 3, conveniently reproduced in W. Price, *op. cit. supra* note 30, App. A; H. Fox, *op. cit. supra* note 30, at 338-42. S.D. White, *op. cit. supra* note 55, at 128-35, details Coke's heavy involvement in passage of this milestone.

63. W. Price, *op. cit. supra* note 30, at 33-34.

64. Letwin, *supra* note 41, at 367.

65. H. Fox, *op. cit. supra* note 30, entitles his Chapter 10 "Resurgence of Monopolies Under Charles I."

dissolved Parliament in 1629 and attempted to rule without it; one historian has called the situation "incredible."[66] Ironically, the monopoly denied Darcy was now given to the Company of Card Makers.[67]

Edward Coke's death occurred in 1634, approximately midway in the period of Charles' autocratic rule. During the eventful years of the first third of what was the most momentous century in English constitutional history, he was a towering figure as successively chief justice of two major courts, an influential member of Parliament in some of its most fateful sessions, and author of the then leading work on English law. For her outstanding biography of Coke, Catherine Drinker Bowen chose well to entitle it *The Lion and The Throne*. It was he who gave permanence to the concept of "due process by law" by asserting its equivalency to *per legem terrae* of chapter 29 of Magna Carta; it was he who contributed significantly to the substantive content of due process that passed to the New World as the English heritage.[68]

Coke's affirmative contribution lay in his insistence that monopoly did not comport with due process. His classical assertion to this effect in the *Second Institute* has been quoted. Largely overlooked, however, is his association of anti-monopoly with chapter 30 as well. Originating as Cap. 41 in Magna Carta of 1215 the provision reads in pertinent part in English translation:

> All merchants are to be safe and secure in leaving and entering England, and in staying and travelling in England, both by land and by water, to buy and sell free from all maletotes by the ancient and rightful customs, except, in time of war, such as come from an enemy country....[69]

In the definitive reissue of Magna Carta in 1225, wherein the number of chapters was reduced by consolidation and omission. Chapter 41 was renumbered 30, immediately following chapter 39 now renumbered 29. The two provisions were thus brought into a closer tie that laid the basis for conception of them as correlatives in later evolution of assertions that freedom of trade was grounded in the Great Charter. Cap. 30 gained greater potentiality when, within one hundred years after 1225, it came by interpretation to embrace

---

66. W. PRICE, *op. cit. supra* note 30, chap. 3, reviews the sixteen years from the Statute to the Long Parliament.

67. Letwin, *supra* note 41, at 367.

68. There are those who to this day challenge Coke's assertion of the equivalency between "law of the land" and "due process." A recent such challenge is that of Jurow, *Untimely Thoughts: A Reconsideration of the Origins of Due Process of Law,* 19 AMER. J. LEG. HIST. 265 (1975). Strength for this position may possibly be found in the persistence of "law of the land" clauses, rather than of "due process" clauses, in the constitutions of numerous American States, remarked *supra* note 1, and in Strong, *Law of the Land,* 3 ENCYC. AMER. CONST. 1130 (1986). However this may be, Professor Jurow concedes that his "thoughts" are "untimely" in the sense that Coke's view prevailed to color subsequent English, and American, constitutional history. It is to be noted that the Jurow thesis in no way questions the interpretation of Magna Carta as including substantive right.

69. Translation of J. HOLT, *op. cit. supra* note 8, at 327. The Latin text is reproduced at 301-03.

English as well as foreign merchants.[70] It has been contended that the two provisions together, located midway among the rights confirmed, in the long run
constituted the heart of Magna Carta.

Closing his commentary on this chapter in Magna Carta Coke observed:

> Upon this chapter, as by the said particulars may appeare, this conclusion is nec-
> essarily gathered, that all monopolies concerning trade and traffique, are against
> the liberty and freedome, declared and granted by this great charter, and against
> divers other acts of parliament, which are good commentaries upon this chapter.[71]

But Coke also took part in buttressing the line of precedent, originating in
chapter 39, that vouchsafed to vassals in the feudal hierarchy their rights in
land and chattels against expropriation by higher authority, be it monarch or
mesne lord. As Chief Justice of Common Pleas he was one of the Judges of
England, along with Popham, Chief Justice of England, and six others who
assembled at Sergeants-Inn to give what amounted to an advisory opinion
"[i]n the session of Parliament held in December anno. 4 Jac. Regis." The
question in *The Case of The King's Prerogative in Saltpetre*[72] was "what prerogative the King had in digging and taking of saltpetre to make gunpowder
by the law of the realm." In conference, as reported by Coke in "headnotes,"
"these points were resolved by them all, *una voce*."

> Although the King cannot take the trees of the subject growing upon his freehold
> and inheritance, nor gravel in the inheritance of his subject, yet he may dig for
> saltpetre and take it.
>
> By the common law every man may come upon his neighbour's land for the
> defence of the realm, and every man may make bulwarks and trenches upon an-
> other's land for defence of the realm; so, for saving a city or town, a house shall
> be pulled down if the next be on fire; and so also the suburbs of a city in time of
> war may be pulled down for the common safety.
>
> The taking of saltpetre is a purveyance of it for the making of gunpowder for
> the necessary defence and safety of the realm; and therefore is inseparably annexed
> to the Crown, and cannot be granted over. The King's servants cannot undermine
> or impair any walls or foundation of any houses of any nature; nor can they dig
> in the floor of the mansion-house for saltpetre; nor can they dig in the floor of any
> barn for the custody of corn, hay, &c.; but they may dig in the floors of stables
> and ox-houses, &c.
>
> After digging, the King's servants must make the places as commodious to the
> owner as they were before.
>
> They must work between sun-rising and sun-setting.
>
> They ought not to place any furnace &c. in any house or building without the
> consent of the owner.
>
> They ought not to stay long in one place, nor return before a long time is passed.
>
> The owner of the land cannot be restrained from digging and taking saltpetre.[73]

---

70. *Id.* at 11-12 Holt notes the extension in the embrace of Chap. 30 and its potentiality.
71. COKE, SECOND INSTITUTE 63. Cited by J. HOLT, *op. cit. supra* note 8, at 12.
72. 12 Co. Rep. 12, 77 Eng. Rep. 1294 (1606).
73. *Id.* at 12, 77 Eng. Rep. at 1294-95.

The "decision," set forth at length following these summations, is as significant for what it clearly implies as for what it says. The subject's rights of property are recognized. Saltpetre on his premises is his to dig or not as he sees fit; only in instances of national jeopardy can the King come upon his land for removal of saltpetre in defense of the Realm, or neighbors lawfully trespass and "take" his property for defense against invading armies or "for the common safety." Even when the King is justified in entering upon the subject's land, his servants must limit themselves to saltpetre deposits and remove them with maximum concern for the disturbed premises and for the peace of the "owner." The rule is inviolability of established rights in property; the exception is the limited one of overriding community or national need.

In his last active years Coke played a critical part in the deepening conflict between Charles I and Commons that marked the latter's formulation of the Petition of Right and the King's artful second response that closed this historic episode.[74] It has been asserted that "[t]echnically the Petition of Right[75] was not a statute but a judicial decision. . . . It secured a striking statement of the supremacy of the law which, however, had yet to be implemented by civil war."[76] The challenged acts of the King included neither expropriative decrees, except as forced loan and billeting of soldiers be regarded as such, nor monopoly grants; the central complaint was arbitrary imprisonment without cause shown and punishment by martial law. Yet early in the recitals are two drawn from chapter 29 of Magna Carta, the first from Henry III's confirmation (1297) and the other from that of Edward III (1354). The first guarantees that liberties of a freeman shall not be violated "but by the lawfull judgment of his peers or by the law of the land"; that following states the guarantee of protection "without being brought to aunswere by due pcesse of lawe."[77] There is breadth here for inclusion of denunciation of both expropriation and monopoly on the basis of contemporary convictions.

In detailed commentary on the Petition it is remarked that, next to rights to protection of the body against arbitrary imprisonment, "[n]o idea was more firmly fixed in the minds of men at that time than the right of the individual to property" in goods, lands, possessions.[78] And opposition to monopoly grants was so intensifying as to place this complaint high on the list of total grievances. It was only that by 1628 these grievances had fused into an issue over the locus of sovereignty. Coke had said during debate on the Petition that "Magna Carta is such a fellow that he will have no Sovereign."[79] The Stuarts,

74. S.D. WHITE, op. cit. supra note 55, devotes chapter 7 to the Parliament of 1628, in which Coke played such a crucial part in formulation of the Petition and its presentation to the King.

75. 6 HALSBURY'S STATUTES OF ENGLAND 471-74 (3d ed. 1969).

76. Smellie, Petition of Right, 12 ENCYC. SOC. SCI. 98, at 99 (1934).

77. 6 HALSBURY, op. cit. supra note 75, at 472.

78. F. RELF, op. cit. supra note 60, at 21-22, 27.

79. Quoted in 5 W. HOLDSWORTH, op. cit. supra note 11, at 451, n. 2.

especially Charles I, were not of a mind willingly to yield their kingly prerogative. Ultimately the issue was resolved in favor of Parliament but only after civil war, regicide, restoration, and revolution.

Violations of the express provisions of the Petition of Right mounted as Charles sought to operate independently of any parliament through the 1630s. Adequacy of revenues was a continuing problem, exacerbated by the need to maintain an army as well as navy in consequence of war with the Scots. The fiscal burden at last became unmanageable and parliamentary elections were called. In the Long Parliament that opened in 1640 it developed immediately that animosity toward monopoly grants as one source of royal revenues had by no means abated. Sir John Culpepper's speech was virulent:

Mr. Speaker:

I have but one grievance more to offer unto you, but that compriseth many. It is a nest of wasps or swarm of vermine which have over-crept the land. I mean the monopolies and Pollers of the people; these like the frogs of Egypt, have gotten possession of our dwellings, and we have scarce a room free from them. They sup in our cup; they dip in our dish; they sit by our fire. We find them in the dye-fat, wash-bowl and powdering tub. They share with the butler in his box. They will not bait us a pin. We may not buy our clothes without their brokage. These are the leeches that have sucked the commonwealth so hard that it is almost hectical. —Mr. Speaker! I have echoed to you the cries of the Kingdom. I will tell you their hopes. They look to Heaven for a blessing on this Parliament.[80]

It was clear the English had had enough. The Long Parliament disqualified all monopolists from sitting, and "called in" a large number of the protested grants. "With this action of the Long Parliament, the internal monopolies ceased to be a political grievance."[81] Nevertheless, Parliament took further action during the reign of James II. *Comyns Digest* records enactment of a statute forbidding all monopolies and giving to those disadvantaged an action for treble damages and double costs.[82] Following this reference is the statement:

So all monopolies are contra to *magna charta*. 2. Inst. 63.[83]

External monopolies were another matter. With the Restoration, attention centered on royal grants for exclusive rights in foreign trade. A number of these traced back to Elizabeth, with some enjoying confirmation under the Stuarts. One of these latter was the patent for sole trade with the East Indies.[84]

---

80. Quoted by John A. Campbell, Brief for Plaintiffs on Reargument, in the *Slaughter-House Cases*, reproduced in 6 P. KURLAND & G. CASPER, LANDMARK BRIEFS AND ARGUMENTS IN THE SUPREME COURT OF THE UNITED STATES: CONSTITUTIONAL LAW 684 (1975).

81. W. PRICE, *op. cit. supra* note 30, at 46.

82. 6 COMYN'S DIGEST 380 (Trade D4, Monopoly) (3d ed. Kyd 1792).

83. *Ibid.*

84. In area the monopoly was tremendous, embracing the Indian and Pacific Oceans. "Other English subjects could trade in those vast regions only under license from the East India Company." Knight, *Chartered Companies,* 3 ENCYC. SOC. SCI. 347, at 349 (1930).

Near the close of the Stuart period the patentee, the East India Co., sued one
Sandys who was "trading hither without license." The relief sought, to stop
Sandys from interfering with the franchise of the Company, was granted in
The Great Case of Monopolies[85] by Lord Chief Justice Jefferies sitting in
King's Bench. For Sandys it was argued that the exclusive grant was void under
Taylors of Ipswich, and the first *Case of Monopolies*. It was also invalid under
the Statute of Monopolies because, contended counsel for Sandys, it did not
fall under any of the exemptions recited in it. Moreover, on analysis it bore all
the evils of monopoly.[86] Underlying the reasoning of those contending for the
plaintiff was the distinction between sole trade within England and that beyond the seas. For this reason the Lord Chief Justice viewed the East India Co.
as having a "good monopoly," one "good for the English economy." Because
Commons had concurred in reaffirmation of the grant, the vindication of monopoly grants in international trade withstood challenge when shortly after
the *Great Case* royal prerogative gave way to parliamentary prerogative with
the Glorious Revolution of 1688. Only in 1792 was the East India trade
thrown open to all comers.

Limitations in English Law on Private Monopolism

Grants made under the prerogative of Crown or Parliament were not the
only avenue to exclusive control of trade in England. Indeed, in first glimpses
of the word "monopoly" the reference is to attempted constriction of the market by private citizens, not to sovereign grants. The beginnings of private effort
are traceable back to the early years of the fifteenth century, with the first decisions recorded in the Year Books. *The Schoolmaster Case* of 1410[87] was an
effort on the part of two masters of a grammar school to employ judicial process to be rid of a competitor whose establishment of a similar school also in
Gloucester was reducing their income. Recovery was denied. This attempt to
maintain an existing monopoly was unusual. It did not surface again until *Hix
v. Gardiner,*[88] decided in the time of James I. More prevalent were efforts to
create conditions of monopoly for the benefit of established artisans. The common form of private action was that of employing contract to bind newcomers
to a pattern of restrictive practices. The first recorded instance of this device

---

85. 10 How. St. Trials 372 (K. B. 1711).

86. A commentator has observed that the East India Co. "guarded its monopoly carefully"; it pursued "the usual practice of monopolists in limiting sales and holding prices
high." T. ASHTON, AN ECONOMIC HISTORY OF ENGLAND: THE 18TH CENTURY 160, 163
(1930).

87. Y. B., 11 Hen. IV, fol. 47, pl. 21 (1410), reproduced in English in M. HANDLER, H.
BLAKE, R. PITAFSKY & H. GOLDSCHMID, CASES AND MATERIALS ON TRADE REGULATION 42
(1975).

88. 2 Bulst. 195, 80 Eng. Rep. 1062 (K. B. 1615).

is found in the *Dyer's Case* of 1415.[89] John Dyer had given bond to the plaintiff that, for opportunity to learn the trade of dyeing, he would not thereafter for the space of a half year, use in the same town with plaintiff their common craft; if he kept his word, the obligation would lose its force. There was a question whether Dyer had honored his commitment but joinder on this issue was of no moment for the court was vehement on the point that the obligation was void.

Between 1415 and 1685, inclusive, eleven known cases of this type were decided.[90] Differences in degrees of restraint, temporal and spatial; in the form of action brought, debt or assumpsit; and in judicial result, void or enforceable, led to much confusion as to what was the law with respect to contracts in restraint of trade. The question rose again in 1711 in the case of *Mitchel v. Reynolds*.[91] Plaintiff sought enforcement of a bond given by defendant in leasing a bake shop to the plaintiff. Defendant had covenanted that for the five-year term of the lease, he would not exercise the trade of a baker within the parish in which the bakehouse was situated or would pay plaintiff the sum of 50 pounds. Defendant conceded violation of his covenant but contended the bond was void in law. Plaintiff demurred.

In Chancery Chief Justice Parker, later Lord Macclesfield, was determined to take the opportunity "to reconcile the jarring opinions." Although these concerned the law governing voluntary restraints he saw fit to commence with a recital of the law of *involuntary* restraints that was the product of earlier conflict over the validity of grants by the Crown. In an opening summary he stated:

Grants or charters from the crown may be

1st, A new charter of incorporation to trade generally, exclusive of all others, and this is void. 8 Co. 121.

2ndly, A grant to particular persons for the sole exercise of any known trade; and this is void, because it is a monopoly, and against the policy of the common law, and contrary to *Magna Charta.* 11 Co. 84.

3rdly, A grant for the sole use of a new invented art, and this is good, being indulged for the encouragement of ingenuity; but this is tied up by the statute of 21 Jac. 1, cap. 3, sect. 6, (2) to the term of fourteen years; for after that time it is presumed to be a known trade, and to have spread itself among the people.[92]

89. Y. B., 2 Hen. V, fol. 5, pl. 26 (1415), reproduced in English in M. HANDLER et al., *op. cit. supra* note 87, at 41.

90. M. HANDLER, CASES ON TRADE REGULATION (2d ed. 1951), summarizes at 149-50 the full opinions in seven of these reproduced in H. OLIPHANT, CASES ON TRADE REGULATION 34-42 (1923). The other four cases are Bragge v. Stanner, Palmer 172, 81 Eng. Rep. 1031 (K. B. 1621); Mercers Case, March N.C. 77, 82 Eng. Rep. 419 (K. B. 1671); Pragnell v. Goff, Style 111, 82 Eng. Rep. 570 (K. B. 1648); Hunlocke v. Blacklowe, 2 Wms. Saund. 156, 85 Eng. Rep. 893 (K. B. 1670).

91. 1 P. Wms. 181, 24 Eng. Rep. 347 (Ch. 1711).

92. *Id.* at 185-86, 24 Eng. Rep. at 348. Citations are omitted.

Later, explaining "the reasons of the differences which we find in the cases,"

> *1st*, With respect to involuntary restraints ...
> As to involuntary restraints, the first reason why such of these, as are created by grants and charters from the Crown and by-laws, generally are void, is drawn from the encouragement which the law gives to trade and honest industry, and that they are contrary to the liberty of the subject.
> *2dly*, Another reason is drawn from *Magna Charta*, which is infringed by these acts of power; that statute says, *nullus liber homo, &c., disseisetur de libero tenemento vel libertatibus, vel liberis consuetudmibus suis, &c.*, and these words have always been taken to extend to freedom of trade.[93]

By contrast

> Voluntary restraints by agreement of the parties, are either—
> *1st*, General, or
> *2dly*, Particular, as to places or persons.
> General restraints are all void, whether by bond, covenant, or promise, &c., with or without consideration, and whether it be of the party's own trade, or not. Particular restraints are either, *1st*, without consideration, all which are void by what sort of contract soever created.
> Or *2dly*, Particular restraints are with consideration. Where a contract for a restraint of trade appears to be made upon a good and adequate consideration, so as to make it a proper and useful contract, it is good.[94]

Under this analysis plaintiff had judgment in *Mitchel v. Reynolds*. The restraint on defendant rested on good consideration in the use of the bakehouse during the term of five years; the restraint was partial, being limited in time and in space. Validity flowed from the fact the restraint was "exactly proportioned to the consideration."

According to the Chief Justice "the reason of the differences in the case of voluntary restraint" is both affirmative and negative. Affirmatively, contracts in restraint of trade, so long as ancillary to a lease, a sale, or a term of employment, and restrain no further than to protect the covenantee, are consistent with legitimate economic and social objectives. On the contrary contracts of overbreadth, non-ancillary, and designed directly to fix prices, restrict production, or apportion territory, are contracts in restraint of competition and nudum pactum.

> *1st*, Negatively; the true reason of the disallowance of these in any case, is never drawn from *Magna Charta*; for a man may, voluntarily, and by his own act, put himself out of the possession of his freehold; he may sell it, or give it away at his pleasure.
> *2dly*, Neither is it a reason against them, that they are contrary to the liberty of the subject; for a man may, by his own consent, for a valuable consideration, part with his liberty; as in the case of a covenant not to erect a mill upon his own lands.

---

93. *Id.* at 183, 24 Eng. Rep. at 349.
94. *Id.* at 187-88, 24 Eng. Rep. at 349.

J. Jones, 13, Mich. 4 Ed. 3, 57. And when any of these are at any time mentioned as reasons upon the head of voluntary restraints, they are to be taken only as general instances of the favour and indulgence of the law to trade and industry.[95]

Mitchel v. Reynolds was a watershed decision on several counts. It reconfirmed that the fatal flaw in grants from the Crown, save where invention was thereby encouraged, lay in their incompatibility with freedom of trade vouchsafed by Magna Carta, chapter 29. With respect to voluntary restraints, on the other hand, freedom from monopoly could not look to Magna Carta for support; the very history of chapter 29 that gave it such potency against Crown prerogative denied it all relevance in the determinately area of voluntary agreements. Protection of competition against monopolistic pressures in that area was left to the courts without a dynamic principle on which to take a stand in its defense. *Mitchel's* requirements for enforceability of restrictive covenants were adequate for a time. A leading decision was *King v. Norris*,[96] 1758, in which a price-fixing agreement among proprietors of formerly competing saltworks was condemned. Yet in the end those requirements proved unavailing for maintenance of competitive patterns.

As industry moved onto a national and world scale with the impact of the Industrial Revolution, the confining concept of "partial restraint" lost vitality. The change in judicial attitude begins to show in *Homer v. Ashford*.[97] A covenant not to compete for fourteen years "in the trade of a saddler's ironmonger" is upheld in favor of the covenantee. Although the area of the restraint consisted of named English cities through which plaintiff travelled, it was found to be partial; a general restraint would have been void. Superficially, there appears to be adherence to the principles of *Mitchel*, yet the plaintiff wins judgment on the following reasoning:

> A merchant or manufacturer would soon find a rival in every one of his servants, if he could not prevent them from using to his prejudice the knowledge acquired in his employ. Engagements of this sort between masters and servants are not injurious restraints of trade, but securities necessary for those who are engaged in it. The effect of such contracts is to encourage rather than cramp the employment of capital in trade, and the promotion of industry. For partial restraints, however, there must be some consideration, otherwise they are impolitic and oppressive.[98]

Consideration need not appear on the deed restraining trade; it is sufficient if shown by the pleadings.

In *Wicken v. Evans*[99] three manufacturers of boxes, each of whom had been selling throughout England, by contract divided the country into three segments. "Each party was to have the exclusive rights to sell in his district during

95. *Id.* at 188-89, 24 Eng. Rep. at 350.
96. 2 Kenyon 300, 96 Eng. Rep. 1189 (K. B. 1758).
97. 3 Bing 321, 130 Eng. Rep. 537 (C. P. 1825).
98. *Id.* at 327, 130 Eng. Rep. at 539.
99. 3 Young & J. 318, 148 Eng. Rep. 1201 (Exchequer 1829).

his life, and the other parties promised not to compete with him during their lives." The Barons of Exchequer managed to view this arrangement as but a partial restraint made on good consideration and hence sustained an action of assumpsit brought against the member who breached the contract by selling outside his area. In 1889 the Court of Appeals had before it the validity of an agreement made between several ship owners plying the China trade that operated to the damage of other shipping companies. Defendants had formed an association, excluding plaintiffs, whereby they gained a monopoly in tea shipments by offering a rebate on goods carried in their holds. Plaintiffs' suit was to no avail.[100] With the Master of the Rolls dissenting, Lords Bowen and Fry affirmed the judgment of Lord Coleridge on the shallow ground that since the defendants formed the association for the purpose of keeping the trade in their own hands and not with the intention of *ruining the plaintiffs' business* by reason of malice or ill will, no action for conspiracy was maintainable. Shortly thereafter, the House of Lords on appeal upheld a worldwide division of territory in weaponry sales on the ground the restraint was no broader than necessary to afford ample protection to the covenantee.[101] Where a combination took close-knit, rather than loose-knit, form, the requirement that contracts restrictive of competition be ancillary was honored in the breach by clever draftsmen. Competitors desirous of eliminating competition would each execute a contract, drawn in favor of a new entity, purportedly partial in restraint and based on adequate consideration with covenant not to compete. But rather than retire from the former business the erstwhile competitors would reappear as stockholders of a monopolistic enterprise.[102] By this device the English road to monopoly was unobstructed and well travelled.

The English heritage included legal principles applicable to two other types of private, unofficial attempts at monopolization. One of these types involved efforts to corner local markets in foodstuff. Technically, three distinct practices were recognized—engrossing, forestalling, and regrating—depending upon the exact time in relation to market operations with respect to which the corner was attempted. Any of the three practices was generally known as forestalling, the objective of which was to elevate market prices.[103] English legislation prohibiting forestalling first appeared in 1266, with later bursts of sta-

---

100. Mogul Steamship Co. v. McGregor, 23 L. R. Q. B. D. 598 (1889), *aff'g* 21 L. R. Q. B. D. 544 (1888).

101. Nordenfeldt v. Maxim-Nordenfeldt Co., L. R. App. Cas. 535 (H. L. 1894).

102. G. Allen, Monopolies and Restrictive Practices chap. 4 (1968), sketches the changes in judicial attitude. A more thorough tracing with citation to other decisions is provided by C. Beach, Monopolies and Industrial Trusts Intro. (1898). The later volume, in chaps. 5-9, provides coverage of the English legislative attack on monopoly that came following WW II—about 60 years after antitrust laws appeared in the United States.

103. Attempts to corner the market in one or another commodity or process appear to have dated from antiquity, with the practice early spoken of as one of monopoly. F. Fetter, The Masquerade of Monopoly 457 (1931).

tutory criminalization until the time of George III when the overlay of prohibitory statutes was repealed.[104] Repeal was the consequence in great part of the writings of Adam Smith who asserted that the forestaller as middleman played a constructive role in England's economy. Not all were in agreement, however. Among the Judges Lord Kenyon was critical of Smith. In each of two decisions,[105] both decided in 1800, the Chief Justice took issue with "Dr. Smith." Asserting that forestalling remained an offense at common law, he declared as follows in one of the opinions:

> I wish Dr. Adam Smith had lived to hear the evidence of today and then he would have seen whether such an offence exists, and whether it is to be dreaded. (Smith's Wealth of Nations, 2 vol. 309. Index-Labour.) If he had been told that cattle and corn were brought to market, and then bought by a man whose purse happened to be longer than his neighbors, so that the poor man who walks the street and earns his daily bread by his daily labour could get none but through his hands, and at the price he chose to demand; that it had been raised 3d., 6d., 9d., 1s., 2s., and more a quarter on the same day; would he have said there was no danger from such an offence?[106]

Lord Kenyon was, however, fighting a losing battle; the views of the classical economist were to prevail. During the reign of Queen Victoria Parliament swept away all English law opposed to forestalling.

In the long history of English opposition to forestalling there is no instance of appeal to Magna Carta even though the offense was always viewed as one of monopolistic practice. The explanation lies in Lord Macclesfield's observation in *Mitchel v. Reynolds*; the attempt at monopoly by forestalling was the product of private action, as with voluntary agreements to restrain trade. Magna Carta provided protections against monopoly by Crown grant. Similar lack of connection with the Great Charter is found in the requirement that only reasonable charges be made by those having a virtual monopoly by reason of the nature of their business. This English rule developed out of two of the many treatises written by Matthew Hale during the early period of the restoration.[107] These two were entitled, *De Jure Maris* and *De Portibus Maris*.[108]

---

104. An overview is provided by Herbruck, *Forestalling, Regrating and Engrossing*, 27 MICH. L. REV. 365 (1929). Jones, *Historical Development of the Law of Business Competition*, 35 YALE L. J. 906 (1926), summarizes English law on forestalling, contracts in restraint of trade, and monopoly patents as a preface to detailed development of American law from the colonial period to the time of publication. The authoritative treatise on forestalling and related practices is said to be ILLINGWORTH, AN INQUIRY INTO THE LAWS, ANTIENT AND MODERN RESPECTING FORESTALLING, REGRATING AND INGROSSING (1800). However, this treatise is not generally available and so has not been examined.

105. Rex v. Rusby, Peake Add. Cas. 189, 170 Eng. Rep. 241 (1800); King v. Waddington, 1 East 143, 102 Eng. Rep. 56 (1800).

106. Rex v. Rusby at 192, 170 Eng. Rep. at 242.

107. E. HEWARD, MATTHEW HALE (1972), recounts the life and accomplishments of one of the most highly respected lawmen of his time. Chap. 14 lists and digests the prolific

In the first Hale declares the King has:

> A *right* of *franchise* or *privilege,* that no man may set up a common ferry for all
> passengers, without a prescription time out of mind, or a charter from the king.
> He may make a ferry for his own use or the use of his family, but not for the
> common use of all the king's subjects passing that way; because it doth in con-
> sequent tend to a common charge, and is become a thing of public interest and
> use, and every man for his passage pays a toll, which is a common charge, and
> every ferry ought to be under a public regulation; viz. that it give attendance at
> due times, keep a boat in due order, and take but reasonable toll; for if he fail in
> these, he in fineable. And hence it is, that if a common bridge be broken, whereby
> there is no passage but by a boat or ferry, it hath been anciently practiced in the
> Exchequer to compel that ferryman, that ferries over people for profit without a
> charter from the king or a lawful prescription, to account for the benefit above his
> reasonable pains and charge.[109]

In *De Portibus Maris* appear the following passages:

> 2. A man for his own private advantage may in a port town set up a wharf or
> crane, and may take what rates he and his customers can agree for cranage, wharf-
> age, houfellage, pefage; for he doth no more than is lawful for any man to do, viz.
> makes the most of his own. And such are coal-wharfs, and wood-wharfs, and
> timber-wharfs, in the port of London and some other ports. But such wharfs cannot
> receive customable goods against the provision of the statute of 1. Eliz. cap. 11.
>
> 3. If the king or subject have a publick wharf, unto which all persons that come
> to that port must come and unlade or lade their goods as for the purpose, because
> they are wharfs only licensed by the queen, according to the statute of 1. El. cap.
> 11. or because there is no other wharf in that port, as it may fall out where a port
> is newly erected; in that case there cannot be taken arbitrary and excessive duties
> for cranage, wharfage, pefage, &c. neither can they be inhanced to an immoderate
> rate, but the duties must be reasonable and moderate, though settled by the king's
> licence or charter. For now the wharf and crane and other conveniences are affected
> with a publick interest and they cease to be *juris privati* only; as if a man set out
> a street in new building on his own land, it is now no longer bare private interest,
> but it is affected with a publick interest.
>
> 4. But in that case the king may limit by his charter and license him to take
> reasonable tolls, though it be a new port or wharf, and made publick; because he
> is to be at the charge to maintain and repair it, and find those conveniencies that
> are fit for it, as cranes and weights.[110]

Whatever basis Matthew Hale had for his assertions respecting the legal requirement of service to all at reasonable charge on the part of those enjoying

---

writings believed to be the product of Hale's pen. He served in three judicial offices: Common Pleas, Exchequer, and King's Bench. His death occurred in the year of the American
Declaration of Independence.

108. These are found in F. HARGRAVE, LAW TRACTS PARS PRIMA AND PARS SECUNDA
(1787).

109. *Id.* at 6-7.

110. *Id.* at 77-78.

a position of private monopoly, the great respect in which he was held led to
judicial acceptance of those assertions as law of the realm. Two decisions make
this clear. *Bolt v. Stennett*[111] was an action in trespass brought by the owner of
a crane located on a quay within the Port of London. Defendant, admitting
use of the crane without plaintiff's consent, justified his action on the grounds
that the quay upon which the crane was erected was "a public, open, and lawful quay . . . necessary for [the] purpose" of importing goods from ships lying
near the quay, upon payment of reasonable compensation by the importers to
the owner of the quay. In a short opinion the court found for defendant, citing
the above-quoted passage in *De Portibus Maris* from which "it is obvious that
Lord Hale considered a public quay to be like a public street, common to all
the King's subjects."[112] A decade later came *Allnutt v. Inglis*[113] where the sitting Judges of King's Bench, with Lord Ellenborough as C.J., in seriatim opinions based their judgments on the principle enunciated by Lord Hale. Those
judgments were that, because under the "actually existing state of things in
the port of London" the London Dock Co. had a virtual monopoly in warehousing imported wines under bond, it was incumbent on the Company to
serve as warehouseman to plaintiff and to charge, not on the basis of its own
published tariffs but at reasonable rates. Decision therefore went for plaintiff,
suing to force performance by the Company as a "business affected with a
public interest."

Hale had written at a time when the issue of the validity of internal monopoly grants by the Crown had been resolved against them and there was waxing
hot the struggle over whether the same fate would befall monopoly grants in
foreign trade. Now there had emerged the issue of control over private monopoly, whether the result of active collaboration of former competitors or of natural forces. Chapter 29 of Magna Carta had in English law appeared relevant
only with respect to publicly induced monopoly, yet as the baneful effects of
private monopoly became more apparent general hatred of monopoly in any
form might well lead to antagonism between Due Process and private restraint
of trade.

---

111. 8 Term. Rep. (Durnford & East) * 606 (summary only), 101 Eng. Rep. 1572 (K. B.
1800).
112. *Id.* at 101 Eng. Rep. 1573.
113. 12 East 527, 104 Eng. Rep. 206 (K. B. 1810).

PART II

RECEPTION ACCORDED SUBSTANTIVE DUE PROCESS OF LAW IN THE NEW WORLD

2. Expropriation by Public Conversion as Denial of Substantive Due Process

What early became of concern in this country were legislative acts expropriating from citizens title to land or to personal property, into the ownership of which they had previously come by operation of valid law.[1] Expropriation was basically of two types: alienation and divestiture. The former was characterized by legislative transfer of rights in property from the prior lawful owner to another individual or to a discrete group. Such actions became described as "taking property from *A* and giving it to *B*." The end result of divestiture was the same as that of alienation—loss of "vested rights" by legislative decree without benefit of reimbursement. The difference was that with divestiture the beneficiary of the taking was not a favored individual or group but the public at large. Instances of each type of attempted expropriation were familiar in the period from Statehood to Nationhood after Civil War. Resistance in the courts was sometimes successful on the basis of conflict with constitutional provisions forbidding special legislation or mandating separation of powers. But common attack, in many instances culminating in invalidation, was predicated on law-of-the-land clauses or their equivalent as due-process-of-law. This was despite misstatements that Due Process had only procedural meaning prior to the Civil War.[2]

---

1. Edward S. Corwin in one of his many writings recounts the instance "of a Massachusetts magistrate in 1657 holding void a tax by the town of Ipswich for the purpose of presenting the local minister with a dwelling house. Such a tax, said the magistrate, 'to take from Peter and give it to Paul,' is against fundamental law." Corwin, *The "Higher Law" Background of American Constitutional Law*, 42 HARV. L. REV. 365, at 395 (1928). Unavailability of the source cited by Corwin makes it impossible to conclude what the magistrate had in mind as fundamental law. From the context in which the citation is made, however, it is reasonable to believe Corwin thought the source was chapter 29 of Magna Carta as understood by Coke. See *id.* at 394.

2. Hamilton, *The Path of Due Process of Law*, in C. READ, THE CONSTITUTION RECONSIDERED 168 (2nd ed. 1968). Hamilton was not alone in this view. R. JACKSON, THE STRUGGLE FOR JUDICIAL SUPREMACY 48 (1941). With regret I must challenge several assertions of "Hamie," whom as a law student I so greatly admired.

Alienation of property rights. Three instances of legislative attempt to take *A*'s property for *B*'s advantage were challenged in judicial proceedings during the 1790s. In two, *Bowman v. Middleton*[3] and *Van Horne's Lessee v. Dorrance,*[4] outright "confirmation" in *B* of title to land belonging to *A* was attempted but judicially rebuffed. In the third instance, *Calder v. Bull,*[5] *B* did benefit from legislative intervention because the Supreme Court could find no constitutional provision on which to rest condemnation. After a will had been denied probate and appeal time had run the legislature of Connecticut directed that a new hearing be held. This time the will was admitted, the judge of probate probably reading the handwriting on the wall. With this dashing of his justifiable expectations of inheritance, the heir went to court crying that his property had been wrested from him by legislative fiat. His plea in the su-

---

3. 1 Bay 252 (C. P. S. C. 1792). Raoul Berger rejects the relevance of this decision because the South Carolina law was held to be "against common right, as well as against *magna charta*." "*Magna Carta*, as we have seen, had no application to acts of the legislature," Berger, "*Law of the Land" Reconsidered*, 74 Nw. U. L. Rev.. 1, 3 (1979). On the same ground Berger lays aside University of North Carolina v. Foy, cited *infra* note 45. *Id.* at 24. I join Mr. Berger in his zeal to demonstrate there is no historical basis in *lex terrae* for judicial indulgence in constitutional policy making but cannot agree on the explanation he advances. It is true that American judges were early puzzled over the proper interpretation to be accorded incorporation in most American constitutions of either "law of the land" or, as Coke had declared to be equivalent, "due process" clauses. Coke, Second Institute of the Laws of England 50, cited *supra* Chapter 1, p. 3, note 1. Yet any grasp of underlying roots of the American Revolution brought realization that legislative supremacy was unacceptable in the New World. With sovereignty vesting in the People, Crown limitation now applied to the Legislative as well as the Executive. The supreme court of New York had figured this out thirty years before *Slaughter-House Cases* (1873), where Justice Miller made the same inexcusable error.

Under our form of government the Legislature is not supreme. It is only one of the organs of that absolute sovereignty which resides in the whole body of the people.

Taylor v. Porter & Ford, 4 Hill 140, 144 (N.Y. Sup. Ct. 1843). Referring then to Article 7, Sec. 1 of the New York Constitution, the court continued:

The words "by the law of the land," as here used, do not mean a statute passed for the purpose of working the wrong. That construction would render the restriction absolutely nugatory, and turn this part of the Constitution into mere nonsense. The people would be made to say to the two Houses: "You shall be vested with 'the legislative power of the State;' but no one 'shall be disfranchised or deprived of any of the rights or privileges' of a citizen, unless you pass a statute for that purpose;" in other words: "You shall not do the wrong, unless you choose to do it."

Id. at 145-46.

4. 2 Dall. 304 (on circuit, 1795) (decision based on Pa. Const.). The State supreme court later took the same view on involuntary "takings." See note 17, *infra*, for Pennsylvania citations.

5. 3 Dall. 386 (1798). It is familiar learning that the Constitution expressly prohibits *ex post facto* legislation by either the States or Congress, and impairment of the obligation of contracts by the States. With ratification of the Fifth and Fourteenth Amendments, due process became the *third* guaranty against retroactivity of legislation. But *Calder v. Bull* limited Ex Post Facto to criminal legislation while the Contract Clause restricted only the States and ultimately lost all potency, leaving the task to due process.

preme court of errors of Connecticut was of no avail; the State remained under Charter with no due process or separation of powers clause; the Fourteenth Amendment was seventy years in the future. He fared no better in the Supreme Court of the United States; yet his determination to carry his claim to that Court produced the celebrated debate between Justices Chase and Iredell over the fundamental question whether the Court possessed authority to reach beyond the bounds of the Constitution for bases of invalidity.

Incensed over the seeming injustice done the heir, Mr. Justice Chase was tempted to invoke natural law to "supplement" the deficiency of the written instrument of governance that had been adopted a decade previously.

> An act of the legislature (for I cannot call it a law), contrary to the great first principles of the social compact, cannot be considered a rightful exercise of legislative authority.... A law that punishes a citizen for an innocent action, or, in other words, for an act, which, when done, was in violation of no existing law; a law that destroys or impairs the lawful private contracts of citizens; a law that makes a man a judge in his own cause; or a law that takes property from A and gives it to B; it is against all reason and justice, for a people to intrust a legislature with such powers, and therefore, it cannot be presumed that they have done it.[6]

Justice Iredell talked his Brother out of his temptation, yet the issue remains central in the question of the future of constitutional review. The Chases of today are pressing for domestication of this awesome power in the bosom of Due Process, contending there is justification for Court engagement in non-interpretive constitutionalism through resort to substantive due process of law.

Justice Chase's assertion that "I will not decide any law to be void, but in a very clear case"[7] may have been occasioned not only by Justice Iredell's position but as well by doubts whether the heir possessed, after the first ruling of the probate court, a quality of "property" worthy of constitutional protection against subsequent legislative vesting in the legatee. Several subsequent cases dealt with the analogous question of the reality of a legislative taking from A for B where the conflicting interests of the involved parties were blunted in one way or another. Two Supreme Court cases, each on appeal from a circuit court, are instructive. *Bank of Columbia v. Okely*[8] presented the question of the constitutionality of a Maryland law that in incorporating a bank in effect gave it power to employ cognovit notes, thus exposing its debtors to summary process on execution where default occurred. In the lower federal court a motion had been made to quash an execution issued under this authority; the grounds were violation of the Seventh Amendment to the Constitution of the United States and of Article 21 of the Maryland Bill of Rights. The latter, reproduced in the opinion, was an exact translation of Magna Carta. Judgment

---

6. *Id.* at 388.
7. *Id.* at 395.
8. 4 Wheat. 235 (1819).

for plaintiff in the lower court was reversed because of the debtor's voluntary acquiesence in foregoing the "ordinary administration of justice" through trial by jury. There could be no unconstitutional taking in such circumstances. A decade later the Supreme Court, in *Wilkinson v. Leland*,[9] gave judgment for the party benefiting from the transfer of property rights (*i.e., B*), convinced that the Rhode Island legislature acted "not to destroy existing rights but to effectuate them."[10]

Terrett v. Taylor[11] involved an early instance of attempted alienation by the Virginia legislature. Story, for the Supreme Court, recognized that pre-revolutionary laws favoring the Episcopal Church could not stand after Virginia's adoption of a constitution protective of religious freedom. However, there was no inconsistency with the new constitution of legislation of 1776 reconfirming to the Church its property which "was in fact and in law, generally purchased by the parishioners, or acquired by the benefactions of pious donors." Vested in the Church, therefore, was "an indefeasible and irrevocable title." In consequence the legislature could not constitutionally wrest title from the Church and lodge it in the parish overseers for aid of the poor, as a statute in 1801 sought to do. Invalidity could not be rested on Due Process limitation on state action, which came only in 1868. The decision consequently has been "assigned" to the Contract Clause but the factual pattern is that of a taking from a private entity, *A*, for the benefit of needy *B*s.

During the 1840s the supreme court of Pennsylvania thrice sustained statutes that factually disadvantaged one party for the benefit of another. All three involved intra-family transfers, which may in part explain the results although the New York courts held the married women's property act of that jurisdiction unconstitutional to the extent it shifted rights of property in married couples as they stood prior to enactment.[12] In *Norman v. Heist*[13] a Pennsylvania law survived challenge on the ground it was "enabling and prospective"; *Menges v. Wortman*[14] concerned an act that cured a defective title; and in *Norris v. Clymer*[15] all parties involved were agreeable to the enactment. One can anticipate for "taking" cases of later date judicial reaction to the circumstances of the legislative action, to the magnitude of the attempted alienation, and to the degree to which the "right" being subjected to transfer is one recognized in the law.

"Normally," observed the Pennsylvania court in *Menges*, "the legislature may not divest the title of an owner and vest it in another."[16] This "general

---

9. 2 Pet. 627 (1829).

10. *Id.* at 661.

11. 9 Cr. 43 (1814).

12. Holmes v. Holmes, 4 Barb. 446 (N.Y. Sup. Ct. 1848); Westervelt v. Gregg, 12 N.Y. 202 (1854); White v. White, 5 Barb 474 (N.Y. Supr. Ct. 1849).

13. 5 Watts & Serg. 171 (Pa. 1843).

14. 1 Pa. St. 218 (1845).

15. 2 Pa. St. 277 (1846).

16. Menges v. Wertman, 1 Pa. St. at 223.

rule" was followed in other States as well as in Pennsylvania.[17] Appearance of the rule as operative against the Congress under the Due Process Clause of the Fifth Amendment came in the contemporary Supreme Court case of *Bloomer v. McQuewan*.[18] Bloomer, assignee of monopoly rights under a patent for a planing machine issued to one Woodworth in 1828, sought to enjoin use of several of the machines by McQuewan who claimed under a license granted by the inventor during the original term of the patent. The license consisted of purchase by McQuewan's assignors of a right to construct and use "a certain number of these machines within the limits of the city of Pittsburg [sic] and Allegheny county."

Under a statute of July 4, 1836[19] authorizing a seven-year extension of patents upon demonstration by the patentees of justification for continuance, Woodworth qualified thereby extending his patent to 1849 from its original termination year of 1842. The 1836 law expressly saved the benefit of the additional time "to the assignees and grantees of the rights to use the thing patented," language that the Court had interpreted in earlier litigation to the effect that "the party who had purchased and was using this planing machine during the original term for which the patent was granted, had a right to continue the use during the extension."[20] By a private Act, Congress on February 26, 1845,[21] extended the Woodworth patent seven more years. Shortly after passage of the private law, Woodworth's administrators assigned all rights under the patent to one Wilson, from whom Bloomer purchased. Bloomer then claimed infringement by McQuewan, who was continuing to use two of the planing machines, on the basis that the latter's rights expired at the end of the first extension since the 1845 law did not contain the "saving" language included in the statute of 1836.

Relief was denied on the following grounds, opinion by Chief Justice Taney:

> The 5th amendment to the Constitution of the United States declares, that no person shall be deprived of life, liberty, or property, without due process of law.
>
> The right to construct and use these planing machines, had been purchased and paid for without any limitation as to the time for which they were to be used. They were the property of the respondents. Their only value consists in their use. And a special act of Congress, passed afterwards, depriving the appellees of the right to use them, certainly could not be regarded as due process of law.
>
> Congress undoubtedly have power to promote the progress of science and useful arts, by securing for limited times, to authors and inventors, the exclusive right to their respective writings and discoveries.

---

17. Taylor v. Porter & Ford, *supra* note 3; Jones Heirs v. Perry, 10 Yerger 58 (Tenn. 1836); Brown v. Hummel, 6 Barr 86 (Pa. 1847); Ervine's Appeal, 16 Pa. St. 256 (1851).

18. 14 How. 539 (1852).

19. 5 STAT. 124, being § 18 of chapter 357, a general statute "for promoting progress of useful arts."

20. Bloomer v. McQuewan, 14 How. at 549.

21. 6 STAT. 936.

But it does not follow that Congress may, from time to time, as often as they think proper, authorize an inventor to recall rights which he had granted to others; or reinvest in him rights of property which he had before conveyed for a valuable and fair consideration.

But we forbear to pursue this inquiry, because we are of opinion that this special act of Congress does not, and was not intended to interfere with rights of property before acquired; but that it leaves them as they stood during the extension under the general law. And in this view of the subject, the appellant was not entitled to the injunction he sought to obtain, and the Circuit Court were right in dismissing the bill.

As the decision on this point disposes of the case, it is unnecessary to examine the other grounds of defence taken by the appellees.

The decree of the Circuit Court must be affirmed.[22]

The fact the Court saved the congressional law from invalidity through exercise of covert constitutional review does not diminish the importance of *Bloomer* in the account of substantive due process as protector against expropriation. The Fifth Amendment now officially contains, as a limitation on Congress, the content state courts had found in state constitutions incorporating either due process or law-of-the-land clauses, or, in New York, both. The absorption rises from technical dictum to outright holding in *Hepburn v. Griswold*,[23] the significance of which for the present analysis is not diminished by the overruling of the decision in the *Legal Tender Cases*[24] through adroit "adjustments" in Court personnel. When in 1864 Griswold sued on a promissory note executed in 1860, Hepburn tendered in payment United States notes issued in 1862 to finance the Civil War. Griswold rejected the tender because on the due date of the promissory note only gold and silver coin were legal tender in payment of private debts. Judgment went to Hepburn in the Kentucky trial court, but reversal on the part of the Kentucky court of appeals was affirmed 5 to 3 in the United States Supreme Court. Basis for the decision favoring Griswold lay in the due process of law provision of the Fifth Amendment.[25]

---

22. Bloomer v. McQuewan, 14 How. at 553-54.

23. 75 U.S. 603 (1869).

24. 79 U.S. 457 (1871). Overruling was achieved by a timely resignation and a judicious appointment. Even in repudiation of *Hepburn* the "adjusted" Court "did not reconsider that portion of the decision relating to due process." B. SIEGARD, ECONOMIC LIBERTIES AND THE CONSTITUTION 51 (1980), citing to 79 U.S. at 553.

25. Decision in the Kentucky court of appeals was not based on the Due Process Clause of Amendment Five, as was that of the Supreme Court in affirming, but on the absence in Congress of any power to impair the obligation of contract save in the exercise of the Bankruptcy Power. Dissenting, Justice Williams contended that by analogy to the Bankruptcy Power, under which Congress can impair pre-existing debt, there is an implication that Congress possesses power to declare what is legal tender by virtue of authority implied from the Necessary and Proper Clause. This reasoning the majority rejected, refusing to infer from absence of a Contract Clause applicable to Congress an intention to enable

The significance of *Davidson v. New Orleans*[26] will be noted in analysis of monopoly by government grant as denial of due process. Although by dictum in a decision sustaining as for a public purpose (*i.e.,* divestiture) an assessment for the draining of swamp lands, Justice Miller nevertheless placed the Court's imprimatur on due process as invalidating a statute declaring without more "that the full and exclusive title of a described piece of land, which is now in A., shall be and is hereby vested in B. . . . ."[27] Seven years later in 1884, another dictum was to the same effect. *Hurtado v. California*[28] directly concerned the reach of Fourteenth Amendment due process with respect to one of the procedural protections specified in Amendment Five; with two dissents State conviction for murder based on an information rather than on indictment by grand jury was held consistent with due process. Yet in the course of the opinion appears the following:

> But it is not to be supposed that these legislative powers are absolute and despotic, and that the amendment prescribing due process of law is too vague and indefinite to operate as a practical restraint. It is not every act, legislative in form, that is law. Law is something more than mere will exerted as an act of power.[29]

Thus the general rules which govern society exclude,

> as not due process of law, acts of attainder, bills of pains and penalties, acts of confiscation, acts of reversing judgments, and *acts directly transferring one man's estate to another*, legislative judgments and decrees, and other similar special, partial, and arbitrary exertions of power under the forms of legislation. Arbitrary power, enforcing its edicts to the injury of the persons and property of its subjects, is not law, whether manifested as the decree of a personal monarch or of an impersonal multitude.[30]

Dictum became holding in *Missouri Pacific Railway Co. v. Nebraska*,[31] decided shortly before the end of the century. On complaint of an association of several growers of wheat and other grains in the environs of Elmwood, Cass County, Nebraska, the State, through its State Board of Transportation, directed the Railroad to lease a segment of its right of way to these complainants for construction by them of an elevator for storage of grains produced by them. The Railroad had previously permitted erection by private parties of two

---

Congress to impair the obligation of a contract like that involved in the litigation at hand.

Subsequent decisions of the Supreme Court have in effect read the Contract Clause into the Fifth Amendment Due Process Clause. Illustrative are Sinking Fund Cases, 99 U.S. 700 (1878); Choate v. Trapp, 224 U.S. 665 (1912); United States v. Northern Pacific R.R. Co., 256 U.S. 51 (1921); Lynch v. United States, 292 U.S. 571 (1934).

26. 96 U.S. 97 (1877). Further analysis will be found in the text *infra* accompanying notes 64-69, chap. 3, pp. 59-60, *Monopoly by Public Grant as Denial of Due Process.*

27. Quoted in full *infra* note 66, chap. 3, p. 60.

28. 110 U.S. 516 (1884).

29. *Id.* at 535.

30. *Id.* at 536 (emphasis added).

31. 164 U.S. 403 (1896).

elevators on railroad right of way but petitioners asserted to the satisfaction of the Board that the capacity of these two was inadequate at certain seasons of the year and that denial to them of a like privilege to build "was an unjust and unreasonable discrimination against them." The Railroad refused to comply with the Board's order, which on resort to the courts was sustained by the supreme court of Nebraska. On writ of error the Supreme Court of the United States reversed, citing *inter alia* to the passage above quoted from *Davidson*.

> This court confining itself to what is necessary for the decision of the case before it, is unanimously of opinion, that the order in question, so far as it required the railroad corporation to surrender a part of its land to the petitioners, for the purpose of building and maintaining their elevator upon it, was, in essence and effect, a taking of private property of the railroad corporation, for the private use of the petitioners. The taking by a State of the private property of one person or corporation, without the owner's consent, for the private use of another, is not due process of law, and is a violation of the Fourteenth Article of Amendment of the Constitution of the United States.[32]

Divesture of Property Rights. Of the divestiture type, the earliest case found is *Respublica v. Sparhawk*,[33] decided by the supreme court of Pennsylvania in 1788. During the struggle for Independence, Pennsylvania's "Board of War," acting on the suggestion of the Continental Congress, had ordered that provisions within the city of Philadelphia of value to the enemy be moved to caches outside in an effort to deny them to the British should they overrun Philadelphia. Into one such depot by name of Chestnut-Hill there were placed among other citizen property 323 barrels of flour belonging to Sparhawk. Not only did British troops enter the City; Chestnut-Hill was overtaken, resulting in the loss to Sparhawk of the greater part of his flour. In the aftermath of victory he sought reimbursement. Beyond dispute as to who was the proper party defendant lay the question whether Sparhawk had any substantive claim. The Commonwealth's attorney general contended that the governmental action taken had been for the general good of the whole community in time of hostilities with England and was therefore not compensable. Sparhawk's counsel, countering that the principles of international law of war did not apply to relations "between a state and its own citizens," insisted that

> justice requires, and the law declares, that adequate compensation should be made for the wrong that is done.... These general principles are fortified by the explicit language of the *Declaration of Rights, Sect....* 8.[34]

That Section (VIII) declared that "no part of a man's property can be justly taken from him, or applied to public uses, without his own consent, or that of

---

32. *Id.* at 417.
33. 1 Dall. 357 (Pa. 1788).
34. *Id.* at 359.

his legal representatives."[35] Understandably, no reliance was placed on the embryonic "law of the land" guaranty of Section IX which sounded in terms of the protection of the criminally accused, specified "liberty" but not "property," and employed "law" in the plural.[36] But why no reliance on Section I that included among "certain natural, inherent, and unalienable rights" those of "acquiring, possessing, and protecting property . . . "?[37] Sparhawk lost his case, yet the guaranty of "due process of law" for rights in property had commenced gestation.

Some five years thereafter the Pennsylvania high court had before it *Isaac Austin v. The Trustees of the University of Pennsylvania.*[38] Attainted for treason, William Austin, Isaac's brother, had suffered confiscation of certain property at the hands of Commonwealth "agents for forfeited estates." It had then been included among divers estates listed for appropriation to the Trustees on action by the Pennsylvania general assembly "agreeably to the directions of the act of assembly establishing the University, passed the 27th November, 1779."[39] Isaac Austin founded his claim chiefly on an Act of 6 August, 1784,[40] that purported to vest in him title to his brother's property. But this enactment was repealed 18 February, 1785,[41] before institution of the suit.

Of the four Justices of the supreme court, three recused themselves for conflict of interest. This left Justice Yeates to resolve the issue. His conclusion was that the repeal was

> for the reasons particularly enumerated in the preamble thereof, and I have no difficulty in declaring for the same reasons, that the former act was unconstitutional. It is however repealed by the same authority which enacted it, and therefore the plaintiff's title cannot be assisted thereby.[42]

The repealing law as available in the Dallas publication later authorized by the Pennsylvania legislature omits the preamble. In consequence, the general assembly's reasons can only be surmised, and the same is true with respect to Justice Keates because of his failure to recite them in his short opinion. In effect was the Pennsylvania Constitution of 1790, with variances from the document of 1776. Section 9 of Article IX now employed the history-freighted language of forbidding deprivation of life, liberty, or property unless by judgment of one's peers or the law of the land. However, if applied as literally

---

35. 8 W. Swindler, Sources and Documents of U.S. Constitutions 278 (1973) (Pa. Const. 1776).

36. *Id.* at 278-79.

37. *Id.* at 278.

38. 1 Yeates 260 (1793).

39. The Act of Establishment is found in 1 A. Dallas, Laws of the Commonwealth of Pennsylvania 815 (1797). By Act of September 22, 1785, 2 *id.* 395, the many appropriations, including that of Austin's property (*id.* at 408), were confirmed to the Trustees.

40. Found in 2 A. Dallas, *op. cit. supra* note 39, at 213.

41. *Id.* at 252.

42. 1 Yeates, *supra* note 38, at 261.

phrased the guaranty reached only the criminally accused.[43] Section 10 of the same Article embraced all propertied persons and required compensation as well as legislative sanction for takings; "nor shall any man's property be taken or applied to public use without consent of his representatives, and without just compensation being made."[44] It may have been the blending of the two restraints that produced the legislative and judicial judgment of unconstitutionality.

Early in the 1800s *Trustees of the University of North Carolina v. Foy & Bishop*[45] presented a second "university" fact pattern. By acts of 1789 and 1794 the State had granted to the University rights in all escheated property and in war-confiscated property if not already sold. Yet by legislation of 1800 the State reneged. The Trustees sued to recover possession and won on the strength of the law-of-the-land clause in the State's original constitution. *B* is now the public; the taking is not to benefit a private individual or individuals but to expropriate for the supposed good of the general citizenry what is deemed to be *A*'s private property. The decision was quite influential with other state courts faced with challenges of laws expropriative in character.

The facts and holding in *Dartmouth College v. Woodward*[46] are familiar. So to many is Daniel Webster's gratuitous observation in argument in the Supreme Court that the New Hampshire legislation constituted a violation of the law-of-the-land clause of that State's constitution.[47] Two subsequent state court decisions followed Webster in invalidating state laws seeking to effect recompositions in the governing bodies of educational institutions for the avowed objective of enhancing public control. One instance, *State v. Hayward*,[48] concerned the Medical Society of South Carolina, a privately organized body originally authorized to license practitioners of physics and surgery and later to offer medical education. Subsequently, the South Carolina legislature passed an act to incorporate the Medical College of South Carolina, all rights, powers, and duties of the Medical Society to be transferred and vested in the new corporation. The new governing board was to be composed of six members named by the Society and six appointed by the Governor. The Society, not having consented to this reorganization, successfully brought *quo warranto*. The Act was held unconstitutional on both the contract and the law-of-the-land clauses in the state constitution. As in *Dartmouth College* there was question whether the Society was a truly private body; both the

---

43. 8 W. SWINDLER, *op. cit. supra* note 35, at 292 (Pa. Const. 1790).
44. *Id.* at 292-93.
45. 5 N.C. 57 (1805).
46. 4 Wheat. 518 (1819).
47. *Id.* at 561, 579-80. The New Hampshire court found no violation of the law-of-the-land clause. Its reasons were two: (1) doubt that any private property was involved; (2) the legislative act under challenge was itself a law of the land. Webster of course successfully challenged each of these grounds on appeal.
48. 3 Rich. 389 (S.C. Ct. App. 1832).

State and the City of Charleston had made appropriations in its support. The decision was again that public financial assistance had not changed a private into a public institution. *Regents of the University of Maryland v. Williams*[49] presented the identical issue and reached the same result of invalidity under Maryland's constitutional provision on law-of-the-land.

For a time protection of private property against divestiture stood in the path of abolition of slavery. An early act of the North Carolina legislature emancipating a slave against the will of the owner was invalidated as contrary to the State's law-of-the-land clause.[50] *Dred Scott v. Sandford*[51] struck down Section 8 of the Missouri Compromise on the basis of the due process provision of the Fifth Amendment. There was some challenge on this ground of Lincoln's Emancipation Act but such was swallowed up in the Northern victory. Here surely was divestiture of property rights of a hated form.

The issue of policy to be followed with respect to consumption of alcoholic beverages has agitated the nation throughout its entire history. The first wave of state prohibition laws came at the middle of the nineteenth century, bringing in its wake several constitutional questions. That of relevance in the present analysis was the validity of this legislation with reference to sales of liquor produced prior to the effective date of enactment. The results of constitutional challenge in the state courts varied in part because of variance in the exact phraseology and approach to the interpretation of the due process, law-of-the-land clauses of the respective state constitutions. The first court to hand down judgment was Vermont's. The prohibitory law survived the test in *Lincoln v. Smith*[52] for the reason that section 10 of the Bill of Rights, after listing many procedural defenses for those accused of crime, concluded with the language "nor can any person be justly deprived of his liberty, except by the law of the land or the judgment of his peers." Omission of the term "property" turned the trick. Yet shortly thereafter the same results came in both *State v. Wheeler*[53] and *State v. Keenan*,[54] where state constitutions succeeding the Charters employed the usual trinity of "life, liberty, or property." Each of the two supreme courts viewed its guaranty to be only of procedural application despite inclusion of "property" because, taken as a whole, the thrust of their identical provisions was protection of the criminally accused.

Contrary to the decisions in New England, the New York court of appeals invalidated that State's prohibition law in the celebrated case of *Wynehamer v.*

---

49. 9 Gill & J. 365 (Md. 1838).

50. Allen's Admr. v. Peden, 4 N.C. 442 (1816).

51. 19 How. 393 (1857).

52. 27 Vt. 328 (1854).

53. 25 Conn. 290 (1856), preceded by State v. Brennan's Liquors, 25 Conn. 278 (1856), holding to the same effect.

54. 5 R. I. 497 (1858), preceded by State v. Paul, 5 R. I. 185 (1858), identical in its holding.

People.[55] New York was unique in having two relevant constitutional provisions in its Bill of Rights. One, using law-of-the-land, had been taken nearly verbatim from Chapter 29 and thus carried a substantive ring, whereas the other was quite similar to the Connecticut and Rhode Island phrasings with their procedural connotations although using the language of due-process-of-law. Both provisions were cited by several of the judges yet the majority rested the decision on the latter.[56] There has been an effort to discredit *Wynehamer* on the ground that a decade later it was overruled by *Metropolitan Board v. Barrie.*[57] Such is blatant inaccuracy to the point of raising a question of professional integrity. In sustaining a revision of the state law that applied only prospectively, *Barrie* but confirmed what all the judges in *Wynehamer* had asserted, namely, that the sole constitutional impediment to temperance legislation was penalization of the sale of liquor on hand on the effective date of prohibition. Invalidation in *Wynehamer* occurred because as a matter of statutory interpretation it was felt the constitutional portion of the law was inseparable from the unconstitutional. The only judicial invalidation of a prohibition law applying to post-enactment transactions was *Beebe v. State,*[58] still another state decision of the 1850's. It is significant that in the opinions in that case there is no reference to a law-of-the-land or due-process-of-law restraint.

That expropriation held violative of due process lay in legislative retroactivity was the apparent predicate of the Supreme Court of the United States in later Prohibition cases. Litigated within the first decade of the Fourteenth Amendment, Iowa and Massachusetts statutes faced the new Due Process Clause which was free of entanglement with procedural protections for the criminally accused such as appear with the Due Process Clause of the Fifth Amendment. In sustaining the Bay State Law the Court made it clear:

> We do not mean to say that property actually in existence, and in which the right of the owner has become vested, may be taken for the public good without due compensation. But we infer that the liquor in this case, as in the case of *Bartemeyer v. Iowa* (18 Wall. 129), was not in existence when the liquor law of Massachusetts was passed. Had the plaintiff in error relied on the existence of the property prior to the law, it behooved it to show that fact. But no such fact is shown, and no such point is taken. The plaintiff in error boldly takes the ground that, being a corporation, it has a right, by contract, to manufacture and sell beer for ever, notwithstanding and in spite of any exigencies which may occur in the morals or the health of the community, requiring such manufacture to cease. We do not so

---

55. 13 N.Y. 378 (1856).

56. Unlike those of Connecticut, Rhode Island, and Vermont, New York's provision on due process was followed by interdiction of the taking of private property for public use without just compensation. Addition of this provision does tend to give the clause as a whole substantive as well as procedural coloration.

57. 34 N.Y. 657 (1866).

58. 6 Ind. 501 (1856).

understand the rights of the plaintiff. The legislature had no power to confer any such rights.[59]

In *Bartemeyer*, decided five years earlier, the Court had cautioned that an attempt to prohibit the sale of liquor lawfully owned prior to the effective date of Iowa's prohibitory law would raise "very grave questions" under the due process clause of the Fourteenth Amendment.[60]

This conception of invalid divestiture, however, did not persist. *Mugler v. Kansas*,[61] decided at the very end of the year 1887, sustained prohibition legislation in its application to beer produced prior to the statute's effective date as well as to beer of later production. Four months later, within the same Term, repudiation of the concept had been carried to legislation prohibiting the manufacture and sale of oleomargarine. The decision was *Powell v. Pennsylvania*[62] wherein, as will be seen, the major issue was state power to destroy in perpetuity production of a product successfully competing with butter.[63] The liquor cases presented no such issue. Prohibition of beer and hard liquor was not sought by a soft drink industry; rather, it was the result of centuries of concern over the social consequences of ready availability of intoxicating beverages. Nor is there, in alienation decisions after *Hepburn v. Griswold*,[64] evidence of retroactivity as the controlling element in the concept of expropriation as denial of due process. Dicta in *Davidson*[65] and *Hurtado*,[66] and the square holding in *Missouri Pacific Railway Co. v. Nebraska*[67] are clear on this point.

An all but unrecognized Supreme Court decision of 1893,[68] unearthed by one commentator,[69] involved resort to substantive due process in invalidation of attempted divestiture of proprietary rights in the public domain. A railroad company operating in Washington Territory had been granted a right of way in public lands by one Secretary of the Interior. Believing that this action was the consequence of deception on the part of the railroad that disqualified it from benefits under federal statute, a succeeding Secretary declared the title a nullity. On a bill in equity by the railroad to enjoin execution of the revocation, the Court observed:

---

59. Beer Co. v. Massachusetts, 97 U.S. at 32-33 (1878).

60. Bartemeyer v. Iowa, 18 Wall. at 133 (1873).

61. 123 U.S. 623 (1887).

62. 127 U.S. 678 (1888).

63. For consideration of *Powell* in this context refer to chap. 5, *infra*, pp. 86-89, text accompanying notes 29-45.

64. Considered in the text at notes 23-25, *supra*.

65. Considered in the text at notes 26-27, *supra*.

66. Considered in the text at notes 28-30, *supra*.

67. Considered in the text at note 31, *supra*.

68. Noble v. Union River Logging Railroad Co., 147 U.S. 165 (1893).

69. Mendelson, *A Missing Link in the Evolution of Due Process*, 10 VAND. L. REV. 125, at 135, n. 68 (1956).

If it were made to appear that the right of way had been obtained by fraud, a bill would doubtless lie by the United States for the cancellation and annulment of an approval thus obtained. [Citations]. A revocation of the approval of the Secretary of the Interior, however, by his successor in office was an attempt to deprive the plaintiff of its property without due process of law, and was, therefore, void.[70]

The usual pattern of divestiture is one in which property is taken from the few for the benefit of many. A variant occurs when the "transfer" is from the many to the few. Ad valorem taxation to support bond issues by state or municipalities to finance internal improvements by private business is the classic example of this variant. The Supreme Court's reaction to this major economic development that swept the country following settlement of the slavery issue was the seminal decision in *Citizen's Loan Association v. Topeka*.[71] It was there determined, opinion by Justice Miller, that taxes for the aid of private enterprise were illegal unless the objective were judicially found to be a "public purpose." The reasoning was that if the purpose was legitimately public in nature this fact would negative the appearance of a taking from *As* (taxpayers) to *Bs* (favored private business). Like most state courts, the Supreme Court drew the line at public utilities, a reasonable decision in view of the unique legal status of public utilities as intermediate between private and public corporations.

The constitutional source of this limitation on governmental aid to privately owned enterprises in the interest of internal economic development *Loan Association* identified as follows:

The theory of our governments, State and National, is opposed to the deposit of unlimited power anywhere. The executive, the legislative, and the judicial branches of these governments are all of limited and defined powers.

There are limitations on such power which grow out of the essential nature of all free governments. Implied reservations of individual rights, without which the social compact could not exist, and which are respected by all governments entitled to the name. [sic] No court, for instance, would hesitate to declare void a statute which enacted that A. and B. who were husband and wife to each other should be so no longer, but that A. should thereafter be the husband of C., and B. the wife of D. Or which should enact that the homestead now owned by A. should no longer be his, but should henceforth be the property of B.[72]

Substantive due process was not the explicit basis of *Loan Association*. One could hardly expect to find the new Due Process Clause cited as authority only one year after Justice Miller had so discounted it in the *Slaughter-House Cases*. The suit against Topeka had been brought under diversity of citizenship, which opened the "whole case" for determination. Decision could thus be

---

70. Noble v. Union River Logging Railroad Co., *supra* note 68, at 176.

71. 20 Wall. 655 (1874).

72. *Id.* at 663. In Cole v. LaGrange, 113 U.S. 1 (1885), like decision was rested on the Missouri constitution.

rested on the underlying constitutional bulwark against expropriation of private property that Justice Chase had invoked in *Calder v. Bull*. But the earlier linkage of the *A* to *B* syndrome with substantive due process would quickly renew under the emergent Due Process Clause of the Fourteenth Amendment.

Alienation/Divestiture of property rights. Once it had been established by *Munn v. Illinois*[73] that Due Process was not offended by state fixation of maximum charges for grain storage where a condition of virtual monopoly obtained among available elevators, applicability of the constitutional principle to railroads immediately followed.[74] Declared the Court in one of these decisions:

> In *Munn v. Illinois, supra*, p. 113, and *Chicago, Burlington & Quincy Railroad Co. v. Iowa, supra*, p. 155, we decided that the State may limit the amount of charges by railroad companies for fares and freights....[75]

Railroads, too, enjoyed virtual monopoly in the trading areas of their respective operations.[76] However, expropriation would occur should the rates legislated under state authority be confiscatory of railroad property rights through failure to provide an adequate return to private ownership. If the effect of non-compensatory rates were viewed as according undue advantage to shippers, the result would take on the coloration of alienation of rights in property. On the other hand, viewing the general public as the ultimate beneficiary from "unreasonably" low rates, the resulting loss to the carrier would have the appearance of expropriation by divestiture. Thus rate regulation constituted a chameleon-like form of expropriation.

The *Railroad Commission Cases* of 1886[77] presented this pattern. With it "now settled" that a State had power to limit the charges made by railroad companies "for the transportation of persons and property within its own jurisdiction," the Court's concern was state power in the face of the Contract and Commerce Clauses of the Constitution.[78] Charters of the railroads involved in the litigation had granted authority to set reasonable rates; there was therefore a question whether later state fixation of conflicting levels of rates impaired the obligation of the contractual grants. *Stone v. Mississippi*[79] had

---

73. 99 U.S. 113 (1877). Discussed textually at notes 11-28, *infra*, chap. 4, pp. 70-73.

74. Chicago, Burlington & Quincy Railroad Co. v. Iowa, 94 U.S. 155 (1877); Peik v. Chicago & Northwestern Railway Co., 94 U.S. 164 (1877); Winona & St. Peter Railroad Co. v. Blake, 94 U.S. 180 (1877).

75. Peik v. Chicago & Northwestern Railway Co., 94 U.S. at 176.

76. F. FETTER, THE MASQUERADE OF MONOPOLY 258 (1931). The principle was to be extended to the so-called "natural" monopolies of electric power, gas, telephone, urban transportation, and water, collectively known as public utilities.

77. Stone v. Farmers' Loan & Trust Co., 116 U.S. 307 (1886); Stone v. Illinois Central Railroad Co., 116 U.S. 347 (1886); Stone v. New Orleans & Northeastern Railroad Co., 116 U.S. 354 (1886).

78. Stone v. Farmers' Loan & Trust Co., 116 U.S. at 325.

79. 101 U.S. 814 (1880). Discussed in text at notes 36, 41, *infra*, chap. 3, p. 54.

made four exceptions to the inalienability of the police power, of which rate regulation was one.[80] This obstacle was overcome by resort to the doctrine of strict construction in the interpretation of charters.[81]

Assertion of violation of the Commerce Clause was founded on the fact that the challenging roads were part of a plan to provide railroad service from the Gulf to the Midwest. If so viewed regulation of their rates would seem to fall on the national uniformity side of the *Cooley Compromise*,[82] with the consequence that the States would be powerless to act even in the absence of congressional action. The very year of the *Commission Cases* the momentous decision in *Wabash, St. Louis & Pacific Railway Co. v. Illinois*[83] had invalidated a prohibition of that State against the hated railroad practice of charging more for a shorter than for a longer freight haul. This time state power was rescued by a different form of strict construction; rate regulation by each of the jurisdictions was viewed separately rather than functionally as parts of a whole, thus grounding the conclusion that this type of state regulation permitted of local variation and accordingly was constitutionally valid under *Cooley*.

Whether regarded as an alienation of property rights or as a divestiture of them, railroad rates set by government at confiscatory levels, the Court saw, would constitute expropriation in violation of substantive due process:

> From what has thus been said, it is not to be inferred that this power of limitation or regulation is itself without limit. This power to regulate is not a power to destroy, and limitation is not the equivalent of confiscation. Under pretence of regulating fares and freights, the State cannot require a railroad corporation to carry persons or property without reward; neither can it do that which in law amounts to a taking of private property for public use without just compensation, or without due process of law. What would have this effect we need not now say, because no tariff has yet been fixed by the commission, and the statute of Mississippi expressly provides "that in all trials of cases brought for a violation of any tariff of charges, as fixed by the commission, it may be shown in defence that such tariff so fixed is unjust."[84]

In the year following the decisions in the *Railroad Commission Cases*, the legislature of Minnesota established a railroad and warehouse commission to which as interpreted by the State's highest court was given power to set, with a finality denying judicial inquiry, the charges to be made for the transportation of property by railroad. In this important respect the Minnesota statute differed from Mississippi's law. On mandamus to the Milwaukee Railroad to observe the tariffs determined by the commission, the state law as construed was challenged as unconstitutional. Although the supreme court of Minnesota

---

80. New Orleans Gas Co. v. Louisiana Light Co., 115 U.S. 650 (1885).
81. Considered textually in notes 30-31, *infra*, chap. 3, p. 53.
82. Cooley v. Board of Wardens, 12 How. 299 (1851).
83. 118 U.S. 557 (1886).
84. Stone v. Farmers' Loan & Trust Co., *supra* note 78, at 331.

sustained the law, reversal was its fate in the Supreme Court of the United States.[85] The deprivation of due process found by the Court was clearly procedural, yet the decision had a substantive quality in its categorical holding that railroads were to be protected by due process from expropriation through attempted imposition of confiscatory rates. It remained only to implement the decision by determination as to how to calculate whether rates fixed by state commissions or legislatures were "reasonable" in terms of the service provided. This required litigation through the 1890s.

No progress was made in *Chicago & Grand Trunk Railway v. Wellman*;[86] there was but repetition of what already had been judicially established. "The legislature has power to fix rates, and the extent of judicial interference is protection against unreasonable rates."[87] In *Reagan v. Farmers' Loan & Trust Co.*[88] the Court's opinion was for the first time marked by detailed consideration of cost figures, yet no formula emerges. That appeared only with *Smythe v. Ames*,[89] invalidating a Nebraska act fixing maximum rates for freights. Fair value of the railroad property being used for the convenience of the public became the test.

And in order to ascertain that value, the original cost of construction, the amount expended in permanent improvements, the amount and market value of its bonds, original cost of construction, the amount expended in permanent improvements, the amount and market value of its bonds and stock, the present as compared with the original cost of construction, the probable earning capacity of the property under particular rates prescribed by statute, and the sum required to meet operating expense, are all matters for consideration, and are to be given such weight as may be just and right in each case. We do not say that there may not be other matters to be regarded in estimating the value of the property. What the company is entitled to ask is a fair return upon the value of that which it employs for the public convenience. On the other hand, what the public is entitled to demand is that no more be exacted from it for the use of a public highway than the services rendered by it are reasonably worth.[90]

---

85. Chicago, Milwaukee & St. Paul Railway Co. v. Minnesota, 118 U.S. 418 (1890).

86. 143 U.S. 339 (1892).

87. *Id.* at 344.

88. 154 U.S. 362 (1894).

89. 169 U.S. 466 (1898).

90. *Id.* at 546-47. Out of this welter of considerations there evolved the formula that the sum of the rates charged the public must equate with the total of operating expenses plus fair return on fair value. In theory this formula accommodated the just interests of both supplier and customer, yet in application it proved hopelessly unworkable. Operating expenses and rate of return presented difficult, but solvable, determinations; fair value, on the other hand, was a can of worms. It lay somewhere between original cost and cost of reproduction, but where? The original cost might include other than prudent investment; cost of reproduction required endless calculations with every change in the price level. The weight to be given each of the two figures as finally ascertained, in setting the "fair value," produced endless debate. The entire valuation process became a ridiculous guessing game, increasingly criticized. Looking ahead, it was not until 1944 that this theoretically sound

At century's end this was the extent of due process protection against ex-propriation. There is paradox in the fact that private property was only par-tially protected against governmental deprivation beyond that which Chief Justice Marshall would have given had he had his way. It is clear from *Fletcher v. Peck*[91] that he would not have restricted the Ex Post Facto prohibition to criminal legislation, as had been done by *Calder v. Bull*[92] before his appoint-ment to the Court. In his view civil retroactivity would have been constitu-tionally invalid without need to resort to Due Process for protection against alienation. And had he been able in *Ogden v. Saunders*[93] to muster a majority for his view of the reach of the Contract Clause, there would have been less occasion for Due Process protection against legislative divestiture. To Mar-shall the Contract Clause was an inhibition to pass laws impairing the obli-gation of contracts, not simply an inhibition to pass retrospective laws; given the proper understanding of Ex Post Facto, the Contract Clause was mere sur-plusage if operative only against retroactive laws. Due Process would differ only in its extension to non-contractual relations, but in the time of John Mar-shall few relations were not deemed contractual in their nature. Witness his holding for the Court in *Fletcher* that the Contract Clause embraced public as well as private contracts.

---

but unworkable formula was junked by Federal Power Comm. v. Hope Natural Gas Co., 320 U.S. 591 (1944).

91. 6 Cr. 87 (1810).

92. See note 5, *supra*, for comment.

93. 12 Wheat. 213 (1827).

3. Monopoly by Public Grant as Denial of Substantive Due Process

There is ample evidence of concern in early America with the monopoly issue that long agitated the Mother Country. In *Coppie of the Liberties of the Massachusetts Collonie in New England*, drawn in 1641, the *Liberty* numbered 9 read: "No monopolies shall be granted or allowed amongst us, but of such new Inventions that are profitable to the Countrie, and that for a short term."[1] Thus one major Colony restated the essence of the Statute of Monopolies as a precaution against Stuart effort to fasten on it exclusive rights of value only to the patentee. After detailed inquiry into the Colonial period, one scholar concluded that "it is obvious from a study of revolutionary records that there was deep-seated hostility among the American colonists to monopoly, and all devices to enhance prices."[2]

The first constitutions of several of the States, including Massachusetts, incorporated in their Declarations of Rights prohibition against the evil.[3] Wording was usually express, asserting the contrariness of monopolies to the "genius" or "spirit" of a free State. Maryland added that "monopolies are odious," an expression familiar from the struggle against them in England. That other of the States did not include express prohibition of monopoly in their Bills of Rights may be explained by sentiments expressed later in a Connecticut case.[4] In a conflict between early gaslight companies for the exclusive right to lay pipes in city streets, that kind of grant was declared to constitute a monopoly. It was of no consequence that Connecticut had "no direct constitutional provision against monopoly" for the "whole theory of a free government is opposed to such grants."[5] It was enough that the Statute of Monopo-

---

1. 5 W. Swindler, Sources and Documents of U.S. Constitutions 48 (1975).

2. Jones, *Historical Development of the Law of Business Competition*, 36 Yale L. J. 42, at 52 (1926). The article continues *id.* 207.

3. Md. Const. XXXIX (1776), in 4 W. Swindler; Mass. Declaration of Rights Art. VI (1780), in 5 *id.* (no exclusive privileges); N.C. Const. XXIII (1776), in 7 *id.*; Tenn. Const. Art. XI, §23 (1796), in 9 *id.*; Va. Declaration of Rights Sec. 4 (1776) in 10 *id.* (no exclusive privileges). The listing in E. Dumbauld, The Bill of Rights 163 (1957) is incomplete.

4. Norwich Gaslight Co. v. Norwich City Gas Co., 25 Conn. 19 (1836).

5. *Id.* at 38.

lies, "which declares such monopolies to be contrary to law and void . . . has always been considered as merely declaratory of the common law."[6]

Absence of constitutional prohibition on monopoly was one of the criticisms of the Constitution as drafted by the Convention of 1787. George Mason, who had unsuccessfully moved for such a prohibition late in the Convention, objected that:

> Under their own construction of the general clause at the end of the enumerated powers, the Congress may grant monopolies in trade and commerce, constitute new crimes, inflict unusual and severe punishment and extend their power as far as they shall think proper. . . . [7]

A pamphleteer attempted to answer Mason's fear on the subject of monopolies by writing that on examination of the Constitution as drafted

> I find it expressly provided, "That no preference shall be given to the ports of one State over the ports of another," and that "citizens of each State shall be entitled to all privileges and immunities of citizens in the several States." These provisions appear to me to be calculated for the very purpose Mr. Mason wishes to secure. Can they be consistent with any monopoly in trade or commerce?[8]

In his response to Mason the pamphleteer was as pathetic in foretelling the future as Mason was prophetic in forecasting the reach of the Commerce Clause implemented by the Necessary and Proper Clause. Mason was far from alone in his objection. The same danger was seen by another Antifederalist:

> By sect. 8 of article I, Congress are to have the unlimited right to regulate commerce, external and internal, and they may therefore create monopolies which have been universally injurious to all the subjects of the countries that have adopted them, excepting the monopolists themselves.[9]

Delegates of five of the ratifying conventions

> [m]indful of the evils of the great commercial monopolies of the Old World, such as the British East India Company and the Dutch East India Company, were desirous that no such monopolies should secure recognition from the United States Government, and to that end they proposed as an amendment to the Constitution an

---

6. *Ibid.* The court did refer to the first section of the State's Bill of Rights, prohibiting "exclusive public emoluments, or privileges . . . " but said nothing of Section 9 forbidding deprivation of life, liberty, or property "but by due course of law." The significance of the independence of these two separate provisions is remarked *infra*.

7. 1 B. SCHWARTZ, THE BILL OF RIGHTS: A DOCUMENTARY HISTORY 446 (1971).

8. *Id.* at 451-52, quoting from *Pamphlets on the Constitution of the United States.* The context makes clear that Mason's concern was the possibility that, absent a prohibition, Northern States could control international shipping to the disadvantage of Southern States.

9. Letters of Agrippa, 1788, reproduced in 1 B. SCHWARTZ, *op. cit. supra* note 7, at 512.

article declaring "that Congress erect no company of merchants with exclusive advantages of commerce."[10]

Jefferson was one of those disappointed that the Constitution as it came from Philadelphia contained no Bill of Rights. Writing twice from Paris in early 1778, he expressed to two correspondents the hope that some ratifying conventions would insist upon annexation of a declaration of rights as the price of acceptance.[11] He thought Virginia would do so. In both letters he stipulated that the declaration should guarantee

> freedom of religion, freedom of the press, freedom of commerce against monopolies, trial by juries in all cases, no suspension of habeas corpus, no standing armies. These are fetters against doing evil which no honest government should decline.[12]

When the Constitution was ratified without the addition of a Bill of Rights, demand turned to pressure for amendment pursuant to the provisions of Article V. Madison's ambivalence at this stage is well revealed in his letter to Jefferson dated October 17, 1788. In view of Madison's key position a paragraph is worthy of quotation.

> Supposing a bill of rights to be proper the articles which ought to compose it, admit of much discussion. I am inclined to think that absolute restrictions in cases that are doubtful, or where emergencies may overrule them, ought to be avoided. The restrictions however strongly marked on paper will never be regarded when opposed to the decided sense of the public, and after repeated violations in extraordinary cases they will lose even their ordinary efficacy. Should a Rebellion or insurrection alarm the people as well as the Government, and a suspension of the Hab. Corp. be dictated by the alarm, no written prohibitions on earth would prevent the measure. Should an army in time of peace be gradually established in our neighborhood by Britn. or Spain, declarations on paper would have as little effect in preventing a standing force for the public safety. The best security agst. these evils is to remove the pretext for them. With regard to Monopolies, they are justly classed among the greatest nuisances in Government. But is it clear that as encouragements to literary works and ingenious discoveries, they are not too valuable to be wholly renounced? . . . Monopolies are sacrifices of the many to the few.

---

10. H.R. Doc. #353, Pt. 2, 54th Cong., 2d Sess. 255 (1897), citing for the House action 1 ANNALS col. 778 (Aug. 1789). Senate action (Sept. 1789) cannot be found in the ANNALS.

11. Letter to Alexander Donald, Feb. 7, 1788, reproduced in 1 B. SCHWARTZ, *supra* note 7, at 612; Letter to C.W.F. Dumas, Feb. 12, 1788, reproduced *id.* at 613.

12. The quotation is from the letter to Donald, *supra* note 11. In the letter to Dumas declaration against suspensions of habeas corpus is omitted. But in each letter "no monopolies in commerce" is included; in Donald's letter this provision immediately follows freedom of religion and freedom of the press, suggesting the importance Jefferson placed on it. In a letter to Madison dated December 20, 1787, Jefferson had first stated his dislike of the absence of these provisions from a Bill of Rights. 12 BOYD, JEFFERSON'S PAPERS 440 (1955), quoted in E. DUMBAULD, *op. cit. supra* note 3, at 9, n. 18 ("restriction against monopolies").

Where the power is in the few it is natural for them to sacrifice the many to their own partialities and corruptions. Where the power as with us is in the many not in the few the danger cannot be very great that the few will be thus favored. It is much more to be dreaded that the few will be unnecessarily sacrificed to the many.[13]

It was no surprise that when a set of amendatory provisions had been drafted, none concerned limitation on monopoly. Jefferson did not give up. His response to the draft Madison had been "so good as to send me," was that:

I like it as far as it goes; but I should have been for going further. For instance the following alterations and additions would have pleased me....[14]

Among these was one reading

Monopolies may be allowed to persons for their own productions in literature and their own inventions in the arts for a term not exceeding ___ years but for no longer term and no other purpose.[15]

Again, Jefferson's advocacy fell short.[16] A final effort was made in the first Congress during debate over the articles of amendment to be submitted to the States. No anti-monopoly provision appearing, it was proposed by Jefferson adherents first in the House and then in the Senate, to add "That Congress erect no company of merchants with exclusive advantages of commerce." But in each instance the proposal was "passed in the negative."[17]

As conversant with English constitutional history as were Jefferson, Richard Henry Lee, Madison, Mason, Wilson and other Founders, it is passing strange that none appeared to connect monopoly with violation of Due Process. Of the State conventions ratifying the Philadelphia draft yet desiring inclusion, by way of amendment, of an article forbidding Congress to create monopolies in commerce, only three proposed, and then as wholly separate, the inclusion of a due process clause.[18] Earlier remarked was the failure of the

---

13. Letter of Madison to Jefferson dated Oct. 17, 1788, to be found in 1 B. SCHWARTZ, *op. cit. supra* note 7, at 614-18. The quoted paragraph appears *id.* at 617-18.

14. Letter of Jefferson to Madison, Aug. 28, 1789, reproduced in 2 B. SCHWARTZ, *op. cit. supra* note 7, at 1140-44. The quoted statement appears *id.* at 1143.

15. This formulation of an anti-monopoly provision follows immediately the statement quoted note 14, *supra.*

16. But that Jefferson was not without support at this juncture in his crusade is shown by the fact that four State Conventions urged inclusion of an anti-monopoly provision in the Federal Bill of Rights. New York proposed "that the Congress do not grant monopolies"; Massachusetts, New Hampshire, and Rhode Island favored the wording "that the Congress erect no company of merchants with exclusive advantages of commerce." 1 ELLIOT, DEBATES IN THE SEVERAL STATE CONVENTIONS 323, 326, 330, 337 (2d ed. 1854).

17. 2 B. SCHWARTZ, *op. cit. supra* note 7, at 1137 (House), 1150 (Senate). Wording of the two proposals was in meaning identical.

18. E. DUMBAULD, *op. cit. supra* note 3, at 190 and 194 (N.Y.), 199 and 200 (N.C.), 183

court in the Connecticut gaslight case to see any connection between the two prohibitions.[19]

The context in which Due Process did work its way into the Constitution as a part of Amendment V in the Bill of Rights would not encourage historical association with anti-monopoly. Unlike preceding formulations, which held close to the wording in Magna Carta, Due Process in Amendment V was closely intertwined with protections for the criminally accused. Provision of these had been another objective of the demand for supplementation of the original instrument that came out of Philadelphia. The linkage between the due process concept and long-standing hostility to monopoly was finally made with the later version of Due Process incorporated within the Fourteenth Amendment where it was expressed free of entangling procedural guarantees.[20] In the interim the stranglehold of monopoly was checkmated by a combination of political forces and judicial doctrines.

Opposition to monopoly, important but not critical in determining the affairs of the first Bank of the United States, became a chief weapon against the second Bank. President Jackson and his lieutenants, who led the movement, attacked the Bank on two scores: since its charter expressly guaranteed that the federal government would create no other banks, it was a monopoly in the strict legal sense; since it was too big and rich, it was also a monopoly in the broader political sense. Thomas Hart Benton of Missouri, the Bank's chief opponent in the Senate, argued accordingly that it was objectionable not only "on account of the exclusive privileges, and anti-republican monopoly, which it gives to the stockholders," but also "because it tends to aggravate the inequality of fortunes" and is "an institution too great and powerful to be tolerated in a Government of free and equal laws." Jackson, when he vetoed the bill renewing the Bank's charter, emphasized the "great evils to our country and institutions [that] might flow from such a concentration of power in the hands of a few men irresponsible to the people." Amos Kendall, who as a member of Jackson's Kitchen Cabinet wrote the first draft of the veto message, in his own public addresses also called the Bank a threat to democracy. . . . In the end this maneuver of repeatedly condemning the Bank as a "monster monopoly," a "moneyed power" that would establish an oligarchy and eventually a monarchy, defeated the Bank's supporters and led to its destruction.

There were other institutions, more numerous and permanent than the central banks, against which public opposition to monopoly was more regularly expressed. Chief among these was the corporation. The view that all corporations are monopolies was as old as the principle that all monopolies are evil, and like it, was founded on English experience.[21]

---

and 184 (Va.). Two of these conventions varied the wording to "exclusive emoluments." But for the Bill of Rights, North Carolina employed the more standard terminology—erection of no "company of merchants with exclusive advantages of commerce." *Id.* at 205.

19. Text at notes 4-6, *supra.*

20. Assisting in the "reunion" may have been favorable resolution of the question whether in America, contrary to England, Due Process restricted legislative as well as executive action.

21. Letwin, *Congress and the Sherman Antitrust Law,* 23 U. OF CHI. L. REV. 221, at 228

Constitutionalized protection against monopoly commenced with the early decision of the Supreme Court of the United States in *Fletcher v. Peck*,[22] in which Chief Justice Marshall interpreted the Contract Clause to include both executed contracts and contracts between a state and an individual. With the philosophy of Rousseau still coloring as "contractual" most every relationship in legal contemplation, here was a powerful constitutional provision for impregnating legislative grants with monopolistic rigidity. To its regret, the State of New York early came to an appreciation of this feature of the Federal Constitution when, tiring of the monopoly granted to Fulton and Livingston for steamboat operation within the State's jurisdiction, it found itself stymied by the Contract Clause.[23] In its courts Ogden, assignee of the original grantees, successfully enjoined Gibbons, though licensed under federal coasting law, from competing in the run between New York City and opposite New Jersey ports. In the Supreme Court of the United States, however, Ogden lost his monopoly on the reasoning of advocate Webster, accepted by Marshall, of the paramountcy of congressional power in instances of commerce among the States. *Gibbons v. Ogden*[24] thus provided one method for breaking the hold of hated monopoly.[25]

The Commerce Clause, however, would not always be available for freeing market competition from monopolistic restriction.[26] Congressional exercise of the commerce power was infrequent until the end of the century, while the constricting effect on state police and taxing power of the negative implication of the Clause inherited from Marshall's dictum in *Gibbons* operated to discourage its broad interpretation.[27] An excellent illustration is provided by

---

(1951). On the other hand, there were political forces pressing in the opposite direction. Thus in the same article, *id.* at 229, n. 50, reference is made to a number of State granted monopolies. L. IACOCCA, AN AUTOBIOGRAPHY 331 (1984), cites a Massachusetts grant of 1643 to a new smelting company of exclusive iron-producing privileges for twenty years to encourage this developing industry. But these were for constructive internal improvements.

22. 6 Cr. 87 (1810).

23. Mendelson, *New Light on Fletcher v. Peck and Gibbons v. Ogden*, 58 YALE L. J. 567 (1949), succinctly depicts the dilemma.

24. 9 Wheat. 1 (1824).

25. Two articles each give lengthy account of the total episode that pitted against each other two of the outstanding legal minds of the early 19th century. Mann, *The Marshall Court: Nationalization of Private Rights and Personal Liberty From the Authority of the Commerce Clause*, 38 IND. L.J. 117 (1962); Campbell, *Chancellor Kent, Chief Justice Marshall, and the Steamboat Cases*, 25 SYR. L. REV. 497 (1974).

26. Jones, *supra* note 2, at 211, states that *Gibbons v. Ogden* "was of great importance, for Massachusetts, New Hampshire, Pennsylvania, Georgia and Tennessee had all granted similar monopolies between 1813 and 1819." The implication is that in each instance interstate commerce, as defined by Marshall, was involved, thus exposing these monopolies to repudiation.

27. This facet of development in the second half of 19th century constitutional law, so damned by critics who could not understand it, is explained in Strong, *Bicentennial Benchmark*, 55 N.C.L. REV. 1, at 43-45 (1976).

Veazie and Young v. Moor.[28] By statute the State of Maine had awarded Moor exclusive rights for seven years on a section of the Penobscot River theretofore unnavigable, provided the grantee would clear the stream for navigation and operate a steamboat on it. Moor complied, only to find Veazie and Young running a boat in competition. The supreme court of the State granted Moor an injunction and damages. Affirming, the Supreme Court of the United States found no conflict with congressional power; the Penobscot runs wholly within the State. To accept defendant's interpretation of the Commerce Clause would extend it inward to control the pursuits of the "planter, the grazier, the manufacturer, the mechanic, the immense operations of the colleries and mines and furnaces of the country. . . . Such a pretension would effectually prevent or paralyze every effort at internal improvement by the several States."[29]

The doctrine of strict construction of contracts, developed with the succession of Roger Taney to the position of Chief Justice, offered some escape from the rigors of the Contract Clause. In the classic case of *Charles River Bridge v. Warren Bridge*[30] the Massachusetts' charter grant to one company to operate a toll bridge over the Charles River was held not to foreclose the State from later authorizing construction of a competing, free bridge. "[A]ny ambiguity in the terms of the contract, must operate against the adventurers, and in favour of the public."[31] Another avoidance technique lay in the established law of municipal corporations to the effect that municipal power (absent home rule) extends only to "reasonable" regulations within clear authority.[32] Of two decisions the later in point of time is the more relevant. On facts strikingly similar to those shortly to come before the Supreme Court in the *Slaughter-House Cases*,[33] a City of Chicago grant of butchering privileges to one concern was on challenge held invalid.[34] The court's reasoning was that if the grant were accepted and bond furnished it would create a contract that tended to monopoly and would therefore be void, the city having no such authority under its charter.[35]

---

28. 14 How. 568 (1852).

29. *Id.* at 574. Defendants' contention of the proper interpretation to be given the Commerce Clause is essentially that now approved by the Court for measuring the reach of congressional authority vis à vis the states.

30. 11 Peter 420 (1837).

31. *Id.* at 544.

32. Mayor of City of Hudson v. Thorne, 7 Paige Ch. Rep. 261 (N.Y. 1838); City of Chicago v. Rumpff, 45 Ill. 90 (1867).

33. 16 Wall. 36 (1873) (to be examined shortly).

34. City of Chicago v. Rumpff, *supra* note 32.

35. Another avoidance device was available in those States whose constitutions carried prohibitions against monopolies. McRee v. Wilmington & Raleigh Rail Road Company, 47 N.C. 186 (1855), held ineffective, against later authorization of a railroad bridge, a monopoly franchise to construct and operate a bridge in perpetuity free of competition within a radius of six miles. The supreme court of North Carolina found it unnecessary to

Any further need for devices of avoidance faded away when in *Stone v. Mississippi*[36] the Supreme Court ruled that in most contracts to which a state is a party there is implied a power on the state's part to alter or amend in the interest of the public good.[37] Although of momentous import the concept of an implied power came analogically from Story's dictum in *Dartmouth College*[38] to the effect express reservation by a state of power to alter, amend, or repeal a corporation's charter could pull the teeth of that holding. In *Beer Co. v. Massachusetts*,[39] decided two years before *Stone*, the Court first relied on an express reservation but then added the new theory of an implied reservation. It was this rejection of the rule of *Fletcher v. Peck* that broke the monopoly the Carpetbag legislature of Louisiana had in 1869 conferred on the Crescent City Live-Stock Landing and Slaughter-House Co. Regaining control of state government, the people of Louisiana had in 1879 adopted a new constitution abolishing monopolies (save in railroad companies) and their legislature had followed with enactment of ordinances opening up the butchering business "to general competition." Crescent City, with time remaining on its 25-year exclusive grant, which had survived attack in the *Slaughter-House Cases*, returned to the Supreme Court confident of a second victory. Decision in the federal circuit court had been favorable; the obligation of the contract with the three parishes gave every assurance of success. But the monopolist had reckoned without *Stone*. Citing it, *Beer Co.* and a third decision, the Court in *Butchers' Union*[40] did not so much as mention *Fletcher*. Now in ascendancy was the new proposition that government cannot bargain away its powers over public health, safety and morals.[41]

It is an irony of history that had *Stone v. Mississippi* been decided a decade earlier there would have been no occasion for the great debate in the *Slaughter-House Cases* of 1873. On challenge, the monopoly grant would have fallen before the constitutional doctrine of implied reservation. As it was, on facts that precluded attack on any of the bases theretofore successful, success against the monopoly would require a fresh approach. Losing in the supreme court of Louisiana, the ousted butchers turned to John Archibald Campbell, a former

---

determine if the 1766 legislative grant was entirely abolished by adoption of the Constitution of 1776 with its express prohibition on monopolies, see note 3, *supra*; it was enough to hold that the railroad was protected against attack by the holder of the earlier monopoly franchise.

36. 101 U. S. 814 (1880).

37. For the exceptions see *infra* note 41.

38. Dartmouth College v. Woodward, 4 Wheat. at 712 (1819).

39. 92 U. S. 25 (1878).

40. Butchers' Union Slaughter-House and Live-Stock Landing Co. v. Crescent City Live-Stock Landing and Slaughter-House Co., 111 U. S. 746 (1884).

41. One year after *Butchers' Union*, four exceptions were made to the rule of inalienability of State police power by New Orleans Gas Co. v. Louisiana Light Co., 115 U. S. 650 (1885): charter alteration, land grants, public utility rates and terms, tax exemptions.

Justice of the Supreme Court of the United States from Alabama who had re-
signed his commission at the outbreak of the Civil War. Conventional learning
in courses and commentary on Constitutional Law stresses Campbell's attempt to induce the Supreme Court to find in the Privileges or Immunities
Clause of the new Fourteenth Amendment the same content Justice Bushrod
Washington had on circuit given the Privileges and Immunities Clause of Article IV, Sec. 2, in the case of *Corfield v. Coryell*.[42] The familiar passage is *Corfield* is as follows:

> We feel no hesitation in confining these expressions to those privileges and im-
> munities which are *fundamental*; which belong of right to the citizens of all free
> governments, and which have at all times been enjoyed by citizens of the several
> States which compose this Union, from the time of their becoming free, independent,
> and sovereign. What these fundamental principles are, it would be more tedious
> than difficult to enumerate. They may all, however, be comprehended under the
> following general heads; protection by the government, with the right to acquire
> and possess property of every kind, and to pursue and obtain happiness and safety,
> subject, nevertheless, to such restraints as the government may prescribe for the
> general good of the whole.[43]

Campbell's reformulation is most succinctly stated at the very close of his
oral argument on Re-argument in the *Slaughter-House Cases*. After summarizing the constitutional effect of Article IV, Section 2, by reference to the facts
and holding in *Ward v. Maryland*,[44] he asserted

> Now, I say that under this Constitution [incorporating the Fourteenth Amendment],
> if the State passes a law which affects the rights or the privileges, or the immunities
> of any citizen of its own population for the benefit of other citizens of its own
> population, this amendment has the effect to give him the same appeal to this
> Court that the Constitution in its original state did to the citizens of another State.[45]

It was a bold contention; a constitutional prohibition against State denial to
out-of-staters of rights accorded its own citizens would have been converted
into one denying to its own citizens, as well as to others, rights deemed fundamental under the *Corfield* test. This contention is repeated in Campbell's
briefs and argument from first to last.[46] Possibly his strategy was, through repetition, to mask the boldness in an appearance of unstartling analogy.

---

42. 4 Wash. C.C. 371, 6 Fed. Cas. 546 (No. 3,230) (Cir. Ct. E.D. Pa. 1823).

43. 6 Fed. Cas. at 551-52.

44. 12 Wall. 418 (1870).

45. 6 P. KURLAND and G. CASPER, LANDMARK BRIEFS AND ARGUMENTS OF THE SUPREME
COURT OF THE UNITED STATES: CONSTITUTIONAL CASES 763 (1975).

46. Dependence in analysis of contentions of counsel in the *Slaughter-House Cases* is
placed on documents collected by 6 P. KURLAND and G. CASPER, in their multi-volume set
first cited *supra* note 45. Materials on the *Slaughter-House Cases* in Volume 6 commence
at 475 and end on 763. Paging used is that of the Editors, not that of counsel.

Campbell had, however, another string to his bow. Durant, for the defendant monopolist, recognized this in his Brief on Re-argument:

> It is contended that the exclusive privileges granted to the Slaughter-house Company by the act are an abridgement of the "privileges and immunities" of the plaintiffs in error as "citizens of the United States, because they have a natural right to keep stock-landings and slaughter-houses, and this act forbids them to do so within certain limits, *and that this act deprives them of property without due process of law," &c.*[47]

The first Brief for Plaintiffs filed by Campbell was replete with denunciation of monopolies. Reviewing in considerable detail the English period under Elizabeth and James I, he wrote at one point that

> This contest of the people with monopolists derives its importance from the fact that it was the first of their great battles for constitutional liberty upon the ground of their common and just rights.[48]

The opposition to monopoly grants on the part of both Parliament and the English courts was stressed; the Statute of Monopolies was summarized; and Popham's opinion in the *Case of Monopolies* reproduced in full. American state decisions were cited for their expressions of antipathy to monopoly. "The Constitution of the United States preserves the only exemption in the English Statute of Monopolies, the privileges for inventors and authors. Many of the State Constitutions have denounced monopolies and exclusive privileges by name."[49] Vigorously challenged were claims of Durant that the Louisiana Act was designed to promote the public health. This was in response to Durant's contention that, conceding the grant to be monopolistic as he in effect did later,[50] it came within the exception recognized for publicly beneficial monopolies.[51]

In this first Brief there was no effective tie of monopoly to denial of substantive due process. Yet association was embryonic. The degree of attention given the English experience could not but implicate the concept of due process; and twice Campbell asserted conflict between the Louisiana monopoly grant and the Constitution of the United States, especially with the newly adopted Amendments.[52] Yet he was flirting not alone with all three prohibitions of Section One of the Fourteenth Amendment but also with the limitation imposed

---

47. *Id.* at 730. (emphasis added.)

48. *Id.* at 557.

49. *Id.* at 560.

50. Charles Allen, another attorney for defendant, denied in his Brief that the grant was a monopoly, and hence that it was free of constitutional taint. *Id.* 588-98.

51. The Supplemental Brief for Defendants, by Durant, consists of documents asserting the improvement of health conditions under the monopoly and denouncing assertions to the contrary by representatives of the ousted butchers. *Id.* 626-38.

52. *Id.* at 546-47; 573.

by the Thirteenth. The Supplemental Brief for Plaintiffs, in which Campbell was joined by attorney Fellows, narrows focus to the Fourteenth Amendment. The conditions of the grant "must be such, that no privilege or immunity of an American Citizen shall be abridged; that no man shall be deprived of life, liberty or property, thereby; and that the equal protection due to every person in the State shall not be denied."[53]

In Plaintiff's Brief Upon the Re-Argument Campbell did return to broad-based attack on the monopoly grant. Part I of the attack is built on the Thirteenth Amendment; Part II consists of argument under the Fourteenth Amendment with occasional return to the Thirteenth because of the close interrelationship said to exist between the two. "The invalidity of this enactment becomes more apparent when we come to consider it in connection with the Fourteenth Amendment to the Constitution. That Amendment was a development of the Thirteenth, and is a more comprehensive exposition of the principles which lie at the foundation of the Thirteenth."[54] Among those principles are rights to life, liberty and property; but also to privileges and immunities, and to equal protection. Part III, devoted largely to analysis and refutation of decision at the level of the supreme court of Louisiana, closes with the assertion that what the colonists wanted for themselves and their posterity was

Freedom. Free action, free enterprise—free competition.... They made no provisions for sinecures, pensions, monopolies, titles of nobility, privileged orders, exempting from legal duty.[55]

Campbell is here getting closer to the antithesis between monopoly and the due process concept of freedom in the common callings. It is in Campbell's oral argument on Re-Argument that substantive due process emerges as the most specific constitutional provision against monopoly.

The case presented to this Court is, that by a legislative edict every man who had been following his profession for years—numbering about one thousand—that those, every one of them, were put under an interdict within three months from the passage of the Act to close up their places of business, and to submit themselves to the control and direction of a corporation just at that time created. Is man's right to pursue his occupation liberty, or is it property?

I should think, that in this country, it could not be denied to be a natural right of the person, and that in the results of that right, or the expectation or hope of results, it was a matter of property, and whether it be the personal liberty and right of a citizen, or whether it be a right of property, then he cannot be deprived of it, by an act of the legislature. No State shall pass any law to deprive him of life, liberty or property, without due process of law. And if the right of a man to choose and prosecute a lawful industry reaches to the rank of a personal privilege, and his hopes and expectations either of happiness or profit shall be classed as property,

53. *Id.* at 579.
54. *Id.* at 649.
55. *Id.* at 682.

then the Fourteenth Amendment to the Constitution stamps with nullity the act of the Legislature of Louisiana on the subject. The other clauses of the Act do, too, in another point of view, for there is not one section of the fourteenth amendment that, in my judgment, is not violated by this action of the Legislature.[56]

The impact on the Court's Reporter of the extended arguments of counsel in the *Slaughter-House Cases* confirms that Campbell's emphasis on English and American hostility to monopoly, which he ultimately related to Due Process, was to him as significant as was his contention based on Privileges and/or Immunities. In the twelve-page summary of the arguments provided by the official Report, Reporter Wallace devotes first attention to the anti-monopoly arguments, then to the background and reasoning respecting Privileges and Immunities, and closes with the essence of the arguments under Equal Protection and Due Process. One sentence suffices for Equal Protection; by an Act "of legislative partiality" seventeen persons are advantaged while a thousand of the same class, equally deserving, are deprived "of the means by which they earn their daily bread."[57] As for Due Process:

> The right to labor, the right to one's self physically and intellectually, and to the product of one's own faculties, is past doubt property, and property of a sacred kind. Yet *this* property is destroyed by the act; destroyed not by due process of law, but by charter; a grant of privilege, of monopoly; which allows such rights in this matter to no one but to a favored "seventeen."[58]

Familiar is the reasoning by which Justice Miller for the Court in the *Slaughter-House Cases* torpedoed Campbell's argument for reversal based on incorporation into the new Privileges or Immunities Clause of the content *Corfield v. Coryell* had given the original Privileges and Immunities Clause. Distinguishing between United States citizenship and State citizenship, Miller assigned to the latter those fundamental rights enunciated in *Corfield* that Campbell was contending were now by the Fourteenth Amendment protected from State action against its own citizens. The Privileges or Immunities of United States citizens were reduced to a category of rights of quite limited significance. This potentially embracive Clause has never recovered from the fateful blow accorded it although there are of late some "stirrings" of revival.[59]

Due Process fared no better. At the outset of his opinion Miller had declared that the Louisiana Act did not prevent the many butchers from continuing in their trade. They were free to butcher and to sell their meats as before, the only requirement now being that their operations must be conducted in the quarters provided by the Crescent City Company on payment of reasonable fees.

---

56. *Id*. at 757-58.
57. 16 Wall. at 56.
58. *Id*. (emphasis in original).
59. Kurland, *The Privileges or Immunities Clause: 'Its Hour Come Round at Last'?* 1972 WASH. U. L. Q. 405.

> The wisdom of the monopoly granted by the legislature may be open to question, but it is difficult to see a justification for the assertion that the butchers are deprived of the right to labor in their occupation, or the people of their daily service in preparing food, or how this statute, with the duties and guards imposed upon the company, can be said to destroy the business of the butcher, or seriously interfere with its pursuit.[60]

There was thus, Miller contended, no expropriation that would suggest the relevancy of due process deprivation in the American meaning of that concept as spelled out in reception of due process from English heritage. Also irrelevant was the English understanding of due process as anti-monopoly, for Miller had followed his claim of no expropriation by putting aside the English experience because it concerned Crown prerogative whereas Parliamentary grants of monopoly never had been questioned.[61] From this it followed with respect to the Due Process Clause that

> under no construction of that provision that we have ever seen, or any that we deem admissible, can the restraint imposed by the State of Louisiana upon the exercise of their trade by the butchers of New Orleans be held to be a deprivation of property within the meaning of that provision.[62]

Justice Miller's assertion of irrelevancy to American constitutional principles of the English condemnation of monopoly for inconsistency with due process, because involving Crown prerogative and not Parliamentary enactment, constitutes one of the most inexcusable performances in judicial annals. Well before 1873 American courts had realized that American legislatures were subject to constitutional limitation.[63] Miller himself recognized this major difference a mere four years later in *Davidson v. New Orleans.*[64] It was "easy to see" from English history, said the Justice for the Court in *Davidson*, that

> Magna Carta's law-of-the-land clause was not intended to protect against the enactment of laws by the Parliament of England. But when in 1866, [sic], there is placed in the Constitution of the United States a declaration that "no State shall deprive any person of life, liberty, or property without due process of law," can a State make anything due process of law which, by its own legislation, it chooses to declare such?[65]

The answer was clear.

---

60. Slaughter-House Cases, 16 Wall. at 61-62.

61. *Id.* at 65-66.

62. *Id.* at 81.

63. Reference is earlier made to this question of the application of constitutional limitation to legislative powers. By mid-century the question had been resolved; the American predicate of popular sovereignty made all branches of government subject to constitutional restraint. *Supra*, chap. 2, p. 30, on *Expropriation by Public Conversion as Denial of Substantive Due Process*, note 3.

64. 96 U. S. 97 (1877).

65. *Id.* at 102.

Immediately following this correction of grievous error, but with no apologies tendered, Justice Miller observed:

> It seems to us that a statute which declares in terms, and without more, that the full and exclusive title of a described piece of land which is now in A., shall be and is hereby vested in B., would, if effectual, deprive A. of his property without due process of law, within the meaning of the constitutional provision.[66]

This gratuitous observation is the more significant since in *Davidson* as in the *Slaughter-House Cases* no expropriation was found by the Court. The assessment for the draining of swamp lands owned in part by the estate of Davidson, was an administrative act that had been preceded by opportunity for notice and hearing, with "full and fair hearing" had. In consequence the case came within *Murray's Lessee v. Hoboken Land and Improvement Co.*[67] wherein the Court had earlier found violation of neither separation of powers nor procedural due process in federal proceedings to distrain moneys owing government by a collector of its revenues. "The court held [in *Murray's Lessee*] that the power exercised was executive, and not judicial; and that the issue of the writ, and the proceedings under it, were due process of law within the meaning of the Constitution."[68] Yet *Davidson* established that expropriation of private property constituted a violation of substantive due process of law under the Fourteenth Amendment.[69]

But how, then, account for the paragraph in *Davidson* in which for the Court Justice Miller finds it "not a little remarkable" that whereas the Due Process Clause in the Fifth Amendment had provoked a paucity of litigation during its then 86 years of presence in the Constitution, the identical provision[70] against the States had in a few years crowded the Court's docket?

> There is here abundant evidence that there exists some strange misconception of the scope of this provision as found in the fourteenth amendment. In fact, it would seem, from the character of many of the cases before us, and the arguments made in them, that the clause under consideration is looked upon as a means of bringing to the test of the decision of this court the abstract opinions of every unsuccessful litigant in a State court of the justice of the decision against him, and of the merits of the legislation on which such a decision may be founded.[71]

---

66. *Ibid.*

67. 18 How. 272 (1855).

68. Davidson v. New Orleans, 96 U. S. at 103.

69. Refer to text of analysis at note 27, chap. 2, *supra*, p. 35.

70. In common with other Justices and most constitutional commentators Miller treats the two provisions as identical. While the words are the same, as employed in Amendment V they are closely associated with other provisions that, with the one exception of eminent domain, are definitely procedural in meaning. Some state courts had denied substantive content to state due process clauses where so entangled with procedural guarantees. Notes 53 and 54 *supra*, chap. 2, p. 39.

71. Davidson v. New Orleans, 96 U.S. at 104.

Commentators have been puzzled, able to offer in explanation only the internal Court conflict that slowed the emergence of substantive due process.[72] For adequate explanation it is necessary to return to further consideration of the momentous *Slaughter-House Cases*.

From the majority opinion of Justice Miller in the *Slaughter-House Cases*, four of the nine members of the Court dissented. All were in general accord with the views set forth by Justice Field in his disagreement. He accepted Campbell's contention that the Privileges or Immunities Clause in the Fourteenth Amendment nationalized the privileges and immunities of the second section of Article IV, rendering fundamental rights applicable against state action without regard to discrimination by any one state against citizens of other states. Then drawing upon the wording of the Civil Rights Act of 1866; the *Corfield* opinion; the *Case of Monopolies*; the English Statute of Monopolies and the decree of Louis XVI, both abolishing monopolies of no public justification; and the opinions in three American State cases noted earlier in this study,[73] Field insisted that freedom from monopoly in the common callings was one of the fundamental rights now constitutionally protected against state action.

> Now, what the clause in question does for the protection of citizens of one State against the creation of monopolies in favor of citizens of other States, the fourteenth amendment does for the protection of every citizen of the United States against the creation of any monopoly whatever.[74]

The separate dissent of Justice Bradley, joined in by Justice Swayne, relates anti-monopoly to due process more closely than does that of Justice Field. Whereas Field relies wholly upon the newly ratified Privileges or Immunities Clause, treating English and American hostility to monopoly as grounding freedom of trade among the fundamental rights, Justice Bradley embraces directly both of Campbell's primary challenges to the Louisiana grant: it collides with the guarantees both of privileges and immunities and of due process of law, adding violation of equal protection for good measure.

> If my views are correct with regard to what are the privileges and immunities of citizens, it follows conclusively that any law which establishes a sheer monopoly, depriving a large class of citizens of the privilege of pursuing a lawful employment, does abridge the privileges of those citizens.
>
> The amendment also prohibits any State from depriving any person (citizen or otherwise) of life, liberty, or property, without due process of law.

---

72. *E.g.*, G. GUNTHER, CASES AND MATERIALS ON CONSTITUTIONAL LAW 507 (10th ed. 1980).

73. Citations accompanying text at footnotes 4 and 32, *supra*, this chapter.

74. Slaughter-House Cases, 83 U.S. at 101. That this statement precedes the references cited does not change the thrust of Field's dissent when treated in summation of his reasoning.

In my view, a law which prohibits a large class of citizens from adopting a lawful employment, or from following a lawful employment previously adopted, does deprive them of liberty as well as property, without due process of law. Their right of choice is a portion of their liberty; their occupation is their property. Such a law also deprives those citizens of the equal protection of the laws contrary to the last clause of the section.[75]

The *Slaughter-House Cases* constituted a major watershed in American constitutional law. A distinguished economist, John R. Commons, saw this more clearly than have constitutional scholars; his analysis was that the majority defined property in terms of its use value, the minority in terms of exchange value.[76] As confirmed by *Davidson*, Miller and those in agreement with him accepted a view of substantive due process as protective of property against expropriation, violation of which they did not find in the Louisiana law, but wholly rejected the concept of substantive due process, pressed by Campbell and embraced most completely by Bradley, as guaranteeing freedom of participation in the common callings. In a word, the majority did not repudiate the American concept of expropriation as a denial of substantive due process; what it did spurn was reception in American constitutional law of the English view of monopoly as deprivation of substantive due process.[77] It was this rejection that must explain the puzzlement of the passage in Miller's opinion in *Davidson* where he alludes to the "strange misconception" about the scope of the Due Process Clause as found in the new Fourteenth Amendment.

When the Crescent City monopoly challenged the abolition by the Louisiana Constitution of 1879 of the "monopoly features in the charter of any corporation now existing in the State," railroads excepted, it fell to Justice Miller to explain the new concept of the general inalienability of the police power, deriving from *Stone v. Mississippi*, that destroyed Crescent City's claim of unconstitutionality.[78] On the judgment against Crescent City there was no disagreement in the Court; *Butchers' Union* was unanimous. However, this result was achieved only by the concurrences of Justices Field and Bradley, Harlan and Woods. In one concurrence Field essentially repeated his views in *Slaughter-House Cases*: "I am of opinion that the act, in creating the monopoly in an ordinary employment and business, was to that extent against common

---

75. *Id.* at 122.

76. J. COMMONS, LEGAL FOUNDATIONS OF CAPITALISM 19 (1924).

77. I credit myself with coming close to realization that two different concepts of Due Process were involved, but missed the point by assuming the broader one somehow grew out of the narrower. Strong, *The Economic Philosophy of Lochner: Emergence, Embrasure and Emasculation*, 15 ARIZ. L. REV. 419, 421-24 (1973). The structure of my casebook, AMERICAN CONSTITUTIONAL LAW (1950), reflected an embryonic appreciation of the dual character of the Due Process concept in the respective contents of chapters 6 and 7 but admittedly it was a case of looking through a glass darkly.

78. Butchers' Union Slaughter-House and Live-Stock Landing Co. v. Crescent City Live-Stock Landing and Slaughter-House Co., 111 U.S. 746 (1884), earlier cited *supra* note 40.

right and void."[79] Bradley, joined by the two new justices, in reiterating his earlier views, specifically related them to Section One of the Fourteenth Amendment.

1. I hold that the liberty of pursuit—the right to follow any of the ordinary callings of life—is one of the privileges of a citizen of the United States. . . .

2. But if the law which created the monopoly in question does not abridge the privileges and immunities of a citizen of the United States to prohibit him from pursuing his chosen calling, and giving to others the exclusive right of pursuing it,—it certainly does deprive him (to a certain extent) of his liberty; for it takes from him the freedom of adopting and following the pursuit which he prefers; which, as already intimated, is a material part of the liberty of the citizen. And, if a man's right to his calling is property, as many maintain, then those who had already adopted the prohibited pursuits in New Orleans, were deprived, by the law in question, of their property, as well as their liberty, without due process of law.

3. But still more apparent is the violation, by this monopoly law, of the last clause of the section "no State shall deny to any person the equal protection of the laws." If it is not a denial of the equal protection of the laws to grant to one man, or set of men, the privilege of following an ordinary calling in a large community, and to deny it to all others, it is difficult to understand what would come within the constitutional prohibition.[80]

Bradley's reliance here on Equal Protection as a constitutional bulwark against monopoly reflects Campbell's resort to this Clause as well as to Due Process, in his arguments in *Slaughter-House Cases*. A monopoly grant can be viewed as having the direct effect of denying equal treatment to all by restricting to a favored one or few opportunities for entry into the calling thus circumscribed. Or, vice versa, major discrimination with respect to entry could suggest monopoly intent. It was on Equal Protection grounds that the Court shortly invalidated a San Francisco ordinance which if the decision of the state supreme court were allowed to stand would have ousted Chinese from the laundry business. Argued and decided with *Yick Wo v. Hopkins*[81] was *Wo Lee v. Hopkins*[82] reversing a decision of the Ninth Circuit[83] which, although find-

---

79. *Id.* at 754-60. The quoted conclusion appears *id.* at 760.

80. *Id.* at 765-66. This summary is immediately followed by a final paragraph of portent for the future.

Monopolies are the bane of our body politic at the present day. In the eager pursuit of gain they are sought in every direction. They exhibit themselves in corners in the stock market and produce market, and in many other ways. If by legislative enactment they can be carried into the common avocations and callings of life, so as to cut off the right of the citizen to choose his avocation, the right to earn his bread by the trade which he has learned; and if there is not constitutional means of putting a check to such enormity, I can only say that it is time the Constitution was still further amended. In my judgment, the present Constitution is amply sufficient for the protection of people if it is fairly interpreted and faithfully enforced. *Id.* at 766.

81. 118 U.S. 356 (1886).

82. *Id.*

83. *In re* Wo Lee, 26 Fed. 471 (C.C.A. 9th, 1886) (Sawyer, J.).

ing the ordinance to be constitutionally discriminatory, had sustained it in deference to the decision in the same case of the supreme court of California.[84] The ordinance required that the laundry business be conducted in brick or stone buildings but vested in a board of supervisors discretion to waive the requirement upon petition.

From the Brief for Defendant[85] and Statement of Facts[86] the following pattern emerges. There were 320 laundries in the city at the time, of which 310 were conducted in wooden buildings. (Ten laundries Chinese managed in brick buildings.) Of this total, 240 laundries were operated by Chinese aliens whose frame structures had scaffolds on the roofs for use in drying the wash. The seventy others, run by Occidentals, were without scaffolds. A second difference lay in the fact that the Chinese laundries were operated on a 24-hour, seven-day-a-week-basis whereas Occidentals did not operate at night or on Sunday. These two distinctions counsel for Defendant stressed as bearing on fire hazards. The point was made: "In towns like San Francisco, constructed largely of wood, the danger from fire is ever present and overshadowing."[87] Cited also were disturbing noises arising from night operation. Further facts bore on the question of alleged discrimination against the Chinese. Yick Wo and 200 of his countrymen had petitioned for waiver but had been denied. Accepting the assertion of counsel for Yick Wo and Wo Lee, the Statement of Facts was that all the petitions of those who were not Chinese, with the exception of Mrs. Mary Meagles, were granted. Defendant's counsel challenged the assertion. "The 'all others' are two, and no more," apparently referring to two large laundries run by Caucasians but employing 40 and 70 Chinese, respectively, whose petitions had been granted.[88]

Contentions of monopoly violative of due process continued in challenges of the ordinance, despite rejection by a lower California court in earlier litigation.[89] Circuit Judge Sawyer in his opinion in Wo Lee,[90] believing it likely

---

84. In the Matter of Yick Wo, 68 Cal. 294, 9 p. 139 (1885). (Sup. Ct. decision accepting opinion of Commissioners.)

85. 9 P. KURLAND and G. CASPER, op. cit. supra note 45, at 17-140.

86. Yick Wo v. Hopkins, 118 U.S. at 356-63.

87. 9 P. KURLAND and G. CASPER, op. cit. supra note 45, at 118.

88. Id. at 125 for Defendant; 118 U.S. at 359 for the inclusive "all" found in the Statement of Facts.

89. Defendant's Brief, id. 29, at 32-37, refers to an earlier litigation in the superior court of San Francisco in which a Mr. White, surely a white, had been arrested for violation of the ordinance and had unsuccessfully sought habeas corpus. The opinion of the court is reproduced in full. White was one of the two Occidentals later granted waiver, inconsistent as this may seem in the absence of further facts. Id. at 54. One of White's contentions, rejected by the court, was that "It [the ordinance] tends to create a monopoly of the laundry business in the hands of those who have or can build brick or stone buildings." Id. at 33.

90. Cited supra note 83, partially reproduced in the Statement of Facts, 118 U.S. at 361-63.

that administration of the ordinance would "close up the many Chinese laundries now existing," clearly reacted to this consideration.

> If this would not be depriving such parties of their property without due process of law, it would be difficult to say what would effect that prohibited result. The necessary tendency, if not the specific purpose, of this ordinance, and of enforcing it in the manner indicated in the record, is to drive out of business all the numerous small laundries, especially those owned by Chinese, and give a monopoly of the business to the large institutions established and carried on by means of large associated Caucasian capital. If the facts appearing on the face of the ordinance, on the petition, and return, and admitted in the case, and shown by the notorious public and municipal history of the times, indicate a purpose to drive out the Chinese laundrymen, and not merely to regulate the business for the public safety, does it not disclose a case of violation of the provisions of the fourteenth amendment to the national constitution, and of the treaty between the United States and China in more than one particular? Does not the petition and return, as clearly as in the *Laundry Case*, present a case within the purview of the observations of Mr. Justice Field quoted from that case? We are ourselves unable to distinguish this case, in principle, from the *Laundry Case*.[91]

The *Laundry Case* was *In re Quong Woo*,[92] a Ninth Circuit decision of 1882. Opinion was by Justice Field, with Judge Sawyer in agreement. Invalidated as a deprivation of petitioner's liberty was an earlier San Francisco ordinance, applicable to all commercial laundries requiring for establishment or continuance the consent of the board of supervisors. That consent was to be granted only upon recommendation of not less than twelve citizens and taxpayers living in the block in which a laundry was, or was to be, located. The ordinance was applicable to Occidentals and Orientals alike, to fireproof buildings as well as to wooden structures. But while facially impartial, the ordinance left no doubt that the intention was to drive the Chinese from the laundry business. The involvement of Field in these Circuit cases is significant; he continues to press his thesis that monopoly constitutes a denial of substantive due process. At the same time, nevertheless, he appreciates the conflict between monopoly and equal protection. Hence he joins Judge Sawyer in continuation of the above passage from *Wo Lee*:

> If this means prohibition of the occupation, and destruction of the business and property of the Chinese laundrymen in San Francisco—and it seems to us this must be the effect of executing the ordinance—and not merely the proper regulation of the business, then there is discrimination and a violation of other highly important rights secured by the Fourteenth Amendment and the treaty. That it does mean prohibition, as to the Chinese, it seems to us must be apparent to every citizen of San Francisco who has been here long enough to be familiar with the cause of an active and aggressive branch of public opinion and of public notorious events. Can

---

91. In re Wo Lee, *supra* note 83, at 474-75.
92. 13 Fed. 229 (C.C.A. 9th, 1882).

a court be blind to what must be necessarily known to every intelligent person in the state?[93]

In the Supreme Court of the United States the issue was viewed as one of racial discrimination. The essence of its opinion is found in its concluding paragraph.

It appears that both petitioners have complied with every requisite deemed by the law or by the public officers charged with its administration, necessary for the protection of neighboring property from fire, or as a precaution against injury to the public health. No reason whatever, except the will of the supervisors, is assigned why they should not be permitted to carry on, in the accustomed manner, their harmless and useful occupation, on which they depend for a livelihood. And while this consent of the supervisors is withheld from them and from two hundred others who have also petitioned, all of whom happen to be Chinese subjects, eighty others, not Chinese subjects, are permitted to carry on the same business under similar conditions. The fact of this discrimination is admitted. No reason for it is shown, and the conclusion cannot be resisted, that no reason for it exists except hostility to the race and nationality to which the petitioners belong, and which in the eye of the law is not justified. The discrimination is, therefore, illegal, and the public administration which enforces it is a denial of the equal protection of the laws and a violation of the Fourteenth Amendment of the Constitution. The imprisonment of the petitioners is, therefore, illegal, and they must be discharged.[94]

These were rather amazing statements to be made by a unanimous Court in light of the telling contentions of Defendant's counsel. The Chinese subjects and white American citizens were not in two major respects operating "under similar conditions." Discrimination there admittedly was, but not "unjust discrimination."[95] Valid differentiation lay in the degree of fire hazard. Counsel reiterated that wooden laundries with scaffolds on the roofs were "highly injurious to the community."[96] So also were the internal fires that never cooled. However, it was the drying scaffolds that presented the greater danger of a conflagration; counsel assured that if each Chinese would take down his scaffold, "each will be fairly treated"[97] but they persisted in "maintaining these forbidden erections."[98] The statement that all Occidentals had been granted waiver, which reinforced the claim of racial discrimination, was inaccurate; only two were known to have received permission.[99]

---

93. In re Wo Lee, *supra* note 83, at 475.

94. Yick Wo v. Hopkins, 118 U.S. at 374.

95. 9 P. KURLAND and G.CASPER, *op. cit. supra* note 45, at 127 (contention of counsel for Defendant).

96. *Id.* at 45.

97. *Id.* at 131.

98. *Id.* at 127.

99. *Id.* at 54, 125. A caveat is justified with respect to total number of laundries, total waivers denied and granted, and all other counts. It is unusually difficult to decipher from available data what were the correct totals.

In his *Path of Due Process of Law*,[100] which came to be the accepted account of what transpired between *Slaughter-House Cases* and *Lochner*,[101] Walton Hamilton asserted that it was with the *Yick Wo* decision that "the Fourteenth Amendment came quietly into constitutional law."[102] The assertion is literally true, *Yick Wo* being the first case of invalidation under the new constitutional provision, but the insistence that it signified more than that proved inaccurate.[103] In the unanimous opinion there is no evidence that Justice Miller had "come over" to the Bradley-Field view of monopoly as a denial of substantive due process; reliance on Equal Protection may well have been a device for achieving agreement on the holding by avoiding that issue. Whether the concurring opinion in *Butchers' Union* would become the prevailing opinion of the Court remained unresolved.

---

100. Hamilton, *The Path of Due Process of Law*, in C. READ, THE CONSTITUTION RE-CONSIDERED 167 (1938, 1968).

101. 198 U.S. 45 (1905), treated extensively, *infra* Parts III and IV.

102. Hamilton, *supra* note 100, at 178 (either edition).

103. Hamilton declared, *id.* at 179: "The right to work at one's chosen occupation had at last become a part of the supreme law of the land." But *Yick Wo* was based on Equal Protection. What blocked the logical "pass" to Due Process is explained *infra* chapter 5, pp. 86-89, text at notes 29-46.

4. Monopoly by Private Contract as Impugned by Substantive Due Process

With the issue of slavery finally resolved by civil war, there followed in the remaining decades of the nineteenth century a great surge in internal economic development in the United States. Surfacing in this revival was again the question of policy with respect to monopoly. Monopoly grants continued, as witness the deviant one by Louisiana.[1] Yet in the very year of the Carpetbagger grant of 1869, the revised constitution of Texas carried a declaration that "Perpetuities and Monopolies are contrary to the genius of a free government and shall never be allowed."[2] The phrasing was identical to that of several of the state constitutional provisions antedating the Civil War, and the intent was probably the same.[3] Yet the wording was capable of application to monopoly attainable through private action in the hospitable environment of rapid economic growth. Of entirely different tenor, the new Georgia constitution of 1877 upgraded from potentiality to actuality the concept of monopoly as product of private concert in contrast to public creation.

> The General Assembly of this State shall have no power to authorize any corporation to buy shares, or stock, in any other corporation in this State, or elsewhere, or to make any contract, or agreement whatever, with any such corporation, which may have the effect, or be intended to have the effect, to defeat or lessen competition in their respective businesses, or to encourage monopoly; and all such contracts and agreements shall be illegal or void.[4]

Two celebrated state court decisions[5] served to further the realization that the chief source of offensive monopoly was coming to be the private, rather than the public, sector of the economy. The Diamond Match Trust attained

---

1. Reference is to the legislative grant to Crescent City Live Stock & Landing Co., litigated in the *Slaughter-House Cases*, analyzed *supra* chap. 3, pp. 54-59, 61-62.

2. Tex. Const., Art. I, Sect. 18 (1869). Wyo. Const., Art. I, Sec. 30 (1889) was of the same tenor.

3. The earlier anti-monopoly constitutional provisions, influenced by English background, were directed wholly at public monopolies.

4. GA. CONST., Art. IV, Sec. 2, para. 4, § 5097 (1877).

5. Richardson v. Buhl, 77 Mich. 632, 43 N.W. 1102 (1889); Richardson v. Standard Oil Co., 44 Ohio St. 137, 5 N.E. 225 (1892).

monopoly position in manufacture and sale of friction matches through a series of restrictive contracts that in combination lodged nationwide control in
the Diamond Match Co. In much the same way the Standard Oil trust had
through contract built itself into a virtual monopoly in production and distribution of petroleum. On challenge, both trusts were held illegal as contrary to
public policy but survived in the form of holding companies.[6]

It is familiar learning that the holding company mechanism came to be the
major method for effecting monopolistic concentrations in industry despite
effort to block this mechanism as illustrated by the Georgia constitutional
provision. It was this device that was employed to consolidate control of the
Great Northern and Northern Pacific Railroads in creation of the Northern
Securities Co. that the United States challenged under the Sherman Act.[7] In
defense, an attorney for Northern Securities by the name of John Johnson read
aright the changing scene in emphasis from public to private monopoly. In his
Brief is this insightful paragraph:

> We concede that a "monopoly," as now understood, involves something more than
> what was understood by Lord Coke; but in modern, as well as in ancient, times,
> the underlying idea, as we have endeavored to show, contains the element of a
> restraint—of exclusion. This is no longer, ordinarily, the result of a Government
> grant; but of contracts between parties having the power to exclude others from
> carrying on a trade or manufacture, which they exercise.[8]

Expansion of the concept to monopoly resulting from private association
produced the paradox of a public right without an effective remedy. For in his
opinion in *Mitchel v. Reynolds* Lord Macclesfield had asserted with respect to
voluntary restraints that freedom from monopoly could not look to Magna
Carta for support; the very history of Chapter 29 that gave it such potency
against Crown prerogative denied it all relevance in the more determinate area
of private voluntary agreements.[9] Attorney John Jewett, contending for Munn
and Scott on rehearing[10] of the Supreme Court decision in *Munn v. Illinois,*[11]
thought this constitutional principle was clear enough.

> It is respectfully denied that there can be any such thing as monopoly, in the sense
> in which it is used in the opinion of the Court, unless it has an origin, actual or
> constructive, in grant from the State. There can be no monopoly in a thing or

---

6. Standard Oil turned immediately to the holding company device; Diamond Match
later.

7. Northern Securities Co. v. United States, 198 U.S. 197 (1904), discussed *infra* this
chapter.

8. Brief of John Johnson in the Northern Securities Case, id., in 15 P. KURLAND and G.
CASPER, *op. cit. supra* chapter 3, note 45, at 436. Attorney Johnson was clearly referring
to monopoly effected by combination of private parties (individuals or corporations).

9. Text at note 95, *supra* chapter 1, pp. 20-21.

10. Neither the opinion of the Court nor the Citators reveal the grant of a rehearing. The
result was clearly reaffirmance.

11. 94 U.S. 113 (1877).

business, which is of common right, no matter how few may avail themselves of that right. When Lord Ellenborough, in *Allnut v. Inglis*, speaks of a *"virtual monopoly,"* he is referring to a monopoly established by law, and not of one, which falls to a man by the accident of his being the only man engaged in a business, which is equally open to any other man, as a matter of personal right. Yet, in this case, the Court has laid down a general rule, which, in its expansiveness, embraces every useful employment and business of the nation, and brings them all into the condition of Government or *legal* monopolies, subject to legislative regulation, not only as to the manner in which the business shall be done, but, also, as to the prices to be charged for services and the use of property.[12]

To Mr. Jewett the Supreme Court in *Munn* had stood the Constitution on its head. In the original argument he had first stressed the significance of the Due Process Clauses in delineating the general principles on which this Nation is founded.[13] In his Further Brief for Plaintiffs in Error[14] he had brought these general principles into concrete application to the facts of *Munn*. These facts were that the State of Illinois had enacted legislation fixing the rates to be charged by grain warehousemen in Chicago; the legislation had been provoked by prior action of these warehousemen in agreeing to abide by rates set by common agreement. Jewett's contention that the law was invalid commenced with the familiar *A* to *B* syndrome, proceeding with predication of his argument squarely on Fourteenth Amendment due process buttressed by the general political principles on which the due process concept had been said to be rested.[15] The view of due process was of a substantive shield against governmental taking of private property.

To the surprise and discomfiture of Attorney Jewett the Illinois statute was sustained. Indeed, he was by the Court, with two dissents, hoisted on his own petard. For his vivid description of the key position occupied by the warehouses in the flow of grain from the producing States of the West through Chicago to the Eastern markets put the Court in mind that

> although in 1874 there were in Chicago fourteen warehouses adapted to this particular business, and owned by about thirty persons, nine business firms controlled them, and that the prices charged and received for storage were such "as have been from year to year agreed upon and established by the different elevators or warehouses in the city of Chicago, and which rates have been annually published in one or more newspapers . . . as the established rates for the year then next ensuing such publication." Thus it is apparent that all the elevating facilities through which

---

12. 7 P. Kurland and G. Casper, *op. cit. supra* chapter 3, note 45, at 688 (Brief on Rehearing 659-96). Mr. Jewett had earlier, *id.* at 670-75, distinguished *Bolt v. Stennett* and *Allnut v. Inglis* with especial attention to the latter in which the London Dock Co. was clearly a legalized monopoly under Parliamentary Acts.

13. Brief for Plaintiffs in Error, 7 P. Kurland and G. Casper, *op. cit. supra* chapter 3, note 45, at 535-72.

14. *Id.* at 573-98.

15. *Id.* at 586-98.

these vast productions "of seven or eight great States of the West" must pass on the way "to four or five of the States on the seashore" may be a "virtual" monopoly.[16]

From access to the private papers of Justice Bradley made available to him, Charles Fairman concluded that it was Bradley who alerted the Chief Justice to Lord Hale's tracts on *De Jure Maris* and *De Portibus Maris*[17] in which, as earlier noted in chapter 1, governmental regulations of charges and usage were justified where "virtual monopoly" obtained. Writing the opinion for the Court in *Munn*, Chief Justice Waite quoted from each of the Hale Tracts,[18] following which extensive quotations were made from two of the opinions in *Allnutt v. Inglis*[19] in which Lord Hale was relied upon for "the law of the subject." Waite was equally reliant upon Hale, closing the references to precedent[20] with repetition of a tribute paid Hale by an early American judge.

> In England, even on rights of prerogative, they scan his words with as much care as if they had been found in Magna Charta; and the meaning once ascertained, they do not trouble themselves to search any further. 6 Cow. (N.Y.) 536, note.[21]

Far from invalidating price fixation beyond the category of common carriers,[22] *Munn v. Illinois* sustained such legislation, given the presence of monopoly.[23] This time substantive due process squared off against private monopoly in constitutional combat; this time substantive due process marched to a different drummer; this time anti-monopoly carried the day. Due Process, the ancient enemy of monopoly, became a sword undergirding, rather than a shield undercutting, governmental power.[24] In view of the crucial role Bradley

---

16. Munn v. Illinois, 94 U.S. at 131 (1877). Jewett in his Brief on Rehearing questioned the Court's figures but conceded them for the sake of argument. However, he did challenge the assertion of resulting monopoly; other warehousemen were free to enter the business, and "fully one-third" of the grain moving through Chicago was not elevated. 7 P. KURLAND and G. CASPER, *op. cit. supra* chap.3, note 45, at 691-92.

17. Fairman, *The So-called Granger Cases, Lord Hale, and Justice Bradley*, 5 STAN. L. REV. 587-92, 651-58, 670-79 (1953).

18. Text supporting notes 107-13, chap. 1, pp. 23-25, *supra*. Some commentators, like Attorney Jewett, have insisted the Court, in invoking Hale's tracts, introduced a forgotten source of questionable relevancy. *Contra* is Scheiber, *The Road To Munn*, in FLEMING AND BAILYN, LAW IN AMERICAN HISTORY 329, at 334-59 (1971). I stand with Scheiber.

19. Note 113, chapter 1, p. 25, *supra*.

20. Munn v. Illinois, 94 U.S. at 126-29.

21. *Id.* at 129.

22. The *Granger Cases*, following the report of *Munn* in 94 U.S. 113.

23. That the presence of monopoly bottomed the decision in *Munn* is the judgment of Hale, *The Constitution and the Price System*, 34 Col. L. REV. 401, at 403 (1934); Hamilton, *Affectation With Public Interest*, 39 YALE L. J. 1089, at 1096-98 (1930); Scheiber, *supra* note 18, at 356-57; see Wyman, *The Law of the Public Callings as a Solution of the Trust Problem*, 17 HARV. L. REV. 156 (1904).

24. The concept is startling because of concentrated attention to Substantive Due Process as a limitation, yet it is within constitutional contemplation. *Cf.* Dellinger, *Of Rights and Remedies: The Constitution as a Sword*, 85 HARV. L. REV. 1532 (1972).

played in the struggle to bring public monopoly to heel through substantive due process, it is difficult not to believe that he was in the forefront of the reading of substantive due process as empowering government to pull the fangs of private monopoly. Dissenting in the *Sinking Fund Cases*,[25] decided shortly after *Munn*, he declared in reaffirming his acceptance of that decision that

> when an employment or business becomes a matter of such public interest and importance as to create a common charge or burden upon the citizen; in other words, when it becomes a practical monopoly, to which the citizen is compelled to resort, and by means of which a tribute can be exacted from the community, it is subject to regulation by the legislative power.[26]

Reaffirmation of the decision in *Munn* by the whole Court, with only Justice Field dissenting on other grounds, occurred six years later in *Spring Valley Water Works v. Schottler*.[27]

> That it is within the power of the government to regulate the prices at which water shall be sold by one who enjoys a virtual monopoly of the sale, we do not doubt. That question is settled by what was decided on full consideration in *Munn v. Illinois*, 94 U.S. 113. As was said in that case, such regulations do not deprive a person of his property without due process of law.[28]

As time ran on, the rule of *Munn*[29] experienced opposition. When further legislation regulating rates of grain warehousemen reached the Supreme Court in *Budd v. New York*,[30] counsel for defendants made a frontal attack.

> As to the judgment of this court in *Munn v. Illinois*, 94 U.S. 113, we submit, with very great respect that the mediaeval rules and instances were allowed too great influence in that judgment. When England was mainly a pastoral and agricultural country, with her trade and commerce in their infancy, all sorts of burdensome restrictions were imposed upon the individual by a paternal theory of government for the supposed benefit of trade. But even at these times and in the midst of this mediaeval darkness, the course of the judges was towards freedom. In the latter part of the eighteenth century there was a general awakening to the false theories which had permitted these impositions. In England Adam Smith's great work was followed by many repeals of vicious regulations, and by an entire cessation of new restraint. In France the edict of Louis XVI liberated trade from corresponding

---

25. 99 U.S. 700 (1878).

26. *Id.* at 747.

27. 110 U.S. 347 (1884).

28. *Id.* at 354. The reference to due process here is to substantive due process in its more familiar role as limitation on state power.

29. J. COMMONS, LEGAL FOUNDATIONS OF CAPITALISM 62 (1924), saw the significance of *Munn* through the eyes of an able economist. "The Munn Case was an innovation in that it recognized a source of power unknown to the common law and unrevealed until property assumed its modern dimensions. The Munn Case decided that the power of property might be restrained in dealings with customers." Theretofore, the issue had been the limits of sovereign power and not of economic power. *Id.* at 34-35 is a similar expression.

30. 143 U.S. 517 (1892).

restrictions. In America the Declaration of Independence set forth the inalienable rights of all men to life, liberty and the pursuit of happiness; that is, among other things to the right to enjoy and acquire property. That the essence of the right of property is in its use and in the power of alienation for use by others is obvious.[31]

The New York law survived the assault yet there were clouds on the constitutional horizon. The opinion for the Court by Justice Blatchford was long and labored; smothered in one paragraph was reliance on the "practical monopoly" involved.[32] Only by reference back to the opinion of the New York court of appeals,[33] whose decision was affirmed, does one find dependence upon the existence of monopolization in grain elevation at Buffalo.[34] And there are now three dissenters, with newly appointed Justice Brewer taking over from Justice Field the burden of challenging the majority's continuing dependence on *Munn*. A paragraph in the Brewer dissenting opinion has an ominous ring to it.

The paternal theory of government is to me odious. The utmost possible liberty to the individual, and the fullest possible protection to him and his property, is both the limitation and duty of government. If it may regulate the price of one service, which is not a public service, or the compensation for the use of one kind of property which is not devoted to a public use, why may it not with equal reason regulate the price of all service, and the compensation to be paid for the use of all property? And if so, "Looking Backward" is nearer than a dream.[35]

Edward Bellamy's *Looking Backward* appeared in 1888. From the vantage point of the year 2000 Bellamy looked back to 1887. Using a familiar literary technique Bellamy has Julian West awakening from a dream of over 100 years to find in the late 19th century a period of moral insensitivity, social disharmony, and economic greed. The contrast between this condition of inhumanity and the tranquillity of life in 2000 A.D. is shocking, for at the later time Utopia has come about by virtue of transformation for the better in human

---

31. *Id.* at 524.

32. *Id.* at 532.

33. People v. Budd, 117 N.Y. 1, 22 N.E. 670 (1889).

34. *Id.* at 10, 22 N.E. at 673. Declared the court:

It is asserted that a combination exists, and has for several years existed, between the elevator owners to maintain excessive charges by fixing a uniform tariff and pooling the earnings, and dividing them ratably among all the elevator owners, although but a part of the elevators are actually operated. (See report of the committee on foreign commerce of the Chamber of Commerce of New York, made in April, 1885.) There is no evidence in the record as to the locations in the port of Buffalo suitable and available for stationary elevators. It is evident that they must be placed where they can be reached by both lake vessels and canal boats, and it may reasonably be assumed that but a limited area (not devoted to other purposes of commerce) is available for the erection of stationary elevators.

The case of *Munn v. Illinois* (94 U.S. 113) is a direct authority upon the question now before us.

35. Budd v. New York, 143 U.S. at 551.

nature. The essence of the book is damning indictment of the time in which he wrote. It followed by sixteen years Samuel Butler's *Erewhon*, a similarly biting criticism of the prevailing order resulting from the Industrial Revolution. The catchy title was coined by spelling *Nowhere* backwards; in turn Thomas More had coined the term utopia from the Greek word meaning nowhere. West learned of the great merits of state socialism in long discussions with a Dr. Leete. A budding love affair between Edith Leete and Julian intermittently gave relief from the heavy conversations on capitalistic versus socialistic economics. The second edition of *Looking Backward*, 1889, edited by Robert Elliott, includes a short but excellent Introduction that takes note of the tremendous impact of the volume not only in the United States but also in England and Europe, including Russia. Justice Brewer's pointed reference to *Looking Backward* appeared but four years later.

Private market control is achievable not only by resort to business combination or to conditions of "natural monopoly"; there is the third route of "cornering the market" through timely purchase from producers for profitable resale at market. It is usually effected by one acting alone, employing contract as the mechanism for gaining control. For centuries alternatively a common law or legislative offense in England,[36] forestalling was no longer unlawful there after 1844. However, in the New World the offense continued as part of reaction to British commercial policies directed against the Colonies. Especially when the offense broadened beyond foodstuffs, its elements and objective were difficult to differentiate from monopoly by private parties attained through the other two devices for exclusion. Gradually, forestalling came to be thought of as monopolization until the two terms became interchangeable in usage.[37] Essentially merged into the concept of monopoly, the doctrine of forestalling lay near the surface of growing awareness of emergent monopoly by private arrangement, as contrasted with historically familiar monopoly by public grant. Impact with substantive due process followed through the latter's antipathy for monopoly. As in the *Munn* framework, the confrontation would be with Due Process as sword, not as shield.

---

36. Refer to chap. 1, pp. 22-23, *supra*, text at notes 103-06.

37. Illustrative is Mass. Laws, chap. 31 (1779) (Province Laws of 1778-1779 entitled "An Act Against Monopoly and Forestalling"). Other instances are cited in Jones, *Historical Development of the Law of Business Competition*, 36 YALE L. J. 42, 207 (1926).

PART III

SUBSTANTIVE DUE PROCESS OF LAW IN AMERICA A CENTURY AFTER RECEPTION FROM ENGLAND

5. Deflections within the Inheritance: Expansion and Contraction

As experience with the inherited content of substantive due process developed in the United States it became ever clearer that it embraced two cores of meaning: anti-expropriation of property interests and anti-monopoly in economic enterprise. With each form of hostility there was internal division. In the case of expropriation the distinction turned on the characterization of the one or ones advantaged by governmentally enforced "takings." With anti-monopoly the difference lay in the public or private character of the entity enforcing conditions of monopoly. The internal bifurcation was by historical origins greater in the latter instance, which explains the devotion of Chapter 3 and Chapter 4 to it while only Chapter 2 is given to the former.

Relative continuity marked judicial approach to expropriation through the nineteenth century. Aside from the short-timed resort to retroactivity as the test of expropriation, the core concept remained one of measuring constitutionality by the severity of the "taking" considering the relationship between the "takor" and "takee" and the nature of the "property" transferred. Increasingly, however, as the century drew to a close substantive due process as anti-expropriative was forced to reckon with the rising tide of state police power. This modifying principle, long in gestation, emerged as the prime mover in the implied reservation of state power to alter or amend all contracts, whether state or private, in the interest of public health, morals, safety—and, ultimately, public welfare. The police power would function as a counter balance in the growing conflict between societal pressures for economic reform and traditional views of individual proprietary rights.

This new pattern was fully developed by the time of *Holden v. Hardy*,[1] decided close to the end of the century. Operators of ore smelters and of underground mines in Utah had challenged a state statute forbidding employment of workers beyond eight hours per day "except in cases of emergency where life or property is in imminent danger." Sustainment of the prohibition by the supreme court of Utah was followed by appeal to the Supreme Court. Over the dissent of Justices Brewer and Peckham, the Court affirmed.

---

1. 169 U.S. 366 (1898).

This right of contract, however, is itself subject to certain limitations which the State may lawfully impose in the exercise of its police powers. . . . While this court has held, notably in the cases *Davidson* v. *New Orleans*, 96 U.S. 97, and *Yick Wo* v. *Hopkins*, 118 U.S. 356, that the police power cannot be put forward as an excuse for oppressive and unjust legislation it may be lawfully resorted to for the purpose of preserving the public health, safety or morals, or the abatement of public nuisances. . . .[2]

The Court found the statute quite clearly related to the public health because of the unusually adverse working conditions obtaining in the two industries covered. The "many authorities which hold that state statutes restricting the hours of labor are unconstitutional . . . have no application to cases where the legislature had adjudged that a limitation is necessary for the preservation of the health of employés, and there are reasonable grounds for believing that such determination is supported by the facts."[3]

The function here judicially "assigned" to substantive due process of law was no part of its historic meanings. On the other hand, it offered the potential of an interface between the acknowledged power of police and the limitation on governmental restraint of the individual vouchsafed by the Constitution of the United States and its satellites in every State. Its essence is balance as opposed to extremism, reconciliation as contrasted with confrontation.[4]

The conception of substantive due process as a sword grounding state power to enact maximum price regulation, although late in emergence, soon came to a crisis in *Brass* v. *North Dakota ex rel. Stoeser*.[5] The issue was not whether *Munn v. Illinois*[6] would be repudiated, it was whether this new facet of Due Process would be held to instances of undoubted monopoly or allowed to undergird all state regulation of maximum—perhaps ultimately even minimum—prices. Abandonment of the monopoly tie that originated the new concept could leave open to governmental power the general fixation of business charges subject only to what limits might evolve from substantive due process in its more traditional role as shield against governmental intervention.

Brass, one of three warehousemen in the tiny town of Grand Harbor, did not seek to be himself a monopolist, nor, so far as the Record reveals, had he and the other two entered into any conspiracy to fix rates. The Court majority

---

2. *Id.* at 391-92.

3. *Id.* at 397-98. Reasoning of this type had surfaced as early as *Powell v. Pennsylvania,* discussed textually at notes 29-46, *infra.* In *Holden,* however, there was no undercurrent of hostile legislative motive that laid open to question the Court's finding of reasonable relationship between the challenged law and the public health.

4. Today's electronic world might describe this balancing of power and limitation as "fine tuning."

5. 153 U.S. 391 (1894).

6. 94 U.S. 113 (1877), considered textually in chap. 4, pp. 70-72, *supra.*

made no claim of monopoly presence.[7] Rather, to the contention of Brass's attorneys that the facts here were significantly distinguished from those in *Budd* and *Munn* where a practical monopoly obtained, as the Court noted in summary of these contentions, the response was of utterly different tenor.

> These arguments are disposed of, as we think, by the simple observation, already made, that the facts rehearsed are matters for those who make, not for those who interpret, the laws. When it is once admitted, as it is admitted here, that it is competent for the legislative power to control the business of elevating and storing grain, whether carried on by individuals or associations, in cities of one size and in some circumstances, it follows that such power may be legally exerted over the same business when carried on in smaller cities and in other circumstances.... [T]he obvious aim of the reasoning that prevailed [below] was to show that the subject-matter of these enactments fell within the legitimate sphere of legislative power, and that, so far as the laws and Constitution of the United States were concerned, the legislation in question deprived no person of his property without due process of law....[8]

In dissent Justice Brewer, with three other justices joining including the faithful Field, does not question *Munn* on its facts but, unable to find any monopolistic element in the North Dakota pattern, he voiced concern over the length to which governmental price fixing would go in the many situations devoid of unquestioned monopoly. Recall that it was this Justice who in *Budd v. New York*[9] had declared odious to him the "paternal theory of government."

> So it is that when any farmer or other individual can at a cost of less than $200 provide himself with all the facilities for storing and shipping the entire product of an ordinary farm, when along the line of a single railroad there are six hundred elevators already constructed, owned, and operated by one hundred and twenty-five different persons, when at every station at which grain is marketed there are from two to ten such elevators, it is held that there exists a monopoly such as justifies control by the public of the prices at which grain shall be stored in any one of these many elevators. [Sic] If this be a monopoly, justifying public control of prices for service, I am at a loss to perceive at what point the fact of monopoly

---

7. That there were 600 elevators in the State located along the line of the Great Northern Railroad was economically irrelevant on the monopoly issue; the distance from Grand Harbor of all but a few of them made it infeasible for Stoeser to haul his grain to any of them. In the county (Ramsey) there were an unidentified number of additional elevators but no data are available as to locations, a significant factor in light of haulage by horse-drawn vehicle in a county of 1248 square miles. However, the fact that two other elevators existed at Grand Harbor created a presumption of competition absent proven allegations of conspiracy among the three to adhere to common rates for storage. Neither Record nor court opinions shed much light on the relations among the three save that Brass in his return to the alternative writ of mandamus issued by the trial court on Stoeser's initiative asserts there was competition among them. Brass v. North Dakota ex. rel. Stoeser, 153 U.S. at 394.

8. Brass v. North Dakota ex. rel. Stoeser, 153 U.S. at 403-04. Note that here again the reference to substantive due process is to that principle as a limitation on state power.

9. 143 U.S. 517 (1892), considered textually in chap. 4, pp. 73-74, *supra*, notes 30-35.

will cease and freedom of business commence. For obviously elevators along the line of that road were as plentiful as other institutions of industry, and as easily and cheaply constructed, and therefore savoring no more of monopoly.[10]

James Carter, renowned advocate famed for his opposition to David Field in the gargantuan debate over the merits of codification of law, saw conflict in the bifurcation of the anti-monopoly aspect of substantive due process. As counsel for the railroads in the valuation quagmire culminating in *Smythe v. Ames*,[11] his Brief contained the following passage:

> Language has sometimes been used, for instance in the case of *Munn* vs. *Illinois* (the determinations in which we do not dispute), which seems to suggest, although it by no means so declares, that the exercise of this power, so far as it seeks to touch prices, is limited to certain pursuits obscurely defined as "affected with a public interest." This is a misleading phrase. The occupations supposed to be thus affected are such as those of millers, innkeepers, ferrymen, carriers &c. But what is meant by saying that these callings are "affected with a public interest?" Is it that they are more necessary or interesting to the public than those of shoemakers, or farmers, or manufacturers of wares in general? No, but only this: that the facilities afforded by these callings are so necessary that the State might properly furnish them itself, and that the number engaged in supplying them is so few that the public is limited in the choice it can make when seeking such services; that is to say, that they are to a greater or less extent monopolies, and these are an undoubted field for the exercise of the police power.
>
> But they are not the only field for its exercise: from the very nature of the power it has no other limitation than the *necessities* of society. The order of reasoning adverted to might, with propriety, be reversed when we are considering the extent of the police power; and instead of saying that whatever things are affected with a public interest may be subjected to the regulation of that power, we might better say that whatever requires the regulation of that power is *affected* with a public interest.[12]

In the first paragraph of this excerpt, Carter is emphasizing the doctrinal underpinning of *Munn* formulated by Chief Justice Waite from the two tracts of Matthew Hale. Magna Carta could not, as Lord Macclesfield had said in *Mitchel v. Reynolds*,[13] provide substantive due process protection against private restraint (monopoly), but this protection could be read from Lord Hale. In this wise, due process of substance became a sword against private monopoly, as contrasted with a shield against monopoly by public dispensation. It

---

10. Brass v. North Dakota ex. rel. Stoeser, 153 U.S. at 410.

11. 169 U.S. 466 (1898), considered textually *supra* chap. 2, p. 45, notes 89-90.

12. 7 P. KURLAND and G. CASPER, LANDMARK BRIEFS AND ARGUMENTS OF THE SUPREME COURT OF THE UNITED STATES: CONSTITUTIONAL CASES 485 (1975). The Carter prophecy pointed to the general validity of price fixing legislation, whereas Justice Brewer and his colleagues in dissent were opposed to the constitutionality of government fixation of price absent a condition of clear monopoly.

13. This landmark decision is thoroughly examined in chap. 1, pp. 19-20, text at notes 91-95.

would have been helpful had Carter used *Brass v. Stoeser* by way of illustration. Brewer & Co. were dissenters because, there being no monopoly on the facts of that case, the majority in their view had no constitutional power from substantive due process as sword to justify the validity of North Dakota maximum price fixation for grain storage. To the dissenters the law was invalid for lack of a demonstrated condition of monopoly. However, were "the order of reasoning" reversed, Carter concludes in his second paragraph, legislation would be constitutional under the police power unless vitiated by substantive due process functioning as a shield against monopoly grant. In a word, by one view legislation is constitutional in the *presence* of monopoly, while in reverse view it is constitutional in the *absence* of monopoly. What to the dissenters the majority had done was to "stretch" the concept of monopoly beyond legitimate limits in order to sustain otherwise invalid law.

In another area of the private sector the role and rule of *Munn* faced early threat of repudiation yet survived initial attack. The occasion for conflict at the level of Fifth Amendment Due Process was enactment by Congress of a national antitrust law. By 1890 great concern had arisen over the growth of industrial combinations, in form both close-knit or loose-knit, that marked the period following the close of the Civil War. Popular demand for protection against excessive prices, restricted production, and poor quality resulting from monopoly control in basic industries led first to state condemnation and then to federal prohibition. The essence of the latter, known as the Sherman Act, lay in two Sections.[14]

> Section 1. Every contract, combination in the form of trust or otherwise, or conspiracy, in restraint of trade or commerce among the several States, or with foreign nations, is declared to be illegal.
> Section 2. Every person who shall monopolize, or attempt to monopolize, or combine or conspire with any other person or persons, to monopolize any part of the trade or commerce among the several States, or with foreign nations, shall be deemed guilty of a misdemeanor....

United States v. Trans-Missouri Freight Association[15] was the first decision to consider the problem of the proper substantive interpretation of the Sherman Act. The bare majority of a divided Court construed Section 1 literally to apply to every contract, combination, or conspiracy in restraint of trade that affected interstate commerce. The result was the illegality of the rate-fixing provisions of the agreement among Western carriers regardless of their asserted reasonableness. The shocking judgment stirred grave apprehension in the business world. In considerably less than two years an essentially identical agreement among Eastern carriers was before the Court in *United States v. Joint Traffic Association*.[16] By agreement of counsel in defense it fell to Attor-

---

14. 15 U. S. C. §§ 1 and 2.
15. 166 U.S. 290 (1897).
16. 171 U.S. 505 (1898).

ney Phelps for the New York Central to challenge the Sherman Act[17] as literally read.

> If the construction of the Anti-Trust act which was adopted by the court in the *Trans-Missouri case* is to stand, it is respectfully insisted that the act, so far as thus interpreted and applied, is in violation of the provisions of the Constitution of the United States, since it deprives the defendants in error of their liberty and their property without due process of law, and deprives them likewise of the equal protection of the laws.
>
> This point was not made on the argument of the *Trans-Missouri case*, because no such construction of the act was anticipated by counsel. Nor was it considered by the court, since it is an unvarying rule that no objection to the constitutionality of a law will be considered, unless raised by the party affected.
>
> The question thus presented is not whether the act in general, or in its application to the many other cases to which it is obviously addressed, is unconstitutional, but whether the agreement here under consideration is one that may be prohibited by legislation, without infringing the freedom of contract and the right of property, which the Constitution declares and protects.[18]

In reply the Solicitor General asserted:

> The doctrine laid down in the case of *Munn* v. *Illinois*, 94 U.S. 113 applies. When a man devotes his property to a public use, to that extent he grants the public an interest in that use.... Congress is entitled to pass judgment upon the tendency of a contract in restraint of trade. If it deems such a contract reprehensible, injurious in its tendencies, it may prohibit it, whether the act will result in a particular case in the establishment of reasonable or unreasonable rates.[19]

Assertion of the applicability of the doctrine of *Munn* is significant. There the intrusion upon monopoly by private contract, while considerable, left the monopolist in possession of a business enterprise entitled to retain earnings at least theoretically equal to a return of capital investment possible under conditions of competition. But sustainment of literal interpretation of the Sherman Act would mean legislative power to destroy completely all business arrangements marked by actual or intended monopoly position. Surely such power was offensive to substantive due process as an extreme expropriation of private property. The Supreme Court, again badly divided, acknowledged the objection labored by Attorney Phelps[20] but turned a deaf ear. A bit of sleight of hand assisted in the result. Common contractual transactions by which businesses were organized, altered and sold, employees secured and re-

---

17. Vagueness in the objectives of the Act raised questions of unconstitutionality on that ground. The challenge failed; present analysis does not call for further attention to this aspect.

18. United States v. Joint Traffice Association, 171 U.S. at 532. The contention is repeated on the next page ending in a recapitulation, *id*. 533-34, stressing that the Act as construed was a deprivation of life and liberty without due process of law.

19. *Id*. at 556-57.

20. *Id*. at 559.

leased, and trade conducted,[21] were read out of that category for purposes of construction of the Act.[22] With them explained away, much of the steam was vented from the vagueness contention as well from that of due process content. The constitutional issue as seen by the majority concerned contracts in restraint of competition and as to them the question was posed:

> Has not Congress with regard to interstate commerce and in the course of regulating it, in the case of railroad corporations, the power to say that no contract or combination shall be legal which shall restrain trade and commerce by shutting out the operation of the general law of competition? We think it has.[23]

The contention that the Sherman Act violated Fifth Amendment Due Process dissolved in thin air. Again, a generation after *Munn*, substantive due process and anti-monopoly were in tandem; legislation attacking monopoly could not possibly be contrary to due process of law. Quite the contrary, by constitutional alchemy substantive due process had, in the face of private monopoly, become a sword, rather than a shield.[24] Walton Hamilton saw this in retrospect when in a symposium on Antitrust he later wrote

> The Sherman Act is thus in accord with the great American tradition. Callings are by law open to all; men have a right to buy and sell in a free and open market.[25]

The title of the article in which he penned this observation gives focus to the picture of consistency between anti-monopoly and due process as disclosed through the early history of antitrust litigation.[26]

However impactful were the foregoing deviations from the traditional essence of substantive due process, they pale in comparison with the abrupt loss of thrust experienced by due process as shield against public monopoly just when this core element was poised to gain full acceptance in the Supreme Court of the United States. From dissenting status in the *Slaughter-House Cases* of 1873 it had shortly moved to concurrent standing in *Butchers' Union*

---

21. The Court provides a detailed listing of these innocuous contracts, *id.* at 567.

22. *Id.* at 567-68. Judge Taft in United States v. Addyston Pipe and Steel Co., 85 F. 271 (C.C.A. 6th, 1898), had offered clarifying analysis by which to distinguish "good" from "bad" contracts of restraint. The former were ancillary to some lawful business operation, whereas the latter were non-ancillary contracts designed to scuttle competition for the purpose of achieving monopolistic control.

23. *Id.* at 569.

24. The Court's disposition of Allgeyer v. Louisiana, 165 U.S. 578 (1897), urged by railroad counsel as requiring the Act's invalidation, is insightful for its disclosure of the judicial process of realignment of due process. *Id.* at 572. The unique part played by *Allgeyer* in the history of substantive due process is shown subsequently.

25. Hamilton, *Common Law, Due Process and Antitrust*, 7 LAW & CONTEMP. PROBS. 24, 41 (1940).

26. Another economist so read Hamilton as sensing "a conception of a basic communion of spirit between due process and free competition." Gould, *Legislative Intervention in the Conflict Between Orthodox and Direct-Selling Distribution Channels*, 9 LAW & CONTEMP. PROBS. 318, 333 (1941).

of 1884, and quickly to apparent majority adoption in *Yick Wo v. Hopkins* only two years later. That *Yick Wo* was decided under the Equal Protection Clause seemed to present no obstacle to ultimate subsumption under substantive due process of the prohibition against monopoly by governmental act. So, in retrospect, thought Walton Hamilton in his widely accepted account of *The Path of Due Process of Law*.[27] "The substance to which 'equal protection' gave a verbal home could pass by contagion into a liberty and a property fortified by 'due process'."[28] Overlooked was the fact that, as earlier observed, there was no evidence that Justice Miller had embraced the Bradley-Field view that government-imposed monopoly was a denial of substantive due process. The reliance on Equal Protection may have been but a device for reaching agreement on the holding by avoiding that "contagion."

Powell v. Pennsylvania,[29] decided shortly after *Yick Wo*, presented the ideal factual pattern for Court embracement of Substantive Due Process as prohibitive of monopoly by governmental action. The issue was the constitutionality of a Pennsylvania statute forbidding the manufacture or sale of oleomargarine. This new product had been developed by a Frenchman in a contest sponsored by Napoleon III to find for the poorer classes a less expensive but palatable breadspread.[30] Mege won the prize; the article gained popular acceptance; and the process was patented in France and England in 1869, and in the United States in 1873. Immediately recognized as a serious competitor of creamery butter, because of lower cost of production, opposition to it became widespread. In this country hostility went beyond the major dairy States. By 1886 half of the existing states had enacted restrictive legislation.[31] Many laws, of which that of Massachusetts[32] was one, forbade the sale of oleo in semblance of butter; Pennsylvania, dissatisfied with that type of restriction, in 1885 enacted complete prohibition[33] as did several other jurisdictions. Resort was also had to the taxing power, applying John Marshall's observation that the power to tax is the power to destroy. The Congressional Act of 1886[34] imposed an excise tax of 2¢ per pound (later increased to 10¢) and license taxes on all engaged in manufacture, distribution, and retailing of the product, the amount declining with successive stages in the process.[35]

---

27. Hamilton, *The Path of Due Process of Law*, in C. Read, The Constitution Reconsidered 167 (1938, 1968).

28. *Id.* at 179.

29. 127 U.S. 678 (1888).

30. Snyder, *Margarine*, in 18 Encyc. Americana 279 (1975).

31. Dewees, *State and Federal Legislation and Decisions Relating to Oleomargarine* 16 (U.S.D.A. 1936).

32. Mass. Pub. Stat. 1881-1882, tit. xi, chap. 56, § 17.

33. Pa. Laws 1885, p. 22, No. 25 (reproduced in the *Powell opinion*, 127 U.S. at 678-80).

34. 24 Stat., chap. 840, at 209-13.

35. Dewees, *supra* note 31. Behn, *The Oleo Margarine Taxes*, 9 Geo. Wash. L. Rev. 837 (1941), traces state anti-oleo taxes to the time of World War II.

The attack on oleomargarine was bitter; the manufacturing process was said to be filthy, the product dangerous to the point of poisonous, the sale fraudulent because of consumer deception. Congressional debate preceding passage of federal law provides a word picture of the intensity of the opposition.[36] Powell's Brief in the Supreme Court[37] effectively countered the extreme, often absurd denunciations of oleo. Quoted was the Report of the Commissioners of Internal Revenue stating that the wholesomeness of the new product was affirmed by eminent chemists and physiologists of Europe and the United States (listing them by name) when prepared from sweet fat of healthy animals and processed in a proper and cleanly manner. Other support could be cited, including refutation of the horror stories regarding foul manufacturing conditions and product unwholesomeness, and hinting that the claim of deception in selling was a red herring.[38] A reading of the Congressional Record and other sources of the period is convincing that the profession of protection for consumers was a sham; riddance of the oleo industry was the clear objective. Ernst Freund, respected scholar of the period, had no doubt that it was the hostility of the dairy interests that led to restrictive legislation against oleomargarine.[39] Once again, as with the New Orleans' butchers and the Chinese laundrymen, monopoly for a favored group was the end sought through state and federal legislation.[40]

---

36. 17 Cong. Rec., 49th Cong., 1st Sess. 4894-940 (microfilm reel #29) (1886).

37. Brief for Plaintiff in Error, Powell v. Pennsylvania, 127 U.S. 678. Record, Microfilm, Part IV, reel #298. On the reel Powell's Brief follows immediately after the Transcript of Record. The offer to prove by Prof. Hugo Blanck the wholesomeness of oleo appears *id.* at 8-9; objection thereto, sustained, at 9-10. Further contentions by Powell are found *id.* at 22-33, including the Report of the Commissioners of Internal Revenue at 28.

38. Bannard, *The Oleomargarine Law.* 2 Pol. Sci. Q. 545, at 548, 551-52(1887); Caldwell, *Oleomargarine*, 134 J. Franklin Inst. 190, at 196-208 (1892); *cf. Comment and Criticism*, in 7 Science 537 (1886) (official German inquiry, finding that when oleo is manufactured under conditions of great cleanliness it is a harmless substitute for butter and that in all manufactories investigated such conditions were present. Absent great cleanliness, there may be danger of disease through communication).

39. E. Freund, The Police Power §282 (1904). This conviction continues to the present day. Thus an account of the history of oleomargarine usage in Chapel Hill, North Carolina, includes the statement that "American dairymen vehemently protested that margarine would ruin the dairy industry, especially if it was colored, so Congress taxed margarine and would not let it be colored. It was 1967 before every state allowed colored margarine." Chapel Hill Newspaper, Section C, page 1, Feb. 17, 1985.

40. Counsel for Powell had urged in his Brief that the legislative consequence was one tending toward monopoly. "While it is not claimed that technically this Pennsylvania Act creates a monopoly, its tendency is toward that and this affords an additional reason why it is in conflict with the 14th Amendment." Brief for Plaintiff in Error, *supra* note 37, at 43. Counsel was correct that in the strict sense monopoly exists only when economic power over a business is concentrated in one entity, as was the fact in *Slaughter-House Cases.* But to his credit he saw that monopoly's characteristic of exclusion of outsiders is not limited to this one situation but obtains in other fact patterns. Where the exclusion is of others from production/marketing of the identical product through concentration of

Had the Bradley-Field view prevailed, the *Butchers' Union* concurrence and the decision in *Yick Wo* would have been cited for precedent and the Keystone State's statute struck down. The then recent decision of the New York court of appeals, *People v. Marx*,[41] provided a perfect model for such opinion. The New York statute of 1884, quoted in the case, was prohibitory, imposing heavy penalties on manufacture or sale of any oleaginous substances "designed to take the place of butter...." Invalidation was unanimous; the following paragraph discloses the reasoning:

> It appears to us quite clear that the object and effect of the enactment under consideration was not to supplement the existing provision against fraud and deception by means of imitations of dairy butter, but to take a further and bolder step, and by absolutely prohibiting the manufacture or sale of any article that could be used as a substitute for it, however openly and fairly the character of the substitute might be avowed and published, to drive the substituted article from the market, and protect those engaged in the manufacture of dairy products against the competition of cheaper substances capable of being applied to the same uses as articles of food.[42]

But no, the Pennsylvania law was sustained, Field alone dissenting. The opinion reflected the line of reasoning taken in the State's Brief.[43] Because the indictment and conviction of Powell were based upon admitted violation of the statutory prohibition against sale of oleo, all offers of proof of the wholesomeness of the product were refused as "immaterial and irrelevant." This was true even of Powell's offer to prove by a Professor Hugo Blanck that the latter saw manufactured the article sold, that pure animal fats were used, that the process of manufacture was clean and wholesome, and that the article sold was as wholesome and nutritious as butter produced from pure milk or cream. The State did not challenge Powell's evidence; rather, objection to its admission, pressed in the State's Brief and sustained by the Court, was that to consider it would constitute a violation of separation of powers. "One branch of the government cannot encroach on the domain of another without danger. The safety of our institutions depends in no small degree on a strict obser-

---

control in few entrepreneurs, the condition is today known as oligopoly. *Yick Wo* presented this factual pattern, as contrasted with the English instances of true monopoly. It is remarkable that Powell's counsel saw functionally-equivalent exclusion where producers of a substitute product, actively competitive, are legislatively fenced from a common market. As will be seen from discussion of cases involving this pattern in chapter 8, *infra*, even Justice Brandeis could not visualize "monopoly" in these circumstances. It is no wonder that the thrust of Powell's contention of invalidity was predicated on the more familiar *A* to *B* syndrome of substantive due process and on denial of equal protection on analogy to *Yick Wo*.

41. 99 N.Y. 29, 1 N.E. 41 (1885).

42. *Id.* at 32.

43. Brief of Defendant in Error, Powell v. Pennsylvania, 127 U.S. 678, Record, Microfilm, Part IV, reel #298, following Brief of Plaintiff in Error.

vance of this salutary rule." [44] From this it was said to follow that the Court was limited to the face of the statute, which professed concern for the protection of the public health; inquiry by the Court into the legislative background to ascertain the actual purpose of the legislation was *verboten* as impermissible inquiry into legislative motive.[45] Confined to this limited vision of the law, the Court, anticipating its reasoning a decade later in *Holden v. Hardy*, cited at the outset of this chapter, found a reasonable relation between the statute and the public health and, accordingly, a valid exercise of the State's power of police consistent with due process of law. In sum, monopoly by public grant was sustained, not repudiated.

The decision was a blow for anti-monopoly due process; the path of progress from dissent in *Slaughter-House Cases* to concurrence in *Butchers' Union*, to final embracement by the Court, that Hamilton thought he saw, was lost with *Powell*.[46] Persevering counsel sought revival in the *Chinese Exclusion Case*[47] which followed *Powell* by one year. It was contended for the unfortunate Ping that "Labor is Property"[48] and accordingly that the "Act of October 1st, 1888, is in contravention of the Fifth Amendment to the Constitution of the United States in this, that it deprives the Appellant of both Liberty and Property without due Process of Law."[49] Prominently cited was Justice Bradley's passage on Due Process in his *Slaughter-House* dissent, quoted above.[50] But the effort, undertaken in admittedly inauspicious circumstances, failed. Congressional power is especially strong in matters of exclusion of aliens, and any tie with monopoly through freedom to engage in the common callings was weak on the facts.

---

44. Powell v. Pennsylvania, 127 U.S. at 685 (quoting Chief Justice Waite in the Sinking Fund Cases, 99 U.S. 700, 718).

45. Since Marshall's time the Court has struggled with the question whether it can or should take account only of legislative profession when there is evidence that other considerations more assuredly explain enactment. The question has arisen in Commerce Clause as well as in cases of Due Process. Despite Chief Justice Warren's claim in United States v. O'Brien, 391 U.S. 367 (1968), that the Court has consistently declined to go behind profession, there is much authority to the contrary. The issue is thoroughly canvassed in chapter 8, *infra*. My view is that motive cannot be considered but that the Court should look behind profession to purpose. Otherwise, escape can be had from all constitutional restraint by legislative use of preambles that label enactments as adopted in the interest of public health, safety, morals, or welfare, whether the assertion is genuine or spurious.

46. Professor Currie, applauding the insight of Field in dissent, declares that "if there was ever a case for substantive due process, this was it. In essence the margarine ban seemed simply a transfer of wealth to the dairy industry, and even Miller in *Davidson* had conceded that a legislature could not give one man's property to another." D. CURRIE, THE CONSTITUTION IN THE SUPREME COURT 378 (1985).

47. 130 U.S. 581 (1889).

48. 9 P. KURLAND and G. CASPER, *op. cit. supra* note 12, at 150.

49. *Ibid.*

50. Text at note 75, chap. 3, pp. 61-62, *supra*. Counsel for Ping are quoting from judicial statements that include the last paragraph of the Bradley passage. *Id.* at 151.

In the tenth edition of his popular *Casebook on Constitutional Law*, Professor Gerald Gunther repeats from earlier editions the observation apropos the *Slaughter-House Cases* that:

> In 1873, a bare majority resisted the dissenters' appeal to social compact and natural law and vested rights ideology; but a generation later, a new majority embraced substantive due process.[51]

Despite his deserved reputation as a careful constitutional scholar, I must fault this assertion in two respects although it reflects the "official view" of constitutional commentators. As for the first portion of the statement, it is by no means established that monopoly due process derived from higher law or some other omnipresence brooding in the jurisprudential sky.[52] To the contrary are the Briefs of John Archibald Campbell in the *Slaughter-House Cases*, confirming understandings of centuries past. In his amazing review of English, French, and other European constitutional history, as well as American, there runs a thread of universal opposition to monopoly. There is no attempt to ground freedom from monopoly in any source but legal history. Only at one point does he cite Adam Smith and then in support of his assertion that there is a property right in human labor. Typical of his resort to historical sources is his reference to the 1776 decree of Louis XVI, inspired by Turgot, followed by that of the French Assembly of 1791, abolishing all monopolies of trades and all special privileges of corporations, guilds, and trading companies. His full familiarity with the English constitutional struggle over monopoly grants was acknowledged by Justice Miller in the majority opinion in *Slaughter-House Cases*. In historical perspective the anti-monopoly content of Due Process is genuine, not spurious.

With respect to the second portion of Professor Gunther's statement, an appreciation of what had transpired "a generation later" is essential in the interest of accuracy. Attention centers on the pivotal case of *Allgeyer v. Louisiana*,[53] decided in 1897. Invalidated was a Louisiana statute imposing a substantial fine on any person, firm or corporation that effected marine insurance on property then within the State where the insurer had failed to comply with state law. Allgeyer & Co. had violated the law by insuring with a non-complying New York company a shipment of cotton bales from New Orleans to foreign ports. The contracts were technically made in New York, and premiums and losses were to be paid there. "The decision of the case demanded no more than the simple comment that an Act of Louisiana had no application to a mat-

---

51. G. GUNTHER, CONSTITUTIONAL LAW 507 (10th ed. 1980). In the 9th edition the statement appears at 553.

52. Among others subscribing to the higher-law—or natural-law—source of anti-monopoly due process are Corwin, *The "Higher Law" Background of American Constitutional Law*, 42 HARV. L. REV. 149, 365 (1928-1929); Grant, *The Natural Law Background of Due Process*, 31 COL. L. REV. 56 (1931); Hamilton, *supra* note 27.

53. 165 U.S. 578 (1897).

ter beyond the jurisdiction of the State."[54] But the opinion for a unanimous Court took a different turn:

> In the privilege of pursuing an ordinary calling or trade and of acquiring, holding and selling property must be embraced the right to make all proper contracts in relation thereto, and although it may be conceded that this right to contract in relation to persons or property or to do business within the jurisdiction of the State may be regulated and sometimes prohibited when the contracts or business conflict with the policy of the State as contained in its statutes, yet the power does not and cannot extend to prohibiting a citizen from making contracts of the nature involved in this case outside of the limits and jurisdiction of the State, and which are also to be performed outside of such jurisdiction. . . .[55]

Precedent for this underlying "privilege of pursuing an ordinary calling or trade" was found in the concurring opinion of Justice Bradley in *Butchers' Union*. The passages quoted have been reproduced earlier in this study.[56] Then follows immediately the sentence that profoundly altered the course of constitutional direction:

> It is true that these remarks were made in regard to questions of monopoly, but they well describe the rights which are covered by the word "liberty" as contained in the Fourteenth Amendment.[57]

The substantive due process the Court now unanimously embraces was of an utterly different order from that espoused by Bradley and Field. They had stood for opposition to monopoly, a position with deep historical roots in Due Process increasingly articulated as espousal of freedom of trade. The essence of freedom of trade was the general right of all to engage in the common callings free from constrictions or prohibitions on entry. In severing this right from its tie with anti-monopoly the Court in one sentence catapulted into an uncharted domain in which substantive due process could become the obstacle to endless instances of legal, economic and social reform. To the extent that Professor Gunther's statement is read as asserting a continuum in the development of substantive due process it disregards this profound break, and thereby does disservice to an understanding of a major segment of American constitutional history.[58]

Of more than historical interest is it to attempt to identify who or what must

---

54. Hamilton, *supra* note 27, at 184.
55. Allgeyer v. Louisiana, 165 U.S. at 591.
56. Text at note 80, *supra* chap. 3, p. 63.
57. Allgeyer v. Louisiana, 165 U.S. at 590. The next paragraph consists of citation to *Powell* v. *Pennsylvania*, the holding in which is distinguished by judicial fiat of the worst sort.
58. Others could be blamed for this grievous error. Thus Walton Hamilton can only be read as asserting a smooth progression from *Slaughter-House Cases* to *Lochner*. Hamilton, *supra* note 27. Professor Gunther is "picked on" because, as a respected constitutional scholar, he has influenced many students of constitutional law.

carry the blame for the breakaway from a quite precise, restricted, well grounded conception of monopoly due process. Not the attorney for Allgeyer & Co.; there is in his Brief no suggestion of a novel reading of the guarantee. He viewed the issue for what it was, a question of legislative jurisdiction[59] within the field of Conflict of Laws.[60] Not Mr. Justice Bradley, who had died in 1892. Not Mr. Justice Field, although accused of paternity by no less than Roscoe Pound in his classic article on liberty of contract,[61] unless Field's failure to take exception to the Court's opinion be regarded as a surrender of former views. As Dean Pound demonstrated there was already abroad in the land by the time of *Allgeyer* an avalanche of state decisions invalidating all manner of laws as violative of freedom, or liberty, of contract.[62] Freedom of contract, in contrast to freedom of trade, called for laissez-faire with respect to all phases of business enterprise. Because the two concepts were often expressed in terms of the right to engage in the common callings, unintended confusion may have been the culprit in the failure to differentiate. But this is a weak reed. The intent is clear to deduce freedom of contract from freedom of trade, thus providing precedential base for a new creed regarding the relationship of government and the individual. A careful rereading of the crucial passage quoted above[63] is convincing.

Stemming from embrace of the economics of Adam Smith[64] and the sociology of Herbert Spencer,[65] a philosophy of individualism had swept the country like the plague. The virus had infected Mr. Justice Brewer, as witnessed by a paragraph from his dissent in *Budd v. New York*, quoted earlier in the text.[66]

---

59. Brief for Plaintiffs in error, Allgeyer v. Louisiana, 13 P. KURLAND and G. CASPER, *op. cit. supra* note 12, at 154-88.

60. Greene, *The Allgeyer Case as a Constitutional Embrasure of Territoriality*, 2 ST. JOHN'S L. REV. 22 (1927).

61. Pound, *Liberty of Contract*, 18 YALE L. J. 454, 470 (1909).

62. *Id.* at 471-78. The earlier of those cases, while they talked the language of freedom of contract, did not employ the phrase. What Pound cites, *id.* at 471, as the pioneer and leading decision, Godcharles v. Wigeman, 113 Pa. St. 427 (1886), condemned a Pennsylvania statute as an attempt by the legislature to do what, in this country, cannot be done; that is, prevent persons who are *sui juris* from making their own contracts. "The Act is an infringement alike of the employer and the employee; more than this, it is an insulting attempt to put the laborer under a legislative tutelage, which is not only degrading to his manhood, but subversive of his rights as a citizen of the United States. He may sell his labor for what he thinks best, whether money or goods, just as his employer may sell his iron or coal, and any and every law that proposes to prevent him from so doing is an infringement of his constitutional privileges and consequently vicious and void." 113 Pa. St. at 437.

63. Text at note 55, *supra*.

64. Viner, *Adam Smith*, in 14 INTER. ENCYC. SOC. SCI. 322 (1968), stressing the pervading influence of this political economist in late 19th century thought.

65. The dominance of the thinking of Spencer in the late 19th century is attested to by a respected scholar. R. HOFSTADTER, SOCIAL DARWINISM IN AMERICAN THOUGHT chap. 2 (1955 ed.).

66. The quotation is found in the text at note 35 of chap. 4, p. 74, *supra*.

Familiar is the denunciation of the Federal Income Tax of 1894[67] by Joseph Choate,[68] who in argument declared it to be communistic, socialistic, and popularistic in defiance of the rights of private property.[69] Expressions of similar hostility to governmental intervention were legion. Under pressure for protection against legislative onslaught Substantive Due Process was seduced into the service of a strange master.[70] Walton Hamilton, completing his trek from *Slaughter-House Cases* to *Lochner*, later sounded a fatalistic note. Speaking of the age in which there occurred the attachment to traditional Substantive Due Process of a spurious content and meaning, he observed:

> In philosophy it was individualism, in government laissez-faire, in economics the natural law of supply and demand, in law the freedom of contract.... An impact that had been irresistible elsewhere should surely have won its way in constitutional law. Its coming seemed inevitable; the constitutional concept which it made its domicile was a mere matter of doctrinal accident.[71]

It had been my hope that research would disclose an explanation of *Allgeyer* that would place it in the stream of development of traditional Due Process embrace. But the issue was not a substantive one; rather, the concern was that of a state's legislative jurisdiction. The twin question of the reach of a state's judicial jurisdiction the Court had faced twenty years before in *Pennoyer v. Neff*.[72] In the parlance of Conflict of Laws the question was one of choice of

---

67. 28 STAT. chap. 349, §§ 27-37 (1894).

68. Pollock v. Farmers' Loan & Trust Co., 157 U.S. 429 (1895).

69. 12 P. KURLAND and G. CASPER, *op. cit. supra* note 12, at 464-67. Choate contended that the income tax was a direct tax; that as such it was required by the Constitution to be apportioned; and that apportionment threatened confiscation of the wealth then concentrated in four Eastern States.

70. Two decisions of the New York court of appeals may have been influential. Matter of Jacobs, 98 N.Y. 98 (1885); People v. Marx, 99 N.Y. 377 (1885), both invalidating state laws as violative of due process. If so, there would be paradox as regards the latter decision for on facts parallel with those in *Powell v. Pennsylvania, supra*, the *Marx* court grounded its decision on the basis of lack of legislative power to prohibit the manufacture of oleomargarine because the product competed with dairy butter in the market. Implicitly, the case is in the tradition of due process hostility to monopoly. *Jacobs*, on the other hand, invalidating legislation forbidding manufacture of cigars in tenement houses, was of the new strain.

71. Hamilton, *supra* note 27, at 189. There can be no questioning of Hamilton's assertion that at the close of the 19th century a creed of individualism had carried the day in private law and the (other) social sciences. But it is one thing for an American court to respond in contract or tort law, where new doctrine can be, as it often is, rejected by legislatures, and quite another to embrace it in constitutional law where because of the supremacy of the judiciary in constitutional interpretation there is no recourse short of constitutional amendment. I have before railed against disregard by some commentators of this false parallelism; the distinction in consequences is so clear as to justify a charge of intended disingenuousness on the part of those who paper over the basic difference in their promotion of a doctrine of "constitutional common law" as one justification for noninterpretivism by the Court.

72. 95 U.S. 714 (1878).

law, the first to come well-defined before the Court. *Allgeyer* has never been overruled on the conflicts issue; however, confinement to its precise facts has left it a derelict on the waters of the law.[73] There is some wonderment that to this alien adjudication the Court attached the dictum that gave to substantive due process a perverse, unhistoric meaning destined to bode ill for the future. It may have been clever judicial politics to fasten the new, embracive content as a dictum on a case not in point, but this explains only the method of introduction and not the motivating force for inclusion. For that Hamilton is probably correct.[74] I for one resent the Court's heed of the siren call, for the door it opened was nothing less than a self-assigned license to engage at will in constitutional noninterpretivism.

---

73. Although *Allgeyer* remains inoperative, the operative principles of American Conflict of Laws derive from Due Process along with Full Faith and Credit.

74. A far-fetched explanation for the appearance of the concept of freedom of contract is that it was a reincarnation of the Contract Clause. For this I of course have no authority, only a hunch arising from the peculiar time sequence involved. It was 1880 when the Clause was sapped of near all vitality by Court embrasure of the doctrine of implied reservation; the first judicial references to "liberty of contract" appeared in the 1880s; the *Allgeyer* opinion with its insidious dictum came down in 1897. This is sufficient justification to entitle one to indulge the speculation.

6. Perversions of Traditional Meaning: Progressive Deterioration

Only five years into the twentieth century the gratuitous dictum in *Allgeyer v. Louisiana*[1] solidified into holding in *Lochner v. New York*.[2] Thus was introduced into constitutional law the first perversion of substantive due process. For the concept of freedom/liberty of contract was alien to historic due process as has been shown in my account of the latter from earliest English origins to 1900.[3] The Justices of the time, steeped in the economics of Adam Smith and the sociology of Herbert Spencer, unabashedly read their philosophy into the Constitution.[4] There is no question but that that philosophy was dominant at the turn of the century.[5] This appears to have been Holmes' view as expressed in his celebrated dissent in *Lochner*;[6] I have elsewhere only questioned his assertion that by 1905 "a large part of the country does not entertain" this philosophy.[7] Elevation of laissez-faireism to constitutional status was possible by confusion of "freedom of trade" as a right to engage in the common callings free of monopoly with "freedom of contract" as a right to carry on a common calling free of governmental restrictions. The two concepts are so distinct as to make it difficult to believe that the confusion was unintentional. Search in case and commentary for an answer to the question of intent has been fruitless.[8] Holmes articulated the distinction but failed to grasp the implications.

---

1. 165 U.S. 578 (1897), considered at the close of chapter 5, *supra*.

2. 198 U.S. 45 (1905).

3. Consideration of the specific point appears at the close of chapter 3, *supra*.

4. In the words of Walton Hamilton, "[t]hey professed with little qualification, an economic creed; and the empty receptacle of 'due process' and the age-old vitality of 'the common right' enabled them to read 'free competition' into the Constitution." Hamilton, *Common Right, Due Process and Antitrust*, 7 LAW & CONTEMP. PROBS. 24, 31-32 (1940).

5. Strong, *Bicentennial Benchmark: Two Centuries of Evolution of Constitutional Processes*, 55 N.C. L. REV. 1, 75 (1976), citing authority of constitutional scholar and of eminent historian.

6. Lochner v. New York, 198 U.S. at 75.

7. Strong, *supra* note 5.

8. Hamilton, *Freedom of Contract*, 6 ENCYC. SOC. SCI.450 (1931), is of no help. This generally accepted account of the conversion of economic theory into constitutional principle makes no reference to the judicial confusion of "freedom of contract" with "freedom of trade" and hence offers no insight into the issue of intent.

Dissenting a generation later in *Adkins v. Children's Hospital,*[9] where the majority invalidated the District of Columbia minimum wage law for women, he observed that "in the present instance the only objection that can be urged is found within the vague contours of the Fifth Amendment, prohibiting the depriving any person of liberty or property without due process of law."[10] Turning to this contention for guidance he said:

> The earlier decisions upon the same words in the Fourteenth Amendment began within our memory and went no farther than an unpretentious assertion of the liberty to follow the ordinary callings. Later that innocuous generality was expanded into the dogma, Liberty of Contract. Contract is not specially mentioned in the text that we have to construe.[11]

Freedom "to follow the ordinary callings," derived from long-standing hostility toward publicly granted monopoly, was far more than "an unpretentious assertion" or an "innocuous generality." It constituted one of the two core meanings of substantive due process developed in centuries of Anglo-American experience. Elsewhere I remark on Holmes' failure to comprehend the reach of anti-monopoly where the hated ogre was the product of private destruction of economic freedom through railroad and industrial combination.[12] It is not unreasonable to lay at his door similar lack of appreciation in the present context although, to borrow one of his own celebrated aphorisms, to do so is "to lay hands on the Ark of the Covenant."[13] In fairness, however, it should be observed that other members of the Court were even more insensitive to the tricky transition than was Holmes. Not only was the upshot an affirmative perversion of substantive due process; it must have played a part in the failure of the Court to give force to the anti-monopoly element resident in the Due Process concept, traced in another portion of this study,[14] that was overshadowed by corruption of "freedom of trade" in the cause of economic dogma.[15]

---

9. 261 U.S. 525 (1923).

10. *Id.* at 568.

11. *Ibid.* In his dissent in Griswold v. Connecticut, 381 U.S. at 518, n. 11 (1965), Justice Black quotes this passage, adding the next two succeeding sentences. However, the context gives no aid in resolving the question whether the "expansion" was intentional.

12. Refer to chapter 9, *infra,* on *Private Monopoly and Substantive Due Process.*

13. Holmes (Brandeis agreeing), dissenting in Springer v. Philippine Islands, 277 U.S. at 211 (1928).

14. Refer to chap. 8, *infra,* on *Public Monopoly and Substantive Due Process.*

15. A distinctly different interpretation of *Lochner* has recently been re-advanced. "[A]n effort to regulate the hours of labor was considered an impermissible taking from *A* in order to benefit *B.*" Sunstein, *Naked Preferences and the Constitution,* 84 COL. L. REV. 1689, at 1717 (1984). By this view the underlying premise of *Lochner* was not hostility to discredited mercantilist thought but to naked wealth transfers. "The notion that legislation is unconstitutional if it represents a naked decision to distribute resources to one group rather than to another came through most clearly in the *Lochner* era." *Ibid.* The *Lochner* period *was* marked by growing fear of socialist doctrine; witness Choate's im-

Lochner's installation of freedom of contract as the new embodiment of substantive due process soon bore bitter fruit. Federal legislation outlawing yellow dog contracts, so detested by Labor, was invalidated in *Adair v. United States*[16] with like result inevitable for state laws of similar import. Citing from *Lochner* Justice Harlan, who had there dissented, referred to the split in viewpoint but explained that:

> [a]lthough there was a difference of opinion in that case as to certain propositions there was no disagreement as to the general proposition that there is a liberty of contract which cannot be unreasonably interfered with by legislation.[17]

After stating the minority position in *Lochner,* the Justice continued:

> While, as already suggested, the rights of liberty and property guaranteed by the Constitution against deprivation without due process of law, is [sic] subject to such reasonable restraints as the common good or the general welfare may require,[18] it is not within the functions of government—at least in the absence of contract between the parties—to compel any person in the course of his business and against his will to accept or retain the personal services of another, or to compel any person, against his will to perform personal services for another.[19]

When a few years later the Kansas law against yellow dog contracts was before the Court in *Coppage v. Kansas*[20] freedom of contract was again center stage.

> The principle is fundamental and vital. Included in the right of personal liberty and the right of private property—partaking of the nature of each—is the right to make contracts for the acquisition of property. Chief among such contracts is that of personal employment, by which labor and other services are exchanged for money or other forms of property. If this right be struck down or arbitrarily interfered with, there is a substantial impairment of liberty in the long-established constitutional sense.[21]

---

passioned denunciation of socialistic and other radical thought in *Pollock v. Farmers' Loan & Trust Co.,* to which reference is made earlier in this study. Chapter 5, *supra*, p. 93, notes 68-69. However, association of *Lochner* with the anti-monopoly core of substantive due process enjoys continued acceptance. *E.g.,* Wonnell, *Economic Due Process and the Preservation of Competition,* 11 HAST. CONST. L. Q. 91 (1983). The relevancy of *Lochner* in both contexts is what makes it central in the account of Substantive Due Process.

16. 208 U.S. 161 (1908).

17. *Id.* at 174.

18. This sentence is a reference to a prior paragraph in the opinion, *id.* at 172, in which it had been asserted that the section of the Congressional Act under challenge "is an invasion of the personal liberty, as well as of the right of property, guaranteed by that [Fifth] Amendment. Such liberty and right embraces the right to make contracts for the purchase of the labor of others and equally the right to make contracts for the sale of one's own labor; each right, however, being subject to the fundamental condition that no contract, whatever its subject matter, can be sustained which the law, upon reasonable grounds, forbids as inconsistent with the public interests or as hurtful to the public order or as detrimental to the common good."

19. Adair v. United States, 208 U.S. at 174.

20. 236 U.S. 1 (1915).

21. *Id.* at 14.

Right of contract then grounded *Adams v. Tanner*[22] in which was held uncon-stitutional the Washington law, promulgated by Initiative, closing private em-ployment agencies, and *Adkins v. Children's Hospital*,[23] where it was said

> There is, of course, no such thing as absolute freedom of contract. It is subject to a great variety of restraints. But freedom of contract is, nevertheless, the general rule and restraint the exception; and the exercise of legislative authority to abridge it can be justified only by the existence of exceptional circumstances.[24]

It was this dogma of freedom of contract that led to invalidation of the min-imum wage law for women despite the fact that, as I will elsewhere contend, "substantive due process was satisfied by proven absence of any expropriation even at the factual level."[25] Opposition to this perversion of the Constitution was growing, however, within as well as beyond the Court. Both *Adkins* and *Adams* were in effect or fact bare majority holdings; the often-told tale of mounting hostility among constitutionalists is recounted by me in an essay at the year of the Bicentennial of Independence.[26]

Contrary to conventional analysis, freedom of contract itself was not the fulcrum of decisions during the last decade of the *Lochner* period. Those de-cisions group into two categories, the price fixing cases and the cases debating the extent to which legislative restrictions might go beyond the constitutional limits of the police power in the interest of effective administration of policies concededly within the scope of that power. Each category merits examination.

The decisions on price fixation by government are considered later in this study[27] because they turned on applications of the rule enunciated in *Munn v. Illinois*. Conveniently ignored by critics is the fact that the Court sustained price fixing nearly as often as it invalidated this form of governmental regula-tion. Invalidation occurred where no monopolistic conditions obtained in the business affected. In this sense the Court was enforcing the economic creed of Smith and Spencer; competitive philosophy was equated to substantive due process and thereby accorded constitutional status. Yet the equation was not as has been assumed. Emphasis was on substantive due process as sword rather than as shield; the issue between the "good guys" and the "bad guys" on the Court was the presence or absence of monopoly in a given factual sit-uation. This is well illustrated by the *New State Ice* case[28] where Oklahoma legislation technically restrictive of market entry rather than of market price

22. 244 U.S. 590 (1917).

23. 261 U.S. 525 (1923).

24. *Id.* at 546.

25. Segment on Employer-Employee Relationships in chap. 7, *infra, Expropriation and Substantive Due Process*.

26. Strong, *supra* note 5, at 51-56.

27. Chapter 9, *infra*, pp. 273-92, on *Private Monopoly and Substantive Due Process*, cited *supra* note 12.

28. New State Ice Co. v. Liebmann, 285 U.S. 251 (1932), considered in chapters 8 and 9, *infra*.

was stricken by the conservative majority because it could see emergence of competitive forces in the ice industry whereas the liberal dissenters were convinced that monopolistic conditions remained in the ascendancy. "The significance of this debate lies not in the question who had the better of the argument but in the fact all the Justices accepted the relevance of monopoly to constitutional adjudication concerning fixation of maximum price."[29] Even Justices Brandeis and Stone had been lured by the fascination of economic debate into temporary tolerance of the underlying premise of *Lochner.* From this lapse into perversion of substantive due process they were shortly rescued under the leadership of none other than Justice Roberts who was of the majority in *New State Ice!*[30]

The second category of cases embraces decisions that not only disclose no dependence on freedom of contract but as well reflect little influence from the economic creed of competitive capitalism. They are cases rejecting the penumbra doctrine enunciated in *Purity Extract Co. v. Lynch*[31] wherein a unanimous Court had, in 1912, sustained a Mississippi prohibition law "which includes in its prohibition the sale of malt liquors." The litigation arose out of a breach of contract. Lynch had entered into an agreement with the company to market in Mississippi its beverage trade-named "Poinsetta" but had repudiated the agreement upon learning of the statutory prohibition. The company in its suit to recover a prepayment required of Lynch countered his defense by contending that the statute deprived it "of its liberty and property without due process of law." The case was tried upon an agreed statement of facts, among which were that "Poinsetta" contained no alcohol and was not intoxicating. For all the Brethren Charles Evans Hughes in his first stint on the Court, after noting the "undoubted" power of the State to "prohibit the selling of intoxicating liquors," delivered himself of the following:

> It does not follow that because a transaction separately considered is innocuous it may not be included in a prohibition the scope of which is regarded as essential in the legislative judgment to accomplish a purpose within the admitted power of the Government.[32]

---

29. This is my conclusion reached in the analysis of *New State Ice* in Strong, *supra* note 5.

30. The appeal of the monopoly test returned again after *Nebbia.* See discussion of Townsend v. Yeomans, 301 U.S. 441 (1937), in chapter 9, *infra.*

31. 226 U.S. 192 (1912).

32. *Id.* at 201. The context in which this assertion is made discloses the Court's sensitivity to the unusual enforcement difficulties that attend the acknowledged power of government, Mugler v. Kansas, 123 U.S. 623 (1877), to outlaw traffic in intoxicants. The quoted excerpt from the Hughes opinion for the Court was followed by the statement that in "dealing with a class of beverages which in general are regarded as intoxicating, [the Mississippi legislature] was not bound to resort to a discrimination with respect to ingredients and processes of manufacture which, in the endeavor to eliminate innocuous beverages from the condemnation, would facilitate subterfuges and frauds and fetter the enforcement of the law." *Id.* at 204. In sustaining the National Prohibition Act of 1919, which covered

The first of the four decisions, *Jay Burns Baking Co. v. Bryan*,[33] rejecting the penumbra doctrine of *Purity Extract* concerned bread weight. The majority had no difficulty with that portion of the Nebraska statute that set minimum weights but found violative of due process the accompanying provision fixing maximum weights designed to prevent the palming off of smaller for larger sizes. The tolerance allowed, two ounces per pound determined by the average weight of not less than 25 loaves twenty-four hours after baking, was deemed arbitrary in view of evidence that conditions of humidity and temperature often prevailing made it impossible to manufacture good bread without frequently exceeding the narrow leeway.

> For the reasons stated, we conclude that the provision, that the average weights shall not exceed the maximum fixed, is not necessary for the protection of purchasers against imposition and fraud by short weights and is not calculated to effectuate that purpose. . . .[34]

Justice Brandeis dissented with the concurrence of Justice Holmes.

> It was not from caprice or love of symmetry [that excessive weights were also prohibited]. It was because experience had taught consumers, honest dealers and public officials . . . that, if short weights were to be prevented, the prohibition of excessive weights was an administrative necessity.[35]

Cited was *Purity Extract* to which the majority had made no reference.

Burns Baking was followed by *Weaver v. Palmer Bros. Co.*[36] invalidating a Pennsylvania law forbidding the use of shoddy in comfortables even when sterilized. After reviewing "much evidence" introduced at trial before a federal three-judge court, the majority concluded:

> This evidence tends strongly to show that, in the absence of sterilization or disinfection, there would be little, if any, danger to the health of the users of comfortables filled with shoddy, new or secondhand; and confirms the conclusion that all danger from the use of shoddy may be eliminated by sterilization.[37]

This time Justice Holmes wrote the dissenting opinion, in which he was joined by Justice Brandeis and a new ally, Justice Stone. Adverting to "the broad statement in *Schlesinger v. Wisconsin* the other day, I do not suppose that it was intended to overrule *Purity Extract & Tonic Co. v. Lynch.* . . . "[38] *Schlesinger*

---

malt liquors whether or not intoxicating, Justice Brandeis quoted the above passages from *Purity Extract* and added a massive documentation of state court and legislative actions that "furnish ground upon which Congress reasonably might conclude that a rigid classification of beverages is an essential of either effective regulation or effective prohibition of intoxicating liquors." Jacob Ruppert v. Caffey, 251 U.S. 254, 288-89 (1920).

33. 264 U.S. 504 (1924).
34. *Id.* at 517.
35. *Id.* at 520.
36. 270 U.S. 402 (1916).
37. *Id.* at 412.
38. *Id.* at 415.

v. Wisconsin,[39] cited for support by the majority, had been decided just one week before *Weaver*. It had stricken, as a deprivation of property violative of due process, a Wisconsin statute creating a conclusive presumption that all gifts made within six years of death were made in contemplation of death and, accordingly, were subject to state inheritance taxes. In his dissent there, joined by Justices Brandeis and Stone, Justice Holmes had conceded

> Of course many gifts will be hit by the tax that were made with no contemplation of death. But the law allows a penumbra to be embraced that goes beyond the outline of its object in order that the object may be secured. A typical instance is the prohibition of the sale of unintoxicating malt liquors in order to make effective a prohibition of the sale of beer.[40]

The reference was unmistakably to *Purity Extract* which is then cited. The majority had well articulated the basis of its contrary position by paraphrasing the defense of the presumption.

> That is to say, "A" may be required to submit to an exactment forbidden by the Constitution if this seems necessary in order to enable the State readily to collect lawful charges against "B." Rights guaranteed by the federal Constitution are not to be so lightly treated; they are superior to this supposed necessity.[41]

Litigation in *Liggett Co. v. Baldridge*[42] presented the question of the validity of a Pennsylvania statute, prospective in effect, requiring that every pharmacy or drug store be owned "only by a licensed pharmacist, and no corporation, association, or copartnership shall own a pharmacy or drug store, unless all the partners or members thereof are licensed pharmacists." Liggett Co., a Massachusetts corporation, was a drug-store chain authorized to do business in Pennsylvania. Challenged as a violation of the due process and equal protection clauses of the Fourteenth Amendment, the law arose from early opposition to chain stores rather than from a legislative conclusion that "administrative necessity" required, for full protection of the public health, the limitation of corporate pharmacies to stockholders licensed as pharmacists.

A bit earlier, when the Court had invalidated on equal protection grounds a statute of Pennsylvania imposing a gross receipts tax on *incorporated* transportation companies[43] Justice Brandeis dissented by taking note of "the fear of growing corporate power" in early Pennsylvania the survival of which might account for effort to discourage resort to the corporate form of organization. So here, there could well be present legislative hostility to a new use of the corporate device that threatened traditional modes of distribution in the retail drug business. Absence of any reference to *Purity Extract Co.* in either

---

39. 270 U.S. 230 (1926).
40. *Id.* at 241.
41. *Id.* at 240.
42. 278 U.S. 105 (1928).
43. Quaker City Cab Co. v. Pennsylvania, 277 U.S. 389 (1928).

majority or dissenting opinion in *Liggett Co.,* and of Justice Stone from among the dissenters, renders uncertain categorizing of *Liggett* with the preceding penumbra cases. On the other hand, the majority relied upon *Burns Baking* and *Weaver,* along with two contemporaneous decisions yet to be reviewed, for its holding of unconstitutionality.[44]

It is familiar learning that in any event the decision is no longer controlling. "The *Liggett* case, being a derelict in the stream of the law, is hereby overruled." *North Dakota State Board of Pharmacy v. Snyder's Drug Stores.*[45] The opportunity came in 1973 when the supreme court of North Dakota struck down a similar law of that State "by reason of our decision in 1928 in *Liggett Co. v. Baldridge,* 278 U.S. 105."[46] "*Liggett,* decided in 1928, belongs to that vintage of decisions which exalted substantive due process by striking down state legislation which a majority of the Court deemed unwise."[47] This characterization of the *Lochner* period as one in which decisions turned on judicial views of the wisdom of legislation has been a favorite with the "liberated" Court and its sycophantic followers among the commentators. It is true the Court had been led astray from the historic principles embedded in substantive due process but there is no justification in depicting it as a "freewheeling Court invalidating in a broad sweep federal and state legislation with which it found itself in disagreement."[48]

One may conclude that Holmes and Brandeis had the sounder position in the penumbra cases, yet it must be conceded the issue raised in those cases presented a debatable question in constitutional limitation. Allowing government to regulate beyond acknowledged limits on the basis of asserted administrative necessity takes on a very different complexion when the interests affected are other than economic. The reaction of a majority of the Court in *Shelton v. Tucker*[49] attests to this. "An Arkansas statute compels every teacher, as a condition of employment in a state-supported school or college, to file

---

44. Liggett v. Baldridge, 278 U.S. at 113. For comment on *Meyer* and *Pierce* refer to text accompanying notes 52 and 53, *infra. Liggett* receives further attention at note 71 of chap. 8, *infra,* pp. 223-24.

45. 414 U.S. 156, 167 (1973).

46. *Id.* at 158. Had the state court grounded its decision solely on the state constitutional provision guaranteeing due process, N. D. Const. Art. I, §12, relying on the majority reasoning in *Liggett,* it could have prevented review by the Supreme Court with its certainty of reversal. The North Dakota trial court had held the statute violative of §12. Reference is made later to the growing resort by state courts to the adequate and independent state ground rule for insulating from Supreme Court review interpretations of State constitutions according greater protection to private interests, at variance with the High Court's construction of facially identical provisions of the federal Constitution. Refer to text at note 78, *infra,* and the reference there given. It is a matter of conjecture whether the North Dakota court failed to appreciate the availability of insulation, or wished to pass to the Supreme Court responsibility for sustaining the legislation.

47. North Dakota State Board of Pharmacy v. Snyder's Drug Stores, 414 U.S. at 164.

48. Strong, *supra* note 5, at 50.

49. 364 U.S. 479 (1960).

annually an affidavit listing without limitation every organization to which he has belonged or regularly contributed within the preceding five years." Over the dissent of four members, led by Justices Frankfurter and Harlan, the law was held unconstitutional for overbreadth. In a footnote[50] it was observed that

> In other areas, involving different constitutional issues, more administrative lee-way has been thought allowable in the interest of increased efficiency in accomplishing a clearly constitutional purpose. See *Purity Extract Co. v. Lynch,* 226 U.S. 192; *Jacob Ruppert v. Caffey,* 251 U.S. 264; *Schlesinger v. Wisconsin,* 270 U.S. 230, 241 (dissenting opinion); *Queenside Hills Co. v. Saxl,* 328 U.S. 80, 83.[51]

Of all the major substantive due process decisions of the *Lochner* reign, *Meyer v. Nebraska*[52] and *Pierce v. Society of Sisters*[53] are most suspect as instances of Court invalidation for conflict with its views of what is wise legislative policy. Yet these two,[54] involving, respectively, prohibition of the teaching in elementary grades of any modern language save English and prohibition of non-public education, not only escaped the wrath of *Lochner*'s critics but, *mirabile dictu,* were resurrected for precedent when the reconstructed Court first indulged in noninterpretivism.[55] Only Justice Holmes, joined by Justice Sanford but not Justice Brandeis, avoided the trap in *Meyer* and even he gave up and yielded to temptation in *Pierce.* In the end, who really was in position to call the pot black?

The *Lochner* brand of constitutional circumscription held sway for nearly thirty years. *Nebbia v. New York* then excised from the Constitution what *Lochner* had read into it.[56] With the grip of freedom of contract and of Smith-Spencer loosened, the test of constitutionality became one of nexus between challenged economic legislation and some head of the police power. Two paragraphs in the opinion of Justice Roberts for the majority identified the degree of nexus required. Earlier it was said that the Fifth and Fourteenth Amendments

> do not prohibit governmental regulation for the public welfare. They merely condition the exertion of the admitted power by securing that the end shall be accom-

---

50. *Id.* at 488, n. 8.

51. In *Queenside Hills,* a 1946 decision upholding a safety regulation for multiple dwellings, Justice Douglas relied upon *Purity Extract* in a situation having nothing to do with administrative necessity for coverage of "wholly innocent" private action.

52. 262 U.S. 390 (1923). *Meyer* provided the rationale as well for Bartels v. Iowa, Bohning v. Ohio, and Pohl v. Ohio, all 262 U.S. 404 (1923).

53. 268 U.S. 510 (1925).

54. Seldom cited is a third decision, Farrington v. Tokushige, 273 U.S. 284 (1927), invalidating a law of the Territory of Hawaii that in forbidding private foreign language schools factually presented a combination of *Meyer* and *Pierce.*

55. Griswold v. Connecticut, 381 U.S. 479, 482 (1965). The *Griswold* case is discussed later in this chapter.

56. This interpretation of the *Nebbia* ruling is more fully advanced by me in chapter 9, *infra,* pp. 291-92.

plished by methods consistent with due process. And the guaranty of due process, as has often been held, demands only that the law shall not be unreasonable, arbitrary or capricious, and that the means selected shall have a real and substantial relation to the object sought to be attained....[57]

Later on, in summary, the Justice declared:

So far as the requirement of due process is concerned, and in the absence of other constitutional restriction, a state is free to adopt whatever economic policy may reasonably be deemed to promote public welfare, and to enforce that policy by legislation adapted to its purpose.... If the laws passed are seen to have a reasonable relation to a proper legislative purpose, and are neither arbitrary nor discriminatory, the requirements of due process are satisfied, and judicial determination to that effect renders a court *functus officio*....[58]

Nebbia thus articulated a test close to, if not identical with, that invoked by Justices Harlan, Day and White in their dissent in *Lochner*. Speaking for the three, the elder Harlan had said "I find it impossible, in view of common experience, to say that there is here no real or substantial relation between the means employed by the State and the end sought to be accomplished by its legislation."[59] Indeed, the *Lochner* majority used the same test, but unable to see any such material connection, suspected "that there was some other motive dominating the legislature than the purpose to subserve the public health or welfare."[60] That motive, they concluded, was to intrude upon the right of contract of both employer and employee. With that "right" now removed, substantive due process was freed of an alien barnacle.

In the restoration substantive due process did not regain its historic core of anti-monopoly; rather, it was transmuted into a counter weight to otherwise unconfined police power in the regulation of private business, much as the expropriation core was "balanced" by infiltration of the police power in a metamorphosis culminating in *Holden v. Hardy*.[61] While this was a pronounced departure from earlier meaning, the new function was within the tradition of due process as shield against excessive intrusion upon economic privacy. What it lost in intensity of bite, it gained in extensity of protection. A requirement that for legislation to pass constitutional muster there must be a showing of reasonable, understood as real and substantial, relationship between the challenged governmental act and constitutional objective offered some responsiveness to the historic role of due process. That degree of nexus would operate to strike a fair balance between public interest and private interest under a Constitution skillfully drawn to give power to govern under a regime of private

---

57. Nebbia v. New York, 291 U.S. 502, 525 (1934).

58. *Id.* at 537.

59. Lochner v. New York, 198 U.S. 45, 69 (1905).

60. *Id.* at 63. "The connection [with the public health], if any exists, is too shadowy and thin to build any argument for the interference of the legislature." *Id.* at 62.

61. For that development refer to chap. 5, *supra*, pp. 79-80, text at notes 1-3.

property.[62] *Nebbia* thus projected a new version but not a perversion of substantive due process.

However, *Nebbia*'s formula for resolution of the conflict between power and limitation did not last. Within fifteen years a radical reformulation had been fashioned, one that surely classified as a perversion of any legitimate meaning of substantive due process consistent with its past. An undercurrent of change appeared with the Court's *per curiam* affirmance, without opinion, of a decision of a three-judge federal court sustaining a Colorado law requiring that restaurant business be conducted in a room separate from one in which merchandising business of any type was conducted.[63] The essence of the opinion of the collegial court is found in two paragraphs:

> While there was a sharp conflict in the opinion of experts in the field of health, hygiene and sanitation, there is substantial evidence that the requirement as to a separate room will tend to promote and protect the public health. Had the same evidence been before the legislature, it could have found either way on the issue and its finding would have been supported by substantial evidence.
>
> Furthermore, despite the opinions of experts to the contrary, we regard the requirement, that restaurants as defined in the statute be conducted in a room separate from the room or rooms in which other departments of a business establishment are conducted, has a reasonable relation to the public health. Such a room can more readily be kept clean and sanitary; it can be kept more free from dust and germ-carrying flies; and, as a less number of persons will enter the room than will enter the general business establishment there will be less of sneezing and coughing therein which all the experts admit may contaminate food. Persons entering a dining room are more apt to be careful of the welfare of others than they would be in a general business establishment.[64]

The talismanic words—reasonable and substantial—from earlier judicial expression are repeated in testing nexus and yet there is a lurking hollowness about the usage. A familiar biblical passage suggests itself: "The voice *is* Jacob's voice, but the hands *are* the hands of Esau." (Genesis 27:22)

The test disintegrated in *United States* v. *Carolene Products Co.*[65] Sustained was the federal statute forbidding distribution in interstate commerce of filled milk made in semblance of milk or cream in any form. Part *Third* of the opinion by Justice Stone opens with disclosure of the slender basis on which the decision rested.

---

62. Over fifteen years ago I urged an even tighter test for resolution of conflicts in the economic as well as civil liberty area in order to provide protective "assurance in optimum degree for all facets of constitutional litigation." Strong, *Fifty Years of "Clear and Present Danger,"* 1969 SUP. CT. REV.41, at 76-80.

63. S. H. Kress & Co. v. Johnson, 299 U.S. 511, *aff'g* 16 F. Supp. 5 (D. Colo. 1936). Appendix A, reproducing the challenged state law, and Appendix B, recording the divided judgment of the state supreme court, follow the opinion of the federal collegial court. *Id.* at 10-14.

64. *Id.* at 7.

65. 304 U.S. 144 (1938).

We may assume for present purposes that no pronouncement of a legislature can forestall attack upon the constitutionality of the prohibition which it enacts by applying opprobrious epithets to the prohibited act, and that a statute would deny due process which precluded the disproof in judicial proceedings of all facts which would show or tend to show that a statute depriving the suitor of life, liberty or property had a rational basis.

But such we think is not the purpose or construction of the statutory characterization of filled milk as injurious to health and as a fraud upon the public. There is no need to consider it here as more than a declaration of the legislative findings deemed to support and justify the action taken as a constitutional exertion of the legislative power, aiding informed judicial review, as do the reports of legislative committees, by revealing the rationale of the legislation. Even in the absence of such aids the existence of facts supporting the legislative judgment is to be presumed, for regulatory legislation affecting ordinary commercial transactions is not to be pronounced unconstitutional unless in the light of the facts made known or generally assumed it is of such a character as to preclude the assumption that it rests upon some rational basis within the knowledge and experience of the legislators.[66]

Appended to the close of the quotation is the famous Footnote 4 in which it is cautioned that a much tighter nexus may be required where "a specific prohibition of the Constitution" is involved or the legislation "restricts those political processes which can be expected to bring about repeal of undesirable legislation.[67] The contrast magnifies the insignificance of the rational nexus text as defined; no matter how great the imbalance in the relevant facts as between those supportive of validity and those contrariwise, constitutionality carries the day. But even this weakening of the test failed to satisfy the newcomer to the Court; "Mr. Justice Black concurs in the result and in all of the opinion except the part marked *Third*."

Carolene Products I[68] introduced a period which Professor Gunther has well described as one of "minimal scrutiny in theory and virtually none in

---

66. *Id.* at 152.

67. *Id.* at 152, n.4. Of late, caution has been urged respecting footnote 4 by two commentators highly qualified to speak on the matter. Powell, *Carolene Products* Revisited, 82 Col. L. Rev. 1087; Lusky, *Footnote Redux,* 82 *id.* 1093 (1982). Justice Powell has the unique advantage of "inside" insight; Professor Lusky, law clerk to Justice Stone when the case was decided, "was privy to events relevant both to the provenance of the Footnote and the spirit in which it was offered." Each commentator stresses that the famous three paragraphs were meant to induce debate on the proper degree of judicial scrutiny to be accorded fact patterns of the types identified, not to promulgate settled resolution of the issue. For present purposes, however, the significance of footnote 4 is the contrast it highlights in comparison with the rational nexus test for review of cases of economic substance. I so conclude although noting Lusky's classing as a "misconception" "the notion that the footnote calls for denial of strict scrutiny in all cases involving property rights or economic interests." *Id.* at 1105.

68. *Carolene Products* I and the second *Carolene* decision, Carolene Products Co. v. United States, 323 U.S. 18 (1944) (*Carolene* II), are considered in chap. 8, *infra,* pp. 226-30, on *Public Monopoly and Substantive Due Process.*

fact."[69] Quoting him further, the *Day-Brite* case[70] "is an especially striking example of the Court's readiness to dismiss due process attacks, even in unusual areas of regulation."[71] Under a Missouri law requiring employers to allow their employees four hours off from work with full pay in order to vote, Day-Brite was fined for failure to recompense one Grotemeyer. The facts of the case were these. The polls on the day of general elections were open from 6 A.M. until 7 P.M. Grotemeyer's shift ran from 8 A.M. to 4:30 P.M., with 30 minutes for lunch, but on election day he was allowed to leave at 3 P.M. Grotemeyer's residence was but 200 feet from his polling place. Thus he had at least one hour before reporting for work, and four hours after work, in which to cast his vote. Like other statutes of the same import, the Missouri law was enacted when the workday ran from 12 to 16 hours thereby providing justification for a released period without sacrifice of pay. But "in the light of contemporary labor developments and improvement in transportation facilities, it is highly questionable whether there is *any* purpose, much less a valid purpose, to this type of legislation now."[72]

The opinion of Justice Douglas for all the Court save Justice Jackson, who couldn't tolerate its extremism, was curt and short:

> The liberty of contract argument pressed on us is reminiscent of the philosophy of *Lochner* v. *New York,* 198 U.S. 45, which invalidated a New York law prescribing maximum hours for work in bakeries; *Coppage* v. *Kansas,* 236 U.S. 1, which struck down a Kansas statute outlawing "yellow dog" contracts; *Adkins* v. *Children's Hospital,* 261 U.S. 525, which held unconstitutional a federal statute fixing minimum wage standards for women in the District of Columbia, and others of that vintage. Our recent decisions make plain that we do not sit as a super-legislature to weigh the wisdom of legislation nor to decide whether the policy which it expresses offends the public welfare. The legislative power has limits, as *Tot* v. *United States,* 319 U.S. 463, holds. But the state legislatures have constitutional authority to experiment with new techniques; they are entitled to their own standard of the public welfare; they may within extremely broad limits control practices in the business-labor field, so long as specific constitutional prohibitions are not violated and so long as conflicts with valid and controlling federal laws are avoided.[73]

For Day-Brite's counsel to challenge the Missouri statute on the "liberty of contract argument" was advocacy near the level of incompetency. It afforded the radicalized Court an opportunity to exhume the *Lochner-Adair-Coppage-*

---

69. G. GUNTHER, CASES AND MATERIALS ON CONSTITUTIONAL LAW 540, n. 1 (10th ed. 1980). The description is taken from Gunther, *A Model for a Newer Equal Protection,* 86 HARV. L. REV. 1, 8 (1972), but in the Casebook he makes it clear that it is equally applicable to economic due process.

70. Day-Brite Lighting, Inc. v. Missouri, 342 U.S. 421 (1952).

71. G. GUNTHER, *op. cit. supra* note 69, at 537.

72. Comment, 47 Nw. L. REV. 252, 254 (1952) (emphasis in the original).

73. Day-Brite Lighting, Inc. v. Missouri, 342 U.S. at 423.

Adkins line of cases for another public whipping, not to disown them for their false premise derived from confusing "liberty of contract" with "freedom of trade" but to contrast them with recent decisions making "plain that we do not sit as a super-legislature to weigh the wisdom of legislation . . . " However, what is plain is that there is being read out of the Constitution the facet of historic substantive due process that offers protection of private interest against raw forms of expropriation. Proof comes in the very next sentence. Limits to legislative power are found in *Tot v. United States,* which invalidated a federal statutory presumption for conflict with *procedural* due process.[74] Only the unversed would miss the obvious implication![75]

With *Day-Brite Lighting* most anything could survive constitutional attack. Prior to his elevation to the Court Felix Frankfurter had declared with clear reference to their substantive content, "The due process clauses ought to go."[76] Now that he has his wish he "concurs in the result" without comment. Even the much heavier economic burden imposed on employers by legislative requirement that for jury duty employees be reimbursed at their regular wage rate, less compensation for service as juror, received scant consideration. In *Dean v. Gadsden Times Publishing Co.,*[77] the Court reversed the Alabama court of civil appeals that had invalidated the law as conflicting with the due process and equal protection guarantees of the Fourteenth Amendment. By predicating its decision on the federal Constitution the Alabama court laid its action open to certain reversal. From this experience it will learn, as other state courts are learning, to base its stricter determinations on the equivalently worded provisions in the Alabama constitution, a procedure that can insulate those determinations under the adequate and independent state ground rule.[78]

---

74. "But the due process clauses of the Fifth and Fourteenth Amendments set limits upon the power of Congress or that of a state legislature to make the proof of one fact or group of facts evidence of the existence of the ultimate fact on which guilt is predicated." Tot v. United States, 319 U.S. 463, 467 (1943). The principle is applicable as well to common-law presumptions and to those operative in civil litigation. F. STRONG, AMERICAN CONSTITUTIONAL LAW 1039-45 (1950).

75. The supreme court of Illinois was alert to what a commentator, cited *supra* note 72, described as "a withering ray upon Constitutional protection" that *Day-Brite* cast. In the face of the Supreme Court action it reaffirmed its earlier decision invalidating under the Illinois Constitution the Illinois "pay while voting" law. Heimgaertner v. Benjamine Electric Mfg. Co., 6 Ill. 2d 152, 128 N.E. 2d 691 (1955), reaffirming People v. Chicago, Milwaukee & St. Paul Ry. Co., 306 Ill. 486, 138 N.E. 155 (1923) (due process and equal protection). Accord: Illinois Central R. R. v. Commonwealth, 305 Ky. 632, 204 S. W. 2d 973 (1947) (taking from A for B unconstitutional under Kentucky Constitution). The supreme court of Missouri in the instant case and some appellate decisions, for which see Comment, *supra* note 72, at 253, n. 7, had sustained the laws.

76. Frankfurter, *The Red Terror of Judicial Reform,* 40 NEW REPUBLIC for Oct. 1, 1924, at 110, reprinted in F. STRONG, *op. cit. supra* note 74, at 301-06.

77. 412 U. S. 543 (1973).

78. Greenhalgh, *Independent and Adequate State Grounds,* in DEVELOPMENTS IN STATE CONSTITUTIONAL LAW chap. 8 (1985) (The Williamsburg Conference of March 9-10, 1984); State v. Jewett, 500 A. 2d 233 (Vt. 1985).

The opinion in *Gadsden* was *per curiam;* decision was rested on *Day-Brite.* There was no reference to the intervening case of *Ferguson v. Skrupa*[79] in which Kansas law limiting to lawyers "the business of debt adjusting" passed constitutional muster. Justice Harlan concurred in the judgment "on the ground that this state measure bears a rational relation to a constitutionally permissible objective."[80] But significantly, the remainder of the Court accepted Justice Black's declaration, "Whether the legislature takes for its textbook Adam Smith, Herbert Spencer, Lord Keynes, or some other is no concern of ours."[81] With this pronouncement Justice Black achieved what he had failed to gain in *Carolene I:* Court repudiation in theory as well as in practice of any constitutional protection of economic interests under substantive due process of law. He had brought the Court to full rejection of *Lochner v. New York.* Only missing from the listing of alternatives open in economic organization was the name Karl Marx! Achieved was a repudiation, bag and baggage, of Substantive Due Process in which presumably all historic versions and perversions had finally been put to rest.

The year was 1963. Two years later came *Griswold v. Connecticut,*[82] opening the era of substantive due process protection of civil and personal rights. Justice Douglas' opinion for the Court, invalidating the Connecticut anti-contraception law, relied upon penumbras of the Bill of Rights. "Various guarantees create zones of privacy." Specified were the First (right of association), Third (prohibition against quartering soldiers in private homes in time of peace without consent of owners); Fourth (protection against unreasonable searches and seizures); Fifth (privilege against self-incrimination); and Ninth (other rights) Amendments. Surely this approach was designed to satisfy Justice Black; but Douglas misunderstood the grand strategy of his Brother, which was to use the Bill of Rights, incorporated into the Fourteenth Amendment, as the outer measure of Due Process and thus bar the Court from its employment otherwise.[83] Not only did the Douglas approach fail to bring

---

79. 372 U. S. 726 (1963).

80. *Id.* at 733.

81. *Id.* at 732.

82. 381 U. S. 479 (1965).

83. Significant efforts in this endeavor were Justice Black's dissents in Adamson v. California, 332 U. S. 46 (1947) (the great debate with Justice Frankfurter over the historic intent of the Fourteenth Amendment with respect to incorporation therein of the Bill of Rights); H. P. Hood & Sons, Inc. v. Du Mond, 336 U. S. 525 (1949) ("a stretching of either [Commerce or Due Process Clause] outside its sphere can paralyze the legislative process . . ."); the principal case ("I like my privacy as well as the next one, but I am nevertheless compelled to admit that government has a right to invade it unless prohibited by some specific constitutional provision"); Harper v. Virginia Board of Elections, 383 U. S. 663 (1966) ("there is no constitutional support whatever for this Court to use the Due Process Clause as though it provided a blank check to alter the meaning of the Constitution as written so as to add to it substantive constitutional changes which a majority of the Court at any given time believes are needed to meet present-day problems").

Black into the majority; it did not discourage other Justices from viewing the issue in substantial part as one of substantive due process justifying invalidation of the Connecticut law. To this seduction Black had responded that

> I do not believe that we are granted power by the Due Process Clause or any other constitutional provision or provisions to measure constitutionality by our belief that legislation is arbitrary, capricious or unreasonable, or accomplishes no justifiable purpose, or is offensive to our own notions of "civilized standards of conduct." Such an appraisal of the wisdom of legislation is an attribute of the power to make laws, not of the power to interpret them.[84]

Only Justice Stewart followed Justice Black in declining the temptation to revive substantive due process as shield against improvident legislation. In addition to joining the Black opinion he had this to say in his own words:

> What provision of the Constitution, then, does make this state law invalid? The Court says it is the right of privacy "created by several fundamental constitutional guarantees." With all deference, I can find no such general right of privacy in the Bill of Rights, in any other part of the Constitution, or in any case ever before decided by this Court.
>
> At the oral argument in this case we were told that the Connecticut law does not "conform to current community standards." But it is not the function of this Court to decide cases on the basis of community standards. We are here to decide cases "agreeably to the Constitution and laws of the United States." It is the essence of judicial duty to subordinate our own personal views, our own ideas of what legislation is wise and what is not.[85]

When eight years later, the constitutionality of strict anti-abortion laws was ripe for decision, Justice Black was gone and major changes in Court personnel had taken place. Through a Justice of recent appointment a different Court with a new Chief Justice rested squarely on Due Process its controversial decision in *Roe v. Wade*.[86]

> A state criminal abortion statute of the current Texas type, that excepts from criminality only a *life-saving* procedure on behalf of the mother, without regard to pregnancy stage and without recognition of the other interests involved, is violative of the Due Process Clause of the Fourteenth Amendment.[87]

Justice Stewart was perplexed and justifiably so.

> In view of what had been so recently said in *Skrupa*, the Court's opinion in *Griswold* understandably did its best to avoid reliance on the Due Process Clause of the Fourteenth Amendment as the ground for decision. Yet, the Connecticut law did not violate any provision of the Bill of Rights, nor any other specific provision of the Constitution. So it was clear to me then, and it is equally clear to me now, that

---

84. Griswold v. Connecticut, 381 U. S. at 513.
85. *Id.* at 530-31.
86. 410 U. S. 113 (1973).
87. *Id.* at 164.

the *Griswold* decision can be rationally understood only as a holding that the Connecticut statute substantively invaded the "liberty" that is protected by the Due Process Clause of the Fourteenth Amendment. As so understood, *Griswold* stands as one in a long line of pre-*Skrupa* cases decided under the doctrine of substantive due process, and I now accept it as such.[88]

Having thus expressed himself with commendable clarity, Stewart embraced the faith he had earlier rejected and concurred in the momentous invalidation.

Two Justices resisted. Justice White, joined by Justice Rehnquist, disagreed sharply.

With all due respect, I dissent. I find nothing in the language or history of the Constitution to support the Court's judgment. The Court simply fashions and announces a new constitutional right for pregnant mothers and, with scarcely any reason or authority for its action, invests that right with sufficient substance to override most existing state abortion statutes.... As an exercise of raw judicial power, the Court perhaps has authority to do what it does today; but in my view its judgment is an improvident and extravagant exercise of the power of judicial review that the Constitution extends to this Court.[89]

With all due respect I find this dissent too mild, sharp as it is. When it is questionable that the Framers intended the judicial branch to exercise affirmative constitutional review beyond vertical testing of state laws[90] nothing but judicial fiat can support what the Court majority has done in *Rowe* and repeated in *City of Akron* v. *Akron Center for Reproductive Health, Inc.*[91]

The episode approaches the ridiculous when this bald return to noninterpretivism is prefaced by Justice Blackmun's assurance in opening the majority opinion in *Roe* that "[w]e bear in mind, too, Mr. Justice Holmes' admonition in his now vindicated dissent in *Lochner v. New York*"[92] to avoid allowing the personal views of Justices to become imbedded in the Constitution. It never occurred to him to heed the celebrated admonition uttered by Justice Stone, dissenting in *United States v. Butler:* "Courts are not the only agency of government that must be assumed to have the capacity to govern."[93] It is trivializing the Constitution to assert, as do defenders of the new perversion of substantive due process, that noninterpretivism in the area of personal liberties is acceptable whereas it was not in *Lochner*'s domain of economic rights. The false principle, that the end justifies the means, is identical.

The deep division within the Court on the fundamental issue of the propriety of constitutional amendment by judicial say-so is reflected in the clash of

---

88. *Id.* at 167-68.
89. *Id.* at 221-22.
90. Strong, *supra* note 5, *passim.*
91. 462 U. S. 416 (1983).
92. Roe v. Wade, 410 U. S. at 117.
93. United States v. Butler, 297 U. S. 1, 87 (1936). The decision invalidated the Agricultural Adjustment Act of 1933.

views of commentators. On three occasions I have entered the lists to break a lance in defense of the position of John Marshall, Learned Hand, and Hugo Black that the proper role of the Supreme Court in our constitutional system is that of constitutional interpreter and not of constitution maker.[94] In the present context it suffices to insist that for the Court to rest its abortion decisions on substantive due process is to pervert that classic formulary from its historic content into the service of an alien level of constitutional review.[95] If judicial activism is to be raised to the new dimension of judicial oligarchy, replacing the method of amendment provided by Article V of the Constitution, this can be done with less offensiveness in the name of the Ninth Amendment that Justice Goldberg "rescued from obscurity" in *Griswold*.[96] That provision was Madison's answer to critics who asserted that any bill of rights however long would inevitably exclude some fundamentals. Let the Court, in reliance on this handy fortuity,[97] rummage among accepted and evolving conceptions of personal liberty and equality to flesh out additional guarantees not incompatible with other safeguards specifically imbedded in the Constitution.

Concededly, resort to the Ninth Amendment presents problems that render its use an act of faith. Dean Ely is convinced that search for unenumerated values of fundamental import can only result in installation of the Justices' own set of values.[98] Professor William Van Alstyne has applied his skillful scalpel to Professor Black's contentions in support of recourse to the beckoning Amendment.[99] And Raoul Berger has effectively discerned the technical pitfalls in resort to the "forgotten Amendment."[100] These are the wording of

---

94. Strong, *supra* note 5, at 97-104 and 113-21; Strong, *Contributions of ERA to Constitutional Exegesis*, 14 GA. L. REV. 389 (1980); Strong, *Levellers in Judicial Robes*, 60 NEB. L. REV. 180 (1981).

95. Epstein, *Substantive Due Process by any Other Name: The Abortion Cases*, 1973 SUP. CT. REV. 159, voices a rejection of *Rowe* that comports with my position. Rejection of revision is ably argued by Easterbrook, *Substance and Due Process*, 1982 SUP. CT. REV. 85, at 90-94. He asserts Professor Perry has conceded that "Judge Bork's arguments are unanswerable." Professor William Van Alstyne's demolishment of noninterpretive theory is equally convincing. Van Alstyne, *Interpreting the Constitution: The Unhelpful Contributions of Special Theories of Judicial Review*, 25 U. OF FLA. L. REV. 207 (1983).

96. Efforts of commentators to rescue the Ninth Amendment from desuetude, antedating Justice Goldberg's heroics, include B. PATTERSON, THE FORGOTTEN NINTH AMENDMENT Part I (1955); Redlich, *Are There "Certain Rights . . . Retained by the People"?* 37 N.Y. U. L. REV. 787 (1962). Written in the early aftermath of *Griswold* were Moore, *The Ninth Amendment—Its Origin and Meaning*, 7 N. ENG. L. REV. 215 (1972); Rhoades and Patula, *The Ninth Amendment: A Survey of Theory and Practice in the Federal Courts Since Griswold v. Connecticut*, 50 DEN. L. J. 153 (1973).

97. J. ELY, DEMOCRACY AND DISTRUST 34-41 (1980); C. BLACK, DECISION ACCORDING TO LAW 43-75 (1981).

98. J. ELY, *op. cit. supra* note 97, chap. 3.

99. Van Alstyne, Book Review, *Slouching Toward Bethlehem with the Ninth Amendment*, 91 YALE L. J. 207 (1981).

100. Berger, *The Ninth Amendment*, 66 CORN. L. REV. 1 (1980).

the provision itself, which suggests closer tie with the Tenth Amendment than with the first eight of the Bill of Rights, and the error of attempted incorporation as a limitation on the States in view of clear intent to the contrary. But faith can undergird remarkable leaps in constitutional exegesis as witness the reading of the Establishment Clause into the Fourteenth Amendment despite the especial awkwardness of this particular incorporation.

The late Professor Robert Dixon felt that *Griswold* and *Roe* could better have been predicated on a concept of "freedom of action" pendent to First Amendment penumbras.[101] These could without inconsistency be found resident in the Ninth Amendment. Professor Tribe has hinted that among other constitutional provisions the Ninth could absorb "rights of privacy and personhood."[102] Judge Ginsburg has assigned the weakness in *Roe* to "concentration on a medically approved autonomy idea, to the exclusion of a constitutionally based sex-equality perspective."[103] That perspective suggests effectuation through the Ninth Amendment provided the justifiable reach of Equal Protection is not alone sufficient.[104] But the substantive due process of Amendment XIV offered no foundation for *Griswold* or *Roe* save as an excuse for the Justices to indulge their own values. As for Substantive Due Process the Court should return to enforcement of the two basic interrelated tenets that have attached to it through centuries of constitutional evolution—that of anti-expropriation and that of anti-monopoly.

---

101. Dixon, *The "New" Substantive Due Process and the Democratic Ethic: A Prolegomenon*, 1976 BRIG. YOUNG L. REV. 43, at 83-87.

102. L. TRIBE, AMERICAN CONSTITUTIONAL LAW §15-3 (1978).

103. Ginsburg, *Some Thoughts on Autonomy and Equality in Relation to* Roe v. Wade, 63 N. C. L. REV. 375, at 386 (1985).

104. Professor Kenneth Karst has recently been a strong advocate of women's rights through greater recognition via Equal Protection. E. g., Karst, *Foreword: Equal Citizenship Under the Fourteenth Amendment*, 91 HARV. L. REV. 1, at 53-59 (1977); Karst, *Woman's Constitution*, 1984 DUKE L. J. 447.

PART IV

THE RESIDUAL LEGACY OF SUBSTANTIVE DUE PROCESS OF LAW

7. Expropriation and Substantive Due Process

Prefatory Note

In modern context actual or seeming governmental expropriation of private economic values can take many guises. It can appear, for instance, in relations as diverse as those of employer and employee, debtor and creditor, family members or community strangers, physician and patient. Other patterns, whether the consequence of societal invention or of legislative design come to mind. The existence of such relationships suggests that for purpose of analysis a host of Court decisions of the past 85 years can be handily grouped in this fashion. On occasion, however, cases group themselves on some other basis, which provides a common denominator for examination. There follows a total of six categories in which litigation has best disclosed twentieth century disposition of allegations that property of A, be A single or plural, has been "taken" by governmental action to the advantage of B, whether B is one or more persons. Chapter 7 closes with a consideration of the price paid in terms of quality of judicial product by the Court's studious and often senseless refusal to predicate decision on grounds of substantive due process of law.

"Taking" Patterns

"Pig-in-the-Parlor" Cases

The second decade of the present century witnessed a passel of cases in which local ordinances sought to oust from cities, or at least from major sections thereof, types of business operations deemed inimical to public values. Such ordinances enjoyed Supreme Court validation with respect to billiard halls,[1] livery stables,[2] laundries emitting dense smoke,[3] and gasoline storage.[4]

---

1. Murphy v. California, 225 U.S. 623 (1912).
2. Reinman v. City of Little Rock, 237 U.S. 171 (1915).

These were instances of pig-in-the-barnyard decisions; the businesses were not inherently bad provided they were kept in their "proper surroundings." But if introduced into a city location they were subject to expulsion upon demonstration that their presence was objectionable to public health, safety, morals, or welfare. These heads of the police power were broadly construed; substantive due process afforded no apparent counterbalance despite the fact the common law recognized property rights in them. To the extent the holdings were validated on the basis of *Mugler v. Kansas*[5] they constituted an extension of constitutional power. Outlawry of the liquor business was never questioned if couched in prospective legislation. The New York court of appeals, by holding, and the Supreme Court, by dictum, originally found invalidity in retroactive prohibition statutes[6] but this substantive due process limitation was overturned in *Mugler*, followed by *Powell v. Pennsylvania*.[7] The modern analog to traffic in liquor is that in drugs, from heroin and cocaine, to hashish, to marijuana. Manufacture and sale of these substances is subject to complete governmental interdiction; no "property" in such business is legally recognized.

A "pig-in-the-parlor" case is one in which a business operation lawful in its original locus has been enveloped by the expansion of a nearby city. In a word, the parlor has come to the pig, not the pig to the parlor. The earliest instance after 1900 appears to have been *Laurel Hill Cemetery v. San Francisco*,[8] where the Court in opinion by Justice Holmes upheld an ordinance forbidding burials within the City/County. The justification given for the prohibition was protection of the health of occupants of nearby dwellings. The Cemetery contended that the popular belief of hazard from interments was "a superstition" but the Court's response was that "the extent to which legislation may modify and restrict the uses of property consistent with the Constitution is not a question for pure abstract theory alone. Tradition and the habits of the community count for more than logic."[9] Counsel for San Francisco had stated in argument that "[t]he prohibition in this case is a prohibition of burials; it is not a direct confiscation of cemeteries."[10] The Court accepted this interpretation: "the or-

---

3. Northwestern Laundry v. City of Des Moines, 239 U.S. 486 (1916).

4. Pierce Oil Co. v. City of Hope, 248 U.S. 498 (1918). The earlier case of Dobbins v. Los Angeles, 195 U.S. 223 (1904), was of the same factual pattern but involved such evident arbitrariness and such suggestion of monopoly objective as to result in invalidation. *Dobbins* is treated *infra* chap. 8, pp. 114-15, text at notes 28-32.

5. 123 U.S. 623 (1887).

6. Wynehamer v. People, 13 N.Y. 378 (1856); Bartemeyer v. Iowa, 18 Wall. 129 (1873); Beer Co. v. Massachusetts, 97 U.S. 25 (1878), are considered in chap. 2, *supra*, pp. 40-41, text at notes 55-60.

7. 127 U.S. 678 (1888). This aspect of *Mugler* and *Powell* is considered in chap. 2, *supra*, p. 41, text at notes 61-67.

8. 216 U.S. 358 (1910).

9. *Id*. at 366.

10. *Id*. at 362 (Argument for Defendant in Error).

dinance in effect merely prohibited burials in existing cemeteries."[11] Thus the local law frustrated receipt of anticipated payments from unsold burial lots estimated to be worth $75,000; however, 40,000 lots had already been sold, the proceeds from which may have equaled—even exceeded—total investment.

Hadacheck v. Los Angeles[12] commonly cited as evidence of such pervasive reach of the police power as virtually to remove substantive due process as a protective shield of property, was even clearer on the limited basis sustaining constitutionality in another pig-in-the-parlor pattern. Hadacheck owned a small tract of land that when purchased by him lay beyond the city limits of Los Angeles but which through municipal expansion had been brought within those limits. As a result the western limit of the tract was the city's boundary to the west, while Wilshire Boulevard constituted its northern border. Hadacheck had bought the three-acre parcel for the bed of clay within it which was of a superior quality for the manufacture of brick. He continued the burning of brick at this location in the face of an ordinance forbidding such usage within a district defined to encompass his tract. For violating the prohibition he was convicted, thereafter challenging his confinement on writ of habeas corpus contending that the ordinance was discriminatory, fostered monopoly, and confiscated his property without due process of law.[13]

Upon answer to the writ it was discharged, remanding Hadacheck to confinement, and his appeal to the supreme court of California failed to bring him his freedom.[14] The State high court distinguished the fact pattern before it from that in the earlier case of *In re Kelso*[15] that had invalidated a city/county ordinance of San Francisco prohibiting the maintenance or operation of a rock and stone quarry within a specified district of the municipality. In *Kelso* the California court had felt that the complete nature of the prohibition, "absolutely" preventing any use of the quarry whatever, in effect took Kelso's property in totality. Here, on the contrary, the prohibition extended only to the brickmaking operations; Hadacheck's ownership of the clay bed remained untouched. In the Supreme Court, which affirmed, this perception again prevailed. "In the present case there is no prohibition of the removal of the brick clay; only a prohibition within the designated locality of its manufacture into

---

11. *Id.* at 364.

12. 239 U.S. 394 (1915)

13. Hadacheck v. Los Angeles, 239 U.S. 394, Record, Microfiche, card 1, at 1-28. The first contention was based on the presence of brick manufacturing by several competitors located in the Boyle Heights section of Los Angeles against which the City had taken no regulatory action. The monopoly contention was one to the effect that the vice of business concentration lies in exclusivity; by removing Hadacheck from the brickmaking business competition would be reduced among the numerous manufacturers of brick located within the City. These contentions the Court rather summarily rejected. Hadacheck v. Los Angeles, 239 U.S. at 412-13.

14. *Ex parte* Hadacheck, 165 Cal. 416, 132 Pac. 584 (1913).

15. 147 Cal. 609, 82 Pac. 241 (1905).

bricks."[16] Counsel for Hadacheck sought valiantly to demonstrate consistency between the case at hand and *Kelso* on the ground that here also the prohibition was absolute because the deposit of clay "cannot be moved to another location."[17] Earlier the contention had been couched in terms of cost; it would be "financially prohibitive to remove the clay to a distant location, burn it, and transport the bricks to places of construction work. To do business in that manner could not possibly compete with other brick manufacturers."[18]

The Supreme Court, however, was not impressed with this line of reasoning. *Kelso* was different and the factual variation was of constitutional dimension. The contention that the brick could not be profitably burned at and marketed from an alternative site, for which Hadacheck's counsel had quoted a passage from the *Kelso* opinion,[19] tended to backfire.

> We can see no valid objection to the work of removing from one's own land valuable deposits of rock or stone that may not be entirely met by regulations as to the manner in which such work shall be done, and this being so, we are satisfied that an absolute prohibition of such removal under all circumstances cannot be upheld.[20]

And counsel for the City had offered in rebuttal an effective observation from a New York case:[21]

> In this country there can be no trouble to find places where brick can be made without damage to persons living in the vicinity. It certainly cannot be necessary to make them in the heart of a village or in the midst of a thickly settled community.[22]

Save for the $25,000 Hadacheck had invested in kilns and structures that presumably could not be relocated, he had been deprived only of opportunity to continue to fire brick at the original site. The Court's reaction was that "[a] vested interest cannot be asserted against [the police power, "one of the most essential powers of government"] because of conditions once obtaining. . . . To so hold would preclude development and fix a city forever in its primitive conditions."[23] The denial to which Hadacheck had been subjected was not the kind of "property" constitutionally protected from taking by substantive due process of law. And although Hadacheck contended that it would be "financially prohibitive" to haul his clay elsewhere for manufacture and marketing of brick, the City denied the assertion[24] and no evidentiary facts were offered to support the allegation. Indeed, Hadacheck's emphasis on the unique qual-

---

16. Hadacheck v. Los Angeles, 239 U.S. at 412.
17. Hadacheck v. Los Angeles, 239 U.S. 394, Record, Microfiche, card 2, at 57-59.
18. *Id.* at 25.
19. *Id.* at 28.
20. *In re* Kelso, 147 Cal. at 613, 82 P. at 242.
21. Hadacheck v. Los Angeles, 239 U.S. 394, Record, Microfiche, card 3, at 64.
22. Campbell v. Seaman, 63 N.Y. 568 (1876). The page in 63 N.Y. given by counsel is incorrect, being 563.
23. Hadacheck v. Los Angeles, 239 U.S. at 410.
24. Hadacheck v. Los Angeles, 239 U.S. 394, Record, Microfiche, card 1, at 37.

ity of his clay for brickmaking suggested doubt about his claimed inability to compete from another site. On these two bases Hadacheck's cry of invalidity rang hollow in the face of public concern for the health, safety, and welfare of citizens threatened with emissions of smoke and dust from the manufacture of building brick at the original stand.

Laurel Hill and Hadacheck concerned instances of partial, "spot" zoning. Comprehensive zoning first came before the Court in Ambler Realty Co. v. Village of Euclid.[25] Industrial development in Cleveland, Ohio, and its environs was moving northeast into Euclid, a suburb originally residential in character. In defense against this industrial expansion threatening to absorb sections of the Village and thereby alter the character of the community, Euclid enacted a zoning ordinance for its entire area, dividing the village into six districts. Unimproved land that Ambler Realty Company had purchased in anticipation of industrial uses, the ordinance largely zoned in U-6, permitting industrial use, but placed the remainder in U-2 (single-family or duplex dwellings) or U-3 (apartments, churches, hotels, schools, and such). The loss to the Company was alleged to be a reduction in value of its tract from $10,000 to $2,500 per acre. For its challenge of the ordinance the Company brought in heavy artillery in the person of Newton Baker, former Secretary of War and founder of the prestigious Cleveland law firm that continues to bear his name. The gist of his contention is found in an opening paragraph of his argument:

> Since the industrial development of a great city will go on, the effect of this attempted action necessarily is to divert industry to other less suited sites, with a consequent rise in value thereof; so that the loss sustained by the proprietors of land who cannot so use their land is gained by proprietors of land elsewhere. In other words, the property, or value, which is taken away from one set of people, is, by this law, bestowed upon another set of people, imposing an uncompensated loss on the one hand and a gain which is arbitrary and unnatural on the other hand, since it results, not from the operation of economic laws, but from arbitrary considerations of taste enacted into hard and fast legislation. Such legislation also tends to monopolize business and factory sites.[26]

Attorney Baker's argument carried the lower federal court, in which injunction was sought and granted, against the ordinance in its totality without awaiting enforcement in any particular. The grounds for invalidation lay in the Fourteenth Amendment's due process and equal protection clauses. On appeal the Supreme Court reversed, with three dissents. Assignment of the majority opinion went to Justice Sutherland who labored at length to find a basis for constitutionality. His answer to Baker's contention, that the facts presented a clear case of taking from As to the benefit of Bs, was that the restriction was conditional and negativistic.

---

25. 272 U.S. 365 (1926).

26. Id. at 371 (Argument for Appellee). Subsequent paragraphs, id. 373-78, set forth the persuasive contentions of this distinguished advocate and public servant.

If it be a proper exercise of the police power to relegate industrial establishments to localities separated from residential sections, it is not easy to find a sufficient reason for denying the power because the effect of its exercise is to divert an industrial flow from the course which it would follow, to the injury of the residential public if left alone, to another course where such injury will be obviated. It is not meant by this, however, to exclude the possibility of cases where the general public interest would so far outweigh the interest of the municipality that the municipality would not be allowed to stand in the way.[27]

Constitutionality was found in familiar limitations on the equitable remedy of injunction. Where that remedy is sought,

as it is here, not upon the ground of present infringement or denial of a specific right, or of a particular injury in process of actual execution, but upon the broad ground that the mere existence and threatened enforcement of the ordinance, by materially and adversely affecting values and curtailing the opportunities of the market, constitute a present and irreparable injury, the court will not scrutinize its provisions, sentence by sentence, to ascertain by a process of piece-meal dissection. . . .

whether there lurks within the interstices any infraction of constitutional protection.[28]

That the Court would scrutinize a comprehensive zoning ordinance in instances of imminent injury to acknowledged property rights was confirmed by the decision two years later in *Nectow v. City of Cambridge.*[29] Nectow sought a mandatory injunction to force the City to permit erection of "any lawful buildings" on a parcel of land lying within 140,000 square feet owned by him. He had outstanding, before passage of the zoning ordinance, a contract to sell the greater part of this tract for $63,000 but the buyer refused to comply because of restrictive zoning of the parcel. Although on each of two sides the adjacent area across a street was residential and so zoned, industrial usage abutted the other two sides with unrestricted areas beyond. A Master found that zoning the land in question as residential "would not promote the health, safety, convenience and general welfare of inhabitants of that part of the defendant city, taking into account the natural development thereof and the character of the district and the resulting benefit to accrue to the whole City. . . . "[30] The trial court ruled against Nectow despite confirmation of the Master's report. A unanimous Supreme Court that included Chief Justice Taft, and Justices Holmes, Brandeis, and Stone, reversed. The Court's short opinion, again by Justice Sutherland, closed with the following statement

That the invasion of the property of plaintiff in error was serious and highly injurious is clearly established; and, since a necessary basis for the support of that

27. *Id.* at 389-90.
28. *Id.* at 395.
29. 277 U.S. 183 (1928).
30. *Id.* at 187 (Master's last finding).

invasion is wanting, the action of the zoning authorities comes within the ban of [the Due Process clause of] the Fourteenth Amendment and cannot be sustained.[31]

Concededly, *Nectow v. City of Cambridge* was not a "pig-in-the-parlor" case. It was more like the "pig-in-the-barnyard" cases, yet not on all fours with them. Its relevance lay in the fact that at some point, albeit it had to be extreme, a fact pattern would run afoul of substantive due process. Following a lapse of over thirty years there did come to the Court another clear "parlor" case in which the private property owner and his lessee believed they had constitutional basis for complaint. This was *Goldblatt v. Town of Hempstead*[32], the opinion in which continues to evoke puzzlement. Goldblatt owned a thirty-eight-acre tract that had been leased for sand and gravel operations since the time of *Ambler* and *Nectow*. Excavation had early reached the water table, creating a water-filled crater that ultimately became a twenty-acre lake of an average depth of twenty-five feet. Around the tract the Town had expanded until, within a radius of 3500 feet, there were more than 2200 homes and four public schools having a combined enrollment of 4500 students. Urban development had engulfed what originally was a parcel surrounded mainly by farmland.

Twice before the Town had sought to be rid of this "blight," ultimately the only operation of its kind within the corporate area. Ordinance No. 16 of 1945 required fencing of the total premises. Goldblatt had complied with a six-foot chain-link fence topped by three strands of barbed wire. Amendment of this ordinance then introduced zoning restrictions that sought to ban further excavation but Goldblatt successfully defended in an injunction suit on the ground of prior non-conforming use. No appeal was taken from this decision at the trial level. The Town's third move was enactment of a revision of Ordinance No. 16 that, in an effort to circumvent the protection of "non-conforming use," imposed a number of restrictions asserted to be in the interest of safety. Excavation below the water table was forbidden; stiffer provisions respecting setbacks from adjoining property lines, the inclines of side walls, and retaining walls were imposed; installation of concrete curbing under the entire 7000 linear feet of fencing was directed; and added was a requirement that all portions of the pit excavated to the maximum permitted level must be refilled.[33]

Litigation commenced in the supreme court of New York with the Town as plaintiff and Goldblatt and his lessee as defendants. Finding that Ordinance No. 16 constituted a valid exercise of the Town's police power, that court enjoined defendants from "conducting sand mining, dredging, and/or pit exca-

---

31. *Id.* at 187-89.

32. 369 U.S. 590 (1962).

33. Goldblatt v. Town of Hempstead, 369 U.S. 590, Record, Microfiche, card 1, at 7-9 (In microform used, Ordinance No. 16 appears on two unnumbered pages of three columns each placed between pages 6 and 10).

vations . . . until such time as (1) a permit for such operations had been issued by the Town of Hempstead pursuant to said Ordinance No. 16 and (2) the defendants shall have corrected the following violations of said Ordinance No. 16:" Listed were five violations embracing all mandates of the ordinance.[34] The appellate division unanimously affirmed the trial court without opinion.[35] Appeal of right was then taken to the court of appeals because of the presence of a constitutional question, defendants insisting the Ordinance constituted a deprivation of property violative of due process of law.

On this appeal, New York's high court split four to three.[36] The emphasis in the majority's short opinion was on the "hazards to both life and property" inherent in "uncontrolled operation of these pits" in consequence of which "restraint need not await an event."[37] "Neither the injunction granted nor the ordinance proscribes future excavation. The injunction merely conditions future operation upon the issuance of a permit from the Town of Hempstead, and the correction of certain violations of the ordinance. There are approximately eighteen acres which are available for excavation."[38] There could therefore be no further sand mining within the twenty acres, already below the water table, and defendants must adjust to the direct safety provisions; but nothing was said about the requirements of curbing and refilling, both of which would be costly. It is accordingly understandable that the majority placed dependence upon *Hadacheck v. Los Angeles* the facts of which were closely analogous on this view of the *Goldblatt* case.

The view of the dissent was markedly different. For them "the record here indicates a systematic attempt to force the defendants out of business."[39] It was noted that the cost of refilling the existing excavation would run beyond a million dollars.[40] The Record could have been cited for the fact the Ordinance called for a curbing eighteen inches in depth[41] to which the fence was to be fastened. From outside the Record it was noted that in the entire history of the pit in question only one drowning had occurred, and that in 1944 prior to installation of the fence required by the Ordinance of 1945.[42] The dissent's summation is found in the following:

No object in the installation of this concrete curbing has been shown except that it would put defendant to the expense of removing the [existing] fence, laying the concrete and constructing a new fence. This, along with the prohibition of exca-

---

34. *Id.* Record, card 1, at 12-14.
35. *Id.* Record, card 3, at 193-95.
36. Town of Hempstead v. Goldblatt, 9 N.Y. 2d 101, 172 N.E. 2d 562 (1961).
37. *Id.* at 104, 172 N.E. 2d at 563-64.
38. *Id.* at 104, 172 N.E. 2d at 563.
39. *Id.* at 107, 172 N.E. 2d at 565.
40. *Ibid.*
41. Goldblatt v. Town of Hempstead, 369 U.S. 590, Record, Microfiche, card 1, at 7 (section 4[c] of the Ordinance), referred to later, *id.* card 6, at 2.
42. Town of Hempstead v. Goldblatt, 9 N.Y. 2d at 110, 172 N.E. 2d at 567.

vation below water level or more than 10 feet below the highway level, and the extension from 10 to 20 feet of the permitted distance between the excavation and the property line and the retrospective requirement of refilling all that had been excavated since 1927, shows that the purpose was expropriation rather than regulation.[43]

On appeal to the Supreme Court of the United States Herbert Goldblatt lost once again. Justices Frankfurter and White did not participate in the Court's decision; the other seven Justices were unanimous in affirmance of the New York court of appeals "on the provisions of the ordinance here invoked."[44] This excluded "such affirmative duties as refilling the existing excavation and the construction of a new fence."[45] The latter, according to facts disclosed below, was necessitated by the Ordinance's requirement of curbing and fencing that would prevent ingress or egress save at gated points. Thus, enforcement of those provisions of the Ordinance forcing upon the owner additional, extremely heavy fixed investment "was not sought in the present litigation . . . These provisions are severable, both in nature and by express declaration, from the prohibition against further excavation."[46] In this posture of the case Goldblatt's reliance on substantive due process[47] was reduced to a claim of invalidity because his lessee could not continue operations under pre-existing conditions. Although the majority of the New York court of appeals had taken the position that neither the ordinance nor the injunction precluded further excavation, surely on the basis that eighteen acres in the plot remained unmined, the Supreme Court upheld prohibition on all further mining on the entire property. The reasoning was twofold:

> If the depth limitation in relation to deepening the existing pit is valid, it follows *a fortiori* that the limitation is constitutionally permissible as applied to prevent the creation of new pits. We also note that even if appellants were able to obtain suitable processing space the geology of the 18-acre tract would prevent any excavation.[48]

Even on this basis Goldblatt's "loss" was one of potential future profits, not of property rights that had in any sense vested.

Again, the parlor had come to the pig, and not the pig to the parlor. No "fault," in a quasi-tortious sense, could be laid at Goldblatt's door; it was "with clean hands" that he was hailed into equity by the Town that wished to be rid of his business in its midst. He had not "asked for trouble" by attempt-

---

43. *Id.* at 109, 172 N.E. 2d at 567.
44. Goldblatt v. Town of Hempstead, 369 U.S. at 598.
45. *Id.* at 597.
46. *Ibid.*
47. Appellants based their claims of the unconstitutionality of the "affirmative duties" of the Ordinance principally on the constitutional provisions against bills of attainder and *ex post facto* legislation. *Ibid.*
48. Goldblatt v. Town of Hempstead, 369 U.S. at 596.

ing to force his kind of operation upon an established urban area, as had the businesses cited in opening this chapter. Yet while private law recognized the thirty-eight acres as his in fee simple, the enhancement in its value was not the product of his acumen but of community development. Even a "liberal" Court would shy from entertaining the views of Henry George, but quaere whether perceptions of that sort do not constitute the inarticulate major premise of Court reasoning in the "parlor" cases where Due Process has made little headway against governmental disturbance of private interests.[49]

The Court's articulated basis for decision lay in a test of the magnitude of adverse impact on Goldblatt. Citing *Pennsylvania Coal Co. v. Mahon*[50] it was recognized that there obtains a limit to uncompensated public deprivation of private property. "This is not to say, however, that governmental action in the form of regulation cannot be so onerous as to constitute a taking which constitutionally requires compensation,"[51] although *Hadacheck* is then cited to demonstrate the lengths to which deprivation can validly go. However, the Court finds it unnecessary to locate the limit of permissibility.

> How far regulation may go before it becomes a taking we need not now decide, for there is no evidence in the present record which even remotely suggests that prohibition of further mining will reduce the value of the lot in question. Indulging in the usual presumption of constitutionality, we find no indication that the prohibitory effect of Ordinance No. 16 is sufficient to render it an unconstitutional taking if it is otherwise a valid police regulation.[52]

This decisive passage is unsatisfactory on two counts. First, no hint is given in explanation of the bald statement that Goldblatt will suffer no reduction in value as a result of the prohibition on continued dredging. It is a non-sequitur to assert that silence in the Record sustains this conclusion, although Professor Tribe appears satisfied with the statement.[53] Secondly, if there is no invalid taking it is because in the counterbalancing of governmental police power and due process limitation the challenged legislation has proved itself to be within "the time-tested conceptional limit of public encroachment upon private interests."[54] This is the fundamental teaching of *Pennsylvania Coal;* there is no occasion for the conditional clause of the second sentence of the passage.

---

49. Trugwell, *Henry George,* 6 ENCYC. SOC. SCI. 630 (1938), provides a succinct account of the life and views of the man who advocated the "single tax" on increases in land value because those gains were the consequences of community productivity, not individual capability.

50. 260 U.S. 393 (1922). This seminal decision is analyzed *infra* in the segment of this chapter 7 styled *A Tale of Two Cites.*

51. Goldblatt v. Town of Hempstead, 369 U.S. at 594.

52. *Ibid.*

53. L. TRIBE, AMERICAN CONSTITUTIONAL LAW 460, n. 3 (1978).

54. The language in quotation marks is that of the Court, 369 U.S. at 594. In itself this is an excellent, succinct definition of the police power.

Contemporaneous with litigation in the dispute between the Town of Hempstead and Mr. Goldblatt and his lessee was similar litigation at the other end of the country. In the California case the City of Los Angeles had by zoning foreclosed gravel, rock and sand removal from 348 acres by Consolidated Rock Products Co. under lease from Valley Real Estate Co. As zoned the area was limited to agricultural and residential uses. The City had won injunctive relief in the trial court, lost on intermediate appeal, but triumphed in the supreme court of California with two dissents. Lessee's appeal to the Supreme Court resulted in dismissal "for want of a substantial federal question." *Consolidated Rock Products Co. v. City of Los Angeles.*[55] At first blush this curt rejection of due process claim would appear to mark the end of constitutional considerations in "pig-in-the-parlor" situations. However, as is always true, the facts are never the same in any two cases.

Consolidated was a hybrid. Two growing suburbs, attractive to sufferers from polluted air and noise of the central city, were moving toward the acreage in question. Quarrying would without question raise quantities of dust and disturb the quietness of resort-type living, although the trial court found that these adverse conditions could be reduced to tolerable levels. That same judge, after viewing the premises, labelled "preposterous" use of the area for purposes permitted by the zoning ordinance. The acreage lay in a watercourse subject to frequent flooding; over millenia river water had built up a deep deposit of sand and rock; bluffs and mountains surrounded the valley. The 348 acres were good for excavation but nothing else. On the other hand, the situation had distinct elements of pig-in-the-barnyard. Although removal of rock, sand, and gravel for commercial sales had taken place at one time, there had been no activity for years. Whether the period of inactivity had been twenty years, as stated by the opinion of the California supreme court, or thirty years according to the intermediate court of appeals, the move to renew removal operations was in effect similar to original action in the face of legislative prohibition.

Overriding these substantive differences was the fact that the active party litigating the issue of constitutionality was the lessee. For it the sole claim of "taking" could be the potentiality of future profits. Apart from this slender toehold, which on precedent was insufficient to ground invalidity, the lessee was litigating another's case. The California courts, while disagreeing on the merits,[56] had paid the question of standing no heed as such, and two Justices of the Supreme Court would have noted probable jurisdiction. Yet the majority of the High Court were of opinion that jurisdictional limitations blocked con-

---

55. 371 U.S. 36 (1962).

56. The two dissenting justices in the supreme court of California wrote no opinion, basing their judgment on the opinion in the intermediate court of appeals where the three participating justices had ruled against the City. That opinion is found in 15 Cal. Rptr. 775 (1961).

sideration of the matter; in these circumstances there could be no *substantial* federal question even if one could be considered on review.

The "best evidence" available concerning the constitutional status of fact patterns of the pig-in-the-parlor variety, and by analogy those of the related pig-in-the-barnyard cousins, consists of two paragraphs found in *Andrus v. Allard*,[57] the decision sustaining federal prohibition of commercial transactions in avian artifacts.

> The regulations challenged here do not compel the surrender of the artifacts, and there is no physical invasion or restraint upon them. Rather, a significant restriction has been imposed on one means of disposing of the artifacts. But the denial of one traditional property right does not always amount to a taking. At least where an owner possesses a full "bundle" of property rights, the destruction of one "strand" of the bundle is not a taking, because the aggregate must be viewed in its entirety. In this case, it is crucial that appellees retain the rights to possess and transport their property, and to donate or devise the protected birds.

> It is, to be sure, undeniable that the regulations here prevent the most profitable use of appellees' property. Again, however, that is not dispositive. When we review regulation, a reduction in the value of property is not necessarily equated with a taking. Compare *Goldblatt v. Hempstead, supra,* at 594, and *Hadacheck v. Sebastian,* 239 U.S. 394 (1915), with *Pennsylvania Coal Co. v. Mahon, supra.** In the instant case, it is not clear that appellees will be unable to derive economic benefit from the artifacts; for example, they might exhibit the artifacts for an admissions charge. At any rate, loss of future profits—unaccompanied by any physical property restriction—provides a slender reed upon which to rest a taking's claim. Prediction of profitability is essentially a matter of reasoned speculation that courts are not especially competent to perform. Further, perhaps because of its very uncertainty, the interest in anticipated gains has traditionally been viewed as less compelling than other property-related interests. Cf., *e.g.,* Fuller & Perdue, The Reliance Interest in Contract Damages (pt. 1), 46 Yale L. J. 52 (1936).[58]

Employer-Employee Relationships

Professor Tribe in his compact treatise on *American Constitutional Law*[59] treats *Lochner v. New York*[60] as an illustration of the familiar syndrome "from A to B." "The Court there summarily rejected any suggestion that New

---

57. 444 U.S. 51 (1979).

* It should be emphasized that in *Pennsylvania Coal* the loss of profit opportunity was accompanied by a physical restriction against the removal of the coal. [Footnote by the Court]

58. Andrus v. Allard, 444 U.S. at 65-66.

59. L. Tribe, American Constitutional Law (1978). Exclusion of coverage of *state* constitutional law makes for compactness impossible with inclusion of state along with *federal* coverage. T. Cooley, Constitutional Limitations (8th ed. 1927), required two volumes for treatment of both fifty years earlier.

60. 198 U.S. 45 (1905), considered in L. Tribe, *op. cit. supra* note 59, chap. 8.

York's limitation of working hours could stand as a 'labor law' intended to benefit bakers at their employers' potential loss, while interfering with the formal contractual freedom of both."[61] On this interpretation the *Lochner* holding constitutes a continuum in the line of cases that preceded 1900 wherein the issue was whether a legislature was "guilty" in the civil sense of a factual transfer to *B* from *A* that rose to the level of an unconstitutional taking.[62] The fallacy in the specifics of the *Lochner* majority decision lies in failure to make the vital distinction between factual and invalid takings. Indeed, a situation where superficially there appears to be a transfer of property value from *A* to *B* may in a transactional sense prove not to be. That is, *A*'s seeming loss is on analysis *de minimis*; in reality the challenged governmental action leaves him whole.

With the retention of Louis Brandeis by the State of Oregon for his assistance in overcoming the threat of invalidity that *Lochner* hung over its program of social legislation, there evolved a means of counterattack. The device was the collection of economic, legislative, and social data demonstrating that the Oregon program could achieve improvement in the conditions of industrial employees without loss to their employers. The Brandeis Brief first appeared in litigation over the constitutionality of the State's limitation of hours of employment of women; the Court took note of it, entering a summary "in the margin."[63] The thrust of this invention in advocacy was convincing evidence that the physiological characteristics of women amply justified a ten-hour maximum workday for them. This initial success dictated employment of the new method in supporting Oregon's maximum hours for men, requiring direct challenge of *Lochner*. The product was a voluminous brief thoroughly investigating every conceivable aspect of matters relevant to the issue.

Because of President Wilson's nomination and the Senate's eventual confirmation of Brandeis for the Supreme Court, the Brief in *Bunting v. Oregon*[64] was submitted under the name of Felix Frankfurter assisted by Josephine Goldmark. The reprint of it in two volumes by the National Consumers' League[65] not only makes for easier availability but enhances the impressive-

---

61. L. Tribe, *op. cit. supra* note 59, at 439. Tribe's reference to Cooley's treatise, at 357, requires care to distinguish between legislative "transfers" where *B* is found deserving on the basis of some common-law principle in contracts, property, or torts, and "transfers" through "mere arbitrary fiat." Expropriation as a denial of substantive due process is concerned only with the latter kind of taking from *A* for the benefit of *B* by legislative decree without justification other than as an exercise of naked power. Where *B* is deserving of recompense from *A* there can be no unconstitutional taking.

62. The expropriation cases before 1900 are analysed in chapters 1 and 2, *supra*. One of the classic cases of early American times was Calder v. Bull, 3 Dall. 386 (1798).

63. Muller v. Oregon, 208 U.S. 412, at 419 (1908). The law was unanimously sustained but "without questioning in any respect the decision in *Lochner v. New York*...." *Id.* at 423.

64. 243 U.S. 426 (1917).

65. Reprinted as The Case for the Shorter Work Day (1916). Available among other

ness of this most celebrated instance of the Brandeis Brief. Volume I presented massive evidence of the dangers of long hours to male employees themselves and to national vitality. In Volume II the benefits of shorter hours were then demonstrated, leading to the conclusion that reduction in hours was the only sensible path for legislators to take in solution of the hazards of long work-days. But what of the economic aspects of reducing hours? The Brief closes with statistical and testimonial evidence to the effect that cost of production is not increased, owing largely to the enhanced efficiency on the part of employees. This demonstration clinched the case for the shorter working day; in actuality such legislation constituted no factual taking from employer for the benefit of his workers. Ergo, there was no taking offensive to substantive due process of law.

So convincing was the Brandeis Brief that counsel for Bunting attacked on the allegation that

[t]he law is not a ten-hour law; it is a thirteen-hour law designed solely for the purpose of compelling the employer of labor in mills, factories and manufacturing establishments to pay more for labor than the actual market value thereof.[66]

This contention stemmed from the law's proviso that "employees may work overtime not to exceed three hours in any one day, conditioned that payment be made for said overtime at the rate of time and one-half of the regular wage."[67] Elaborating on the contention, counsel pitched his assertion of the law's invalidity on the following syllogistic reasoning:

In this case the employee was receiving a regular wage of 40 cents per hour, on its face a living wage, and there was no basis for an arbitrary demand that he be paid 60 cents per hour for three hours of his time. The effect is to take money from the employer and give it to the laborer without due process or value in return.[68]

For the bare Court majority, three Justices dissenting and Justice Brandeis not participating, Justice Mckenna rejected the contention advanced. The Oregon law was an effort to set a maximum on hours of labor, nothing more; the proviso was but a means of enforcement of the ten-hour limitation. Thus correctly characterized, "our judgment of it is that it does not transcend constitutional limits." The "taking" issue had been by-passed, first by Bunting's counsel in averting challenge of the law as a regulation of hours, and then by the Court's refusal to view the statute as a wage law. This made it possible to

---

libraries in the Law Library of the University of North Carolina at Chapel Hill cataloged Tr/B942c vols. 1 and 2.

66. Bunting v. Oregon, 243 U.S. at 429 (Argument for Plaintiff in Error, quoted in the opinion of the Court, *id*. at 436).

67. *Id*. at 434.

68. *Id*. at 429-30 (Argument for Plaintiff in Error). The Court quoted a paraphrase, *id*. at 436: "It is a ten-hour law for the purpose of taking the employer's property from him and giving it to the employee; it is a thirteen-hour law for the purpose of protecting the health of the employee."

avoid an attempt to explain *Lochner*, leaving it unreversed in the back waters of constitutional law. And the issue of the constitutionality of minimum wage legislation was left to contemporaneous constitutional litigation.

In that litigation, involving federal as well as state action, minimum wage fixation fared well on the surface. The third leg in Oregon's program for improvement in working conditions, a minimum wage law for women sustained by the state's supreme court, survived appeal to the Court by 4 to 4 vote, with Justice Brandeis continuing in his policy of non-participation.[69] At the same time a majority of the Court upheld, in *Wilson v. New*,[70] a congressional act designed to avert a threatened nationwide rail strike. Maximum hours were permanently set at eight; provisionally, wages were to be no lower than theretofore received for longer hours of work. The wage provisions did not pass master without challenge. Eminent counsel for New and other Receivers of the railway challenging the law described the section on wages in these words:

It is a direct taking of the carrier's property without compensation and the transfer of the same to private individuals.[71]

Dissenting Justices in an opinion by Justice Day were of like view.

Such legislation, it seems to me, amounts to the taking of the property of one and giving it to another in violation of the spirit of fair play and equal right which the Constitution intended to secure in the due process clause to all coming within its protection, and is a striking illustration of that method which has always been deemed to be the plainest illustration of arbitrary action, the taking of the property of A and giving it to B by legislative fiat. Davidson v. New Orleans, 96 U.S. 97, 104.[72]

This time the "taking" claim was faced but explained away by the majority that found basis for constitutionality in the by then accepted proposition that "the business of common carriers by rail" generates a "public interest" that in turn "begets a public right of regulation to the full extent necessary to secure and protect it."[73]

---

69. Stettler v. O'Hara, 243 U.S. 629 (1917). This decision came down on the same day, April 9, 1917, as did that in *Bunting v. Oregon, supra* note 64.

70. 243 U.S. 332 (1917).

71. *Id.* at 337 (Argument for Appellees). The thesis is continued *id.* at 338. Counsel were Walker Hines and John Johnson.

72. *Id.* at 370. Citation of *Davidson* in support of this assertion discloses that Justice Day understood that holding, which has been misunderstood by most commentators. My analysis is found in chap. 2, p. 35, text at notes 26-27; chap. 3, pp. 60-61, text at notes 70-72, both *supra*.

73. Wilson v. New, 243 U.S. at 347. Reference to this basis I made in *The Economic Philosophy of Lochner*, 15 ARIZ. L. REV. 419, at 441, n. 113 (1973), written before I realized the significance of substantive due process as sword in governmental legislation against private monopoly. Revelation has produced chap. 4, *supra*, and chap. 9, *infra*, concerning *Private Monopoly and Substantive Due Process*. From this it follows that reliance on that line of decisions was ill founded.

It certainly cannot be said that the act took away from the parties, employers and employees, their private right to contract on the subject of a scale of wages since the power which the act exerted was only exercised because of the failure of the parties to agree and the resulting necessity for the lawmaking will to supply the standard rendered necessary by such failure of the parties to exercise their private right.[74]

While the 1917 decisions seemed to support the constitutionality of minimum wage legislation, uncertainty remained. The Oregon law had been upheld only on the technical ground of affirmance by an equally divided Court; the federal law passed the constitutional test on the questionable basis of what Justice Day for a third of the Court rejected as "justification by emergency." In consequence the issue was in limbo until the Court's decisive utterance in *Adkins v. Children's Hospital.*[75]

In support of the District of Columbia law there had been presented another voluminous Brandeis Brief of two volumes; again the document carried the name of Felix Frankfurter, assisted this time by Mary Dewson who like Josephine Goldmark was a staff member of the National Consumers' League.[76] Of a total length of over one thousand pages, the Brief was divided into three Parts. Part First, entitled *The Successful Working of Minimum Wage Legislation,* first detailed the administration of minimum wage laws, by data drawn principally from the American States and the Canadian Provinces. There followed sections presenting conclusions reached from these data. Among these were sections stressing the effect of minimum wage levels on worker efficiency and cost of production.[77] The evidence adduced was compelling on the point that higher wage scales resulted in increased productivity, leaving the deduction that employers were in no way disadvantaged by minimum wage legislation. The parallel with maximum hours was striking.[78] A finding of the constitutionality of the District of Columbia minimum wage law should therefore have followed from demonstration of the absence of any "taking" from the Hospital for the benefit of its employees.

This absence a bare majority of the Court denied in a familiar passage:

---

74. Wilson v. New, 243 U.S. at 357.

75. 261 U.S. 525 (1923).

76. Reprinted as DISTRICT OF COLUMBIA MINIMUM WAGE CASES, OCTOBER TERM 1922. Available among other law libraries in the Law Library of the University of North Carolina at Chapel Hill cataloged Tr/A236b vols. 1 and 2.

77. The most pertinent sections of the Brief were 2, 5, and portions of 6(1) of Part First consisting of pages 301-33, 387-439, 449-52, 457-80.

78. Commencing Volume 2, Part Second of the Brief set forth the minimum wage laws then on the books of American states, Canadian provinces, Great Britain and other countries. Part Third concluded the argument by pressing the need for minimum wage legislation in the District (and generally in the United States) on the basis of considerations other than economic.

The law takes account of the necessities of only one party to the contract. It ignores the necessities of the employer by compelling him to pay not less than a certain sum, not only whether the employee is capable of earning it, but irrespective of the ability of his business to sustain the burden, generously leaving him, of course, the privilege of abandoning his business as an alternative for going on at a loss. Within the limits of the minimum sum, he is precluded, under penalty of fine and imprisonment, from adjusting compensation to the differing merits of his employees. It compels him to pay at least the sum fixed in any event, because the employee needs it, but requires no service of equivalent value from the employee. It therefore undertakes to solve but one-half of the problem. The other half is the establishment of a corresponding standard of efficiency, and this forms no part of the policy of the legislation, although in practice the former half without the latter must lead to ultimate failure, in accordance with the inexorable law that no one can continue indefinitely to take out more than he puts in without ultimately exhausting the supply.[79]

The position of the five Justices in insisting on a value of service standard rather than one of cost of living has been roundly condemned by commentators.[80] The fallacy in the majority reasoning lay not in insistence upon distinguishing between the two standards but in the assumption that necessarily a quantitative difference always obtains between them. Convincing factual evidence that increased productivity is the consequence of minimum wage floors at substandard levels of pay negates that assumption and undercuts the claim of a taking. This was the teaching of the Brandeis Brief.

Unfortunately, the dissent of Chief Justice Taft, in which Justice Sanford joined, failed to grasp the economic dynamics of the situation. It was essentially restricted to inability to see why *Muller v. Oregon* did not control. The separate Holmes dissent carried one paragraph suggesting economic insight and yet it too stressed the precedential control of *Muller* and *Bunting*.[81] In consequence there was no effective response to the majority whose invalidation of the District statute must be laid to the continuing grip of the freedom-of-contract dogma that blinded them from comprehending that substantive

---

79. Adkins v. Children's Hospital, 261 U.S. at 557.

80. Often cited is Powell, *The Judiciality of Minimum-Wage Legislation*, 37 HARV. L. REV. 545 (1924). The author was the celebrated Thomas Reed Powell, later of fame as professor of Constitutional Law at Harvard Law School. His conclusion was damning. "As a flagrant instance of insufficient reasons and of a judgment widely regarded as an indefensible judgment, the minimum wage decision has few, if any, rivals. While many may doubt the long-run wisdom of minimum-wage legislation, few have been heard to approve the authoritative declaration of its constitutional invalidity. The decision has evoked a more nearly unanimous chorus of disapproval than any other decision in years." *Id.* at 572.

81. Justice Brandeis is recorded as having taken "no part in the consideration or decision of" the case or its companion, *Adkins v. Lyons*. The unofficial explanation has always been that his daughter Elizabeth was a member of the District's Minimum Wage Board. In taking no part even in consideration of the case Brandeis denied to colleagues of both majority and dissent his knowledge of economic behavior.

due process was satisfied by proven absence of any expropriation even at the factual level.[82]

Only in 1937, after an aborted attempt in 1934,[83] did the issue of constitutionality of minimum wage legislation again come squarely before the Court in *West Coast Hotel v. Parrish*.[84] As earlier, the law involved was restricted to women. Defending the Hotel against a suit by one of its chambermaids for the difference between wages paid her and those prescribed by the Washington law, counsel offered a short and precise contention that went straight to the mark.

> The statute was passed in 1913, long before the decision of this Court in the *Adkins* case. It is in no sense an emergency measure.
>
> It sets up but one standard, that is, the wage must be adequate for the maintenance of the adult woman worker. It does not require that the wage have any relation to the reasonable value of the worker's services. The *Adkins* case, 261 U.S. 525, and like cases decided subsequently, condemn such legislation.[85]

In support of the statute no Brandeis type of Brief was filed; however, the Attorney General of Washington and two assistant attorneys general were on counsels' brief for plaintiff as amici curiae on behalf of the State.

The Court was again badly split but this time the five prevailing Justices supported constitutionality. The dissenters followed the format advanced by Hotel's counsel. For them *Adkins* still held the answer. Incorporated in their dissent is the long paragraph from their prevailing opinion in *Adkins* that has been quoted above in analysis of that case, together with the paragraph following to the same effect. The fallacy in that reasoning has been remarked. Vindication of the Washington law by Chief Justice Hughes for the new majority largely pursued, until the last paragraph of his opinion, the line of thought taken by his predecessor in his dissent in *Adkins*. But then the successor to Taft launched an emotionally charged attack upon employers of female workers hardly in keeping with his image. The "recent economic experience" was said to have "brought into a strong light" the *exploitative* behavior of employers in their relations with women employees "relatively defenseless against the denial of a living wage." "What these workers lose in wages the taxpayers

---

82. Collins and Friesen, *Looking Back on Muller v. Oregon*, 69 A.B.A.J. 294, 472 (1983), provides a colorful and detailed account of the initial efforts to secure the constitutionality of maximum hour-minimum wage legislation in which the State of Oregon played a leading part. Final validation of minimum wage laws came later, as the text recounts.

83. Morehead v. New York ex. rel. Tipaldo, 298 U.S. 587 (1934), rejecting an attempt to distinguish the New York law from that of the District of Columbia invalidated in *Adkins*. "No application has been made for reconsideration of the constitutional question there decided." *Id.* at 604.

84. 300 U.S. 379 (1937).

85. *Id.* at 380 (Argument for Appellant).

are called upon to pay. The bare cost of living must be met."[86] Continuing in this vein, the righteous Chief Justice asserted

> [i]t is unnecessary to cite official statistics to establish what is of common knowledge through the length and breadth of the land. While in the instant case no factual brief has been presented, there is no reason to doubt that the State of Washington has encountered the same social problem that is present elsewhere. The community is not bound to provide what is in effect a subsidy for unconscionable employers. The community may direct its law-making power to correct the abuse which springs from their selfish disregard of the public interest.[87]

What this says in essence is that there is an apparent taking from the employer, measured by the difference between what he voluntarily pays and what he would be required to pay under minimum wage law, but his anti-social behavior denies him relief under substantive due process. *A* is at fault, and *B* is receiving only what is his rightful due. Justice Brandeis was one of the majority of five, yet he may have despaired at the outburst. Were he not at the end of his tenure he might have concurred in the result but explained his position on the sound economic reasoning he had advanced years before as advocate.

The long-mooted issue of the validity of minimum wage legislation at last was for the nonce resolved, as earlier had been the question of squaring maximum hours with substantive due process. In *United States v. Darby Lumber Co.*,[88] sustaining the Fair Labor Standards Act, attention was centered on the federalistic issue. Darby's assertion of violation of the Fifth Amendment by reason of the Act's provisions for minimum wages and maximum hours received short shrift. Less than a paragraph sufficed to reject this challenge.

> Since our decision in *West Coast Hotel Co. v. Parrish*, 300 U.S. 379, it is no longer open to question that the fixing of a minimum wage is within the legislative power and that the bare fact of its exercise is not a denial of due process under the Fifth more than under the Fourteenth Amendment. Nor is it any longer open to question that it is within the legislative power to fix maximum hours. *Holden v. Hardy*, 169 U.S. 366; *Muller v. Oregon*, 208 U.S. 412; *Baltimore & Ohio R. Co. v. Interstate Commerce Commission* [221 U.S. 612]. Similarly the statute is not objectionable because applied to both men and women. Cf. *Bunting v. Oregon*, 243 U.S. 426.[89]

---

86. The quoted assertions are those of the Chief Justice as is use of the term "exploitation." *Id.* at 399.

87. *Id.* at 399-400.

88. 312 U.S. 100 (1941).

89. *Id.* at 125. Citation of *Baltimore & Ohio R. v. I.C.C.* after *Holden* and *Muller* is an oddity. Decided in 1911 it played no part in the conflict over the constitutionality of maximum hours limitation. Nowhere in *Bunting* was it cited; in the Brandeis Brief, *supra* note 65, only the Congressional Act under which it was decided is listed, *id.* at 7 of Volume 1, in cataloging American Legislation Limiting the Hours of Labor for Men. That Act prescribed a maximum of 16 hours after which the railroad employee should have at least 10 hours off duty. In the words of Justice Hughes when first on the Court as an Associate

It is commonly assumed that maximum-hour and minimum-wage legislation, having finally been sustained after initial holdings of unconstitutionality, presents no further problem at the constitutional level. Probably not, yet sustainment on one set of facts does not guarantee validity when the fact pattern differs. Supreme court decisions attest this. Altered circumstances may render constitutional a law otherwise invalid;[90] true also is the reverse, a law first held valid may by force of circumstances later become unconstitutional.[91] Minimum wage laws, at least, could not today be sustained either as they should have been in *Adkins* or as they were in *West Coast Hotel*. The current strength of labor unions and decades of employer adjustment to state and federal underpinning of wages at the lower end of the wage scale have forced from the field the unconscionable employer of Hughes' wrath, even discounting the possibility of improvement in the humanization of American business. At the same time the Brandeis-Frankfurter thesis that minimum wages would so enhance worker productivity as to offset the added cost of labor, economically sound in the days of sweated wages, has little relevance with federal minimum wage of broad coverage at $3.35 per hour.

Maximum hour and minimum wage restrictions are today at such levels that further reduction in the one or increase in the other would place the issue of their validity in a new posture. A reduction in the workday below eight hours, say to six hours daily for a 30-hour week, surely could not enhance productivity in proportion to the added cost to the employer. Studies of fatigue, a major cause of industrial accidents in a machine technology, reveal that the rate increases after about eight hours. Consequently, reduction in hours below eight per day would not significantly improve productivity from that aspect. Examination of economic literature discloses disagreement among economists regarding the merits of any further increase in minimum wage levels. Because none addresses directly the question whether increase

---

Justice,

> The fundamental question here is whether a restriction upon the hours of labor of employees who are connected with the movement of trains in interstate transportation is comprehended within this sphere of authorized legislation. This question admits of but one answer. The length of hours of service has direct relation to the efficiency of the human agencies upon which protection to life and property necessarily depends. ... And in imposing restrictions having reasonable relation to this end there is no interference with liberty of contract as guaranteed by the Constitution. *Chicago, Burlington & Quincy Railroad Company* v. *McGuire*, 219 U.S. 549.

Baltimore & Ohio R. Co. v. Interstate Commerce Comm., 221 U.S. at 618-619.

McGuire, also a 1911 decision, sustained an Iowa law forbidding limitation of liability in contracts between employer and employee against contention of violation of the Fourteenth Amendment. Was Justice Stone belatedly suggesting that at least as to maximum hours the issue of the validity of legislative limitation had actually been settled prior to *Bunting v. Oregon?* The decision to cite in point, in view of the history of case development, was *Bunting*.

90. Abie State Bank v. Bryan, 282 U.S. 765 (1931).
91. Chastleton Corp. v. Sinclair, 264 U.S. 543 (1924).

would induce "taking," it becomes necessary to secure by deduction whatever light on this query can be gleaned. There appears to be general agreement that higher minima would create disemployment but disagreement as to its seriousness.[92] It is said that mounting wage scales tempt employers to find "offsets" to higher costs of labor, resulting in less desirable fringe benefits and working conditions.[93] Interest in minimum wage legislation seems now to focus on its use to alter the distribution of income, with the conclusion that it is not particularly effective for this objective.

In seeking assistance from economic sources, I am indebted to Professor Lester Thurow for reference to what is in his judgment "the best analysis of the economic impacts of the minimum wage." The study is the work of Edward Gramlich of the University of Michigan.[94] The excerpts that follow give the essence of the analysis:

> Minimum wages do, of course, distort relative prices, and hence compromise economic efficiency, but so do all other attempts to redistribute income through the tax-and-transfer system. The important question is not whether minimum wages distort, but whether the benefits of any income redistribution they bring about are in some political sense sufficient to outweigh the efficiency costs.[95]
>
> For adults, however, the tenuous argument in favor of minimum wages is preserved. There is indeed some disemployment effect, but not enough to make low-wage adults worse off on balance.... Yet the spillover of benefits into high-income families—who are not likely to become tomorrow's low-income families—is not trivial and does sharply reduce the efficiency of the minimum wage as a means of redistributing income. The inflationary potential of large increases in the minimum wage is likely to become serious long before the redistributive potential becomes significant.[96]

Although discounting the hazard of disemployment, Professor Gramlich feels that higher minimum wages would create "a whole series of other complications...."[97] "At some point these complications make it unwise to boost the minimum wage any more, and that point is likely to be not much above the present minimum."[98] His "own view" is that

> as long as minimum wages are kept low relative to other wages, they are not terribly harmful and in fact even have slightly beneficial effects both on low-wage workers and on the overall distribution of income.[99]

---

92. R. POSNER, ECONOMIC ANALYSIS OF LAW 106-10 (2nd ed. 1977); cf. J. PETERSON, MINIMUM WAGES Intro. (1981).

93. W. WESSELS, MINIMUM WAGES, FRINGE BENEFITS, AND WORKING CONDITIONS chap. 1 (1980).

94. Gramlich, *Impact of Minimum Wages on Other Wages, Employment, and Family Incomes* 409, in BROOKINGS PAPERS ON ECONOMIC ACTIVITY (#2, 1976).

95. *Id.* at 410.

96. *Id.* at 449. The intervening pages are devoted to statistical analysis that fortunately it is not necessary to understand for present purposes.

97. *Id.* at 451.

98. *Id.* at 450.

99. *Ibid.*

These passages seem to damn with faint praise. Even so, two commentators on the Gramlich analysis believe him overly tolerant of minimum wages. As one concluded: "I find that Gramlich's arguments in favor of minimum wages are not supported by the evidence. His most interesting and novel findings strengthen the case against minimum wages. The economic support for the minimum-wage program remains very weak indeed."[100]

Further enhancement of minimum wage levels cannot longer be constitutionally sustained on grounds either of unconscionable employer exploitation or of greater employee-motivated productivity.[101] The economics of minimum wages has become complex and indeterminate. In the newly-advanced justification of minimum wage legislation as an instrument for redistribution of income, elements of factual taking are implicated. The transfer of value from A to B is openly intended and applauded. Whether invalidity would be found in this goal depends on the Supreme Court's resolution of basic conflict between rights to property and rights to equality as epitomized in the split-Court decision of *Harris v. McRae*.[102]

Contemporaneous with initial state legislation looking to maximum hours and minimum wages in the employment relationship was the legislative push for workmen's compensation as an alternative to common law rules governing liability for industrial injuries. Toward the close of the nineteenth century there had evolved first in Germany under Bismarck and then in England, the concept that injured workers should be compensated on the basis of relation to employment, not on negligence.

From 1902 onward many legislators clamored for a similar change of law in this country. They argued that the mechanization of the country had made injuries inevitable; that industry and not charity or savings should pay for industrial injuries;

---

100. Michael L. Wachter in commentary, *id.* at 459.

101. While some economists "reject the view that the quality of labor input can contribute to explaining the post-1973 productivity slow down," it is clear by inference that labor productivity has not recently increased. HENDRICK, ed., INTERNATIONAL COMPARISONS OF PRODUCTIVITY AND CAUSES OF THE SLOWDOWN chaps. 1 and 2 (1984). *Id.* chap. 9 considers possible improvements in labor productivity resulting from recent business embrasure of the "participative ethic" which metamorphoses the labor-management relation into one of co-partnership in industrial production. Increase in labor productivity should stem from worker satisfaction with part direction of an enterprise. There is evidence of such in current instances of employee ownership. Rosen, *Esop's Fables* in PUBLIC CITIZEN 21 (Fall, 1983). But the relevancy of minimum wage enhancement by legislation is in this revolutionary context of industrial democracy highly questionable.

102. 448 U.S. 297 (1980). Elsewhere I commended the majority opinion in *Harris* which held that Congress was under no constitutional obligation to underwrite abortions for indigent women. Justice Stewart was firm despite the dissent of four. "Nothing in the Due Process Clause supports such an extraordinary result" as translating "the limitation on governmental power implicit in the Due Process Clause into an affirmative funding obligation...." *Id.* at 318. Strong, *Levellers in Judicial Robes,* 60 NEB. L. REV. 680 (1980). *Contra:* Perry, *Why the Supreme Court was Plainly Wrong in the Hyde Amendment Case: A Brief Comment on* Harris v. Roe, 32 STAN. L. REV. 1113 (1980).

that simple justice required the abolition of the old common-law defences for industrial injuries.[103]

In a word, the cost of injuries unavoidable in the new era of machine technology should be treated as one of the necessary costs of production.[104] Early opposition of employers and insurers found sufficient refuge in the prevailing concept of freedom of contract to stir contest over the constitutionality of at least compulsory compensations acts. Washington's and Wisconsin's first acts were sustained[105] but not so New York's.[106] These three decisions came in 1911.[107] In *Ives* the New York court of appeals predicated invalidity on the Fourteenth Amendment Due Process Clause as well as upon the State's due process clause.

It was immediately recognized that this action blocked review by the Supreme Court because the jurisdictional statute provided only for review where the federal claim had been denied, *i.e.*, where the state law had been sustained. Correction followed in Congress by enactment of the Judiciary Act of 1914, providing for review in either situation.[108] That same year the New York legislature perfected by reenactment a second try following state constitutional amendment. This effort to meet constitutional obstruction was successful in the courts of the State, where clearly a changed perception prevailed in response to economic understanding and careful legislative drafting.[109] In the same year that *Bunting v. Oregon* sustained the constitutionality of maximum hour legislation for men,[110] *New York Central R.R. Co. v. White*[111] affirmed the lower holding of constitutionality. The heart of the unanimous decision is disclosed in the following excerpts from a long paragraph.

> Nor is it necessary, for the purposes of the present case, to say that a State might, without violence to the constitutional guaranty of "due process of law," suddenly set aside all common-law rules respecting liability as between employer and employee, without providing a reasonably just substitute. . . . No such question is here presented, and we intimate no opinion upon it. The statute under consideration sets aside one body of rules only to establish another system in its place. If the employee is no longer able to recover as much as before in case of being injured

---

103. S. Horovitz, Injury and Death Under Workmen's Compensation Laws 6 (1944).

104. Wambaugh, *Workmen's Compensation Acts: Their Theory and Their Constitutionality*, 25 Harv. L. Rev. 129 (1911), is in its concise coverage true to its title.

105. State *ex. rel.* Davis-Smith Co. v. Clausen, 65 Wash. 156, 117 P. 1101 (1911); Borgnis v. Falk Co., 147 Wis. 327, 133 N.W. 209 (1911).

106. Ives v. South Buffalo Ry. Co., 201 N.Y. 271, 94 N.E. 431 (1911).

107. The three decisions were followed by State Journal Co. v. Workmen's Compensation Board, 161 Ky. 562, 170 S.W. 437 (1914) (invalid under Ky. Const.).

108. Act of Dec. 23, 1914, c. 2, 38 Stat. 790.

109. Matter of Jensen v. Southern Pacific Co., 215 N.Y. 514, 523-28, 109 N.E. 600, 602-04 (1915), followed in the *New York Central* case, *infra* note 111.

110. Text at notes 64-68, *supra*.

111. 243 U.S. 188 (1917).

through the employer's negligence, he is entitled to moderate compensation in all cases of injury, and has a certain and speedy remedy without the difficulty and expense of establishing negligence or proving the amount of the damages.... On the other hand, if the employer is left without defense respecting the question of fault, he at the same time is assured that the recovery is limited, and that it goes directly to the relief of the designated beneficiary. And just as the employee's assumption of ordinary risks at common law presumably was taken into account in fixing the rate of wages, so the fixed responsibility of the employer, and the modified assumption of risk by the employee under the new system, presumably will be reflected in the wage scale. The act evidently is intended as a just settlement of a difficult problem, affecting one of the most important of social relations, and it is to be judged in its entirety. We have said enough to demonstrate that, in such an adjustment, the particular rules of the common law affecting the subject-matter are not placed by the Fourteenth Amendment beyond the reach of the law making power of the State; and thus we are brought to the question whether the method of compensation that is established as a substitute transcends the limits of permissible state action.[112]

In a nutshell what the Court found was a trade off between employer and employee. Both gained from abandonment of fault as basis for liability. Provided the compensation schedules were adequate, as the Court here found, there were no circumstances supportive of a taking, either from the employee or from the employer. However, that due process limitations lurked in the background became apparent in subsequent litigation. In two decisions concerning the Utah Act,[113] both involving injury in necessary crossing of railway tracks to reach the employer's plant, the Court sustained awards on the ground that "employment includes not only the actual doing of the work, but a reasonable margin of time and space necessary to be used in passing to and from the place where the work is to be done."[114] Yet the second case, where the crossing occurred in railroad right of way rather than on a public road, came "nearer the border line."[115]

Four years later the question of constitutionality arose in litigation under the Federal Longshoremen's Act which, like the state compensation laws but unlike the Federal Employers' Liability Act, abandoned the fault basis of liability.[116] Because the Act "applies only when the relation of master and servant exists" Chief Justice Hughes for the majority saw no constitutional infirmity under the Due Process Clause of the Fifth Amendment; *New York Central* was directly in point. But the clear inference was that the employment relation set

---

112. *Id.* at 201-02.
113. Cudahy Co. v. Parramore, 263 U.S. 418 (1923); Bountiful Brick Co. v. Giles, 276 U.S. 154 (1928). Attorney Horovitz, see note 103, *supra*, represented the widow in *Bountiful Brick*.
114. Bountiful Brick Co. v. Giles, 276 U.S. at 158.
115. *Id.* at 159.
116. Crowell v. Benson, 285 U.S. 22 (1932).

the boundary.[117] With this a dissent of three, led by Justice Brandeis, disagreed.

> Without doubt the word "employee" was used in the Longshoremen's Act in the sense in which the common law defines it. But that definition is not immutable; and no provision of the Constitution confines the application of liability without fault to instances where the relation of employment, as so defined, exists.[118]
>
> . . . .
>
> It is not to be assumed that congress, having power to amend and revise the maritime law, is prevented from modifying those criteria and enlarging the liability imposed by this Act so as to embrace all persons who are engaged or engage themselves in the work of another, including those now designated as independent contractors.[119]

"Without doubt" the Brandeis view would prevail today. Indeed, *NLRB v. Hearst Publications,*[120] sustaining the Labor Board in classifying newsboys as "employees," provided the precedent in 1944. By traditional understanding, newsboys were independent contractors. Only Justice Roberts, who had joined Brandeis in the *Crowell* dissent, now dissented but clearly on grounds of statutory interpretation, not unconstitutionality. At this point the Court has left to the states the issue of the ultimate limits to which workers' compensation laws can be extended. The leading treatise on this type of legislation[121] includes a chapter on "Statutory Employees" in which in turn is a section on *Constitutionality of nonemployee coverage.*[122] There it is recorded that state statutes making newsboys "employees" by legislative fiat "seem to have encountered no difficulty."[123] However, "[t]rouble arose"

> when Wisconsin also declared legislatively that any person on a golf course for purposes of caddying was deemed to be an employee of the golf course. This was held, in the *Wendlandt* case, to be "unconstitutional as violative of due process of law in that it attempts to set up a relation of employer-employee that is absolutely contrary to fact."[124]

---

117. The decision in *Crowell v. Benson,* along with three others of the same period, is best known for evolution of the doctrine of "constitutional fact." Constitutional facts, because decisive of constitutionality, there required an independent review by the Court of an administrative finding. Whether injury arose in the course and out of the employment was to the majority such a "fact" inasmuch as Due Process limited liability to instances of the employment relation. Justice Brandeis disagreed because in his judgment Due Process did not impose this limitation. Strong, *The Persistent Doctrine of Constitutional Fact,* 46 N.C. L. REV. 225 (1968), is an analysis of this unique doctrine which is further considered *infra* chap. 8, pp. 240-41.

118. Crowell v. Benson, 285 U.S. at 82.

119. *Id.* at 83.

120. 322 U.S. 111 (1944).

121. A. LARSON, WORKMEN'S COMPENSATION LAW (ed. 1982).

122. *Id.* §49.22.

123. *Ibid.* p. 9-62.

124. *Ibid.* p. 9-63. Full citation of the *"Wendlandt case"* is Wendlandt v. Industrial Comm., 256 Wis. 62, 39 N.W. 2d 854 (1949).

No case within the last thirty-five years, although all commentators stress the tendency of courts to indulge in *liberal* interpretation of the basic statutes, is cited by the treatise as even hinting at the possibility of invalidity. The *Wendlandt* decision itself is criticized in the following passage:

> Unless (as is true in some jurisdictions) the state constitution limits compensation legislation to employees, there is no reason why the legislature's power cannot extend to a simple declaration that compensation coverage is extended to a particular category of admitted non-employees, since, although the opposite view was at one time urged in the early days of constitutional uncertainty, it is now well settled that the constitutionality of compensation legislation rests not upon the private employment contract but upon public welfare and police powers.[125]

The passage reflects patent ignorance of constitutional principles! A state's police power does not provide an open sesame to unlimited legislative authority to play fast and loose with private property; the guaranty of due process sets bounds at the point where "taking" occurs. The two fundamental principles of power and limitation are always in counterbalance. A sure test would come were "public welfare" deemed to require a legislative or judicial interpretation of the employment relation as embracing all accidents or occupational diseases, however and whenever caused, falling within the period from date of employment to time of termination. Assume, for instance, the following: a trained mechanic, X, has been on the payroll of Ford Motor Co. for 16 years. He is known to all as an "employee" of Ford. His specific task has always been that of mounting the wheels and tightening the lugs on the left-hand side of cars passing him on the assembly line. For several years he has devoted a week of his paid vacation to a fishing trip with Y to one of the many Michigan Lakes. He looks forward to these trips as respite from the monotony of the assembly line. The division of chores between X and Y as they camp on lakeshore is for the latter to build a cooking fire after a hard day of fishing while X procures water from the lake. On one occasion X slips and falls into deep water, drowning before his companion can rescue him. Is his widow able to recover for death during "the course of employment"?

It could be that an affirmative answer is already at hand on analogy from *Usery v. Turner Elkhorn Mining Co.*,[126] a decision of 1976. With Justice Powell *dubitante,* the Court found no constitutional infirmity in the retroactive application of the Black Lung Benefits Act of 1972 with respect to claims in the nature of workers' compensation made for death or total disability owing to pneumoconciosis. Unquestionably the disease had been contracted from coal dust while the claimants had been employed in the mines of the company, but at a time prior to enactment of the federal statute. Assertion of constitutional invalidity pressed by several coal operators was predicated on the Due Process

---

125. A. LARSON *op. cit. supra* note 121, p. 9-65 of §49.22.
126. 428 U.S. 1 (1976). The Chief Justice concurred in the judgment; Justice Stevens did not participate.

Clause of the Fifth Amendment. While a century earlier legislative retroactivity had been thought to be the key to violation of property due process,[127] the essential ingredient of the guarantee both before and later was conceived to be not so much a matter of the timing of governmental intervention as of its overall dislocation of proprietary interests. Justice Black's pronouncement in *Ferguson v. Skrupa* notwithstanding,[128] the Constitution does premise a regime of private property. Concededly, "the declining centrality of private property to modern constitutional adjudication" leads courts to view some allocations A to B not as "naked wealth transfers, but legitimate efforts to promote the public good."[129] Yet there is a limit short of raw expropriation: it is significant that Justice Black did not include the name of Karl Marx among those whose economic theories a legislature "may take for its textbook."

In the present-day relationship of employer-employee, provision for retirement or termination benefits looms large. The functional conception of "employment" embodied in the instance just illustrated surely embraces the terminal aspects of extended periods of contractual association; it cannot end abruptly with the last day of "work." *Allied Structural Steel Co. v. Spannaus*[130] skirts the lurking constitutional question. Recitation of the factual pattern and decision is reserved for later consideration in this chapter on expropriations and substantive due process. The case was argued and decided on the Contract Clause, the majority of the Justices agreeing with Allied that a Minnesota law imposing heavier assessments than the employer had voluntarily assumed in its pension benefits plan impaired the obligation of contract. Writing for the Court Justice Stewart premised that the Contract Clause "is not a dead letter" and must be accorded its due weight in a state's "exercise of its otherwise legitimate police power."[131] The statute made serious inroads on existing contractual relationships without evidencing any major economic or social problem that could justify it. Thus unlike decisive decisions on hours, wages, and worker's compensation, the invalidation in *Allied* was of no general dimension as concerns constitutional power and limitation in employer-employee relations. This is not to say, however, that, with employment pension funds involving legions of workers and running into the billions of dollars,[132] attempted "adjustment" of rights along broad legislative lines might not result in factual taking challenged as passing constitutional limits. But for the present *Allied* is significant for the dissent of Justice Brennan, in which he was joined by Justices White and Marshall. He quickly comes to the point of irreconcilable difference with the majority:

---

127. Refer to text at notes 55-67 of Chap. 2, pp. 40-41, *supra*.
128. Refer to text accompanying notes 79 and 81 of Chapter 6, p. 109, *supra*.
129. Sunstein, *Naked Preferences and the Constitution*, 84 Col. L. Rev. 1689, at 1729 (1984). Professor Sunstein's thought-provoking analysis is well worth careful attention.
130. 438 U.S. 234 (1978).
131. *Id.* at 241, 242.
132. R. Lynn, The Pension Crisis 50, 52 (1983).

Today's decision greatly expands the reach of the [Contract] Clause. The Minnesota . . . Act does not abrogate or dilute any obligation due a party to a private contract; rather, like all positive social legislation, the Act imposes new, additional obligations on a particular class of persons. In my view, any constitutional infirmity in the law must therefore derive, not from the Contract Clause, but from the Due Process Clause of the Fourteenth Amendment.[133]

That on the facts of this case "I think that any claim based on due process has no merit" does not mitigate from the significance of the Justice's insistence that it is due process that has applicability here *and* that the Due Process Clause does limit "a State's power to enact such laws" as Minnesota's.[134] Left for commentary at the close of this chapter is this non-sensical Court resort to the Contract Clause in a determination to avoid predication of unconstitutionality upon the due process concept.

A Tale of Two Cites
(with apologies to Charles Dickens)

Two decisions of the 1920s, one early in the decade, the other toward the end, are classic examples of Court disposition of claims of expropriation. It is common in casebook and textbook to set them in juxtaposition, for the latter sustained the Cedar Rust Act of Virginia not long after the invalidation of the Kohler Act of Pennsylvania. The Kohler Act had sought to prohibit coal companies owning mineral rights in urban land to extract coal deposits therefrom under homes built upon the surface. Surface rights had been purchased at reduced prices under split ownership. Virginia's law, when locally implemented, required the state entomologist to effect the cutting down within two miles of an apple orchard of all red cedars on private property either actually or potentially infected with cedar rust "balls." In springtime these "balls" opened to release spores that, carried by winds, infected both the fruit and the leaves of most varieties of apple tree, first stunting fruit growth and ultimately killing the tree through defoliation. In *Pennsylvania Coal Co. v. Mahon*[135] Justice Brandeis had alone dissented from the opinion of Justice Holmes for the Court; in *Miller v. Schoene*[136] both Holmes and Brandeis joined in the unanimous opinion written by Justice Stone.

The superficial conflict in result dissolves upon close examination. In a suit by the Mahons to enjoin the coal company from mining the coal under their dwelling, as forbidden by the Kohler Act, the company was represented in argument by John W. Davis, conceded to be one of the most outstanding advocates of the period. Arguing persuasively that the Act "takes the property of the Coal Company without due process of law," Davis concluded that even

133. Allied Structural Steel Co. v. Spannaus, 438 U.S. at 251.
134. *Id.* at 262.
135. 260 U.S. 393 (1922).
136. 276 U.S. 272 (1928).

[i]f every word in the preamble of the Kohler Act were true there would still be no justification for the uncompensated transfer of the beneficial use of the supporting coal from defendant to plaintiff. No emergency will justify the transfer of property or a tangible property right from one citizen to another without just compensation.[137]

On the Brief for the State of Pennsylvania, as *amici curiae*, its Attorney General contended for an opposite interpretation of the Act.

It contains no provision requiring any mine owner to leave coal in place. If natural support other than coal in the pillars be available, or if artificial support be provided, every pound of coal may be removed from the mines.

Nor does it transfer the right of support from owner of the coal to the surface owner. This right, license or estate in the land is nothing more than an immunity from civil liability for damages to the surface owner. Under the Kohler Act, this immunity continues.[138]

The opinion of Justice Holmes that grounded reversal of the supreme court of Pennsylvania opened with a paragraph picturing the constitutional framework within which the issue at bar must be resolved.

Government hardly could go on if to some extent values incident to property could not be diminished without paying for every such change in the general law. As long recognized, some values are enjoyed under an implied limitation and must yield to the police power. But obviously the implied limitation must have its limits, or the contract and due process clauses are gone. One fact for consideration in determining such limits is the extent of the diminution. When it reaches a certain magnitude, in most if not all cases there must be an exercise of eminent domain and compensation to sustain the act. So the question depends upon the particular facts. The greatest weight is given to the judgment of the legislature, but it always is open to interested parties to contend that the legislature has gone beyond its constitutional power.[139]

Viewing the case as one "of a single private house," "[t]he extent of the public interest is shown by the statute to be limited, since the statute ordinarily does not apply to land when the surface is owned by the owner of the coal."[140] "On the other hand the extent of the taking is great. It purports to abolish what is recognized in Pennsylvania as an estate in land—a very valuable estate—and what is declared by the Court below to be a contract hitherto binding the plaintiffs."[141] The conclusion was the same treating the case "as one

---

137. Pennsylvania Coal Co. v. Mahon, 260 U.S. at 404. It was later said of the Kohler Act that in effect it gave "to the grantees a security in the enjoyment of the surface which they had not bargained nor paid for ...." Marblehead Land Co. v. Los Angeles, 47 F. 2d 528, at 532 (C.C.A. 9th, 1931).

138. Pennsylvania Coal Co. v. Mahon, 260 U.S. at 410.

139. *Id.* at 413.

140. *Id.* at 413-14.

141. *Id.* at 414.

in which the general validity of the act should be discussed."[142] Against this background, Holmes continued in a crucial passage.

> The general rule at least is, that while property may be regulated to a certain extent, if regulation goes too far it will be recognized as a taking. It may be doubted how far exceptional cases, like the blowing up of a house to stop a conflagration, go—and if they go beyond the general rule whether they do not stand as much upon tradition as upon principle. [Citation omitted] In general it is not plain that a man's misfortunes or necessities will justify his shifting the damages to his neighbor's shoulders. [Citation omitted] We are in danger of forgetting that a strong public desire to improve the public condition is not enough to warrant achieving the desire by a shorter cut than the constitutional way of paying for the change. As we already have said, this is a question of degree—and therefore cannot be disposed of by general propositions. But we regard this as going beyond any of the cases decided by this Court. The late decisions upon laws dealing with the congestion of Washington and New York, caused by the war, dealt with laws intended to meet a temporary emergency and providing the compensation determined to be reasonable by an impartial board. They went to the verge of the law but fell short of the present act. *Block* v. *Hirsh,* 256 U.S. 135. *Marcus Brown Holding Co.* v. *Feldman,* 256 U.S. 170. *Levy Leasing Co.* v. *Siegel,* 258 U.S. 242.[143]

Seldom in constitutional cases were Justices Holmes and Brandeis in disagreement. Here, in one of the few, Justice Brandeis dissented because his view of the case as made by the record and briefs was much different. "For aught that appears the value of the coal kept in place by the restriction may be [comparatively] negligible."[144] "The restriction here in question is merely the prohibition of a noxious use. The property so restricted remains in the possession of the owner. The State merely prevents the owner from making a use which interferes with paramount rights of the public."[145] This paramountcy he found in the safety of the citizens of Scranton, individually and collectively. He recognized that

> [e]very restriction upon the use of property imposed in the exercise of the police power deprives the owner of some right theretofore enjoyed, and is, in that sense, an abridgment by the State of rights in property without making compensation. But restriction imposed to protect the public health, safety or morals from dangers threatened is not a taking.[146]

Justice Brandeis' doubt that the amount of the taking was serious flew in the face of Holmes' insistence that it was great. The majority opinion stressed the magnitude of the taking to overt exclusion of other relevant factors. Yet one senses from the opinion a feeling that the coal company had conducted itself

---

142. *Ibid.*

143. *Id.* at 415-16. The rent control laws are considered in chap. 9, *infra,* p. 277, on *Private Monopoly and Substantive Due Process.*

144. Pennsylvania Coal Co. v. Mahon, 260 U.S. at 419.

145. *Id.* at 417.

146. *Ibid.*

in almost exemplary fashion. There was no evidence of corporate overreaching; the contractual dealings with the Mahons and other purchasers were devoid of any non-disclosure to purchasers. Buyers knew or should have realized the risks involved in purchasing only surface rights at reduced prices. The company gave timely notice of intent to mine at risk to users of the surface. This relationship between the parties is in marked contrast to that in *Miller*. The only factor moderating that contrast could be that the landholdings of the coal companies in the region were so extensive that those desiring to purchase real estate for home construction may often have had no alternative but to buy from the coal interests on their terms.

Brandeis' reliance for constitutionality upon heads of the police power must be carefully understood. Not every exercise of regulatory power can be valid or there is nothing left of due process restriction. What is correct to assert is that a *valid* exercise of the police power is not a taking, which is a tautological way of stating limits of the police power as constrained by substantive due process. What is "valid" requires a weighing (or balancing) of private and public concerns.

Professor Tribe in his treatise on *American Constitutional Law* asserts that in *Pennsylvania Coal* "the Court did *not* hold that the statute violated due process of law as a taking from the coal company for the private benefit of the homeowner. Instead, the majority found for the coal company solely because it had not been compensated for the 'taking' of its property (its subsurface mining rights) for public benefit by the mining restriction statute."[147] Three commentators in their intensive study of *The Taking Clause* insist that in *Pennsylvania Coal* Holmes rewrote the Constitution by, and should be overruled for, introducing a balancing test into adjudication under that holding.[148] Concededly, analysis in this context is unusually difficult because the term "taking" "doubles" in constitutional law. It is express in the Fifth Amendment applicable technically to Congress. Yet as I have shown[149] it has been an integral element of American substantive due process since reception from England, and thus is embedded in both the Fifth and Fourteenth Amendments. And since 1897 the Taking Clause itself has been merged into the due process guarantee of the Fourteenth Amendment.[150] No wonder there is confusion regarding these two inhibitions on expropriation; keen appreciation of the double entendre is essential to adequate understanding.[151]

---

147. L. Tribe, American Constitutional Law 444 (1978). The italicized "not" and the quotation marks around "taking" are his.

148. F. Bosselman, D. Callies, and J. Banta, The Taking Issue chaps. 8 and 12 (1973).

149. Chap. 2, *supra*.

150. Chicago, Burlington & Quincy R.R. v. Chicago, 166 U.S. 226 (1897).

151. Confusion appears in G. Gunther, Constitutional Law 544-45 (10th ed. 1980), at the commencement of a Section entitled *Eminent Domain and the "Taking-Regulation" Distinction.* "Among the earliest 'specific' Bill-of-Rights-guarantees absorbed into the 14th Amendment's due process guarantee was the Fifth Amendment command that private

The principle of eminent domain, that government cannot lawfully appropriate private property to itself except for a use devoted to the public weal and on payment of full market value, has its own distinct history. Parallelism with due process taking is close, especially in origins, and yet with differences great enough to preclude practically all cross citation in decisional development.[152] In its evolution the primary issues of application have concerned the qualities of "property" subject to taking, the extent to which there must be a literal transfer of the object taken, how much beyond public user the concept of public use extends, and the appropriate measure of the compensation to be paid the transferee by the body possessed of this special power of sovereignty.[153] Due process taking, by contrast, is at the core of the concept of expropriation as one arm of historic due process evolving through centuries of English and American development. Both constitutional principles set limits to the lengths to which legislatures can validly transfer private property from *A* to *B*. But the consequence of unconstitutional taking under due process is nullification of the attempted transfer, whereas with eminent domain compensation must attend transfers made for legitimated *public* uses.

In *Pennsylvania Coal* the judicial action was instituted by the Mahons, who sought by injunction to prevent the company from mining in such a way as to

---

property shall not 'be taken for public use, without just compensation.' " Appended to this statement is a footnote: "See Chicago, B. & Q. R.R. v. Chicago, 166 U.S. 226 (1897) (just compensation), and Missouri Pac. Ry. v. Nebraska, 164 U.S. 403 (1896) (property may not be taken for 'private' rather than 'public' use)." The text continues: "State and federal resorts to the power of eminent domain are common, and a prolific source of constitutional litigation. . . ."

The first citation is to the case in which the Court read into the Due Process Clause of the Fourteenth Amendment the Eminent Domain provision express in the Fifth. Note 150, *supra*. However, the *Missouri* case had nothing to do with eminent domain. There the Court invalidated an attempt by the State of Nebraska to force the railroad to yield a section of its right-of-way for the benefit of a group of wheat growers who sought to build thereon an elevator for the storage of grain. The bald effort to transfer *A*'s property to *B* was held a "taking" in violation of substantive due process. The decision is properly "placed" in chap. 2, p. 41, *supra*. Quotation from the opinion is explicit:

The taking by a State of the private property of one person or corporation, without the owner's consent, for the private use of another, is not due process of law, and is a violation of the Fourteenth Article of Amendment of the Constitution of the United States.

Id. at 417 of 164 U.S. Citations omitted save for Loan Association v. Topeka, 20 Wall. 655; Davidson v. New Orleans, 96 U.S. 97, 102; Cole v. La Grange, 113 U.S. 1.

152. This can be seen by comparing the evolution of eminent domain as detailed by F. BOSSELMAN, D. CALLIES, AND J. BANTA, *op. cit. supra* note 148, chaps. 5, 6, 7, with chaps. 1 and 2, *supra*. With both excess and inverse condemnation of today the kinship of due process and eminent domain again becomes close.

153. Excellent analyses of these elements of eminent domain are provided by Dunham, *Griggs v. Allegheny County in Perspective: Thirty Years of Supreme Court Expropriation Law*, 1962 SUP. CT. REV. 63 (1962); Stoebuck, *A General Theory of Eminent Domain*, 47 WASH. L. REV. 553 (1972).

cause the subsidence of their dwelling. In the pleadings no base was laid for an award of damages as compensation to the company for desisting; the defense was a claim of statutory infirmity. The outcome of the suit was Court reversal of the decree in equity the Mahons had won from the supreme court of Pennsylvania. These features of the litigation are proof positive that Holmes for the majority viewed the case as one of a due process taking, provoking invalidation of the Act.[154] The statute had gone "too far," that is, it had stretched beyond what elsewhere he had vividly called "the petty larceny of the police power."[155] No reimbursement is constitutionally required for bounded exercises of the police power; if there were such a requirement "Government hardly could go on . . . . " Yet Government must often go on, which it can provided the purpose is public and compensation is paid in the course of condemnation proceedings. This is taking under the power of eminent domain, to which Holmes clearly had reference when he spoke of "the constitutional way of paying for the change."[156]

Critics of Holmes' opinion disclose their own analytic deficiencies, not his. Differentiating between the power of police and the power of eminent domain, Holmes placed them in perspective. Constitutional commentators of the new breed too often show their irritation at limitations on governmental power; they hint that government is stymied in its quest for greater public well-being if substantive due process blocks supposed advancement under the police power. Clearly this is not the constitutional design; the issue is always that of who is to pay for transfers of private property, the owners adversely affected or the group/community that enjoys the gain. Holmes' insight made constitutional room for uncompensated exercises of the police power. Yet when the "larceny" extends from "petty" to "grand" a technical taking occurs which requires that government, if it elects not to desist, must show a publicly ori-

---

154. Attorney Davis had argued four points:
   1. The Kohler Act impairs the obligation of the contract between the parties.
   2. The Kohler Act takes the property of the Coal Company without due process of law.
   3. The Kohler Act is not a bona fide exercise of the police power.
   4. If surface support in the anthracite district is necessary for public use it can constitutionally be acquired only by condemnation with just compensation to the parties affected.

Record and Briefs, Pennsylvania Coal Co. v. Mahon, 260 U.S. 393, Microfiche, card 4, at 5. *Id.* at 33 he concluded:

   The Kohler Act is not a police regulation because obviously intended not for the public but a favored and restricted class of private citizens; secondly, it is not merely a regulation of mining but primarily a transfer of a property right . . . from one citizen to another. It is not a valid exercise of the right of eminent domain because not exercised for the public generally and provides no compensation whatever to the party whose property is taken.

155. G. GUNTHER, *op. cit. supra* note 151, at 545, gives the source of this Holmesian phrase.

156. The short passages in quotation marks are from the Holmes opinion.

ented justification and pay appropriate compensation. Thus Holmes demonstrated the interplay in the Fifth and Fourteenth Amendments between due process as the test of taking and eminent domain as the price of exaction.[157] Commentators continue to fail to grasp this vital interaction, attempting to treat the Substantive Due Process Clause and the Just Compensation Clause in splendid isolation.[158] The *Pennsylvania Coal* opinion is a classic statement on the fundamental "play" of private versus public interest.[159]

An opportunity for authoritative enlightenment in this fuzzy area seemed at hand with the docketing on the Court's calendar of the litigation from California styled *San Diego Gas & Electric Co. v. San Diego*.[160] Rezoning by the City of San Diego had thrown into a category of "open-space," restricted essentially to parkland hopefully to be purchased with proceeds from a bond

---

157. For this insight he may have had the assistance of a classic scholar in constitutional law. Ernst Freund, The Police Power §511 (1904), stated the distinction incisively:

> Under the police power, rights of property are impaired not because they become useful or necessary to the public, or because some public advantage can be gained by disregarding them, but because their free exercise is believed to be detrimental to public interests; it may be said that the state takes property by eminent domain because it is useful to the public, and under the police power because it is harmful, or as Justice Bradley put it, because "the property itself is the cause of the public detriment."
>
> From this results the difference between the power of eminent domain and the police power, that the former recognises a right to compensation, while the latter on principle does not.

158. Stoebuck, *Police Power Takings and Due Process*, 37 Wash. & Lee L. Rev. 1057 (1980); Note, 58 Tex. L. Rev. 1447 (1980); Comment, 28 N.Y. L. Sch. L. Rev. 1137 (1984).

159. It is apparent that Justice Holmes felt some uncertainties about his opinion. Not only had Justice Brandeis dissented but an anonymous editorial in 33 New Republic 136 (Jan. 3, 1923) written by Dean Acheson, one-time law clerk to Brandeis, had favored the Brandeis position. Wrote Holmes to Harold Laski, "I fear that I am out of accord for the moment with my publicly-minded friends in another way. Frankfurter generally writes to me about any important opinions of mine and he has been silent as to the one I sent you in which Brandeis dissented; probably feeling an unnecessary delicacy about saying that he disagrees. Of course, I understand the possibility of thinking otherwise—I could not fail to, even if Brandeis had agreed. But nevertheless when the premises are a little more emphasized, as they should have been by me, I confess to feeling as much confidence as I often do. I always have thought that old Harlan's decision in *Mugler v. Kansas* was pretty fishy. But I am not going to reargue the matter now." 1 Holmes-Laski Letters 473 (Howe ed. 1953).

R. Epstein, Takings: Private Property and the Power of Eminent Domain 63 (1985), makes the flat statement that the case "contains elaborate language by Holmes, which he later regretted in correspondence, that where regulation goes 'too far' it will be treated as a taking for which compensation must be paid." Cited for this assertion is 2 Holmes-Pollock Letters 108 (Howe ed. 1941). Holmes' comment, found on the following page (109), does not support Professor Epstein. There is no indication of regret with respect to the central theme of his *Pennsylvania Coal* opinion, for which refer to the textual quotation at note 143, *supra*. Despite this minor slippage the volume provides scholarly analysis.

160. 450 U.S. 621 (1981).

issue, much of a parcel of land the Company had bought in anticipation of construction of a nuclear plant. The bond issue had failed to win voter approval, leaving the parcel of no usable value to the Company. There ensued a suit in inverse condemnation brought by the Company that alleged a taking of its property without just compensation in violation of the Federal and California constitutions. The remedies sought were damages, mandamus, and declaratory relief. As Justice Rehnquist was later to observe in his concurrence,

> The procedural history of this case in the state courts is anomalous, to say the least, and it has resulted in a majority of this Court concluding that the California courts have not decided whether any taking in fact has occurred...and Justice Brennan concluding that the [California] Court of Appeal has held that the city of San Diego's course of conduct could not effect a "taking" of appellant's property.[161]

To those who specialize in the technicalities of federal jurisdiction may be left the issue as to whether the California courts had reached a final judgment within the requirement of the federal jurisdictional statute limiting appeal from state courts.[162] A bare majority thought not, thus requiring dismissal. Four were of opposite view, thus bringing them to the merits.[163] Their opinion, by Justice Brennan, took the form of a dissent because of their disagreement with the California position that "A landowner may not 'elect to sue in inverse condemnation and thereby *transmute an excessive use of the police power into a lawful taking* for which compensation in eminent domain must be paid.'"[164] Stated as an issue it was "whether a government entity's exercise of its regulatory police power can ever effect a "taking" within the meaning of the Just Compensation Clause."[165] The response of the four Justices was in the affirmative, contrary to that of the courts of California.

The Brennan-led dissent was premised upon two propositions. One was that Court decisions respecting the exercise of eminent domain had both materially broadened conception of the kinds of property right subject to taking, and minimized insistency on physical invasion. Threefold reference to *United States v. Causby*[166] is highly suggestive in this regard. Little overt reference was made to the contemporaneous expansion of public user to a broad spectrum of public uses; presumably this is such familiar learning that Justice Brennan left to implication a fuller exposition of it.[167] *Berman v. Parker*[168] enunciates

---

161. *Id*. at 636.

162. 28 U.S. C. § 1257.

163. The Court was as evenly divided as is possible in an odd-numbered tribunal inasmuch as Justice Rehnquist, concurring on jurisdictional grounds, would on the merits "have little difficulty in agreeing with much of what is said in the dissenting opinion of Justice Brennan." 450 U.S. at 633-34.

164. San Diego Gas & Electric Co. v. San Diego, 450 U.S. at 641-42 (emphasis in original.)

165. *Id*. at 647.

166. 328 U.S. 246 (1946).

167. Some attention is paid to present breadth, 450 U.S. at 656.

168. 348 U.S. 26 (1954).

the new standard.[169] Now absent, therefore, were the former impedimenta to relating a due process taking to taking by eminent domain.

Establishment of this interconnection left for Justice Brennan consideration of the range of remedies available for "taking." In *Pennsylvania Coal* the Court's decree enjoined enforcement of the Kohler Act, thus employing nullification as the traditional remedy for due process taking. On the other hand, in eminent domain proceedings the remedy for a taking is always compensation to the aggrieved. But invalidation for regulatory taking can often be unsatisfactory, reasoned the Justice. "Invalidation unaccompanied by payment of damages would hardly compensate the landowner for any economic loss suffered during the time his property was taken."[170] "Invalidation hardly prevents enactment of subsequent unconstitutional regulations by the government entity."[171] Justice Brennan concluded that the Taking Clause answered in the negative "the question whether a government entity may constitutionally deny payment of just compensation to the property owner and limit his remedy to mere invalidation of the regulation instead."[172]

Accordingly, the Justice found no difficulty with his proposal of a "constitutional rule" requiring payment of just compensation "once a court finds that a police power regulation has effected a 'taking.' . . . "[173]

> It should be noted that the Constitution does not embody any specific procedure or form of remedy that the States must adopt: "The Fifth Amendment expresses a principle of fairness and not a technical rule of procedure enshrining old or new niceties regarding 'causes of action'—when they are born, whether they proliferate, and when they die." *United States v. Dickinson, supra,* 331 U.S., at 748. Cf. *United States v. Memphis Cotton Oil Co.,* 288 U.S. 62, 67-69 (1933). The States should be free to experiment in the implementation of this rule, provided that their chosen procedures and remedies comport with the fundamental constitutional command. See generally Hill, The Bill of Rights and the Supervisory Power, 69 Colum. L. Rev. 181, 191-193 (1969). The only constitutional requirement is that the landowner must be able meaningfully to challenge a regulation that allegedly effects a "taking," and recover just compensation if it does so. He may not be forced to resort to piecemeal litigation or otherwise unfair procedures in order to receive his due. See *United States v. Dickinson, supra,* [331] U.S., at 749.[174]

San Diego Gas & Electric had provided Justice Brennan with opportunity to advance judicial understanding of a murky area of constitutional law. Basically he had reaffirmed "Justice Holmes' opinion for the Court in *Pennsylvania Coal Co. v. Mahon*"[175] against the continuing criticism that it was un-

---

169. The two sources cited *supra* note 153 identify the major modifications in doctrine.

170. San Diego Gas & Electric Co. v. San Diego, 450 U.S. at 655.

171. *Id.* at 655, n. 22.

172. *Id.* at 653. See *id.* at 646 for differing wording to the same effect.

173. *Id.* at 658.

174. *Id.* at 660.

175. *Id.* at 649. The first sentence of the new paragraph, *ibid,* constitutes the full statement of the reaffirmation.

sound and ought to be repudiated.[176] Put to rest was the unfortunate inheritance from *Mugler v. Kansas*, that an exercise of the police power can never constitute a taking, which had misled Justice Brandeis into dissent in *Mahon* and deluded those who likewise fell into the verbal trap. On its face the statement is a truism; its falsity lies in its assumption that the police power is limitless whereas it is bounded by substantive due process of law.[177] It is to Justice Brennan's credit that he saw the fallacy others had missed; as a member of the Court that had buried economic due process in *Ferguson v. Skrupa* he was an unlikely prospect! That background, however, explains his failure to grasp the great insight of Holmes in *Pennsylvania Coal* that like all brilliant perceptions is simple in its construct: If in the counterbalancing of the thrust of police power and the restraint of substantive due process government action goes "too far," there is a taking that spells invalidity. The essence of constitutionalism is that there is a limit to the extent to which the political group can lawfully impose upon the individual the cost of improvement in the general interest. However, because "government must go on," it is not held hostage by reason of the finding of an invalid taking. That finding means only that government cannot proceed without paying. If government's objective is to achieve a legitimately public purpose, payment to the private owner(s) of just compensation for what is needed in the interest of the whole society removes the obstruction to progress. In short, the Due Process Clause determines the taking, the Taking Clause the price of an exaction. The two constitutional provisions function in tandem, each fulfilling its unique office in a unitary transaction.

Failure of Justice Brennan to grasp this Holmesian insight I ascribe to lack of grounding in a historic core of substantive due process. For centuries there had been found resident in that inheritance from Magna Carta the general principle that the property of *A* should not be taken by government for the benefit of *B*.[178] So determined had been the reconstructed Court to eradicate all vestiges of the earlier perversions of substantive due process that in the excess of the endeavor it had, in the vernacular, thrown out the baby with the bathwater.[179] Chief Judge Breitel of the New York court of appeals had seemed to capture the essence of the Holmesian vision[180] yet this had come about only

---

176. Refer to text at notes 147 and 148, *supra*.

177. The elder Justice Harlan cannot be faulted for his assertion in Mugler v. Kansas, 123 U.S. 623, at 668-69 (1887), that exercise of the police power cannot constitute a taking. Liquor, like prostitution, has no claim on substantive due process for protection against prohibition. It was Harlan's application of the assertion in instances like Powell v. Pennsylvania, 127 U.S. 678 at 683 (1888), where private property could make that claim, that caused misunderstanding. Yet to Holmes even *Mugler* was "fishy." Note 159, *supra*.

178. Chap. 2, *supra*, of this study demonstrates the vitality of this principle in the New World upon inheritance from English constitutional development.

179. Refer to chap. 6, *supra*, on *Perversions of Traditional Meaning*.

180. Fred. F. French Investing Co. v. City of New York, 39 N.Y. 2d 587, at 594, 350 N. E. 2d 381, at 385 (1976).

"metaphorically," which for Justice Brennan destroyed its reality. He rejected the Breitel "interpretation of the Pennsylvania opinion" because it not only "tamper[s] with the express language of the opinion" but also "ignores the coal company's repeated claim before the Court that the Pennsylvania statute took its property without just compensation."[181] With due respect, however, I can find in the pages of John W. Davis' Brief for the Coal Company which the Justice cites no such emphasis for this latter assertion.

There the troubling question rested, to rise again in 1985.[182] A rather complicated fact pattern involving a developer's plan for residential clustering had resulted in a § 1983 suit for relief for alleged violations of the just compensation guarantee and of substantive due process. The federal district court had granted to defendants a directed verdict on the latter claim but allowed a jury award of damages on the alternate claim, only to grant a judgment *non obstante veredicto* on the ground that a temporary deprivation cannot, as a matter of law, constitute a taking. A divided court of appeals reversed, holding that "temporary denial of property could be a taking" and relying upon the dissent in *San Diego Gas & Electric Co. v. San Diego* ... that "damages are required to compensate for a temporary taking."[183] With only Justice White dissenting and Justice Powell not participating, the Court in opinion by Justice Blackmun determined that the case was not ripe for resolution. Justice Brennan, with Justice Marshall concurring, joined "the Court's opinion without, however, departing from my views set forth in *San Diego*. . . ."[184]

In testing for prematurity Justice Blackmun separately considered "the claim under the Just Compensation Clause" and "respondent's claim under the due process theory that petitioners espouse." In each instance the absence of ripeness was found in the fact that after the regional planning commission had disapproved a plat of the yet undeveloped portion of the subdivision the developer had failed to seek variances as was his privilege but instead resorted to suit in court. In so doing he had left unresolved the final and dispositive position the administrative agency would take with respect to the land in question.

> In sum, respondent's claim is premature, whether it is analysed as a deprivation of property without due process under the Fourteenth Amendment, or as a taking under the Just Compensation Clause of the Fifth Amendment. We therefore reverse the judgment of the Court of Appeals. . . ."[185]

For the present analysis the outcome of this latest litigation is significant only as it reveals continuing failure to catch the essence of Holmes' opinion in

---

181. San Diego Gas & Electric Co. v. San Diego, 450 U.S. at 649, n. 14. *Cf.* note 154, *supra.*

182. Williamson County Regional Planning Comm. v. Hamilton Bank of Johnson City, 105 Sup. Ct. 3108 (1985).

183. *Id.* at 3116.

184. *Id.* at 3124.

185. *Ibid.*

Pennsylvania Coal v. Mahon. The case is several times cited yet there is no advance in understanding beyond Justice Brennan's effort. Indeed, if anything the dichotomy in treatment as opposed to Holmes' conception of the operational unity of the two Clauses is more pronounced. This may well explain the short Brennan concurrence suggesting uneasiness on his part lest the new opinion show signs of analytical retrogression.

In *Miller v. Schoene,* considerable testimony at the trial and in argument on appeal concerned the effect on value of land from which red cedars were cut. Counsel for the Millers sought in vain to introduce the judgment of friendly witnesses to the effect that removal would diminish land value by five to seven thousand dollars.[186] Relying on the statutory language of the authorization to remove the cedars, the trial judge refused the proffer. Counsel did, however, get these figures into the Record by stating what his witnesses would have testified, and took exceptions to the ruling of the trial court.[187] On the other hand, witnesses on behalf of the defendant entomologist were permitted to testify that in their opinion the Miller land was worth more with the cedars removed. Explanation lay in assertion that grass for grazing cannot grow under red cedars because of density of the foliage, but does rejuvenate with the cedars gone.[188] The effect of this on the Virginia court of appeals, which affirmed the trial court finding for Defendant, was marked. "The evidence tends to show that the land is more valuable without them than with them."[189] Indeed, "No land is taken."[190]

The impression left by the Record with respect to the cedars themselves is similar. Smaller ones could be marketed in Washington as Christmas trees, larger ones sold as fence posts; yet their value was not appreciable. But what value the downed cedars had belonged to the owners. "Not a stick of the cedar tree is taken by the Entomologist."[191] There was no expense to the owners in cutting; this was county expense ultimately to be borne by the orchardists. In ordering destruction of the cedars on Miller land the trial court allowed $100 in damages for injury to the land caused by the operation[192] although there had been testimony that no damage would occur if the task were properly done in dry weather so that the sod was not torn up.[193] In these circumstances where was a "taking" of which the Millers could complain?

---

186. Miller v. Schoene, 276 U.S. 272, Record, Microfiche, card 1, at 13; card 2, at 144, 148 (Brief for Plaintiffs in Error.)

187. Record, card 2, at 144. The Four Certificates of Exceptions were identical in stating the alleged loss to be from five to seven thousand dollars. *Id.* at 150-51.

188. Record, card 1, at 65-67, 72; card 2, at 124; card 3, at 7, 38 (Brief of Defendant in Error).

189. Record, card 2, at 160 (opinion, Va. Ct. App.).

190. Record, card 3, at 37 (Brief of Defendant in Error).

191. *Id.* at 6.

192. Record, card 2, at 151-53.

193. *Id.* at 123. One witness said $25 was sufficient.

At one point in Defendant's Brief in the Supreme Court reference is made to the "offending cedars."[194] Seldom has the Court had before it as clear an instance of offensiveness on the part of an *A* who is seeking constitutional protection against an alleged taking for *B*. In *Pennsylvania Coal* the company had dealt straightforwardly with the Mahons, selling the surface rights at a lower figure because reserving to itself the coal deposit below and giving adequate notice when ready to mine the pillars of coal supporting the surface from subsidence. In *Miller v. Schoene*, by contrast, the State was seeking to protect the orchardists from inroads generated, however innocently, by the owners of nearby red cedars. *B* was not benefiting at the expense of *A* but only being protected from *A*'s threatened destruction of his, *B*'s, valuable property. Tort law might well support suit for injunction by the apple owners against owners of the cedars.

The classic case is *Georgia v. Tennessee Copper Co.*[195] wherein Georgia as quasi-sovereign was successful in securing protection against sulphureous gases destructive of "forest, orchards, and crops" in five Georgia counties. The short opinion by Holmes suggests that on original jurisdiction a State, if it has a cause of action at all, "is somewhat more certainly entitled to specific relief than a private party might be."[196] On the other hand, there exist unusual problems of "standing" in invoking original jurisdiction. The cases of nuisances at private or interstate law at least are relevant in demonstrating that in *Miller v. Schoene* the relationship between *A* and *B* was inverted from the usual pattern, thus further negativing the Millers' claim of an invalid taking from them for the benefit of neighboring orchardists.[197]

Quite understandably, the Millers sought to rely on *Pennsylvania Coal Co. v. Mahon*. "The American theory of government has no room for the view that one man's property can be taken or destroyed to enhance the property value or financial prosperity of another."[198] Yet counsel for the Millers in Assignments of Error at the constitutional level, in both the Virginia court of appeals and the Supreme Court of the United States, inartfully drafted them as follows:[199]

(1) The statute violates due process by depriving plaintiffs of their property;
(2) The statute violates equal protection ...
(3) In that it amounts to the taking of the property of your petitioners for the benefit of private owners of apple orchards.

Thus the basic claim of taking was not specifically grounded in due process, as precedent from Holmes would have dictated. Whether this had any adverse effect on the judicial mind is not likely and yet one may wonder.

---

194. Record, card 3, at 37.
195. 206 U.S. 230 (1907).
196. *Id.* at 237.
197. L. Tribe, *op. cit. supra* note 147, at 462, grapples with this aspect of *Miller*.
198. Miller v. Schoene, 276 U.S. 272, Record, Microfiche, card 3, at 10-12.
199. *Id.*, card 2, at 154-55, 176-77.

The decisions of the Virginia courts,[200] affirmed by the High Court, were without question correct. Even had the trial court allowed directly in evidence plaintiffs' claim of a diminution of from 5 to 7 thousand dollars in the value of the land, there was the testimony of a number of witnesses for the entomologist that the value would be enhanced, not diminished by removal. Moreover, these latter explained why enhancement would result[201] whereas in the Record there was only tangential basis given to support the proffered testimony of diminution[202] which, furthermore, was not great in comparison with the intrinsic value of the 225 acres that were involved. So with the cedars separate from the land. Felling, removal of the brush, and any possible damage to the sod involved no expense for the Millers; their only demonstrable loss was of "scenic value," as ephemeral a form of property as the heir's rights in *Calder v. Bull.*[203] Add that the cedars were offenders, causing heavy losses for the orchardists and dependent employees, and that the customary pattern of expropriation by reason of a taking from *A* for *B*'s benefit is scrambled.

The difficulty with the decision in *Miller v. Schoene* in not with the result reached. There was no disagreement in a Court that included Holmes as well as Brandeis. Unanimity is understandable on the facts; the claim of real diminution in value from loss of the red cedar trees was shaky at best. There was no "taking" but only an instance of petty larceny under the police power. The difficulty with the case lies in the opinion for the full Court written by a recent appointee to the High Bench. Justice Stone's approach to resolution of the litigation lay in a contrast of the small value of the red cedars "as compared with that of the apple orchards of the state. Apple growing is one of the principal agricultural pursuits in Virginia. The apple is used there and exported in large quantities. Many millions of dollars are invested in the orchards, which furnish employment for a large portion of the population. . . . "[204] Emphasizing this comparison the former Dean of Columbia Law School was led to conclude that

it will not do to say that the case is merely one of a conflict of two private interests and that the misfortune of apple growers may not be shifted to cedar owners by ordering the destruction of their property; for it is obvious that there may be, and that here there is, a preponderant public concern in the preservation of the one

---

200. Miller v. Schoene, 146 Va. 176, 135 S.E. 669 (1926), *aff'g* decision of the circuit court of Virginia. The Cedar Rust Act had been sustained on other grounds in Bowman v. State Entomologist, 128 Va. 351, 105 S.E. 141 (1920), and Kelleher v. Schoene, 14 F. 2d 341 (W.D. Va. 1926).

201. Refer to text at note 188, *supra.*

202. Removal of the cedars would eliminate shade for grazing cattle. However, this was answered by pointing to the presence of walnut and other trees that provided shade without destroying the growth of grass beneath them.

203. 3 Dall. 386 (1798), discussed in chap. 2, *supra*, pp. 30-31, following citation note 5.

204. Miller v. Schoene, 276 U.S. at 279.

interest over the other. [Citations omitted] And where the public interest is involved preferment of that interest over the property interest of the individual, to the extent even of its destruction, is one of the distinguishing characteristics of every exercise of the police power which affects property.[205]

A perceptive current analyst detects in the Stone opinion an unsettling quality. "*Miller* in one sense reflects a familiar point. At least in the absence of a physical taking, if a statute falls within the police power there is generally no violation of the takings clause, even if no compensation is paid. In another sense, however, the decision went far beyond this conventional understanding. In *Miller*, those whose cedar trees had been destroyed may not have been committing a public nuisance at common law."[206] Disturbingly absent is any consideration of conflicting values. Irrelevant are the substance of the "property" interest that is shifted from A to B, the magnitude of the transfer, or the nature of the causal relationship obtaining between the two interests. In this view the test for possible expropriation is sapped of its historic vitality; given a conclusory finding of the locus of that fuzzy element known as "public interest" and further inquiry is abated. The type of reasoning is similar to common failure in eminent domain proceedings to comprehend that the measure of compensation does not lie in the gain to the condemnor but in the loss to the condemnee.

An impressive revisit to Holmes' opinion in *Pennsylvania Coal* v. *Mahon* would be more sympathetic toward Justice Stone's grounding of validity in *Miller v. Schoene*.[207] Against a background in philosophic thought the author paints a picture of underlying conflict in views concerning "rights" in private property. Holmes is said to reflect the more traditional conception founded in acceptance of acquisitiveness as the motivating force in human behavior. The conflicting view is of ownership imbued with a sense of civic responsibility, reflected in Stone's approach. By this view Holmes' test of diminution in value to A in a taking for B is too narrow in perspective and overly simplistic in application. A persuasive case is made in support of this criticism; a differing balance between public and private considerations may be in order today. However, any such "adjustment" is a far cry from dismissal of all effective limitation on redistribution of property interests, which one senses is the inarticulate major premise of the *Miller* opinion.

---

205. *Id.* at 279-80. The string of Supreme Court decisions cited in support of the Justice's assertion has a common denominator in the concept of nuisance. Familiar, *e.g.*, are Mugler v. Kansas, 123 U.S. 623 (1887); Hadacheck v. Los. Angeles, 239 U.S. 394 (1915); Village of Euclid v. Ambler Realty Co., 272 U.S. 365 (1926).

206. Sunstein, Naked Preferences and the Constitution, 84 COL. L. REV. 1689, at 1725 (1984). R. EPSTEIN, *op. cit. supra* note 159, at 113-15 expresses similiar skepticism regarding the Stone opinion.

207. Rose, Mahon *Reconstructed: Why the Takings Issue is Still a Muddle,* 57 SO. CALIF. L. REV. 561 (1984). Bryden, *But Cf.,* 1 CONST. COMMENTARY 183 (1984) (Editor's Note), a third revisit to *Pennsylvania Coal,* may be dismissed as superficial.

The only case in English constitutional history that could be cited as supportive of Stone's outreach of government power is *The Case of the King's Prerogative in Saltpetre*.[208] Dated 1606 it was in effect an advisory opinion given by Coke, Popham, and other Judges of England concerning the authority of James First to take saltpeter for production of gunpowder from deposits on the private property of his subjects. The "decision" is considered in the course of analysis of Magna Carta in chapter 1.[209] Sovereign power to take private property without compensation was there limited to defense of the realm from invading armies or to safety of a city from conflagration. Holmes' familiar exception in *Pennsylvania Coal* to unconstitutional taking, the blowing up of a house to stop a conflagration, suggests agreement with the English Judges. But, Justice Stone seemingly swept all semblance of restraint before him by asserting that "preferment of [the public] interest over the property interest of the individual, to the extent even of its destruction, is one of the distinguishing characteristics of *every* exercise of the police power *which affects property*."[210]

Technically, no fault can be found with the proposition that every exercise of the police power is constitutional. This is but a truism. Yet there is a hollow ring to the statement as phrased, for it recognizes no limit on sovereign power provided a public interest can be spotted. This is *Mugler* talk, which misled Justice Brandeis into differing with Holmes in *Pennsylvania Coal v. Mahon*. It is highly significant that only three months after *Miller v. Schoene*, in the same year, Brandeis was in agreement with Holmes when the latter opened his dissent in *Springer v. Philippine Islands*[211] with the following paragraph:

> The great ordinances of the Constitution do not establish and divide fields of black and white. Even the more specific of them are found to terminate in a penumbra shading gradually from one extreme to the other. Property must not be taken without compensation, but with the help of a phrase, (the police power) some property may be destroyed for public use without paying for it, if you do not take too much. When we come to the fundamental distinctions it is still more obvious that they must be received with a certain latitude or our government could not go on.[212]

That Justice Brandeis had come to terms with Holmes' insight is confirmed by two momentous decisions of the 1930s in which he wrote the opinions invalidating federal[213] and state[214] legislation on principles of substantive due process of law. In neither did a present public interest prevent a balancing with private interest to set a limit on governmental exercise of the police power.[215]

---

208. 12 Co. Rep. 12, 77 Eng. Rep. 1294 (1606).
209. Chap. 1, *supra*, pp.15-16, text following citation at note 72.
210. Miller v. Schoene, 276 U.S. at 280 (emphases added).
211. 277 U.S. 189 (1928).
212. *Id*. at 209-10.
213. Louisville Joint Stock Land Bank v. Radford, 295 U.S. 555 (1935).
214. Thompson v. Consol. Gas Utilities Corp., 300 U.S. 55 (1937).
215. These cases are considered in other segments of this chapter.

Justice Stone's failure to join in the *Springer* dissent, as had Justice Brandeis, may be justified by the fact the issue at hand was a question of indirect rather than of direct constitutional limitation. However, nothing would have prevented his notation of agreement with Holmes' first paragraph while disagreeing with him on application of the constitutional principle of separation of powers. Suspicion that he remained unconverted arises when one notices that his assertion that the limitless preferment of public interest over private is a distinctive characteristic of exercises of the police power which affect property. Exactly ten years later it was this same Justice who fashioned the opinion in *Carolene Products I*[216] with its celebrated footnote 4 that launched the double standard in constitutional review of permissiveness respecting economic legislation contrasted with that restrictive of civil liberties. A decade is not overly long a period for gestation of radical misconception.[217]

Buyer-Seller Relationships

The plight of farmers, which for producers of certain agricultural products like wheat was an aftermath of World War I, in the Great Depression became even more serious for all agriculturists including specialists such as dairymen. State and federal legislation designed to succor this section of the economy inevitably produced instances of seeming factual taking that generated questions of constitutionality under substantive due process. Challenge, however, if attempted proved fruitless.

In order to overcome a distressed market in fluid milk, resulting from gross disparity between supply and demand, the New York Milk Control Act established a Milk Control Board with power to fix minimum and maximum prices for retail sales of milk to consumers. The Board fixed the price at nine cents for a quart of milk, which Nebbia, a Rochester grocer, undercut. The law was sustained 5 to 4 in *Nebbia v. New York*.[218] In a rambling statement of dissent for the "gang of four" Justices, Justice McReynolds finally came upon, as the basis for the law's invalidity, a finding of unconstitutional taking from consumers for the benefit of dairymen producers.

> Not only does the statute interfere arbitrarily with the rights of the little grocer to conduct his business according to standards long accepted—complete destruction may follow; but it takes away the liberty of twelve million consumers to buy a necessity of life in an open market. It imposes direct and arbitrary burdens upon those already impoverished seriously with the alleged immediate design of affording special benefits to others.
>
> . . . .

---

216. United States v. Carolene Products Co., 304 U.S. 144 (1938).

217. For this context, *Carolene I* is considered in chap. 6, *supra*, pp. 105-106, text at notes 65-67.

218. 291 U.S. 502 (1934), subjected to critical analysis chapters 8 and 9, *infra*.

The Legislature cannot lawfully destroy guaranteed rights of one man with the prime purpose of enriching another, even if for the moment, this may seem advantageous to the public.[219]

Later federal effort on behalf of dairy farmers under a section of the Agricultural Marketing Agreement Act of 1937, authorizing marketing orders fixing minimum prices to be paid producers of intrastate milk, appears to have been challenged solely on federalistic grounds. The Court in *United States v. Wrightwood Dairy Co.*[220] sustained the Act without reference to the possible bearing of Fifth Amendment due process. By this time but one of the "gang" remained on the Court.

In the Agricultural Adjustment Act of 1933 Congress declared the existence of an economic emergency, owing to the disparity between the prices of agricultural and of other commodities, with consequent destruction of farmers' purchasing power. As a solution the Secretary of Agriculture was empowered to reduce the acreage or production for market of any basic agricultural commodity, and to provide for rental or benefit payments through agreements with producers. With respect to these agreements for payments to farmers, an excise tax was imposed upon the first domestic processing, to be paid by the processor. The tax was to be "at such rate as equals the difference between current farm price for the commodity and the fair exchange value . . . ," defined as the price necessary to give the same purchasing power as in the base period. Primary challenge of the Act was on federalistic grounds and it was on this basis that the law fell, albeit with strong dissent on the part of Justices Stone, Brandeis, and Cardozo. *United States v. Butler.*[221]

However, in oral argument before the Court George Wharton Pepper for the Receivers of Hoosac Mills Corp. contended that the Act also offended the Due Process Clause of the Fifth Amendment.

On the other hand, if I am wrong in my main contention and if Congress may lawfully regulate such production—on the general welfare theory or some other equally vague— it by no means follows that the entire cost of the regulatory process may be taken out of the pockets of the processors. . . . It is all very well to think of the promotion of the agricultural industry as a public purpose; but to integrate the industry for purposes of regulation by treating the handler and producer as having interlocking interests and then to compel the stronger group to extend financial aid to the weaker comes perilously close to taking A's property and giving it to B. Something like this was attempted by Congress in the Railroad Retirement Act, where strong roads were expected to make up the deficiencies of the weak. This exaction from the processor might be justified if there were any ascertainable relation between the rate of tax and the activity in respect of which the excise is levied. But when it appears that the tax rate is determined by the width of the gap between what the farmer's income is and what Congress thinks it ought to be, it

219. *Id.* at 557-58.
220. 315 U.S. 110 (1942).
221. 297 U.S. 1 (1936).

begins to look as if the processor were brought upon the scene merely in order to have his pocket picked for the benefit of the farmer. It would be hard enough on the processor to have to submit to assessment merely to increase the producer's income; but when we reflect that the increase is accomplished by using the proceeds of the tax to raise the price which the processor has to pay for his raw material, the question arises whether this is the due process which the Fifth Amendment guarantees. It seems clear to me that it is not due process to measure an excise on processing by a deficiency in producer's income.[222]

In the printed argument for the Government the Fifth Amendment drew little attention. There was no direct response to Pepper's contention of a due process taking from processors for the benefit of producers; reliance was placed upon familiar decisions blocking judicial inquiry into the relationship between the exaction and the appropriation of revenues received therefrom.[223] Neither majority nor dissenting opinion made any reference to the contention.[224]

Having first sustained the Agricultural Adjustment Act of 1938 as a constitutional exercise of congressional power even as to wheat consumed on the farm, because such wheat "overhangs the market,"[225] the unanimous Court was forced to face the contention of violation under the Fifth Amendment. Disposal of the contention that any taking had occurred required little analysis.

It is agreed that as a result of the wheat programs [Farmer Filburn] is able to market his wheat at a price "far above any world price based on the natural reaction of supply and demand." We can hardly find a denial of due process in these circumstances, particularly since it is even doubtful that appellee's burdens under the program outweigh his benefits. It is hardly lack of due process for the Government to regulate that which it subsidizes.[226]

---

222. *Id.* at 42-43

223. *Id.* at 14-15. This printed argument was signed by the Attorney General, Solicitor General (later Justice) Reed, two Assistant Attorneys General, and several others of the Department of Justice including Alger Hiss.

224. Note may be taken here of Attorney Pepper's "suggestion" that "the processing exaction is a far more marked departure from what is usually regarded as permissible in taxation than was the case in Nichols v. Coolidge, 274 U.S. 531 (1927), in Hoeper v. Tax Commission of Wisconsin, 284 U.S. 206 (1931), or in Heiner v. Donnan, 285 U.S. 312 (1932)." *Id.* at 44. These decisions, together with Schlesinger v. Wisconsin, 270 U.S. 230 (1926), constituted pre-*Nebbia* judicial reaction to legislative attempts at intra-family transfers of property. In *Hoeper*, taxation to the husband of the wife's income was invalidated, Holmes, Brandeis and Stone dissenting. *Hoeper* is considered in a later segment of this chapter, p. 186. The other three cases concerned due process limits on inclusion in a decedent's estate, for purposes of death taxes, of private property conveyed prior to death. There was agreement within the Court where the transfer occurred prior to enactment of the taxing provision, *Nichols*, but disagreement as to transfers after enactment where conclusively made in contemplation of death. *Schlesinger* and *Heiner* (5th and 14th Amendments).

225. Wickard v. Filburn, 317 U.S. 111 (1942).

226. *Id.* at 130-31.

Justice Hugo Black's third-of-a-century career as an Associate Justice of the Supreme Court of the United States was marked by two cases disclosing his early and his late attitude toward the Contract Clause. In *Wood v. Lovett*[227] he led the dissent from a decision invalidating a Depression-spawned statute of Arkansas; in *El Paso v. Simmons*[228] he was the sole dissenter in a decision that sustained Texas law enacted in the very year that *Wood* had been decided. Through study of Justice Black's twin dissents in these contrary holdings under the Contract Clause insight can be gained into the relation of this Clause to the Due Process Clauses.

The Contract Clause was functionally a specific prohibition on governmental expropriation of a major form of private property. Paired with the Commerce Clause it was a powerful protector of property interests through most of the nineteenth century. Yet with *Stone v. Mississippi*[229] it was doctrinally undercut to become largely a paper tiger.[230] With that keen insight that was often his,[231] Holmes realized its new impotency; in consequence it was as though the Clause had never been incorporated into the Constitution.[232] In the years of the 1930s, just prior to the nomination and confirmation of Hugo Black, the Court had in effect followed Holmes to the point of merging the essence of the Contract Clause into Substantive Due Process. The decisional instruments were *Home Building & Loan Association v. Blaisdell*[233] and *Lynch v. United States*.[234] *Blaisdell* was formally predicated on the Contract Clause but the reasoning was clearly from Due Process. *Lynch* confirmed that due process was the controlling constitutional provision. Absence of a Contract Clause operative against Congress was of no moment there; through due process the opinion exhibited exactly the same reasoning process apparent in *Blaisdell*. Rigidity in approach was replaced by a weighing of relevant considerations, with the magnitude of the attempted "taking" assuming center stage. The intellectual path back to Holmes in *Pennsylvania Coal Co. v. Mahon* is striking.[235]

---

227. 313 U.S. 362 (1941).

228. 379 U.S. 497 (1965).

229. 101 U.S. 814 (1880).

230. The great significance of *Stone* v. *Mississippi*, the principle of which was carried to *private* contracts in Manigault v. Springs, 199 U.S. 473 (1905), is stressed in chap. 3, *supra*.

231. A disappointing exception is noted in chap. 6, *supra*, p. 96, text at notes 9-13; another is considered in chap. 9, *infra*, pp. 266-69, text at notes 21-38.

232. Noble State Bank v. Haskell, 219 U.S. 104, 109-10 (1911); Marcus Brown Holding Co. v. Feldman, 256 U.S. 170, 198 (1921); Phillips Petroleum Co. v. Jenkins, 297 U.S. 629, 634-35 (1936). Note, 32 COL. L. REV. 476 (1932), provides a detailed account of the Contract Clause before and after its deflation.

233. 290 U.S. 398 (1934).

234. 292 U.S. 571 (1934). *Blaisdell* and *Lynch* are examined *infra* in the Debtor-Creditor segment of this chapter.

235. The seminal decision in *Pennsylvania Coal* is thoroughly examined *supra* in the segment of this chapter subtitled *A Tale of Two Cites*.

In the *Lovett* case Wood had at tax sale purchased land from the State of Arkansas, relying upon an enactment of 1935 that cured all irregularities in the tax proceeding by virtue of which the State had recouped delinquent taxes owed by the former owner. In 1937 the law of two years earlier was repealed. As observed by Justice Roberts who for a majority of five had reversed the State supreme court's sustainment of the repudiating act, the purpose of the 1935 enactment "was to assure one willing to purchase from the State a title immune from attack on grounds theretofore available."[236] For Justice Black, dissenting for himself and two others newly come to Court,[237] the entire episode was quite understandable. The 1935 legislature "was persuaded of the wisdom of such a step."[238] But the later legislature "became convinced that the law had worked directly contrary to the state's policy of obtaining the benefits believed to flow from continuity of possession by home owners and farmers. . . ."[239] Therefore, "sound policy dictated its repeal."[240]

The majority did not stop to consider how adverse to the interests of the purchaser at tax sale was the opening of his title to attack on the ground of possible deficiencies in the tax sale. General experience with unprotected tax titles is that they are not dependable, yet this might not be true at this particular sale. Under traditional Contract Clause doctrine the degree of impairment of the substantive obligation was irrelevant, and here clearly there had been *some* impairment. Q.E.D. Justice Black also purported to be reaching his decision under that Clause but his proffered reasoning discloses due process weighing of factors.

> If under the Contract Clause it is justifiable to seek to find "a rational compromise between individual rights and public welfare," *Home Building & Loan Assn. v. Blaisdell, supra,* at 442, then it seems to me that this is a case for the application of that principle.[241]

The "rational compromise" he had already found in the immediately preceding sentence. The repeal of 1937 was

> a law which, without depriving purchasers of the right to recover their money outlay, with interest, sought to make the way easy for former home owners and property owners of all types to reacquire possession and ownership of forfeited property.[242]

The joker here is "money outlay." Bids at tax sales are normally at the amount of the tax delinquency; stated baldly, that amount is notoriously low compared with the market value of the property involved. This defrocks the

---

236. Wood v. Lovett, 313 U.S. at 368.
237. Douglas and Murphy, J.J.
238. Wood v. Lovett, 313 U.S. at 373.
239. *Ibid.*
240. *Ibid.*
241. *Id.* at 386.
242. *Ibid.*

assertion of reasonableness in the so-called compromise. Under the 1937 repeal the only "rights" assured to those who bought at tax sales in reliance on the law of 1935 are the amounts bid at the tax proceedings plus interest; the far greater values of the properties in question are up for grabs. The only defense that could be made to this judicial sleight of hand is that those greater values were so tainted by cupidity as to justify their return to the former owners. But if such defense had any economic grounding it was incumbent on Justice Black to demonstrate that the property rights of purchasers beyond payment made at tax sale were not of a quality to warrant constitutional protection. His failure to undertake such a demonstration was a concession to the weakness of the contention.

The facts in *El Paso v. Simmons* were these: Simmons sued the City in diversity to determine title to certain Texas land that in 1910 the State had sold in a major distribution of public land to private ownership. The contract called for a small down payment, for forfeiture on nonpayment of interest, but for reinstatement by the defaulting purchaser at any time upon payment of delinquent interest provided no rights of third parties had intervened. Thirty-seven years later Texas amended the law to limit the reinstatement right to five years from the forfeiture date. Five years and two days after forfeiture Simmons tendered payment of back interest and filed for reinstatement. The State refused the proffer, relying on the statutory amendment, and subsequently sold the land to the City of El Paso. For all the Court save Justice Black, Justice White found no constitutional violation. Technically, decision was based on the Contract Clause; however, the reasoning was again typical of due process analysis.

With discovery of great oil and gas deposits in Texas, the unlimited reinstatement rights made inevitable speculation in land ownership. The result was "the imbroglio over land titles in Texas. The long shadow cast by perpetual reinstatement gave rise to a spate of litigation between forfeiting purchasers and the State or between one or more forfeiting purchasers and other forfeiting purchasers."[243] This state of affairs was a far cry from the original intention to encourage settlement of the vast public domain and to provide revenues to underwrite a public school system. Surely, felt the majority, the State was not powerless to "restore confidence in the stability and integrity of land titles and to enable the State to protect and administer its property in a businesslike manner."[244] "Laws which restrict a party to those gains reasonably to be expected from the contract are not subject to attack under the Contract Clause, notwithstanding that they technically alter an obligation of a contract."[245]

El Paso was decided in the year that marked Justice Black's break with Justice Douglas over the legitimacy of what has come to be called constitutional

---

243. El Paso v. Simmons, 379 U.S. at 513.
244. *Id.* at 511-12.
245. *Id.* at 515.

noninterpretivism. The momentous decision was *Griswold v. Connecticut*[246] invalidating the Nutmeg State's statute prohibiting the practice of contraception by married couples. The Douglas opinion reveals clear marks of an effort to explain the conclusion of unconstitutionality in such a way as to satisfy Justice Black. Black rejected the bid in no uncertain terms. Endorsing the views of "the late Judge Learned Hand," he insisted that the proper role for the Justices was to construe "the Constitution as written," leaving alteration to the mechanism provided by the "Constitution makers." "That method of change was good for our Fathers, and being somewhat old-fashioned I must add it is good enough for me."[247] For issues under the Contract Clause this position clearly dictated judicial adherence to the strict language of the constitutional provision. Just as he had contended with respect to the First Amendment, so with the Contract Clause: no means no.

Although "compelled to dissent from the Court's balancing away the plain guarantee"[248] of the Contract Clause, Justice Black could not resist a factual challenge of the majority's assertion that "the promise of reinstatement . . . was not the central undertaking of the seller nor the primary consideration for the buyer's undertaking."[249] At least at first blush this surprising downgrading of the reinstatement obligation is difficult to accept and the Justice directly challenged what he labeled as a "guess."

> To my way of thinking it demonstrates a striking lack of knowledge of credit buying and selling even to imply that these express contractual provisions safeguarding credit purchasers against forfeitures were not one of the greatest, if not the greatest, selling arguments Texas had to promote purchase of its great surfeit of lands.[250]

To Justice Black, and to me, this was excessive balancing in favor of the State. But how, then, account for his dissent in *Wood v. Lovett*? In a footnote he offered the explanation "that the state law, in that case, which protected purchasers of land against loss even though their titles were based only on quit claim deeds, should have been upheld under *Blaisdell*."[251] Yet *Blaisdell* was relied upon by the majority in *El Paso*, forcing Justice Black to "explain" that key decision, "which the Court seems to think practically read the Contract Clause out of the Constitution. . . ."[252]

What to conclude from this account of Mr. Justice Black's intellectual acrobatics? With deference to his memory my conclusion is that he lost stature by dissenting in *El Paso*. The time had long passed for rigid interpretation of

---

246. 381 U.S. 479 (1965), earlier considered in chap. 6, *supra*, pp. 109-10, text at notes 82-85.
247. *Id.* at 522.
248. El Paso v. Simmons, 379 U.S. at 517.
249. *Id.* at 514.
250. *Id.* at 530.
251. *Id.* at 527, n. 17.
252. *Id.* at 523.

the Contract Clause. Since 1880 it was destined to play a role in the constitutional structure different from that originally conceived; its new function was to be as definer of a type of property right claiming major protection under substantive due process. *Blaisdell* signalled acceptance of this basic shift in constitutional doctrine although the old façade was retained. I believe Black as a young Justice sensed the new pattern, found it congenial, and sought to apply its teaching in *Wood* against a throwback to discarded understanding. I find unacceptable the result he reached there, agreeing only that his approach to resolution of the constitutional issue was in accord with the new assignment given to the Contract Clause.

While I join Justice Black in disagreement with the *El Paso* majority on their downgrading of the significance of the provision for unlimited reinstatement, two other considerations operate in counterbalance to make the decision a close one. The profits realized by purchasers were windfall in character, not of the quality of property right likely to weigh heavily in determining the presence or absence of an unconstitutional taking although arguably constituting a factual "transfer." Secondly, in its move to rectify the imbroglio resulting from the early legislation, the State, far from cut-off of the period of reinstatement, allowed five years from date of forfeiture. In the circumstances this would seem to have been ample for determination of action on the part of purchasers. Speculative opportunities were put an end to by the later cut-back; and yet, as the majority concluded, an invalid taking could hardly obtain when parties were restricted "to those gains reasonably to be expected from" the contracts.[253]

A brace of recent decisions involved frustration for wholesale suppliers of natural gas who had sought by contract to protect their pricing structures in transactions with retailers. In the first in date of decision, *Energy Reserves Group, Inc v. Kansas Light & Power Co.,*[254] the Natural Gas Policy Act of 1978, replacing earlier federal regulation, provided for gradually rising price ceilings based on an "inflation adjustment factor" in addition to other market considerations. For newly discovered or newly produced gas the price set for December, 1978, was $2.078 per million BTU's. Another section of the Act set at $1.63 per million BTU's the December, 1978, ceiling price for categories of natural gas not otherwise covered. Kansas then enacted what it called a Natural Gas Price Protection Act permitted by a section of the federal law allowing a State to establish for the intrastate market a maximum lawful price for the first sale of natural gas produced in such State on condition its price did not exceed the applicable maximum lawful price set under the Federal Act. The Kansas Act, if valid, operated to limit escalation to the $1.63 level. Energy Reserves asserted that prohibition of increase to the higher level of $2.078 im-

---

253. *Id.* at 515.
254. 459 U.S. 400 (1983).

paired the obligation of each of the two contracts made with it by Kansas Light & Power.

Disposition of the appeal discloses how slender the reed of the Contract Clause has become. "The threshold determination is whether the Kansas Act has impaired substantially ERG's contractual rights. Significant here is the fact that the parties are operating in a heavily regulated industry."[255] In this context

> the contracts expressly recognize the existence of extensive regulation by providing that any contractual terms are subject to relevant present and future state and federal law. This latter provision could be interpreted to incorporate all future state price regulation, and thus dispose of the Contract Clause claim. Regardless of whether this interpretation is correct, the provision does suggest that ERG knew its contractual rights were subject to alteration by state price regulation. Price regulation existed and was foreseeable as the type of law that would alter contract obligations. . . . In short, ERG's reasonable expectations have not been impaired by the Kansas Act.[256]

This disposed of the challenge without more, as three members of the Court insisted in concurrence.[257] Yet the majority proceeded to add the following:

> To the extent, if any, the Kansas Act impairs ERG's contractual interests, the Kansas Act rests on, and is prompted by, significant and legitimate state interests. Kansas has exercised its police power to protect consumers from the escalation of natural gas prices caused by deregulation. The State reasonably could find that higher gas prices have caused and will cause hardship among those who use gas heat but must exist on limited fixed incomes. [258]

It had been said earlier in the opinion:

> The requirement of a legitimate public purpose guarantees that the State is exercising its police power, rather than providing a benefit to special interests.[259]

As a constitutional provision intended for protection of property interests created through contract, the Contract Clause is in shambles, with another blow yet to come in *Exxon Corp. v. Eagerton*.[260] That litigation arose from the action of Alabama in raising its severance tax on oil and gas produced within the State and forbidding producers to pass this increase on to purchasers. In the Court's own words, on appeal from sustainment in the court below,

> the pass-through prohibition did restrict contractual obligations of which appellants were the beneficiaries. Appellants were parties to sale contracts that permitted them

---

255. *Id.* at 413.
256. *Id.* at 416.
257. *Id.* at 421.
258. *Id.* at 416-17.
259. *Id.* at 412.
260. 462 U.S. 176 (1983).

to include in their prices any increase in the severance taxes that they were required to pay on the oil and gas sold. The contracts were entered into before the pass-through prohibition was enacted and their terms extended through the period during which the prohibition was in effect. By barring appellants from passing the tax increase through to their purchasers, the pass-through prohibition nullified *pro tanto* the purchasers' contractual obligations to reimburse appellants for any severance taxes.[261]

But clear as was the taking, reliance on the Contract Clause was unavailing. In a unanimous opinion Justice Marshall shot down the constitutional challenge by citation of the established principle from *Stone v. Mississippi*[262] and other standard decisions to the effect that private parties by contract cannot prevent a legislature from enacting law for the public good,[263] here the protection of consumers from excessive prices.[264] *Exxon Corp. v. Eagerton* was a case for substantive due process, although the result might well have been the same because of the meager protection now afforded retroactivity by Due Process. But the Court's continuing play to the grandstand made it impossible to resort to the pertinent provision of the Constitution. The Court's opinion is practically, although not technically, an advisory opinion inasmuch as the tax increase had been repealed by the time the issue reached the Court. This would have been a propitious occasion for the Court to come off the double standard, which grows in insubstantiality as time passes.[265]

---

261. *Id.* at 189.

262. See note 230, *supra*, for reference to the significance of this momentous decision.

263. Reliance was placed on the precedent provided by Producers Transportation Co. v. Railroad Comm., 251 U.S. 228 (1920), where, according to Justice Marshall, "the Court upheld an order issued by a state commission under a newly enacted statute empowering the commission to set the rates that could be charged by individuals or corporations offering to transport oil by pipeline. The Court rejected the contention of a pipeline owner that the statute could not override preexisting contracts." Exxon Corp. v. Eagerton, 462 U.S. at 193.

264. Professor Epstein's criticism of *Eagerton* is telling.

The Court in *Eagerton* sought to justify the legislation by noting that its provisions apply to "all oil and gas producers." Yet on this point, at least, the argument runs into the teeth of the contract clause: "No state shall . . . pass any . . . Law impairing the Obligation of Contracts." The words "pass any law" encompass such general legislation as well as legislation favoring a single producer. Indeed, the very fact that the Alabama legislation pits consumers, producers, and royalty owners against each other reinforces the need for judicial intervention. Otherwise, the statute effectively becomes a tool whereby a successful faction is able to ensure a payoff to all of its members. *Eagerton*, on its facts, is a textbook case in which the Constitution requires judicial nullification of legislation, even by a court that denies the contract clause any prospective application. *Eagerton*, as decided, is a clear example of how the unprincipled manipulation of necessary limitations on the contract clause can lead to the judicial nullification of the constitutional text.

Epstein, *Toward a Revitalization of the Contract Clause*, 51 U. OF CHI. L. REV. 703, at 740 (1984).

265. Professor William Van Alstyne, one of the ablest constitutional scholars, has dem-

Debtor-Creditor Relationships

The Great Depression threatened financial ruin for many classes of debtors. Among these were owners of mortgaged property, both urban and rural. The response of Government to appeals for relief of mortgagors was enactment of moratorium legislation. Of state statutes, that of Minnesota was illustrative. Enacted in April of 1933 the law[266] was to remain in effect "only during the continuance of the emergency and in no event beyond May 1, 1935." Within that time frame a foreclosure court, upon application of a mortgagor, was authorized to extend the normal one-year period of redemption "for such additional time as the court may deem just and reasonable."

On hearing, the court was to determine the reasonable value of the income on the property involved, or if without income, the reasonable rental value thereof, and to direct the mortgagor "to pay all or a reasonable part of such income or rental value, in or toward the payment of taxes, insurance, interest, and mortgage indebtedness at such times and in such manner" as should be determined by the court. The mortgagor was to remain in possession if he met these conditions but on the other hand the integrity of the mortgage indebtedness was unimpaired and the rights of the mortgagee to judicial sale, to bid at such sale, and to deficiency judgment were maintained, provided the mortgagor failed to redeem during the extended period. In a debate over the proper approach to constitutional interpretation the Court sustained the statute 5 to 4 in *Home Building & Loan Ass'n v. Blaisdell*.[267]

Decision was rested on the Contract Clause but with clear indication that the same result would have ensued under Due Process. It should have been decided on the latter basis, for as Holmes had pointed out well before 1934 the momentous decision in *Stone v. Mississippi* had deflated the Contract Clause to the point that it offered no major protection to private property not available from Due Process.[268] It was almost as though that Clause had never been included in the Constitution.[269] A decision of the same year as *Blaisdell* un-

---

onstrated the superficiality of the distinction underlying the double standard. Van Alstyne, *The Recrudescence of Property Rights as the Foremost Principle of Civil Liberties*, 43 LAW & CONTEMP. PROBS. 66 (1980).

266. Minn. Laws 1933, c. 339.

267. 290 U.S. 398 (1934).

268. Marcus Brown Holding Co. v. Feldman, 256 U.S. 170, 198 (1921); Noble State Bank v. Haskell, 219 U.S. 104, 109-10 (1911).

269. Professor Robert Hale of Columbia came to this conclusion at the close of an exhaustive examination of decisions under the Contract Clause. Remarking that "there is at least a tendency for the contract clause and the due process clause to coalesce," he observed:

Although there is no clause expressly forbidding the federal government to pass laws impairing the obligation of contracts, any federal law impairing them in a manner which the Supreme Court deemed unreasonable would doubtless be held to be a dep-

derwrote this conclusion by another route. *Lynch v. United States*[270] concerned the constitutionality of congressional legislation of 1933, called the Economy Act because enacted in response to federal financial difficulties arising from the Depression. A clause of §17 in this Act read that "all laws granting or pertaining to yearly renewable term insurance are hereby repealed."[271]

The provision clearly applied to policies of this description that had been issued during World War I pursuant to the War Risk Insurance Act of 1917. In consolidated suits brought by beneficiaries of two insureds it was "claimed that the Act deprived them of property without due process of law in violation of the Fifth Amendment." The issue was whether Congress intended to revoke the remedy, which would destroy judicial jurisdiction inasmuch as it had not given consent to suit, or to repudiate the obligation of the contracts. A unanimous Court concluded that the latter had been the intent and held against the Government. "War Risk Insurance policies are contracts of the United States" and "being contracts, are property and create vested rights."[272]

It was clear that the Act would fall but the wording of the pronouncement warrants full quotation in view of the question of constitutional interpretation first raised in *Pennsylvania Coal Co. v. Mahon*.[273]

> The Fifth Amendment commands that property be not taken without making just compensation. Valid contracts are property, whether the obligor be a private individual, a municipality, a State or the United States. Rights against the United States arising out of a contract with it are protected by the Fifth Amendment. United States v. Central Pacific R. Co., 118 U.S. 235, 238; United States v. Northern Pacific Ry. Co., 256 U.S. 51, 64, 67. When the United States enter into contract relations, its rights and duties therein are governed generally by the law applicable to contracts between private individuals. That the contracts of war risk insurance were valid when made is not questioned. As Congress had the power to authorize the Bureau of War Risk Insurance to issue them, the due process clause prohibits the United States from annulling them, unless, indeed, the action taken falls within the federal police power or some other paramount power.[274]

---

rivation of property without due process, contrary to the Fifth Amendment. And a state law which impaired obligations in a manner which the Court deemed reasonable would be held valid. The fact that a person is deprived of a contract right rather than a different sort of property may make legislation seem to the judges more, or less, reasonable in a particular case. But the results might be the same if the contract clause were dropped out of the Constitution, and the challenged statutes all judged as reasonable or unreasonable deprivations of property.

Hale, *The Contract Clause: III*, 57 HARV. L. REV. 852, at 890-91 (1944).

270. 292 U.S. 571 (1934).

271. 48 STAT. 9. The clause in question is quoted in the Brandeis opinion, 292 U.S. at 575.

272. Lynch v. United States, 292 U.S. at 576, 577.

273. 260 U.S. 393 (1922), discussed, *supra*, in the segment of this chapter, *A Tale of Two Cites*.

274. Lynch v. United States, 292 U.S. at 579.

Although the first sentence of this paragraph cites to the Eminent Domain portion of the Fifth Amendment, the very next reference to this Amendment has to be to its due process provision; *Northern Pacific*, decided in 1921, was the latest of those prior cases establishing that, while the Federal Government is not bound by a Contract Clause, it is subject to approximately the same limitations by virtue of the Due Process Clause of Amendment Five.[275] In the remainder of the paragraph reliance is clearly placed on due process as a protector of property interests not within valid exercises of delegated federal authority that are the rough equivalent of state police power. Frankly, Justice Brandeis stated the law of the Constitution backward. Holmes' statement in *Pennsylvania Coal* had put it correctly: if government goes too far under cover of the police power there is a due process taking resulting in nullification, yet government can have its way if the purpose is public and rightful compensation is paid the takee. Recalling that Brandeis dissented in *Pennsylvania Coal*, a charitable view of this paragraph is that in the earlier case his mind was running on a different track.

With respect to the merits, the taking in *Lynch* was complete whereas in *Blaisdell* the substance of the mortgagee's claim remained untouched. The conflicting results in the two cases are therefore consistent with the factor of magnitude that plays a central part in determining presence or absence of expropriation.[276] Consistency is further demonstrated by contrasting with *Blais-*

---

275. Writing for the Court recently, Justice Brennan makes the statement "We have never held, however, that the principles embodied in the Fifth Amendment's Due Process Clause are coextensive with prohibitions existing against state impairments of pre-existing contracts." Pension Benefit Guaranty Corp. v. R. A. Gray & Co., 467 U.S. 717, at 733 (1984). Supporting the statement is citation to Philadelphia, Baltimore & Washington Railroad v. Schubert, 224 U.S. 603 (1912). Rejecting constitutional challenge of the Federal Employer's Liability Act of 1908, the Court there observed that a private party had no power to contract out of future Congressional legislation. But the Contract Clause, certainly since 1880, affords no such power with respect to State legislative action, as the Justice made plain in his dissent in Allied Structural Steel Co. v. Spannaus, 438 U.S. 234, at 251 (1978). The error is the more puzzling when it is noted that *Spannaus* is cited by him in the immediately preceding sentence. Supporting my assertion in the text are the following: the *Central Pacific* and *Northern Pacific* cases cited in the quotation at footnote 274, *supra*; Choate v. Trapp, 224 U.S. 665 (1912); Sinking Fund Cases, 99 U.S. 700, 718 (1878).

276. At odds with this textual statement is the view of one who spent a total of 25 years as an American legislator.

In the last analysis nearly every law transfers something from A to B. It matters not whether this advantage be tangible or fancied, large or small. Somebody gains, somebody loses, for you cannot create an advantage out of a vacuum. This makes the whole question one of degree, and there is no principle, no fundamental right, in a matter of degree.

R. Luce. Legislative Problems 60 (1935, reprinted 1971).

Whatever merit may be found in political discourse for Luce's assertion that there is no

dell the Court's decisions on the original and the amended Frazier-Lemke Acts. These successive enactments constituted congressional reaction to the plight of farm debtors as a consequence of persistent decline in farm prices aggravated by Depression conditions. Constitutionality of the first Act was tested in litigation styled *Louisville Joint Stock Land Bank v. Radford.*[277] In a unanimous opinion written by Justice Brandeis the statute was found violative of the Fifth Amendment.

> As here applied it has taken from the Bank the following property rights recognized by the Law of Kentucky:
> 1. The right to retain the lien until the indebtedness thereby secured is paid.
> 2. The right to realize upon the security by a judicial public sale.
> 3. The right to determine when such sale shall be held, subject only to the discretion of the court.
> 4. The right to protect its interest in the property by bidding at such sale whenever held, and thus to assure having the mortgaged property devoted primarily to the satisfaction of the debt, either through receipt of the proceeds of a fair competitive sale or by taking the property itself.
> 5. The right to control meanwhile the property during the period of default, subject only to the discretion of the court, and to have the rents and profits collected by a receiver for the satisfaction of the debt.[278]

Radford's contention that "the Bank retains every right in the property to which it is entitled" Brandeis rejected as resting

> upon the unfounded assertion that its only substantive right under the mortgage is to have the value of the security applied to the satisfaction of the debt. It would be more accurate to say that the only right under the mortgage left to the Bank is the right to retain its lien until the mortgagor, sometime within the [statutory] five-year period, chooses to release it by paying the appraised value of the property.[279]

---

principle or fundamental right involved in the extent to which legislation attempts transfers from *A* to *B*, constitutional theory is highly sensitive to matters of degree. Such sensitivity is of the very essence of the concept of expropriation, long at the heart of substantive due process in English and American constitutionalism. This is the unquestioned lesson to be learned from critical analysis of centuries of constitutional history; the lesson is repeated in the period under consideration. It could not be otherwise in a polity committed to preservation of private property as well as to public authority to govern through the police power, the power to tax, and the power to take property by eminent domain but only for public use upon paying just compensation.

277. 295 U.S. 555 (1935). Sandwiched between *Blaisdell* and *Radford* were decisions invalidating two Arkansas statutes for inconsistency with the Contract Clause. W.B. Worthen Co. v. Thomas, 292 U.S. 426 (1934) (opinion by C. J. Hughes); W.B. Worthen Co. v. Kavanaugh, 295 U.S. 56 (1935) (opinion by Cardozo, J.). Each of the statutes was grossly destructive of rights of creditors. *Blaisdell* was distinguished in each instance; both opinions reflected due process analysis although formally invoking the Contract Clause; both decisions were unanimous.

278. *Id.* at 594-95.

279. *Id.* at 596.

Radford's inevitable reliance on *Blaisdell* "lends no support to his contention."

> There the statute left the period of the extension of the right of redemption to be determined by the court within the maximum limit of two years. Even after the period had been decided upon, it could, as was pointed out, "be reduced by order of the court under the statute, in case of a change in circumstances...."(p. 447); and at the close of the period, the mortgagee was free to apply the mortgaged property to the satisfaction of the mortgage debt. Here, the option and the possession would continue although the emergency which is relied upon as justifying the Act ended before November 30, 1939.[280]

Immediate amendment of the Frazier-Lemke Act, duly challenged in *Wright v. Vinton Branch of the Mountain Trust Bank*,[281] was construed to be preservative of rights 1, 2, and 4. Allegations of the mortgagee that the legislation remained destructive of rights 3 and 5 were met by findings of the reasonableness of these provisions as worded in the amendment supported by the assertion that in *Radford* it "was not held that the deprivation of any one of these rights would have rendered the Act invalid, but that the effect of the statute in its entirety was to deprive the mortgagee of his property without due process of law."[282] Decision was again unanimous, this time in favor of constitutionality.

The Court, through Justice Brandeis, did take note of some differences in constitutional basis between this holding and that in *Blaisdell*:

> The question which the objections raise [here] is not whether the Act does more than modify remedial rights. It is whether the legislation modifies the secured creditor's rights, remedial or substantive, to such an extent as to deny the due process of law guaranteed by the Fifth Amendment.[283]

But in thrust the amendment brought the federal law in line with the Minnesota statute; essentially, the two enactments temporarily extended the normal period of redemption, and while this feature kept the mortgagees out of possession for a longer time they were assured of protection both of their caretaker interests during ouster and specifically of the security of the physical property that had been pledged as collateral for the loans.

A contemporary writer offers an analysis of the economic facts underlying the Minnesota statute that makes the *Blaisdell* result an extremely difficult one to judge.[284] In three insightful paragraphs[285] Professor Epstein views the state

---

280. *Id.* at 597-98.
281. 300 U.S. 440 (1937).
282. *Id.* at 457.
283. *Id.* at 470.
284. Epstein, *Toward a Revitalization of the Contract Clause*, 51 U. OF CHI. L. REV. 703 (1984).
285. *Id.* at 737-38.

legislative effort as one to "undue the mischief" resulting from massive deflation caused by federal contraction of the money supply; yet finds in the moratorium action a failure to consider the "financial arrangements that the mortgagees relied upon to obtain their own funds," thus possibly depriving them of the hedge in their own borrowing "that lay at the core of their financial strategy"; to conclude that

> [h]ad Hughes written the right kind of opinion, *Blaisdell* would have reflected an inevitable struggle with an intractable set of facts, but the opinion would have announced no broad interpretive principle.... Instead, *Blaisdell* trumpeted a false liberation from the constitutional text that has paved the way for massive government intervention that undermines the security of private transactions. Today the police power exception has come to eviscerate the contracts clause.[286]

Whether or not one accepts the conclusion, the analysis is valuable for its disclosure of economic factors lying below the surface of the *Blaisdell* case. The teaching is equally valuable for in-depth consideration of *Radford* and *Wright* as well as other facets of the expropriation issue.

At first blush surprising is the fact, generally unnoticed, that nowhere in the opinion in *Radford* is mention made of substantive due process. In the federal court of appeals, which was reversed, the issue was clearly understood as being one of bankruptcy power versus due process limitation;[287] in *Wright*, as the above quotation demonstrates, the Court itself was deliberating in terms of "the due process of law guaranteed by the Fifth Amendment." And the reasoning of Justice Brandeis for the Court in *Radford* is pure due process. Yet the conclusion of unconstitutionality is rested on the very last provision of the Amendment.

> The province of the Court is limited to deciding whether the Frazier-Lemke Act as applied has taken from the Bank without compensation, and given to Radford, rights in specific property which are of substantial value[288].... As we conclude that the Act as applied has done so, we must hold it void. For the Fifth Amendment commands that, however great the Nation's need, private property shall be not thus taken even for a wholly public use without compensation. If the public interest requires, or permits, the taking of the property of individual mortgagees in order to relieve the necessities of individual mortgagors, resort must be had to proceedings by eminent domain; so that, through taxation, the burden of the relief afforded in the public interest may be borne by the public.[289]

---

286. *Id.* at 738.

287. Louisville Joint Stock Land Bank v. Radford, 74 F. (2d) 576, 580-81 (C.C.A. 6th, 1935).

288. Quite significant is the citation at this point of Loan Ass'n v. Topeka, 20 Wall. 655, 662, 664 (1874). Analysis of this seminal case is found in chap. 2, *supra*, p. 42, text associated with notes 71 and 72.

289. Louisville Joint Stock Land Bank v. Radford, 295 U.S. at 601-02.

Surprise turns to understanding by reference back to Holmes' landmark opinion in *Pennsylavania Coal v.Mahon*.[290] Justice Brandeis is getting the hang of the duality in the Fifth Amendment. Logically, analysis commences with the assertion of propertied parties that a "taking" has occurred because the facts demonstrate that the police power has been pushed beyond limits. If a taking is judicially found, the offending statute is a nullity unless provision is made for just compensation, which "saves" it in the general public interest. The Brandeis opinion although long is somewhat elliptical in the sense that he does not stop to observe that since an unconstitutional taking has been found the Act falls; he passes directly to the fact it could be saved by payment of just compensation (the presence of a *public* purpose being clear) but the "Frazier-Lemke Act does not purport to exercise the right of eminent domain."[291]

Political subdivisions of the States, as well as private entities, were forced by the Depression to default on their obligations. Once again both federal and state legislatures sought to provide means of relief. Two decisions of the Court, each providing for composition of debts under specified statutory conditions, responded to the crisis. First in time was *United States v. Bekins*, [292] decided in 1938. Congress had the year before added Chapter X to the Bankruptcy Act. Major conditions to relief by debt composition included state consent, procedural protections, approval of submissions by 51 percent of the creditors and confirmation of the plan by two-thirds thereof, and a specific finding by the court that the plan of composition "is fair, equitable, and for the best interests of the creditors." By far the greater constitutional issue in *Bekins* was the federalistic one; the Fifth Amendment question was dispatched with one sentence.[293] Four years later, in *Faitoute Iron & Steel Co. v. City of Asbury Park*,[294] a similar holding of constitutionality was the consequence of challenge to a New Jersey enactment providing for composition of the debts of municipalities unable by reason of Depression circumstances to meet their obligations. The state law required for approval of an adjustment 85 percent of the creditors, favorable action by the municipality and by a state Municipal Finance Commission, and a judicial finding of the presence of four specified conditions of fiscal inability and creditor protection. Contrasting the facts of *Faitoute* with those found in *Kavanaugh*,[295]

[h]ere we have just the opposite...with the result that that which was a most depreciated claim of little value has, by the very scheme complained of, been saved

---

290. Refer back to text at footnote 273, *supra*, supporting text consideration.

291. Louisville Joint Stock Land Bank v. Radford, 295 U.S. at 596.

292. 304 U.S. 27 (1938).

293. Given the circumstances, the citation to the Fifth Amendment must have been to the Due Process Clause, not that of Eminent Domain. The federal law was upheld.

294. 316 U.S. 502 (1942).

295. W.B. Worthen Co. v. Kavanaugh, 295 U.S. 56 (1935), commented on in note 277, *supra*.The Arkansas statute had been invalidated.

and transmuted into substantial value. To call a law so beneficent in its consequences on behalf of the creditor who, having had so much restored to him, now insists on standing on the paper rights that were merely paper before this resuscitating scheme, an impairment of the obligation of contract is indeed to make of the Constitution a code of lifeless forms instead of an enduring framework of government for a dynamic society.[296]

During the Depression era the Court was faced with recurrence of the issue first met in the *Legal Tender Cases* of 1871.[297] Involved in modern context was the difficult question of the extent of congressional power over the nation's monetary system in face of the restrictions flowing from Due Process. The problem was precipitated by the Congressional Joint Resolution of June 5, 1933, nullifying gold clauses in private and public obligations including obligations of the United States. "Every obligation, heretofore or hereafter incurred, whether or not any such provision is contained therein or made with respect thereto, shall be discharged upon payment, dollar for dollar, in any coin or currency which at the time of payment is legal tender for public and private debts."[298] Gold clauses were a delight of creditors because of all commodities gold for centuries had been the most stable in value; the gold clause thus came the closest to guaranteeing that payment at maturity would in purchasing power equal the value loaned. "The gold clause merely prevents the borrower from availing itself of a possibility of discharge of the debt in depreciated currency."[299] *Norman v. Baltimore & Ohio Railroad Co.*[300] determined the validity of the Resolution in application to money contract obligations between private parties; *Perry v. United States*[301] made the decision with respect to similar obligations of the United States. In each instance the action of Congress was sustained 5 to 4.

Norman had sued on a coupon from a gold-clause bond issued by the Baltimore & Ohio Railroad. The New York court of appeals had sustained the trial court in limiting recovery "to the face of the coupon, dollar for dollar, in currency." On appeal to a United States court of appeals was a like ruling, with respect to other railroad bonds with gold clauses, decreed by a federal district court in a bankruptcy proceeding. There had thus been "taken" from these obligees the difference between the gold standard of value per dollar

---

296. Faitoute Iron & Steel Co. v. City of Asbury Park, 316 U.S. at 515-16. The passage could only have been penned by Justice Felix Frankfurter, the third appointee of President Franklin Roosevelt in his "reconstruction" of the Court.

297. 12 Wall. 457 (1871), considered *infra* note 302.

298. 48 STAT. Part I, 112-13. Nebolsine, *The Gold Clause in Private Contracts*, 42 YALE L. J. 1051 (1933), written just before the Resolution, provides background on the gold clause and possible alternatives for creditor protection.

299. Quoted by the dissenters from a decision of the Permanent Court of International Justice, Perry v. United States, 294 U.S. at 363.

300. 294 U.S. 240 (1935).

301. 294 U.S. 330 (1935).

(25.8 grains .9 fine) and the lower standard of value (15 5/21 grains .9 fine) resulting from devaluation of the dollar. Stated otherwise, they had been frustrated in their effort to receive on the bonds in purchasing power what they had lent to the obligors. The magnitude of their "loss" would be measured in the extent of the depreciation of the currency between date of purchase and date of maturity. The gain or benefit to the obligors lay in release from their obligation to pay on their debts at the higher values commanded by gold clauses. But this was not the case of an ordinary transfer from A to B for the latter's advantage. Overreaching was the power of Congress to establish a uniform monetary system.

The Court adverted to the *Legal Tender Cases* for guidance.[302]

[T]he Court, in the legal tender cases, recognized the possible consequences of such enactments in frustrating the expected performance of contracts,—in rendering them "fruitless or partially fruitless.".... The conclusion was that contracts must be understood as having been made in reference to the possible exercise of the rightful authority of the Government, and that no obligation of a contract "can extend to the defeat" of that authority. *Knox v. Lee*, supra, [12 Wall.] pp. 549-551.

On similar grounds, the Court dismissed the contention under the Fifth Amendment forbidding the taking of private property for public use without just compensation or the deprivation of it without due process of law. That provision, said the Court, referred only to a direct appropriation.... The Court referred to the Act of June 28, 1834, by which a new regulation of the weight and value of gold coin was adopted, and about six per cent. was taken from the weight of each dollar. The effect of the measure was that all creditors were subjected to a corresponding loss, as the debts then due "became solvable with six per cent. less gold than was required to pay them before." But it had never been imagined that there was a taking of private property without compensation or without due process of law. The harshness of such legislation, or the hardship it may cause, afforded no reason for considering it to be unconstitutional. *Id.*, pp. 551, 552.[303]

Reasoning from the *Legal Tender Cases*, the Chief Justice concluded thusly in *Norman*:

We are not concerned with consequences, in the sense that consequences, however serious, may excuse an invasion of constitutional right. We are concerned with the constitutional power of the Congress over the monetary system of the country and its attempted frustration. Exercising that power, the Congress has undertaken to establish a uniform currency, and parity between kinds of currency, and to make that currency, dollar for dollar, legal tender for the payment of debts. In the light of abundant experience, the Congress was entitled to choose such a uniform monetary system, and to reject a dual system, with respect to all obligations within the range of the exercise of its constitutional authority. The contention that these

---

302. 12 Wall. 457 (1871), overruling Hepburn v. Griswold, 8 Wall. 603 (1869), considered in chap. 2, *supra*, p. 34, text at notes 23-25.
303. Norman v. Baltimore & Ohio Railroad Co., 294 U.S. at 304-06.

gold clauses are valid contracts and cannot be struck down proceeds upon the assumption that private parties, and states and municipalities, may make and enforce contracts which may limit that authority. Dismissing that untenable assumption, the facts must be faced. We think that it is clearly shown that these clauses interfere with the exertion of the power granted to the Congress and certainly it is not established that the Congress arbitrarily or capriciously decided that such an interference existed.[304]

Perry v. *United States* concerned redemption of a Liberty Loan Bond issued by the United States itself during World War I. These bonds carried a provision that both interest and principal were payable "in United States gold coin of the present standard of value," *i.e.*, in dollars of 25.8 grains of gold .9 fine. On presentment after the bonds were called for redemption Perry demanded payment on the basis of the express obligation. The Treasury refused to comply with that demand, offering to pay only the face of the bonds in legal tender currency of 15 5/21 grains of gold .9 fine per dollar. Justification was based on the Congressional Joint Resolution, which Perry asserted was unconstitutional "as it operated to deprive [him] of his property without due process of law." On suit in the Court of Claims against the United States for the difference in dollar payment, that court certified to the Supreme Court the question whether Perry was "entitled to receive from the United States an amount in legal tender currency in excess of the face amount of the bond?"

In an opinion for himself and four other Justices, Chief Justice Hughes agreed with Perry that the Joint Resolution, in nullifying gold clauses in United States obligations, was unconstitutional.

> There is a clear distinction between the power of Congress to control or interdict the contracts of private parties when they interfere with the exercise of its constitutional authority, and the power of the Congress to alter or repudiate the substance of its own engagements when it has borrowed money under the authority which the Constitution confers.[305]

But in the end Perry fared no better than did Norman; in impairment of the contract relationship he had suffered no recoverable damages!

> Plaintiff has not shown, or attempted to show, that in relation to buying power he has sustained any loss whatever. On the contrary, in view of the adjustment of the internal economy to the single measure of value as established by the legislation of the Congress, and the universal availability and use throughout the country of the legal tender currency in meeting all engagements, the payment to the plaintiff of the amount which he demands would appear to constitute not a recoupment of loss in any proper sense but an unjustified enrichment.

> Plaintiff seeks to make his case solely upon the theory that by reason of the change in the weight of the dollar he is entitled to one dollar and sixty-nine cents in the present currency for every dollar promised by the bond, regardless of any

---

304. *Id.* at 316.
305. Perry v. United States, 294 U.S. at 350-51.

actual loss he has suffered with respect to any transaction in which his dollars may be used. We think that position is untenable.[306]

If the dubious reasoning of the bare majority in the gold clause cases does not "wash," as for the minority of four, speaking through Justice McReynolds it did not, then those cases must be understood as applications in the present century of England's *Case of the King's Prerogative in Saltpetre.*[307] In *Norman* and *Perry* there was a crisis in the national economy as serious in its own way as the threat of foreign invasion or internal rebellion three hundred years earlier. To fall back on this explanation of the exception to substantive limitation of governmental power is more justified than that necessary to ground Justice Stone's seemingly limitless reach of the police power in explaining sustainment of the Virginia statute in *Miller v. Schoene.*[308] Apple production, while of great significance to the economy of the State of Virginia, presented no crisis condition. *Korematsu v. United States,*[309] to arise a decade later, came closer to a condition of national crisis, yet in the after-light of World War II there will always be dispute concerning the gravity of danger of Japanese invasion. To the one in whose honor essays have been published under the title of *Power and Policy in Quest of Law,*[310] Fifth Amendment Due Process experienced a low point with sustainment of the Japanese Exclusion Order despite any evidence of disloyalty after Pearl Harbor among citizens or aliens of Japanese ancestry.[311]

The very predicate of the *A* to *B* syndrome is that if the appearance of a taking is belied by the facts there is no denial of substantive due process. Two decisions of the 1940s, one coming early in the decade and the other toward the end, found no taking on economic facts far less debatable than those accepted in the gold clause cases. *Gelfert v. National City Bank*[312] sustained a New York statute amendatory of traditional mortgage law which allowed a deficiency judgment to a mortgagee who in a foreclosure proceeding after default bid in the security on the loan at a low value. Replacement of old § 1083 of the Civil Practice Act by a revised version of the same section in 1938

---

306. *Id.* at 357-58.

307. 12 Co. Rep. 12, 77 Eng. Rep. 1294 (1606), considered in chap. 1, *supra,* p. 15, at note 70.

308. 276 U.S. 172 (1928), discussed at length textually, *supra,* pp. 155-59, at notes 186-210, in the portion of this chapter entitled *A Tale of Two Cites.*

309. 323 U.S. 214 (1944).

310. See the Introduction to the 1985 volume by editors McDougal and Reisman.

311. PERSONAL JUSTICE DENIED 3 (1982) (Report of the Commission on Wartime Relocation and Internment of Civilians). Rostow, *The Japanese American Cases—A Disaster,* 54 YALE L. J. 489 (1945), deserves great commendation for his courageous denunciation of *this* infamy. Of the three dissenters in *Korematsu* only Justice Murphy was a "liberal." The other two were Jackson and Roberts, J.J. Where were Justices Black and Douglas at the "moment of truth"?

312. 313 U.S. 221 (1941).

in effect denied a deficiency judgment where the court determined that the "fair and reasonable market value of the mortgaged premises" equalled or exceeded the amount of the debt. The Court had previously sustained a Depression-originated law of North Carolina that did not displace traditional remedy,[313] and an earlier New York law of displacement but enacted as an emergency measure.[314]

The essence of the unanimous opinion by Justice Douglas is found in the following passage.

> Mortgagees are constitutionally entitled to no more than payment in full. *Honeyman* v. *Jacobs, supra.* They cannot be heard to complain on constitutional grounds if the legislature takes steps to see to it that they get no more than that. . . . Certainly, so far as mortgagees are concerned, the use of the [legislative] criterion of "fair and reasonable market value" in cases where they obtain the property for a lesser amount holds promise of tempering the extremes of both inflated and depressed market prices. And so far as mortgagors are concerned, it offers some assurance that they will not be saddled with more than the amount of their obligations. To hold that mortgagees are entitled under the contract clause to retain the advantages of a forced sale would be to dignify into a constitutionally protected property right their chance to get more than the amount of their contracts. *Honeyman* v. *Jacobs, supra.* The contract clause does not protect such a strategical, procedural advantage.[315]

With the advent of World War II mobilization of productive capital on an unprecedented scale became as essential as mobilization of manpower. The latter was effected through the Selective Service process. With respect to war production Congress chose from among several alternatives that of dependence on private enterprise subject to protection against profiteering. The method selected was rapid deployment of capital by contract with provision for later recapture of what war experience revealed to be "excess profits." "The Renegotiation Act was developed as a major wartime policy of Congress comparable to that of the Selective Service Act."[316] Recovery by the Government of excessive profits was sustained by the Court in *Lichter v. United States.*[317]

> One of the primary purposes of the renegotiation plan for redetermining the allowable profit on contracts for the production of war goods by private persons was the avoidance of requisitioning or condemnation proceedings leading to govern-

---

313. Richmond Mortgage & Loan Corp. v. Wachovia Bank & Trust Co., 300 U.S. 124 (1937).

314. Honeyman v. Jacobs, 306 U.S. 539 (1939), cited at beginning and end of the quotation from *Gelfert*, text *infra* note 315.

315. Gelfert v. National City Bank, 313 U.S. at 233-34.

316. Quoted from *Lichter v. United States*, cited *infra* note 317, at 754.

317. 334 U.S. 742 (1948). Combined with *Lichter* for decision were two other cases from United States courts of appeal.

mental ownership and operation of the plants producing war materials. A refund to the Government of excessive earnings of railroad carriers under the recapture provisions of § 15a of the Transportation Act of 1920, 41 Stat. 488, has been sustained by this Court. *Dayton-Goose Creek R. Co. v. United States*, 263 U.S. 456. The collection of renegotiated excessive profits on a war subcontract also is not in the nature of a penalty and is not a deprivation of a subcontractor of his property without due process of law in violation of the Fifth Amendment.[318]

In both *Gelfert* and *Lichter* measurement of the excess in the hands of the creditor was judgmental. Should the worth of the mortgaged property in *Gelfert* be overvalued, or the extent of the excess profits in *Lichter* be misjudged as greater than the actual amount, theoretically there would be some taking. However, the judicial process was to be trusted in the one instance, while in the other the administrative process satisfied procedural due process when accompanied by the availability of redetermination in the Tax Court. Even were a factual taking shown it would surely not rise to an unconstitutional taking.

"In 1977, for the first time in nearly forty years, the Court invalidated a state law as violating the Contract Clause, in *United States Trust Co. v. New Jersey*, 431 U.S. 1. The prevailing opinion in the 4 to 3 decision was by Justice Blackmun. Justice Brennan, joined by Justices White and Marshall, submitted a vehement dissent."[319] The contract took the form of a covenant in legislative form between the States of New York and New Jersey and "holders of any affected bonds" that indebtedness incurred to construct the World Trade Center and to purchase the Hudson-Manhattan Railroad would be secured by rentals, tolls, and other revenues of the Port Authority without diversion to financing mass transit. Twelve years later the two States repudiated the covenant by legislative repeal in response to pressures that the Authority participate in efforts to solve the overriding transportation problem.

For the majority Justice Blackmun, recognizing that the Contract Clause was no longer accorded rigid interpretation yet continued to yield some protection of "property interests" in Contract, took *Blaisdell* and *El Paso*[320] as the guides for finding the dividing line between permissible and impermissible impairments. "The extent of impairment is certainly a relevant factor in determining its reasonableness. But we cannot sustain the repeal of the 1962 covenant simply because the bondholders' rights were not totally destroyed."[321] "It was with full knowledge of these concerns [the pressures to involve the Port

---

318. *Id.* at 787-88.

319. Quoting G. GUNTHER, CONSTITUTIONAL LAW 562 (10th ed. 1980). Not only had it been 40 years since invalidation under the Contract Clause, it had been 30 years since major litigation on any aspect of "taking" except for Armstrong v. United States, 364 U.S. 40 (1960) ("taking" violating Fifth Amendment just compensation clause found by split Court).

320. *Blaisdell* is considered earlier in this segment, *El Paso* in that on *Buyer-Seller Relationships*, of the present chapter.

321. United States Trust Co. v. New Jersey, 431 U.S. at 27.

Authority in mass transit] that the 1962 covenant was adopted. Indeed, the covenant was specifically intended to protect the pledged revenues and reserves against the possibility that such concerns would lead the Port Authority into greater involvement in deficit mass transit."[322]

"The Court rightly held," concludes Professor Epstein, "that in this 'financial' matter the state was free to make a binding contract limiting its own power, since the state had other available means to subsidize the growth of mass transit without placing a special burden on the bondholders. . . . There is no reason to allow the state to trick a group of individuals into parting with money on one set of conditions only to find that it is bound by another."[323] But while critic Epstein agrees with the result in *United States Trust Co.*, the opinion "is far too muddy in leaving open the possibility that contracts could be impaired if the impairment were 'reasonable and necessary' to accomplish some important public purpose. . . . The proper approach in such cases is for the state to condemn the covenant if it wishes, paying just compensation for what it takes."[324]

At three points in his dissent Justice Brennan contended that the impact of the repeal on the bondholders was minimal. Twice the basis of contention was analysis of the factual background in the case itself, aided by reference to the judgments of the New Jersey courts that had found no unconstitutional impairment.[325] In the other instance, his conclusion derived from comparison of this case with prior decisions on the "modern" Contract Clause.[326] But what gave vehemency to the dissent was the portion in which he detected a fundamental alteration in Court philosophy.[327] For one thing "today's decision is markedly out of step with this deferential philosophy" present in earlier Contract Clause decisions commencing with *Blaisdell*. One senses that the Justice does not mind Court employment of the balancing test as long as it almost always results in favor of Government; he is irritated because here to his way of thinking the test misfired.

But this is only prelude to his concern that the majority is retrogressing to the "heyday of economic due process associated with *Lochner v. New York* . . . and similar cases long since discarded . . . [where] this Court treated 'the liberty of contract' under the Due Process Clause as virtually indistinguishable from the Contract Clause."[328] Recall that the year of this decision was not

---

322. *Id.* at 31-32. The bracketed phrase is taken from the sentence immediately preceding.

323. Epstein, *supra* note 284, at 720-21.

324. *Id.* at 720, n. 45.

325. United States Trust Co. v. New Jersey, 431 U.S. at 41-44, 61-62 (dissent).

326. *Id.* at 55-58.

327. *Id.* at 59-61.

328. *Id.* at 61.

overly far removed from *Ferguson v. Skrupa*,[329] wherein Justice Black offici-
ated at the presumably final interment of substantive due process. One can
almost see Justice Brennan in terror at the prospect of the supposedly deceased
ogre rising from its copper coffin in the midst of the solemn burial proceedings!

> In more recent times, however, the Court wisely has come to embrace a coherent,
> unified interpretation of all such constitutional provisions, and has granted wide
> latitude to "a valid exercise of [the States'] police powers," *Goldblatt* v. *Hempstead*,
> 369 U.S. 590, 592 (1962), even if it results in severe violations of property rights.
> See *Pittsburgh* v. *Alco Parking Corp.*, 417 U.S. 369 (1974); *Sproles* v. *Binford*, 286
> U.S. 374, 388-389 (1932); *Miller* v. *Schoene*, 276 U.S. 272, 279-280 (1928); cf.
> *Williamson* v. *Lee Optical Co.*, 348 U.S. 483, 488 (1955). If today's case signals
> a return to substantive constitutional review of States' policies, and a new resolve
> to protect property owners whose interest or circumstances may happen to appeal
> to Members of this Court, then more than the citizens of New Jersey and New
> York will be the losers.[330]

Despite their concern in the Port Authority case that the Court was in the
process of reverting to Lochnerism, Justice Brennan and his two colleagues
went along with Justice Blackmun who drew the assignment to write the opinion in *Webb's Fabulous Pharmacies, Inc. v. Beckwith*.[331] The Court was unanimous that a Florida statute transgressed the Fourteenth Amendment in attempting to vest in a county rights to interest on monies deposited in the
registry of the county court pursuant to interpleader. At the closing of an
agreement by Eckerd's to purchase essentially all the assets of Webb's Fabulous Pharmacies it appeared that the latter's debts were greater than the purchase price. With this disclosure Eckerd's filed in the circuit court of Seminole
County a complaint interpleading both Webb's and Webb's creditors and
tendering the purchase price to Beckwith, the clerk of that court.

After court appointment of a receiver for Webb's, that officer successfully
moved for transfer to him of the principal amount in the registry less the
clerk's statutory fee; but interest on the principal, now aggregating more than
$100,000, was retained by the clerk under claim of ownership. The receiver
then moved the court to direct payment to him of this amount. Ruling favorably to the receiver, the court declared that Webb's creditors, not the clerk or
the county, were the rightful parties entitled to this accumulated interest.
However, on appeal the supreme court of Florida reversed the circuit court,

---

329. 372 U.S. 726 (1963), for caustic comment on which refer to chap. 6, *supra*, p. 109,
text at notes 79-81.

330. United States Trust Co. v. New Jersey, 431 U.S. at 61. Note especially the citation
of *Miller v. Schoene* at the pages of the Stone opinion criticized in another segment of this
chapter, *supra*, captioned *A Tale of Two Cites*. Criticism of *Lee Optical* appears in chap.
6, *supra*, pp. 107-08, and later in this chapter.

331. 449 U.S. 155 (1980).

rationalizing that while on deposit in the registry the interest was "public money," not "private property." Accordingly, the statute on which Beckwith relied was held constitutional.

Justice Blackmun came quickly to the conclusion that the statute effected an unconstitutional expropriation.

> Neither the Florida Legislature by statute, nor the Florida courts by judicial decree, may accomplish the result the county seeks simply by recharacterizing the principal as "public money" because it is held temporarily by the court. The earnings of a fund are incidents of ownership of the fund itself and are property just as the fund itself is property. The state statute has the practical effect of appropriating for the county the value of the use of the fund for the period in which it is held in the registry.[332]

Clearly, Beckwith's claim to the interest on behalf of the court registry and the county was irrational; the money "belonged" to the creditors. There was no disagreement among the Justices; the Florida law was invalid. It was a case for invocation of substantive due process if ever there was one. But no, continued Justice Blackmun,

> To put it another way: a State, by *ipse dixit*, may not transform private property into public property without compensation, even for the limited duration of the deposit in court. This is the very kind of thing that the Taking Clause of the Fifth Amendment was meant to prevent. That Clause stands as a shield against the arbitrary use of governmental power.[333]

As though the Due Process Clauses had not served this function over time! The "Taking Clause of the Fifth Amendment" was of course inapplicable on the facts of *Webb*'s; only because this guaranty has been read into the Due Process Clause of the Fourteenth Amendment was it relevant to the decision. Even then the remedy under the Taking Clause, award of just compensation, made no sense in this case; the appropriate remedy, which the Court invoked, was that of nullification under due process of law. It is true these anomalies did not here cause any miscarriage in result and yet they make the Court look silly in going to such lengths to avoid grounding the decision on the constitutional provision dictated by pertinent precedent. As long as the Court relies upon substantive due process in resolving civil liberties issues, for which historic basis is less clear, it is ridiculous to play ostrich where precedent runs its roots deep in English as well as American constitutional history.

Legislatively Imputed Relationships

Where factual expropriation is evident there normally must obtain some element of plausible relationship between *A* and *B* to avoid a finding of uncon-

---

332. *Id.* at 164.
333. *Ibid.*

stitutional taking. The early case of *Bowman v. Middleton*[334] is a classic instance of raw, unmitigated transfer of rights in land by legislative fiat in the absence of any apparent justification. A majority of the unreconstructed Supreme Court thought it had come upon another such instance in *Hoeper v. Tax Commission,*[335] wherein Wisconsin sought by statute to tax to Mr. Hoeper the combined income of him and of Mrs. Hoeper, who had brought to their marriage a separate estate. Declared the prevailing opinion

> We have no doubt that, because of the fundamental conceptions which underlie our system, any attempt by a state to measure the tax on one person's property by reference to the property or income of another is contrary to due process of law as guaranteed by the Fourteenth Amendment.[336]

Justice Holmes was correct in dissenting, joined by Justices Brandeis and Stone. "This case cannot be disposed of as an attempt to take from one person's property to pay another person's debts. The statutes are the outcome of a thousand years of history."[337] Under a Constitution recognizing rights in private property there is a limit to taxing one person on a stranger's income; but at common law and since, husband and wife are not strangers to each other.

Two years after *Hoeper* a closely divided Court determined in *Burnet v. Wells*[338] that the limit to governmental power of attribution had not been exceeded. Mr. Wells had created several irrevocable trusts to pay for insurance on his life, the proceeds of the trusts to be paid after his death for the benefit of his dependents. Meantime income from the trust funds was to be used by the trustee to pay the premiums on the insurance. The Commissioner of Internal Revenue assessed to Wells this income which he had failed to report. In the federal court of appeals the settlor was successful in his challenge of the assessments, the court relying on *Hoeper,* but suffered reversal on certiorari. For the bare majority of the Supreme Court Justice Cardozo placed reliance on the distinguishing of *Hoeper* that the Court had made a month before in *Reinecke v. Smith,*[339] as well as on the fact that "the use to be made of the income of the trust was subject, from first to last, to the will of the grantor announced at the beginning."[340] But reliance on *Reinecke* was questionable, for there the settlor held, jointly with the trustee, the power to revoke or modify the trust. The emerging "gang of four" sharply dissented in *Burnet:*

> The powers of taxation are broad, but the distinction between taxation and confiscation must still be observed. So long as the Fifth Amendment remains un-

---

334. 1 Bay (S. C. C. P. 1792), cited chap. 2, *supra*, p. 30, note 3.
335. 284 U.S. 206 (1931).
336. *Id.* at 215.
337. *Id.* at 219.
338. 289 U.S. 670 (1933). An excellent critique of this decision is found in Note, 22 IOWA L. REV. 390 (1937).
339. 289 U.S. 172 (1933).
340. Burnet v. Wells, 289 U.S. at 682.

repealed and is permitted to control, congress may not tax the property of A as the property of B, or the income of A as the income of B.[341]

For several years following, the Court was faced with claims of unconstitutional taking in competitive relationships.[342] In three of five leading decisions these claims were successful. The first in point of time was *Nashville, Chattanooga & St. Louis Ry. v. Walters*.[343] As the carrier conceded, many earlier cases had sustained imposition on railroads of the entire cost of grade separation. Yet here imposition of one-half of the cost was successfully challenged as a violation of substantive due process. Explanation lay in the changing circumstances respecting crossing accidents. In a long opinion replete with economic data, Justice Brandeis for the majority stressed the altered attitude from that of the dangerousness of rail operation to concern for safety on cross-country highways. The particular grade separation in litigation was part of a state-federal plan for a through highway running parallel to the Railroad that would divert carriage to truckers who were paying little toward highway costs compared to heavy taxation of railroads. The underpass in question was not needed for local traffic nor as a feeder to railway traffic. The greater danger now, Justice Brandeis contended, was from high-speed motor vehicle competition. Justices Cardozo and Stone disagreed, but gently, surely because the Court's opinion was by Brandeis himself.

That this decision was something of a judicial aberration is suggested by a later Court ruling involving imposition on the Santa Fe and Southern Pacific railroads of 50% of the cost of grade separations. A completely new complement of Justices upheld the assessments in *Atchison, Topeka & Santa Fe Ry. Co. v. Public Utility Comm*.[344] The opinion of course insisted that *Nashville* was not out of line, that it had been decided on the "special facts" shown which included the keen competition afforded the railroad by highway users. Here considerations of public safety were found to be clearly present.[345] But for all the effort at reconciliation, query whether much remained of Brandeisian concern for the disadvantaged competitor in a "taking" conflict.

Where to lay the blame for the condition of American railroads following World War I will forever be debatable, but that it was economically bad is

---

341. *Id.* at 683.

342. One such instance of competitive relationship had arisen prior to the *Hoeper-Burnet* cases on familial relationships. Ann Arbor Railroad Co. v. United States, 281 U.S. 658 (1930), presented the question of the validity of the Hoch-Smith Resolution of Jan. 30, 1925, whereby Congress sought to aid depressed agriculture by directing the Interstate Commerce Commission to reduce to the lowest possible minimum the rate structure for rail shipments of agricultural products. The Court by exercise of covert review avoided the "serious question" of the constitutionality of this factual taking from carrier for the advantage of shipper.

343. 294 U.S. 405 (1935).

344. 346 U.S. 346 (1953).

345. *Id.* at 353-54.

agreed. The intolerable situation led to inclusion by Congress in the Transportation Act of 1920 of the famous recapture provisions under which one-half of "excess earnings" of the stronger roads were to be captured by the Interstate Commerce Commission for use of these monies in loans to weaker roads as a means of their economic rehabilitation. This taking from As for the benefit of Bs was necessitated by the fact that rates had to be equalized among competing roads. Inevitable challenge of this legislation led to litigation culminating in *Dayton-Goose Creek Ry. Co. v. United States*.[346] Unanimity prevailed in a Court that included Holmes and Brandeis as well as the four Justices who a decade later were for a time to obstruct the New Deal. The opinion sustaining constitutionality was by the genial Chief Justice William Howard Taft; he readily observed that the Court had been "greatly pressed" by the contention that recapture "is a plain appropriation of [carrier] property without any compensation" in violation of Fifth Amendment due process but analysis showed that neither complaining carriers nor shippers were the worse off for the strengthening of the weaker roads to everyone's gain.[347]

When the issue of the validity of the Railroad Retirement Act of 1934 was before the Court in *Railroad Retirement Board v. Alton Railroad Co.*,[348] *Dayton-Goose Creek* figured prominently because of the provisions for pooling monies exacted from the carriers for payment of retirement benefits. It was distinguished by the majority, which found the law unconstitutional.

> This case is relied upon as sustaining the principle underlying the pension act, but we think improperly. The provision was sustained upon the ground that it must be so administered as to leave to each carrier a reasonable return upon its property devoted to transportation, and the holding is clear that if this principle were not observed in administration, the Act would invade constitutional rights.[349]
>
> This court has repeatedly had occasion to say that the railroads, though their property be dedicated to the public use, remain the private property of their owners, and that their assets may not be taken without just compensation. The carriers have not ceased to be privately operated and privately owned, however much subject to regulation in the interest of interstate commerce. There is no warrant for taking the property or money of one and transferring it to another without compensation whether the object of the transfer be to build up the equipment of the transferee or to pension its employees.[350]

However, to the four dissenters, of whom Justice Brandeis was one, *Dayton-Goose Creek* was directly apropos. After asserting its applicability in principle,[351] Chief Justice Hughes, who authored the vigorous dissent, continued:

> A distinction is sought to be made because the carriers, which were required to contribute, were permitted to retain a reasonable return upon their property. But

346. 263 U.S. 456 (1924).
347. *Id.* at 484-85.
348. 295 U.S. 330 (1935).
349. *Id.* at 358.
350. *Id.* at 357.
351. *Id.* at 386 (dissent).

what the strong roads were compelled to contribute were their own earnings resulting from just and reasonable rates—earnings which they were as clearly entitled to retain for their own benefit as the moneys which in the present instance are to be devoted to retirement allowances. The fact that the recapture provisions failed of their purpose and have been abandoned does not disturb the decision as to constitutional power.[352]

In contrast is a frequently overlooked decision of 1937 in which the still unreconstructed Court was fully agreed in finding an invalid taking from *A* for *B*'s benefit. The instance was *Thompson v. Consolidated Gas Utilities Corp.*[353] where the Texas Railroad Commission had decreed that vertically integrated oil companies must on certain conditions allow the use of their pipelines by non-integrated independent producers. "[T]he sole purpose of the limitation which the order imposes upon the plaintiff's production is to compel those who may legally produce, because they have market outlets for permitted uses, to purchase gas from potential producers whom the statute prohibits from producing because they lack such a market for their possible product."[354] As a consequence Consolidated's allowable volume of natural gas would be reduced below its own requirements resulting from ownership of pipeline facilities and possession of advantageous marketing contracts. The reaction of a unanimous Court, through Justice Brandeis, was terse. "Our law reports present no more glaring instance of the taking of one man's property and giving it to another."[355]

In point of time, *Thompson* was sandwiched between two Court decisions respecting challenges to state unemployment insurance laws. Wisconsin had pioneered this new concept in legislation with an enactment of 1932 imposing upon industrial employers a payroll tax the proceeds of which were to be disbursed in relief of unemployment among those formerly employed by them. While the proceeds were earmarked for a common fund, each covered employer was assigned his separate account to which were charged payments made to his own ex-employees. However, some of the states that followed Wisconsin, including Alabama and New York, adopted a pooled-fund arrangement whereunder benefits were to be paid eligible employees irrespective of their former employers. This legislative disregard of the unemployment experience of individual employers precipitated claims of invalidity under Due Process and Equal Protection of the Fourteenth Amendment. The New York law of 1935 was challenged in three suits consolidated for decision under the style of *W. H. H. Chamberlin, Inc. v. Andrews, Industrial Commissioner.*[356] The New York court of appeals sustained the law, two of seven judges dissenting.

---

352. *Ibid.*
353. 300 U.S. 55 (1937).
354. *Id.* at 77.
355. *Id.* at 79.
356. 271 N.Y. 1, 2 N.E. 2d 22 (1936).

On appeal, *"Per Curiam:* The judgments in these cases are severally affirmed by an equally divided Court."[357]

Explanation for this 4 to 4 result is found in the fact that Justice Stone was absent from the Bench at the time of argument and decision in *Chamberlin.* But he was present for consideration of the attack on the Alabama law by Gulf States Paper Corp. and Southern Coal & Coke Co. in *Carmichael v. Southern Coal Co.*[358] and wrote the opinion that broke the tie in the divided Court. Speaking for himself and two of the other Justices in disagreement, Justice Southerland declared that

> from the constitutional point of view, in so far as it involves the ground upon which I think the Alabama act should be condemned, I entertain no doubt that the Wisconsin plan is so fair, reasonable and just as to make plain its constitutionality; and that the Alabama statute, like the New York statute involved in *Chamberlin, Inc. v. Andrews,* 299 U.S. 515, affirmed by an equally-divided court during the present term, is so arbitrary as to result in a denial both of due process and equal protection of the laws.[359]

However, a differing view carried the day despite the contention of counsel of both corporations that, as concisely put for Southern Coal & Coke, "[t]he State Act takes private property from one class for the use of another. . . ."[360] For present analysis the gist of Stone's long opinion is found in Part Third of *"Validity of the Tax Under the Fourteenth Amendment."*

> *Third. Want of Relationship Between the Subjects and Benefits of the Tax.* It is not a valid objection to the present tax, conforming in other respects to the Fourteenth Amendment, and devoted to a public purpose, that the benefits paid and the persons to whom they are paid are unrelated to the persons taxed and the amount of the tax which they pay—in short, that those who pay the tax may not have contributed to the unemployment and may not be benefited by the expenditure.[361]
> . . . .
> Even if a legislature should undertake, what the Constitution does not require, to place the burden of a tax for unemployment benefits upon those who cause or contribute to unemployment, it might conclude that the burden cannot justly be apportioned among employers according to their unemployment experience. Unemployment in the plant of one employer may be due to competition with another, within or without the state, whose factory is running to capacity; or to tariffs, inventions, changes in fashions or in market or business conditions, for which no employer is responsible, but which may stimulate the business of one and impair or even destroy that of another. Many believe that the responsibility for the business cycle, the chief cause of unemployment, cannot be apportioned to individual em-

---

357. Chamberlin v. Andrews, 299 U.S. 515 (1936).
358. 301 U.S. 495 (1937).
359. *Id.* at 531 (dissent).
360. *Id.* at 499.
361. *Id.* at 521 (majority opinion).

ployers in accordance with their employment experience; that a business may be least responsible for the depression from which it suffers the most.[362]

Chamberlin, Thompson, and Carmichael were decided on the eve of the Rooseveltian "reconstruction of the Supreme Court." By early 1938 Justices Sutherland and Van Devanter had retired, Justices Black and Reed appointed and confirmed. Justice Brandeis remained, as did Justices Butler and Mc-Reynolds. Alteration in constitutional position had thus commenced and yet Court personnel was for the interim a mixture of old and new. The President's plan for augmentation of the number on the High Court, designed to introduce "new blood," had been rejected by Congress but although he had lost that battle time was on his side. It was in this milieu that the Court heard argument and decided *New York Rapid Transit Corp. v. City of New York.*[363] The tax was one on gross receipts, revenues to be segregated for the exclusive purpose of "relieving the people of the City of New York from the hardships and suffering caused by unemployment." Once again the facts presented the classic pattern of factual taking from *A* for *B*, *A*s being the local public utilities and *B*s the City's victims of the Great Depression. The opinion of the Court unanimously sustaining the tax, challenged as violative of the Contract Clause and of the Due Process and Equal Protection Clauses of the Fourteenth Amendment, was devoted to the contentions of unequal protection and impairment of the Transit Corporation's fateful five-cent-fare contract with the City. The due process claim received short shrift; the finding of no denial of equal protection "also disposes of the Corporation's contention that the Local Laws constitute a deprivation of due process, as being measured without regard to the net income of or ruinous effect on the taxpayers, and as laying on a particular class a burden which should be borne by all."[364]

New York Rapid Transit was a case in which the relationship between *A* and *B* was more tenuous than in any prior situations. Absent was even the attenuated nexus supporting unemployment insurance laws of the pooled-fund type. The fictitious rule in tax adjudication that the object of an exaction is always revenue enabled the Court to play ostrich to the obvious fact that here the purpose of raising the funds was to devote the proceeds to relief of those forced out of employment by business stagnation. The admittedly heavy burden of the tax, as compared with that on other businesses, together with the absence of any evidence that blame for the economic depression attached peculiarly to public utilities, made a strong case of invalid taking but for the judicial blinders. However, as an instance of "taking" it was poorly argued on behalf of the Transit Company. In the Jurisdictional Section on Statement and Specification and Error appellant's Brief did specify deprivation of due pro-

---

362. *Id.* at 523-24. R. EPSTEIN, *op. cit. supra* note 159, at 311-12, is critical of the Stone opinion in *Carmichael* for its "sell-out" to the police power.

363. 303 U.S. 573 (1938).

364. *Id.* at 587.

cess as well as violation of the Contract and Equal Protection Clauses.[365] Yet in the Argument, Points I and II dealt solely with aspects of alleged unequal treatment by the taxing law[366] while Point III was devoted entirely to assertions of impairment of the obligation of the contract between the corporation and the city under Article I, Sec. 10.[367] Only in a passing observation in the course of contentions regarding the absence of equal protection was there even a glimmer of sensitivity to the taking aspect. The Court's opinion clearly reflected counsel's failure to develop a due process argument. The other issues, especially under Equal Protection, were significant on the facts but in totality the advocacy was faulty nevertheless.

Statutes in half the States, requiring "pay for voting," at bottom involve a similarly strained relation. True, they represent alleged police power enactments, imposing on employers not only the burden of released time for employee voting but as well recompensing them for time not worked, thus shallowly appearing as a facet of the employment connection. In sustaining one of these laws in *Day-Brite Lighting, Inc. v. Missouri*,[368] Justice Douglas for the Court majority relied upon superficiality in analogizing the statute to minimum wage legislation for women. "The present statute contains in form a minimum wage requirement."[369] This attenuated reasoning was too much for Justice Jackson who in dissent insisted that "there must be some limit to the power to shift the whole voting burden from the voter to someone else who happens to stand in some economic relationship to him."[370] Realism compels recognition that the "economic relationship" alleged here was solely a convenient handle for enforcement of a policy of enticement to exercise of the franchise; it is but a handy means to an end unrelated to the tie of employer-employee. Shed of disguise, *Day-Brite* gave constitutional blessing to legislative expropriation on the slender basis of civic relationship without reliance on any judicial blindfold such as that invoked in the tax cases.

With *Day-Brite* most anything could survive constitutional attack. Even the much heavier economic burden imposed on employers by legislative requirement that for jury duty employees be reimbursed at their regular wage rate, less compensation for service as juror, received scant consideration. In a short *per curiam* opinion, *Dean v. Gadsden Times Publishing Co.*,[371] the Court reversed the Alabama court of civil appeals that had invalidated the law as conflicting with the due process and equal protection guarantees of the Four-

---

365. Brief for Appellant, Rapid Transit Corp. v. New York, 303 U.S. 573, Record, Microfiche, card 4, at 2, 15.

366. *Id.* at 17-60.

367. *Id.* at 60-93.

368. 342 U.S. 421 (1952), vigorously criticized *supra* chap. 6, pp. 107-08, text from note 70 through note 75.

369. *Id.* at 423-24.

370. *Id.* at 427.

371. 412 U.S. 543 (1973).

teenth Amendment. By predicating its decision on the federal Constitution the Alabama court laid its action open to certain reversal. From this experience it will learn, as other state courts are learning, to base its determinations on its own reading of similarly worded provisions in the Alabama constitution, a procedure that can insulate those determinations under the adequate and independent state ground rule.[372]

Limitation of the liability of a private atomic power plant, in the event of a "nuclear incident," presented a fact pattern roughly the converse of that in *New York Rapid Transit*. The congressional amendment of the Atomic Energy Act "takes" from residents surrounding these plants their rights under state tort law in order to induce private enterprise to undertake the production of electric power by nuclear fission. In the earlier case the taking was from utility stockholders for the benefit of the unemployed; here the taking is from those in the path of nuclear disaster for the enticement of utility investors. Initially, challenge to the $560 million limit for any single incident was successful. In the Western District of North Carolina, before Judge James McMillan, the Carolina Environmental Study Group won declaratory relief against the Atomic Energy Commission.[373] Satisfied that plaintiffs had standing, Judge McMillan held the Price-Anderson Act invalid on substantive due process grounds, with added reasons under Equal Protection. "The Act violates the Due Process Clause because it allows the destruction of the property or the lives of those affected by nuclear catastrophe without reasonable certainty that the victims will be justly compensated."[374] Defendant reliance on the reasoning of "an exchange of burdens and benefits," citing *New York Central Railroad Co. v. White*,[375] which seemed apropos, was rejected by Judge McMillan. "There is no *quid pro quo*,"[376] he declared, specifying nine reasons for this conclusion. The last of these concerned the statutory proviso that, were a nuclear accident to cause damage beyond the liability limit, Congress "will take whatever action is deemed necessary and appropriate to protect the public from the consequences of a disaster of such magnitude." To this the Judge responded "Mr. Micawber would like that idea."[377]

On direct appeal, however, the trial court was reversed. *Duke Power Co. v. Carolina Environmental Study Group, Inc.*[378] A third of the Court was rightly

---

372. Greenhalgh, *Independent and Adequate State Grounds*, in DEVELOPMENTS IN STATE CONSTITUTIONAL LAW chap. 8 (1985) (Williamsburg Conference of March 9-10, 1984); State v. Jewett, 500 A. 2d 233 (Vt. 1985).

373. Carolina Environmental Study Group v. United States Atomic Energy Comm., 431 F. Supp. 203 (W. D. N. C. 1977).

374. *Id.* at 222.

375. 243 U.S. 188 (1917), quoted at length textually in the segment of this chapter, *supra*, pp. 139-40, note 112, styled *Employer-Employee Relationships*.

376. Carolina Environmental Study Group v. United States Atomic Energy Comm., 431 F. Supp. at 223.

377. *Id.* at 224.

378. 438 U.S. 59 (1978).

troubled over the standing issue, but the Chief Justice powered his way over that hurdle to reach and resolve the substantive question without dissent. A closing paragraph catches the essence of the opinion.

> In the course of adjudicating a similar challenge to the Workmen's Compensation Act in *New York Central R. Co. v. White*, 243 U.S., at 201, the Court observed that the Due Process Clause of the Fourteenth Amendment was not violated simply because an injured party would not be able to recover as much under the Act as before its enactment. "[H]e is entitled to moderate compensation in all cases of injury and has a certain and speedy remedy without the difficulty and expense of establishing negligence or proving the amount of the damages." The logic of *New York Central* would seem to apply with renewed force in the context of this challenge to the Price-Anderson Act. The Price-Anderson Act not only provides a reasonable, prompt, and equitable mechanism for compensating victims of a catastrophic nuclear incident, it also guarantees a level of net compensation generally exceeding that recoverable in private litigation. Moreover, the Act contains an explicit congressional commitment to take further action to aid victims of a nuclear accident in the event that the $560 million ceiling on liability is exceeded. This panoply of remedies and guarantees is at the least a reasonably just substitute for the common-law rights replaced by the Price-Anderson Act. Nothing more is required by the Due Process Clause.[379]

Fortunately for all, the country has been spared the tragedy of a nuclear disaster resulting from meltdown of an atomic plant. Three-Mile-Island came close; hopefully, lessons from that near catastrophe lessen the Damoclean threat. Moreover, economic developments are discouraging the bringing on line of additional nuclear plants; even some projects underway at the cost of millions of dollars have been abandoned. The ultimate employment of new technology for substitution of fossil fuel lies in fusion rather than fission of the atom, thereby avoiding exceptional hazard to the public safety. Thus, there has been no "taking" of life or property in this context, with increasing likelihood there never will be. Absence of any factual taking renders moot the issue of unconstitutional taking. In this view the judgment of the Supreme Court was correct on the merits. But this very mootness undercuts the base for Court assumption of jurisdiction. No wonder the Chief Justice felt it incumbent on him to devote to the jurisdictional question three of the four Parts of his opinion. The result enhances one's skepticism as to whether the "rules" supposedly governing the Court's employment of its adjudicating power have any firm basis in constitutional design. District Judge McMillan's perspective in this litigation, on the basis of which he found an unconstitutional taking, provided sounder ground for justifying the exercise of federal judicial power. The Supreme Court's tight-rope act would not have been convincing as a circus performance. Circumstances simply mandated reaching the "right" result however rough the jurisprudential terrain.

---

379. *Id.* at 92-93. The above analysis was written before the Chernobyl disaster.

Because "the Price-Anderson Act does, in our view, provide a reasonably just substitute for the common-law or state tort law remedies it replaces," the Court in *Duke Power* said it did not need to resolve the question whether a satisfactory *quid pro quo* is constitutionally necessary.[380] Recent state legislation capping damage awards in medical malpractice suits does, however, pose this issue. In this context there is no provision of a specific remedy for the party negligently injured. Left to that party in place of the full measure of damages as determined by a jury is the satisfaction of preservation of the traditional compensatory system in tort believed threatened by escalating malpractice insurance rates that induce or force diminution in the ranks of medical specialists. Thus the offset provided does not save the injured party harmless in any direct sense; its benefits run not to those now seeking full recovery but to other claimants who may thereby be protected against inability to secure any private recovery at all. It scarcely qualifies in the usual understanding of trade-off. Assertion, therefore, that there is a fair substitute on analogy to workers' compensation legislation is unpersuasive.

The supreme court of Illinois first burst this bubble in a paragraph so convincing as to be quoted verbatim by the supreme court of New Hampshire.

> Defendants argue that there is a societal *quid pro quo* in that the loss of recovery potential to some malpractice victims is offset by "lower insurance premiums and lower medical care costs for all recipients of medical care." This *quid pro quo* does not extend to the seriously injured medical malpractice victim and does not serve to bring the limited recovery provision within the rationale of the cases upholding the constitutionality of the Workmen's Compensation Act.[381]

At the same time neither court, Illinois categorically and New Hampshire by inference, committed itself to the proposition, as stated by the former, "that under no circumstances may the General Assembly abolish a common law cause of action without a concomitant *quid pro quo*." Similar reservation has been make by the supreme court of North Dakota:

> We do not hold, or even suggest, that no right may be limited or withdrawn without providing a quid pro quo. Ohio says that such a quid pro quo must be given, but Idaho, Wisconsin, and Nebraska disagree.[382]

In the presence of a demonstrably adequate *quid pro quo* there can be no factual taking, *a fortiori* no unconstitutional legislative "transfer" from A for

---

380. Duke Power Co. v. Carolina Environmental Study Group, Inc., 438 U.S. at 88.

381. Wright v. Central Du Page Hospital Assoc., 63 Ill. 2d 313, 328, 347 N.E. 2d 736, 742 (1976). Adoption by the New Hampshire supreme court appears in Carson v. Maurer, 120 N.H. 925, 943, 424 A. 2d 825, 837-38 (1980).

382. Arneson v. Olson, 270 N.W. 2d 125, 134 (N. D. 1978). Citations to the four cited cases follow: Simon v. St. Elizabeth Medical Center, 3 Ohio Ops. 3d 164, 170, 355 N.E. 2d 903, 910 (Com. Pl. 1976); Jones v. State Board of Medicine, 97 Idaho 859, 869, 555 P. 2d 399, 409 (1976); State ex rel. Strykowski v. Wilkie, 81 Wis. 2d 491, 520, 261 N.W. 2d 434, 447-448 (1978); Prendergast v. Nelson, 199 Neb. 97, 120, 256 N.W. 2d 657, 671 (1977) (but quid pro quo found in assurance of collectibility of any judgment recovered).

B's benefit. But absent that balance an invalid taking may be present. As observed by a Texas court of appeals, "it is safe to reflect, we think, that where a true quid pro quo does exist, it strengthens the statute's constitutionality."[383] Resort to the post-*Nebbia* test of rational nexus where economic interests are involved in constitutional adjudication provides a means of short-circuiting assertions of "taking" violative of substantive due process. Decisions of the supreme court of California, *Fein v. Permanente Medical Group,*[384] and of the high court of Indiana, *Johnson v. St. Vincent Hospital, Inc.,*[385] are illustrative. Satisfied that the state limitation law "is achieving its intended goal" of "preserving the availability of health care services . . . to the benefit of the entire community including the badly injured plaintiff," the Indiana court concluded:

> Accordingly, we find that the limitations upon patient recoveries is [sic] not arbitrary and irrational, but furthers [sic] the public purposes of the Act in a manner consistent with due process of law guaranteed by our state and federal constitutions.[386]

Appeal of the California decision to the Supreme Court of the United States was dismissed "for want of a substantial federal question," Justice White alone dissenting.[387]

However, these validations of state capping laws have been achieved on the flimsy basis provided by the perversion of Substantive Due Process heretofore criticized.[388] The state courts that have invalidated similar statutes, usually on denial of Equal Protection provisions of State and/or Federal Constitutions,[389] have faced up to a concern over constitutionality reflected in Justice White's conclusion "that the federal question presented by this appeal is substantial."[390] Analysis on the basis of the core principle resident in expropriative

---

383. Baptist Hospital of Southeast Texas, Inc. v. Baber, 672 S. W. 2d 296, 298 (C.A. Tex. 1984).

384. 38 Cal. 3d 137, 695 P. 2d 665 (1985).

385. 273 Ind. 374, 404 N.E. 2d 585 (1980).

386. *Id.* at 396, 404 N.E. 2d at 599.

387. Fein v. Permanente Medical Group, 106 Sup. Ct. 214 (Oct. 15, 1985).

388. Refer to chap. 6, *supra.*

389. Arneson v. Olson, *supra* note 382, is unusual in that, while holding the North Dakota law invalid under the equal protection clauses of both State and Federal Constitutions, 270 N.W. 2d at 136, the opinion opened with the declaration that "North Dakota has never renounced substantive due process as a constitutional standard," the Supreme Court to the contrary. *Id.* at 132.

390. This concern is well expressed in *Carson v. Maurer,* cited *supra* note 381, where the court, overruling its prior view, concluded that "rights involved herein are sufficiently important to require that the restrictions imposed on these rights be subjected to a more rigorous judicial scrutiny than allowed under the rational basis test." 120 N.H. at 932, 424 A. 2d at 830. The court realized that its position differed from that of the Supreme Court but "we are not confined to federal constitutional standards and are free to grant individuals more rights than the Federal Constitution requires." *Id.* at 932, 424 A. 2d at 831. In the *Fein* case from California, the appeal of which the Supreme Court dismissed,

due process discloses unusual uncertainty in determining presence or absence of a true *quid pro quo*.

Immediately presenting itself is the quality of the property right possessed by the negligently injured party. The right to recover damages for injuries arising from medical malpractice existed at common law. However, a common-law right is not free from legislative modification; one office of statutes is that of altering the product of judicial law making. Guest statutes have been sustained on the ground that "the Constitution does not forbid the creation of new rights, or the abolition of old ones recognized by the common law, to attain a permissible objective."[391] The California statute capping damages was in effect prior to Fein's first chest pain; there could, therefore, be no upsetting of settled expectations concerning extensive damages for the negligence that later intervened by reason of faulty medical diagnosis. Had Fein been awarded full damages prior to the statute's enactment, he would have had a vested interest rating high on a scale of property rights. The "right" being one of remedy, it is otherwise subject to adjustment although not to the extent of destruction. *Duke Power* is not a precedent for total extinction of this kind of economic interest.

None of the capping statutes denies all relief, as was true of the guest statutes and those denying remedy for alienation of affections. The caps range in monetary measure from $200,000 to $500,000. Magnitude of "taking" cannot be judged from dollar figures, however; the statutes vary in coverage of categories of damages and in patterns of jury largesse. The California law set the limit of noneconomic loss at $250,000; the jury award for this type of recompense was $500,000, thus requiring a 50 percent cut back. Legislative caps of lesser or greater maxima could result in greater or lesser taking depending upon the amounts of award, the ages of the injured, and the degrees of their incapacitation. In any event the higher awards would experience the most severe diminutions. It is these features of across-the-board limitations on recovery that have led several state courts to invalidate on grounds of equal protection, or functionally equivalent, constitutional provision. Reducing an award by one-half from the judgment of the jury nears the limit of validity if it does not "go too far" in instances of total permanent disablement.

In instances of medical malpractice the originating relationship of physician-patient has a personal and professional cast quite at variance with the relationships present in the situations so far considered save for that involving immediate family. The situation alters drastically when the association sours by reason of the physician's negligence. *A* then has at common law a right to full adjudicated damages from *B*. By statute, however, *B* has a liberty to de-

---

Chief Justice Bird and Justice Mosk were of similar view to that in *Carson,* the latter expressing vigorous irritation at the two-tier adjudicative framework of either rational nexus or strict scrutiny.

391. Silver v. Silver, 280 U.S. 117, at 122 (1929).

cline payment beyond the maximum legislatively set, leaving *A* powerless to recover the remainder of the damages judicially fixed.[392] There is thus fashioned an imputed relationship by which *A* is required to assume a portion of *B*'s responsibility. It is not the situation where the legislative (or judicial) branch replaces contributory negligence with comparative negligence, for there the premise is that *A* has been partially to blame for the negligent behavior and, therefore, *B* should not be forced to carry the total burden.[393]

Imputing this "reverse" relationship in medical malpractice cases is not easy to vindicate. *A*'s responsibility seems as far-fetched as that of the New York public utilities in *New York Rapid Transit*. With *Day-Brite Lighting* legislative imputation of relationship is in effect without limit but state courts could be expected to follow Justice Jackson in calling a halt short of such extreme. Only an unquestioned crisis in health care provision in a particular state would provide a strand of connection supporting the imputed relationship in the malpractice context. Analogy would have to be traced through Holmes' exception in *Pennsylvania Coal Co.*—demolition of a structure to stop a conflagration—back to the *Case of Salt Petre* in the time of Coke.[394]

What Price the Avoidance of Expropriative Due Process?

Review of Supreme Court cases of the past forty-five years discloses the lengths to which the reconstructed Court has gone to avoid decision on the basis of substantive due process where alleged expropriation of property values has been at issue. Resurrection of the Contract Clause and the "dusting off" of the Taking Clause have provided the major substitutes for adjudication. The headlong quest for purification from "tarnished" Due Process has produced strained, if not erroneous, results. For those on Court and off who glory in this circumvention the price has of course been of no concern. The end is felt to justify the means. But from the point of view of responsible juridical constitutionalism the picture is not satisfying.

---

392. Allegations of violation of separation of powers do not appear noticeably in response to legislative capping of damage awards in medical malpractice litigation as they have in cases of legislative "tampering" with traditional judicial power to determine criminal sentencing after conviction—as for example with mandatory imprisonment for drinking or drug violations.

393. Although published prior to the recent wave of capping statutes, *Comment*, 1975 DUKE L. J. 1417, contributes materially to identification of considerations relevant to analysis under expropriative due process.

394. That episode in English antecedents is related in chap. 1, *supra*, pp. 15-16. In the present chapter there is reference to the *Case* in the course of commentary on the opinion of Justice Stone in *Miller v. Schoene*, *supra*, p. 159, and of Chief Justice Hughes in *Perry v. United States*, *supra*, p. 180.

Justice Black's attempted return in *El Paso*[395] to the early rigidity of the Contract Clause was ill fated. Nearly a century of *Stone v. Mississippi* made impossible a return to the Marshallian stance. Insistence on extreme and outmoded doctrine made the Justice's position so untenable as to be wide open to rejection. His contention for invalidity would have been much stronger precedentially and psychologically had he based it on the dynamics of substantive due process. But the majority, too, would have done better had it faced the issue head-on in *El Paso*, relying on substantive due process rather than employing the Contract Clause as a front.

As Holmes had seen, *Stone v. Mississippi* did not just open a way around the Contract Clause; it removed the provision from the decisional scene save for four exceptions that by the narrowness of their applications tended to "prove the rule." Possibly a direct approach, uninhibited by contract-related suppositions, would have discouraged the attempt to justify validity in part on the absurd assertion that investors did not weigh heavily the unlimited period for reinstatement. Adjudication would have been far more satisfactory in quality of analysis had all the Justices repudiated the "pledge" not to invoke due process in an economic context. Would that the Court had had the good sense to return to the "model" of *Pennsylvania Coal Co. v. Mahon*, where Justice Holmes passed over the Contract Clause to judge the Company's claim of taking by the time-honored tests for expropriation under substantive due process of law.

In a trio of recent cases the high cost of avoidance has received some attention at the hands of several members of the Court. One of this trilogy was *Allied Structural Steel Co. v. Spannaus*.[396] There Minnesota sought to impose upon any employer of 100 or more employees that had established a pension benefits plan what was denominated a "pension funding charge" if the employer either terminated its plan or closed a Minnesota office. The charge was assessed if the pension funds were not sufficient to cover full pensions for all employees who had worked at least 10 years. Allied's plan, to which it alone contributed but which was terminable by it at any time and for any reason, was not as extensive in its coverage. A few months following the legislative enactment Allied gave notice that it was closing its in-state office, whereupon it was notified of the assessment of a charge of approximately $185,000. Challenge ensued in a federal statutory court, the company claiming that the law unconstitutionally impaired its contractual obligations to its employees under its voluntary pension agreement. Judgment went for the state but the Supreme Court reversed on the ground asserted by Allied.

---

395. El Paso v. Simmons, 379 U.S. 497 (1965), considered in the segment of this chapter, *supra*, pp. 165-67, on *Buyer-Seller Relationships*.

396. 438 U.S. 234 (1978), first considered in this chapter, *supra*, pp. 143-44.

Justice Stewart's opinion for the majority discloses the difficulty of applying the Contract Clause since its undercutting by *Stone v. Mississippi*. On the one hand, "it is to be accepted as a commonplace that the Contract Clause does not operate to obliterate the police power of the States."[397] "Nonetheless, the Contract Clause remains part of the Constitution. It is not a dead letter."[398] Accordingly, "[if] the Contract Clause is to retain any meaning at all . . . it must be understood to impose *some* limits upon the power of a State to abridge existing contractual relationships, even in the exercise of its otherwise legitimate police power."[399] Inquiry must therefore be directed to the substantiality or severity of the impairment. "[The] statute in question here nullifies express terms of the company's contractual obligations and imposes a completely unexpected liability in potentially disabling amounts."[400] Moreover, the law "has an extremely narrow focus"; it "was not even purportedly enacted to deal with a broad, generalized economic or social problem."[401] "It is not necessary to hold that the Minnesota law impaired the obligation of the company's employment contracts 'without moderation or reason or in a spirit of oppression.' "[402] "But we do hold that if the Contract Clause means anything at all, it means that Minnesota could not constitutionally do what it tried to do to the company in this case."[403]

For himself and Justices White and Marshall, Justice Brennan vigorously dissented. To him the Act "was designed to remedy a serious social problem arising from the operation of private pension plans."[404] And "in no sense" did the Act "impose 'sudden and unanticipated' burdens."[405] Primarily, however, Justice Brennan was in fundamental disagreement with the majority's understanding of the reach of the Contract Clause. For him the Minnesota Act did "not implicate the Contract Clause in any way. The basic fallacy of today's decision is its mistaken view that the Contract Clause protects all contract-based expectations, including that of an employer that his obligations to his employess will not be legislatively enlarged beyond those explicitly provided in his pension plan."[406] The law in question did not dilute an obligation, it added one. "In my view, any constitutional infirmity in the law must therefore

---

397. *Id*. at 241.

398. *Ibid*.

399. *Id*. at 242 (emphasis in original).

400. *Id*. at 247.

401. *Id*. at 248, 250.

402. *Id*. at 250. The quoted expression Justice Stewart took from the opinion of Justice Cardozo for the Court in its invalidation of the Arkansas moratorium law in W.B. Worthen Co. v. Kavanaugh, 295 U.S. 56, 60 (1935) ("Not even changes of the remedy may be pressed so far as to cut down the security of a mortgage without moderation or reason or in a spirit of oppression.")

403. *Id*. at 250-51.

404. *Id*. at 252.

405. *Id*. at 254.

406. *Id*. at 255.

derive, not from the Contract Clause, but from the Due Process Clause of the Fourteenth Amendment."[407]

Although Justice Brennan, relying on *Usery v. Turner Elkhorn Mining Co.*,[408] rather summarily asserted "that any claim based on due process has no merit,"[409] he is nevertheless deserving of commendation for pressing on the majority the relevance of Due Process. Indeed, the credit might be doubled, for he made the effort despite repetition in *United States Trust*[410] of his loathing of Lochnerism. He did not allow this antipathy to blind him to the contribution that attention to substantive due process can make in the economic sphere. However, his gesture did not commend itself to five of the Justices. Premising decision on an embracive interpretation of the Contract Clause,[411] the majority forced that constitutional provision to carry the burden of invalidity which could have been more convincingly borne by the due process concept (although clearly not to Justice Brennan's satisfaction). Recognized was the familiar fact of history that "the Contract Clause receded into comparative desuetude with the adoption of the Fourteenth Amendment, and with the development of the large body of jurisprudence under the Due Process Clause of that Amendment in modern constitutional history."[412] However, continued adherence to the double-standard commitment that substantive due process was invocable solely in non-economic litigation prevented resolution of the issue on the more resilient constitutional ground. Miscarriages of this kind can in the end produce only bad jurisprudence.

The question inevitably arises as to why Justice Brennan did not, in the synchronous case of *Penn Central Transportation Co. v. New York City*,[413] take a position comparable to that he took in *Allied*. Under the City's Landmarks Preservation Law Grand Central Terminal had been designated a "landmark" and the block it occupies a "landmark site." Subsequently, as owner of the terminal, Penn Central entered into a lease with Union General Properties, Inc., under which the latter was to construct over the Terminal a multi-story office building. When the Landmarks Preservation Commission rejected plans for this construction Penn Central and UGP, rather than appealing the ruling, sued in a New York supreme court asserting that this application of the Landmarks Law took property without just compensation in violation of the Fifth and Fourteenth Amendments and as well arbitrarily deprived them of prop-

---

407. *Id.* at 251.

408. The citation to *Turner Elkborn* is 428 U.S. 1 (1976).

409. *Id.* at 262-64.

410. United States Trust Co. v. New Jersey, 431 U.S. 1 (1977), considered in the segment of this chapter, *supra*, pp. 182-84, on *Debtor-Creditor Relationships*.

411. The majority position on the reach of the Contract Clause is supported by Epstein, *Toward a Revitalization of the Contract Clause*, 51 U. OF CHI. L. REV. 703, at 722-23 (1984).

412. Allied Structural Steel Co. v. Spannaus, 438 U.S. at 241.

413. 438 U.S. 104 (1978).

erty without due process of law in violation of the Fourteenth. The trial court granted declaratory and injunctive relief but was reversed by the appellate division. To quote the Court in its ultimate review

> The New York Court of Appeals affirmed. 42 N.Y. 2d 324, 366 N.E. 2d 1271 (1977). That court summarily rejected any claim that the Landmarks Law had "taken" property without "just compensation," *id.*, at 329, 366 N.E. 2d at 1274, indicating that there could be no "taking" since the law had not transferred control of the property to the city, but only restricted appellants' exploitation of it. In that circumstance, the Court of Appeals held that appellants' attack on the law could prevail only if the law deprived appellants of their property in violation of the Due Process Clause of the Fourteenth Amendment.[414]

Despite this basis of decision in New York's highest court the Supreme Court formally limited its consideration to the Taking Clause of the Fifth Amendment as incorporated into the Fourteenth Amendment.[415] The Court split 6 to 3 over whether there had been an eminent domain taking. Yet in debate on this issue both majority and dissent cited willy nilly without heed to possible distinction eminent domain cases and due process cases. *Pennsylvania Coal* received attention, distinguished by the majority[416] while found quite apposite by the dissenters.[417]

One can understand why Justice Brennan, who wrote the prevailing opinion holding that the Taking Clause had not been violated, failed to press for analysis on due process grounds; judging from the position of most members of the Court as exhibited in *Allied* he could not have induced four to join him. He could have written separately—presumably a concurring opinion—had he not been foreclosed by a view to be found in a footnote he dropped in his dissent in *Allied*.

> I recognize that the only question presented by appellant is whether the Minnesota Act violates the Contract Clause. See Jurisdictional Statement 2. However, I think that a due process claim is fairly subsumed by the question presented and, under the circumstances, elementary fairness requires that I address the due process claim. This reasoning does not apply to the other possible challenges to the Act— *e.g.*, ones based on the "Taking" Clause or on the Commerce Clause—for these others involve rather different considerations from those involved in the Contract and Due Process Clause analysis.[418]

---

414. *Id.* at 120-21. Note the absence of the term "taking" in reference to Due Process. If Due Process is offended the Court speaks of a deprivation; the term "taking" is employed only with respect to the Taking Clause. This play with words is contrary to usage that prevailed until recent Court revival of some protection for property interests by pressing into service ill-fitting constitutional substitutes for Substantive Due Process. The Court is attempting to stage Hamlet without Hamlet!

415. *Id.* at 122.

416. *Id.* at 130, n. 27.

417. *Id.* at 152.

418. Allied Structural Steel Co. v. Spannaus, 438 U.S. at 262-63, n. 9.

Because the Taking Clause, like the Contract and Due Process provisions, is a type of direct constitutional limitation, there would appear to be no reason why challenge under it could not be "subsumed by the question presented," as readily as under Due Process. The considerations involved would seem no different. With respect to the Commerce Clause, on the other hand, different considerations might well apply because that clause is one of the primary indirect limitations of the Constitution.[419] The objective of limited government is the same but achieved by a distinct route. We are not given any explanation why the Due Process Clause of the Fourteenth Amendment cannot be "fairly subsumed" under the Jurisdictional Statement in *Penn Central* even if properly construed as limited to claims under the Taking Clause.[420] In a very real sense Justice Brennan had for himself and five colleagues introduced due process considerations by placing reliance upon, or distinguishing, so many decisions based on Fourteenth Amendment Due Process rather than on the Taking Clause imported from the Fifth Amendment.[421]

---

419. Use of the terms "direct" and "indirect" constitutional limitation is explained in Strong, *Judicial Review; A Tri-Dimensional Concept of Administrative-Constitutional Law,* 69 W. VA. L. REV. 111 (1967). A similar differentiation between the two major types of constitutional limitation is made by Epstein, *supra* note 411, at 715-17.

Kaiser Aetna v. United States, 444 U.S. 164 (1979), is one of the cases that on analysis involved both the indirect limitation of federalism, which is not a concern in this study, and the direct limitation of substantive due process. In Justice Blackmun's dissent, for himself and Justices Brennan and Marshall, are passages intimating that wherever the National Government's navigational servitude reaches, Congress is empowered to act without hindrance. *Id.* at 187 (full paragraph), 188 (opening sentence of new paragraph). I cannot be certain that the opening sentences of Part III negate this unwarranted view of the Constitution. The majority of six, in opinion by Justice Rehnquist, are clear that the Commerce Clause as a grant of power to Congress is subject to constitutional limitations. For them the more relevant limitation is not the indirect, federalistic one although Justice Blackmun slips into the error of thinking it is, but the direct limitation of the Taking Clause. *Id.* at 172-73 (the sentences commencing on the third line of the text and running two lines over to the next page), 174 (first two sentences under "B"). In my judgment the majority might better have relied on the direct limitation of substantive due process for determining the presence of a taking, which in a sense they did by looking to *Pennsylvania Coal.*

The structure of the American Constitution is again stressed by me in Strong, *Court vs. Constitution,* 54 N.C. L. REV. 125 (1976).

420. The Statement is reproduced, 438 U.S. at 122-23, n. 24.

421. A year after *Penn Central* Justice Brennan wrote for the full Court in Andrus v. Allard, 444 U.S. 51 (1979), which determined the validity of retroactive applications of the Eagle Protection Act and the Migratory Bird Treaty Act. The three-judge district court in which challenge was made held retroactivity unconstitutional in violation of Fifth Amendment economic substantive due process for depriving owners of pre-existing avian artifacts of opportunity to profit from these relics. United States v. Allard, 397 F. Supp. 429 (D. Mont. 1975). On direct appeal however, according to Justice Brennan, "appellees have used the terminology of the Takings Clause." 444 U.S. at 64, n. 21. This shift in basis of attack obliged the Justice, enabling him to avoid predicating reversal on banished grounds. Why counsel adopted this strategy can only be surmised. Probably it was thought wise to

There are signs in the *Penn Central* litigation of misconceptions respecting pertinent constitutional provisions that can cloud judicial vision and possibly skew decisional results. In rejecting out of hand plaintiffs' claim of taking without compensation "since the law had not transferred control of the property to the city," the New York court of appeals was misled by early interpretations of the Taking Clause that required literal appropriation by *B* of property from *A*.[422] This restricted view has been altered by leading cases such as *United States v. Causby*,[423] where continuing intrusion by military planes into the air space above Causby's chicken farm was held to have constituted a taking of Causby's property requiring payment of just compensation. Justice Brennan satisfied himself that that situation arising from United States flight operations during World War II was distinguishable from the fact pattern of *Penn Central*. However, this history of the Taking Clause could cause a warped understanding of that provision's applicability.

This is exactly what happened in *Loretto v. Teleprompter Manhattan CATV Corp.*[424] With the advent of cable television New York enacted a law requiring a landlord to permit a cable television company to install its facilities on the landlord's rental property. The New York courts sustained the statute but a split Supreme Court reversed on a finding of violation of the "Takings Clause." The majority, in an opinion by Justice Marshall, conceded that the intrusion was minor. But this fact was not critical, said he; what was decisive was the fact of permanent physical attachment to the landlord's premises. "Our constitutional history confirms the rule, recent cases do not question it, and the purposes of the Taking Clause compel its retention."[425] By joining, along with Justice White, in Justice Blackmun's dissent, Justice Brennan avoids the majority's errors in interpretation of the Taking Clause yet in so restricting himself he fails to provide the constitutional insight that would come from analysis in terms of Due Process[426]

---

indulge the Court in its hostility toward substantive due process in economic contexts.

However, it is possible counsel's research disclosed that, while at one point in the nineteenth century the essential vice of undue process equated with retroactivity, this doctrine died with *Mugler v. Kansas* and *Powell v. Pennsylvania*. Refer to chap. 2, *supra*, p. 41, text at notes 61 and 62, for full consideration. But resort to the Taking Clause availed nothing. "*Everard's Breweries v. Day*, 265 U.S. 545 (1924), involved a federal statute that forbade the sale of liquors manufactured before passage of the statute. The claim of a taking in violation of the Fifth Amendment was tersely rejected." Andrus v. Allard, 444 U.S. at 67.

422. Pumpelly v. Green Bay Co., 80 U.S. 166 (1871), is often cited as the early embodiment of this reading of the Taking Clause.

423. 328 U.S. 256 (1946).

424. 458 U.S. 419 (1982).

425. *Id.* at 426.

426. A notator has observed that "something seems wrong when that same doctrine [the special preciousness of the right to possess, use, and dispose] compensates a landlord for losing the use of one-eighth of a cubic foot of space on her building but denies compensation to another owner who has lost the right to develop (at substantial profit) the airspace

The Taking Clause is of immense significance for it is *the* constitutional provision that bottoms the right of private property. By clear implication private property may not be taken by government for private use. If taken for public use the owner is to receive just compensation. However, the Clause gives no hint as to what constitutes a "taking"; it only decrees the protection of private property from uncompensated taking. In this respect it functions much as does the Tenth Amendment, which postulates a federal government but gives no indication of the division between federal and state powers. As I have shown,[427] historically it has been substantive due process that has drawn the line between taking and nontaking. Holmes grasped this constitutional fundamental by his differentiation between petty larceny of the police power and governmental intrusion that goes too far and thereby becomes a taking which must be compensated to be constitutional. Police Power and Due Process are in continuous counterpoise, determining the limits to which government may go in fostering the public welfare without cost to the public. *Pennsylvania Coal Co. v. Mahon* is a seminal case because it well articulated these basic principles of constitutionalism.

Despite Justice Holmes, however, these principles continue to be misunderstood, even in high places. Thus the majority opinion in *Loretto* opens and closes with error. Justice Marshall noted at the outset that the New York court of appeals judged the law to serve a legitimate public purpose "and thus is within the state's police power. We have no reason to question that determination. It is a separate question, however, whether an otherwise valid regulation so frustrates property rights that compensation must be paid."[428] This is a *non sequitur*; if the exercise of the police power be valid, then *a fortiori* there has been no taking and the constitutional question is at an end. At the opinion's close there is a footnote. "In light of our disposition of appellant's takings claim, we do not address her contention that § 828 deprives her of property without due process of law."[429] But once a taking has been found, there is no place for further inquiry under due process; there remains under the Taking Clause only the question what compensation is due in the circumstances, public purpose being here assumed.

On the other hand, the dissent was weak only because it was limited to rebutting the majority on the interpretation of the Taking Clause. To base decision on that provision is akin to deciding half a case—and the second half at that. Technically, the Taking Clause simply dictates what must ensue when a taking has been found. It is necessary to look elsewhere to determine whether there has been a taking. This is more properly judged by examination of sub-

---

over its railroad terminal building." Note, 62 N.C. L. Rev. 153, 160 (1983). It does seem as though the dissents had the better result in both *Loretto* and *Penn Central*.

427. Chapters 1 and 2, *supra*.

428. Loretto v. Teleprompter Manhattan CATV Corp., 458 U.S. at 425.

429. *Id.* at 441, n. 20.

stantive due process decisions on one side and the other that have pricked out the boundary line over time. The Court has sensed this by turning to due process cases in supplementation of the inadequacies of so-called "taking" (eminent domain) decisions. Recall Justice Brennan's extensive resort to them in *Penn Central.*

In *Loretto* the magnitude of the taking was slight; the Teleprompter firm was guilty of no offensive practices, adhering to the procedures required by the statute; the original installation for "crossovers" to other rental structures occurred prior to Loretto's purchase of the rental property in question while the later cable drop on her building was desired by one of her tenants; Loretto's conflicting statements do not negate the reasonable belief that if anything the installation enhanced the sale value of her property.[430] Thus on substantive due process analysis there was no unconstitutional taking, albeit a technically factual one. Accordingly, it seems clear the dissent reached the correct result. But how much more convincing that judgment would have been had it been based, not on search for an answer from Taking Clause guidance, but on the instructive teachings of due process of law.[431]

Justice Brennan had meantime in *San Diego*[432] recognized the essentiality of *Pennsylvania Coal* to an understanding of the relationship of the Due Process and Taking Clauses, thereby achieving significant progress in appreciating the implications of that nexus. Unhappily, his analysis did not lead him to the pith of Holmes' genius. In the Court's next face-off with the puzzlement attending the interplay of the two clauses, Justice Blackmun's opinion in *Williamson County Regional Planning Comm.*[433] marked no advance in understanding, appearing even to losing ground from the level of comprehension Justice Brennan had achieved.[434] However, in the latest bout with this consti-

---

430. The conflicting statements are recorded in the two opinions, *id.* at 437-38, n. 15 (majority), *id.* at 452, n. 9 (dissent). The likelihood of increased value by reason of the cable connection reminds of testimony in *Miller v. Schoene* that the Miller land would be more valuable with the red cedars removed.

431. Epstein, *Not Deference, But Doctrine: The Eminent Domain Clause,* 1982 SUP. CT. REV. 351, is a critically constructive analysis of *Loretto* and of Texaco, Inc. v. Short, 454 U.S. 516 (1982), the latter a decision announced earlier in the same Term. While his focus is on the Taking Clause Professor Epstein's insights are cast against a broad background impacting due process and other constitutional provisions applicable to "matters of economic regulation" where the Court has depended on deferential attitude toward legislation rather than developing sound doctrine. His excellent analysis constitutes a major contribution toward improvement in constitutional theory; further improvement could be achieved by making resort to substantive due process fully central to adequate grasp of the function of the Taking Clause.

432. Refer *supra* to the segment of this chapter titled *A Tale of Two Cites,* pp. 150-53, text at notes 160-77.

433. Cited and summarized *supra* this chapter, p. 154, text at notes 182-85.

434. Grasping the Holmes vision requires mastery in constitutional theory. Justice Blackmun has said of himself, "I'm not a 'jurisprude.' I couldn't be an expert in jurisprudence if I wanted to be ... I don't have the intellect for it." Jenkins, *A Candid Talk with Justice Blackmun,* N.Y. Times Magazine of February 20, 1983, 20 at 61.

tutional enigma there is a ray of hope that in the end the Court will understand Holmes and abandon its stubborn resistance to recognition of the role substantive due process should play in resolution of the relationship between the Due Process Clause and the Taking Clause of Amendment Five.

The litigation that holds this promise is that concerning the constitutionality of congressional legislation known as the Multiemployer Pension Plan Amendments Act of 1980, supplementing the Employee Retirement Income Security Act of 1974. ERISA established a pension plan termination insurance program under which a government-owned agency styled the Pension Benefit Guaranty Corporation collects insurance premiums from covered private retirement plans of single-employers or multi-employers and with these proceeds provides payments to employee participants where their plans terminate without sufficient assets to support guaranteed benefits. Upon evidence that a number of multiemployer plans were experiencing extreme financial hardship, Congress became concerned lest employer withdrawals jeopardize the statutory scheme. Enactment of MPPAA followed, imposing upon a withdrawing employer limited retroactive liability to pay whatever share of a plan's unfunded liabilities is attributable to his participation in that plan.

When an Oregon construction firm, participant in a multiemployer pension plan through a collective-bargaining agreement, withdrew, PBGC assessed withdrawal liability. Refusing payment, the firm brought suit asserting that in retroactivity MPPAA was violative of Fifth Amendment Due Process. The challenge was rejected in *Pension Benefit Guaranty Corp. v. R. A. Gray & Co.*,[435] with Justice Brennan responding for the Court in terms of substantive due process analysis. There has followed, against a similar factual background, an equally unsuccessful attack on MPPAA based on the Taking Clause. In *Connolly v. Pension Benefit Guaranty Corp.*,[436] Justice White spoke for the full Court holding the conclusion "not inconsistent with our prior Taking Clause cases."[437] Although the relationship of the Clauses remains disjunctive rather than conjunctive, there is in the sum of the two cases a gain in comprehension in the acceptance of equivalency as between the two. A bit more encouraging is Justice O'Connor's concurrence, in which she is joined by Justice Powell. As the newest member of the Court, her appoinmtment still recent, she should not be dogmatically committed to that insistence on avoidance that has blurred the vision Holmes saw in the functional interconnection of the two Clauses. It is true she has not taken the ultimate intellectual step of fusing the Clauses into an operational unity whereby the one is the determinant of invalid taking while the other dictates the price of government exaction that has "gone too far." Yet in the manner of her references to the twin provisions she seems so close to squaring the circle!

---

435. 467 U.S. 717 (1984).

436. 106 Sup. Ct. 1018 (1986).

437. *Id.* at 1026.

8. Public Monopoly and Substantive Due Process

Governmental embracement of monopoly, as contrasted with privately created monopoly,[1] can result from either adoption of state socialism or favoritism accorded certain private enterprisers to the exclusion of business rivals.

Monopoly by Public Ownership

Government's own entry into business enterprise was occasioned by two considerations. One was growing reaction to abuses of "the hand that fed them" in the period of public aid to private business that marked the internal economic development of the United States. Not surprisingly, first steps in public ownership appeared in the area of the so-called natural monopolies, where abuses of public trust were most manifest and the economics of public utility operation actively discouraged competition. A further consideration inducive to public ownership, of contrary nature, was the failure of competitive enterprise to serve the full economic needs of a developing society.

A significant response was enactment by the legislature of Maine of legislation authorizing city or town to establish and maintain "a permanent wood, coal and fuel yard" for sale at cost of these sources of heating in a severe climate. Sustainment of the law by the state supreme court was followed by affirmance in the Supreme Court of the United States. This breakthrough by *Jones v. City of Portland*[2] was shortly followed by *Green v. Frazier*[3] where the

---

1. Chap. 9, *infra*, pp. 265-73, on *Private Monopoly and Substantive Due Process*, traces the hostility of substantive due process toward concentration of economic power by private enterprise.

In economic terminology favoritism to a group of three or more would create an oligopoly; to two, a duopoly. However, legal literature employs the term "monopoly" to describe any situation in which effective competition has been supplanted. Fateful consequences in antitrust law have flowed from this looseness but for present analysis it will be condoned.

2. 245 U.S. 217 (1917).

3. 253 U.S. 233 (1920).

Court upheld a program of the Non-Partisan League of North Dakota, projected by statute, extending public financing to banking, manufacturing and warehousing of agricultural products, and residential lending. This major expansion in the constitutionality of public ownership was quickly confirmed by favorable decisions on financing of a municipal subway system,[4] of Colorado's construction of the Moffat Tunnel,[5] and of a municipal filling-station.[6] After a review of these developments, an able commentator concluded: "As far as the Supreme Court is concerned there is no real limit to state and municipal activity in the field of business enterprise."[7] The same conclusion could be deduced respecting federal authority within federalistic limits after litigation concerning the Tennessee Valley Authority.[8]

Government ownership does not necessarily connote public monopoly in the definitional sense of a "form of economic enterprise in which the elimination of competition—the essential characteristic of monopoly—is sanctioned by public authority."[9] Government ownership may be undertaken or subsequently embraced as a market mechanism for moderating pricing by private industry. Termed "yardstick enterprise" it is used as an alternative to public price fixation. This was apparently the objective of the city of Lincoln, Nebraska, in entering the business of gasoline retailing;[10] the classic illustration is sales of electric power by the Tennessee Valley Authority. However, public ownership tends to be monopolistic, whether by original design or through the operation of economic forces.[11] Resort to government ownership for purposes

---

4. City of Boston v. Jackson, 260 U.S. 309 (1920).

5. Milheim v. Moffat Tunnel Improv. Dist., 262 U.S. 710 (1923).

6. Standard Oil Co. v. City of Lincoln, 275 U.S. 504 (1927), aff'g 114 Neb. 243, 207 N.W. 172 (1926).

7. McAllister, *Public Purpose in Taxation*, 18 CALIF. L. REV. 241, 248 (1930). May, *Government Ownership*, 7 ENCYC. SOC. SCI. 111-12 (1932), provides an extensive list of public ownership by the early 1930s.

8. Ashwander v. Tennessee Valley Authority, 297 U.S. 288 (1936); Tennessee Electric Power Co. v. Tennessee Valley Authority, 306 U.S. 118 (1939).

9. The definition of monopoly is that of Gross, *Monopolies, Public*, 10 ENCYC. SOC. SCI. 619 (1933).

10. That the City of Lincoln entered the filling station business to provide yardstick competition is suggested by the contemporaneous legislation of neighboring South Dakota, S.D. Laws 1925, chap. 184, authorizing the State to enter this business upon a finding that the retail prices of gasoline at private stations were "unreasonable and excessive." However, the supreme court of South Dakota held the statute invalid, White Eagle Oil & Refining Co. v. Gunderson, 48 S.D. 608, 205 N.W. 614 (1925), contrary to the decision of Nebraska's supreme court in Standard Oil Co. v. City of Lincoln, cited *supra* note 6. The *White Eagle* opinion cites to numerous state court invalidations of attempts at state socialism.

11. Market Street Railway Co. v. California Railroad Comm., 324 U.S. 548 (1945), is illustrative. Older citizens will recall the two sets of tracks that once occupied San Fran-

of yardstick competition could not possibly evoke opposition from substantive due process in light of the latter's historic core of anti-monopoly.[12] Government ownership with intent to supplant private enterprise by public monopoly, although theoretically in conflict with that core, incurred no constitutional opposition for lack of precedent in point.[13]

---

cisco's Market Street until the competition of the municipal street cars forced the private company out of business. Said the Court in litigation over the sale price of the private lines to the city: "The due process clause has been applied to prevent governmental destruction of existing economic values. It has not and cannot be applied to insure values or to restore values that have been lost by the operation of economic forces." *Id.* at 567.

12. The affinity of antitrust doctrine and substantive due process is noted in chap. 9, *infra*, entitled *Private Monopoly and Substantive Due Process*.

Counsel for preferred stockholders of Alabama Power Co., challenging the constitutionality of T.V.A. sales of electric power, advanced contentions under the Fifth as well as the Tenth Amendment. Ashwander v. Tennessee Valley Authority, *supra* note 8, at 293, citing, *inter alia*, Adair v. United States, 208 U.S. 161, 180 (1908), discussed in chap. 6, *supra*. However, federalistic considerations were in such ascendancy that the issue of government ownership as such received no overt attention by the Court. In the second assault on T.V.A.'s constitutional legitimacy, counsel for Tennessee Power asserted invalidity under the Fifth, Ninth, and Tenth Amendments. Tennessee Electric Power Co. v. T.V.A., *supra* note 8, at 121. And Butler and McReynolds, JJ., in their dissent stressed that "[t]he issues also include the question whether, as applied, the Act is void because the execution of defendants' program will deprive complainants of their property without due process of law in contravention of the Fifth Amendment." *Id.* at 147. But Government counsel contended that "[t]he sale of power by the Authority and its wholesale customers does not constitute regulation, and the loss of appellants' business, if any, is not a 'taking' of their property under the Fifth Amendment," *id.* at 131, and the Court majority squelched the issue by finding lack of standing to sue. Certainly T.V.A. litigation did nothing to suggest that as to government ownership the Court would construe the Fifth Amendment Due Process Clause differently from that of the Fourteenth Amendment.

13. E. Freund, The Police Power §§ 666, 667 (1904). Counsel for the attacking taxpayers in the *Portland* case, *supra* note 2, contended "that the establishment of the municipal woodyard is not a public purpose, that taxation to accomplish that end amounts to the taking of the property of the plaintiffs in error without due process of law." Jones v. City of Portland, 245 U.S. at 221. Cited in support of the contention was Citizens' Savings & Loan Association v. Topeka, 20 Wall. 655 (1874), considered in this study chap. 2 and again in chap. 7, *supra*. The citation was inapt as those treatments demonstrate; *Loan Association* had nothing to do with public ownership.

Further evidence of lack of precedent in due process for invalidating government ownership with the likely consequence of public monopoly is indicated by each of two early landmark decisions, one state the other federal. Opinion of the Justices, 150 Mass. 592, 24 N.E. 1084 (1890), sustained municipal provision to private citizens of gas or electricity for lighting. Reference to due process was conspicuous by its absence. In South Carolina v. United States, 199 U.S. 434 (1905), the Court in assuming state power to adopt a dispensary system for distribution of liquor hinted that further state involvement in business enterprise might develop to the point of management of "all business," *id.* at 454-55, yet gave no indication that such extensions would be beyond state power. However, the issue directly facing the Court was federal power to levy excise taxes on state business activity. Accord, on principle, New York v. United States, 326 U.S. 572 (1946).

Monopoly by Public Grant to Private Interests

Monopoly in private hands effected through public grant to a single entity or to a favored group had evoked an altogether different reaction from the dynamic of substantive due process of law. Entrenched in English constitutionalism as a consequence of the epochal struggles in the time of Coke, hostility to monopoly grants had come to the New World. Attacked first on general constitutional principles and then in reliance on the Contract Clause, a particularly detested such grant locked horns with substantive due process in the titanic conflict of the *Slaughter-House Cases* earlier depicted in this study.[14]

Due Process as Shield Against Monopoly Grants: Forces in Conflict

Crescent City's butchering monopoly survived by one vote. Yet from the powerfully articulated position taken by the minority of four Justices[15] the anti-monopoly facet of substantive due process attained concurrent status eleven years later in *Butchers' Union*[16] and in another two its thesis had won the Court's approval, *Yick Wo v. Hopkins*.[17] As Walton Hamilton was to say of this development, "[t]he right to work at one's chosen occupation had at last become a part of the supreme law of the land. The substance to which 'equal protection' gave a verbal home could pass on by verbal contagion into

---

14. 16 Wall. 36 (1873). A large portion of chap. 3, *supra*, is devoted to examination of this momentous decision.

15. It is to be noted that in Bartemeyer v. Iowa, 18 Wall. 129 (1873), which was submitted on printed arguments at the time of argument in the *Slaughter-House Cases*, both Justice Bradley and Justice Field reasserted very categorically the view that Due Process shielded against governmental monopoly in the form of grants to private interests. In *Bartemeyer* Justice Miller affirmed the supreme court of Iowa in sustaining the early prohibition law of that State. Justices Bradley and Field concurred. Declared the former:

> When [vested rights of property] are not in question, the claim of a right to sell a prohibited article can never be deemed one of the privileges and immunities of the citizen. It is *toto coelo* different from the right not to be deprived of property without due process of law, or the right to pursue such lawful avocation as a man chooses to adopt, unrestricted by tyrannical and corrupt monopolies. . . .

> The monopoly created by the legislature of Louisiana, which was under consideration in the *Slaughter-House Cases*, was, in my judgment, legislation of this sort and obnoxious to this objection. But police regulations, intended for the preservation of the public health and the public order, are of an entirely different character. So much of the Louisiana law as partook of this character was never objected to. It was the unconscionable monopoly, of which the police regulation was a mere pretext, that was deemed by the dissenting members of the court an invasion of the right of the citizen to pursue his lawful calling.

18 Wall. at 136-37. Justice Field's like view is found in the full paragraph *id.* at 138.

16. Butchers' Union Slaughter-House and Live-Stock Landing Co. Crescent City Live-Stock Landing and Slaughter-House Co., 111 U.S. 746 (1884).

17. 118 U.S. 356 (1886), fully considered *supra* chap. 3, text at notes 81-99.

a liberty and a property fortified by due process."[18] True, *Yick Wo* was decided on Equal Protection. However, in light of historical background it was reasonable to believe, with Hamilton, that the anti-monopoly principle would become embedded in Substantive Due Process. Had not ex-Justice Campbell in his forceful contentions in *Slaughter-House Cases* found antipathy to monopoly in both those provisions of the Fourteenth Amendment?

But the expected was not to be. Hard upon *Yick Wo* the Court in *Powell v. Pennsylvania*[19] upheld, against a due process challenge, state legislation that by prohibiting the manufacture and sale of oleomargarine designed to take the place of butter achieved a monopolistic position for the latter as a breadspread.[20] Essentially the same result then followed from Court sustainment of federal[21] and state[22] prohibition of the manufacture and sale of colored oleomargarine; a white breadspread is psychologically unpalatable. An admitted advantage attends criticism after the fact. Yet one cannot but wonder why counsel for Powell argued denial of "rights of liberty and property without due process of law"[23] rather than pressing the anti-monopoly aspect of substantive due process so ready at hand. The irony is heightened by the fact the Court cited both *Butchers' Union* and *Yick Wo*, on which the contention would have been grounded, but in support of state power to legislate for the public health and the public morals!

Understandable is the failure to correct the mistake in *Plumley*, where the strong basis for challenge appeared to lie with the Commerce Clause.[24] The

---

18. Hamilton, *The Path of Due Process of Law*, in C. READ, THE CONSTITUTION RECONSIDERED 167, at 179 (1938, 1968).

19. 127 U.S. 678 (1888), for detailed consideration of which refer to chap. 5, *supra*, pp. 86-89, text at notes 29-46.

20. Although long accepting with other commentators Walton Hamilton's analysis in *The Path of Due Process of Law*, cited *supra* note 18, I now question whether it may have contributed to the confounding that eventuated between freedom of trade and freedom of contract, to result in the major perversion of substantive due process discussed in chap. 6, *supra*. "Hamie" never intended this result yet his intellectual transition from the Equal Protection of *Yick Wo* to "the liberty and property" of Due Process took him off course from concentration on the latter as embodying hostility toward monopoly. Basis for my questioning is found in his failure to make any reference to *Powell v. Pennsylvania* and its implications. As his further tracing of the path of due process makes clear, his attention is focused on the cases involving asserted expropriation of property and those parenting the alien doctrine of freedom of contract.

21. McCray v. United States, 195 U.S. 27 (1904) (heavily differential excise tax on colored oleo).

22. Capital City Dairy Co. v. Ohio, 183 U.S. 238 (1902).

23. Powell v. Pennsylvania, 127 U.S. at 683. I am assuming counsel was thinking of expropriation. If, however, he had in mind the anti-monopoly core of Due Process he should have been explicit.

24. Plumley v. Massachusetts, 155 U.S. 461 (1894). In *Plumley*, the oleo having been shipped into Massachusetts from Illinois in the original packages, the "vital question"

issue did come to a head in the *McCray* litigation where a retailer in oleomargarine had knowingly purchased from the Ohio Butterine Co. a fifty-pound package of colored oleo to which were affixed revenue stamps at the rate of one-fourth cent per pound rather than ten cents for like weight specified for colored oleo. In a suit by the United States for the statutory penalty under the Oleomargarine Act of 1886, McCray defended on both the Fifth and Tenth Amendments: although in form a tax, in actuality the exaction was not designed to raise revenue but to suppress the manufacture of oleomargarine in aid of the butter industry, thereby contravening both direct and indirect limitations on the power of Congress. While conceding that both the Fifth and Tenth Amendments qualify all other provisions of the Constitution, the Court, with three dissents, found no violation of either.

The explanation was twofold. Precedent arguably "demonstrated that the motive or purpose of Congress in adopting the acts in question may not be inquired into...."; [25] this disposed of the contention that Congress had usurped the reserved powers of the States. As for the Fifth Amendment "no instance is afforded from the foundation of the government where an act, which was within a power conferred, was declared to be repugnant to the Constitution, because it appeared to the judicial mind that the particular exertion of constitutional power was either unwise or unjust."[26] The best McCray's counsel had done with the Fifth was to insist that arbitrary discrimination "against oleomargarine in favor of butter, to the extent of destroying the oleomargarine industry for the benefit of the butter industry, [was] violative of 'those fundamental principles of equality and justice which are inherent in the Constitution of the United States.' "[27] Again, counsel had failed to make the crucial connection with the anti-monopoly core of due process. Why this artlessness? The dissenting Justices, in failing to write an opinion, left no clue as to whether they saw the connection.

Within six months of its decision in *McCray* the Court pronounced judgment of invalidity in *Dobbins v. Los Angeles.*[28] *Dobbins* presented the Court with the question whether the city council of Los Angeles could prevent the construction of a gas works within a specified district in which in pursuance of plaintiff's contract with Valley Gas & Fuel Co. erection had commenced with approval of the board of fire commissioners but which the council then

---

was seeming conflict with congressional power under the Commerce Clause. "This is the only question the learned counsel for the petitioner urges upon our attention, and in view of the decision in *Powell v. Pennsylvania*, 127 U.S. 678, is the only one that we need to consider." *Id.* at 467. Justice Harlan wrote the opinion in *Plumley*, as he had in *Powell*. Clearly, he regarded the Fourteenth Amendment issue as having been resolved by *Powell*.

25. McCray v. United States, 195 U.S. at 59.

26. *Id.* at 54.

27. *Id.* at 30 (Statement of the Case, for Defendant).

28. 195 U.S. 223 (1904).

constricted to plaintiff's loss. Plaintiff averred not only that the larger district was "devoted almost exclusively to manufacturing enterprises" but that "the action of the municipal authorities complained of was taken for the purpose of protecting the . . . Los Angeles Lighting Company in the enjoyment of its monopoly."[29] Reviewing the averments of the bill, to which the city had demurred, a unanimous Court concluded:

> This action is strongly corroborative of the allegations of the bill that the purpose was not police regulation in the interest of the public but the destruction of the plaintiff's rights and the building up of another company still within the privileged district after the passage of the amendment. Being the owner of the land and having partially erected the works the plaintiff in error had acquired property rights and was entitled to protection against unconstitutional encroachments which would have the effect to deprive her of her property without due process of law. It is averred in the bill of complaint that the district within which the works were being erected was one given over to manufacturing enterprises, some of which were fully as obnoxious as gasworks possibly could be; that it contained large spaces of unoccupied lands, worthless except for manufacturing purposes, and by clear inference that there was nothing in the situation which rendered it necessary, in order to protect the city from a noisome and unhealthy business, to decrease the area within which gasworks could lawfully be erected.[30]

Counsel for the defendant city contended that "[t]he motives of a legislative body in enacting a law cannot be inquired into by the courts."[31] The Court's response is significant to the consideration of this critical issue.

> Whether, when it appears that the facts would authorize the exercise of the power, the courts will restrain its exercise because of alleged wrongful motives inducing the passage of an ordinance is not a question necessary to be determined in this case, but where the facts as to the situation and conditions are such as to establish the exercise of the police power in such manner as to oppress or discriminate against a class or an individual the courts may consider and give weight to such purpose in considering the validity of the ordinance. This court, in the case of *Yick Wo v. Hopkins*, 118 U.S. 356, held that although an ordinance might be lawful upon its face and apparently fair in its terms, yet if it was enforced in such a manner as to work a discrimination against a part of the community for no lawful reason, such exercise of power would be invalidated by the courts.[32]

Impact of Conflict: Framework for Analysis

No two cases are ever identical on their facts, which with rare insight Thurman Arnold saw as opening a vista of stare indecisis. Four distinctions differentiate *Dobbins* from *McCray*. The ordinance challenged constituted an at-

---

29. *Id.* at 225 (Statement of the Case, for Plaintiff).
30. *Id.* at 239-40.
31. *Id.* at 233.
32. *Id.* at 240.

tempted exercise of regulatory power, not of taxing power. It was state action, not congressional enactment. The law had the effect of perpetuating monopoly by preventing what economic literature labels *commodity competition*, competition among providers of a given product or service. The federal act, like the Massachusetts and Pennsylvania laws in *Plumley* and *Powell*, effected outlawry of *substituted competition*, competition among rival products for the same market. Fourthly, by demurrer to the complaint alleging monopoly, defendant conceded that the purpose of the local enactment was preservation of monopoly theretofore enjoyed by Los Angeles Lighting Co.; there was no occasion to look behind the face of the ordinance. Assuming judicial employment of Coke's "artificial reasoning of the law" one concludes that the identical Court found in these differences between *Dobbins* and *McCray* the basis for contrary conclusions as to constitutionality. The two contemporaneous holdings thus provide framework for inquiry into the following eighty years of Court decisions on monopoly by public grant (or withholding) and substantive due process of law.

   Police Power vs. Taxing Power;[33] *Federal Power vs. State Power.* Because tax revenues constitute the very lifeblood of any political body, it would seem reasonable for the Court to manifest greater reluctance in questioning ulterior purpose of taxing acts than in exercises of the police power. Editor Gunther, however, finds in modern decisions on congressional power a tendency to the contrary.[34] There is the *Child Labor Tax Case,*[35] in which Justices Brandeis and Holmes joined in looking behind the congressional label to invalidate on the ground of forbidden purpose and effect; *United States v. Constantine*[36] although with dissent by them; and the fact that while the federal tax on wagers was sustained in *United States v. Kahriger*[37] Justice Jackson had serious doubts and Justice Frankfurter dissented in an opinion that, although he did not join it, Justice Douglas agreed expressed his views "that this tax is an attempt by the Congress to control conduct which the Constitution has left to the responsibility of the States."[38]

   Examination of Court adjudication in instances of state regulation or taxation, largely concerned with discrimination against oleomargarine,[39] dis-

---

   33. Technically, only the States have powers of police; Congress has only enumerated power, *e.g.*, to regulate commerce among the States, to tax and spend for the general welfare. However, with the vast expansion of Congress's power with respect to interstate commerce it has become increasingly common practice to think of Congress as also having a general power of police.
   34. G. GUNTHER, CONSTITUTIONAL LAW: CASES AND MATERIALS 213-24 (10th ed. 1980).
   35. Bailey v. Drexel Furniture Co., 259 U.S. (1922).
   36. 296 U.S. 287 (1935).
   37. 345 U.S. 22 (1953).
   38. *Id.* at 40.
   39. Aside from oleo cases there was Quong Wing v. Kirkendall, 223 U.S. 59 (1912), up-

closes no distinction between the two types of enactment as regards reference to ulterior purpose.[40] Against the contention of the taxpayer in *McCray v. United States*[41] that the Court should intervene "if a lawful power may be exerted for an unlawful purpose," the judicial response was that separation of the powers of government forbade intrusion by one branch upon the province of another.[42] Inasmuch as the Constitution does not directly impose on the States the principle of separation of powers, it might therefore be thought there would be wider berth for Court inquiry where state taxation or regulation was under challenge. However, the possibility of any such distinction was negatived in *A. Magnano Co. v. Hamilton*,[43] which upheld against due process attack a Washington state tax of fifteen cents per pound on butter substitutes. There was no dissent from the proposition that

> [e]xcept in rare and special instances, the due process of law clause contained in the Fifth Amendment is not a limitation upon the taxing power conferred upon Congress by the Constitution... And no reason exists for applying a different rule against a state in the case of the Fourteenth Amendment.... Collateral purposes or motives of a legislature in levying a tax of a kind within the reach of its lawful power are matters beyond the scope of judicial inquiry. *McCray v. United States, supra,* 56-59.[44]

---

holding a Montana law that imposed a license for operation of hand laundries but exempting the steam laundry business. *Cf. In re* Yot Sang, 75 Fed. 983 (D. Mont. 1896), invalidating earlier Montana law taxing hand laundries more heavily.

40. Prohibition under the police power of production and sale of all oleo margarine or of oleo colored in imitation of butter: Powell v. Pennsylvania, *supra* note 19; Plumley v. Massachusetts, *supra* note 24; Capital City Dairy Co. v. Ohio, *supra* note 22 (per quo warranto proceedings). Discouragement or prohibition under the taxing power: Hammond Packing Co. v. Montana, 233 U.S. 331 at 333-34 (1914) (State "may express and carry out its policy [against oleo margarine] as well in a revenue as in a police law."); A. Magnano Co. v. Hamilton, 292 U.S. 40, at 44 (1934); Carmichael v. Southern Coal & Coke Co., 301 U.S. 495, at 512 (1937). Glenn v. Field Packing Co., 290 U.S. 177 (1933), was a *per curiam* affirmance of a three-judge federal district court that had invalidated a 10¢ per pound state tax on oleomargarine for violation of the Kentucky constitution. There are conflicting decisions from state courts on prohibition of oleomargarine by state taxation. *E.g.*, Flynn v. Horst, 356 Pa. 20, 51 A. 2d 54 (1947) (invalid); Ludwig v. Harston, 65 Wyo. 137, 197 P. 2d 252 (1948) (valid).

41. 195 U.S. 27, cited *supra* note 21.

42. *Id.* at 54-55. *Cf.* note 44, *infra*.

43. 292 U.S. 40 (1934), cited *supra* note 40.

44. *Id.* at 44. Note that the pages cited from *McCray* are not those cited *supra* note 42, thus discounting the influence of separation-of-powers doctrine in *McCray*.

Because *Dobbins* involved a Los Angeles ordinance, somewhat lesser judicial reluctance to question legislative profession might stem from the requirement familiar in the law of municipal corporations that, wholly apart from constitutional limitations, a municipal ordinance must stand the test of "reasonableness." However, I find no evidence of this factor at work in the context under present examination.

Exclusion of Market Competition Among Rival Entrepreneurs/Products. Of the four distinctions that differentiate *Dobbins* from *McCray* the first two are of little, if any, significance as the preceding paragraphs demonstrate. Not so the third and fourth. Each of these requires extensive and intensive examination. With respect to the third, monopoly by exclusion from a common market of competition between marketers of identical goods is far more familiar than is exclusion of competition among rival products. In defining "competition" the economist Walton Hamilton stressed the former with only passing reference to the latter.[45] Product (substituted) competition is somehow less apparent to the untrained eye; certainly the phenomenon was much later in recognition. The monopolies of Coke's time, against which he inveighed, were always grants to favored individuals in a given business; and the early monopoly grants in this country, culminating in that to the Crescent City Co. attacked in the *Slaughter-House Cases*, were of this type.[46] Supreme Court treatment of commodity competition cases after *Dobbins* follows in the ensuing paragraphs.

In a closing segment of the majority opinion in *Lochner v. New York*, which is seldom noted, assertion that legislative "interference . . . with the ordinary trades and occupations of the people seems to be on the increase,"[47] is supported by citation to three state court decisions each invalidating laws requiring restrictive licensing of those seeking to enter the trade of horseshoeing.[48] That these attempted curbs on market entry came from three distinct geographical areas of the nation and for the time represented a uniquely common calling suggests early legislative indulgence in anti-competitive favoritism. In a comprehensive review of marketing barrier enactments, appearing in 1941, it is stated that "[s]ince the turn of the century, state licensing legislation in some form has encompassed virtually every conceivable type of profession, industry, business, trade and occupation."[49] Citations provided in this survey

---

45. Hamilton, *Competition*, 4 ENCYC. SOC. SCI. 141 (1931).

46. The English grants are reviewed in chap. 1, the 19th century American grants in chap. 3, of this study.

47. Lochner v. New York, 198 U.S. at 63.

48. Bessette v. People, 193 Ill. 334, 62 N.E. 215 (1901); People v. Beattie, 96 App. Div. 383, 89 N.Y. Supp. 193 (1904); In re Aubrey, 36 Wash. 308, 78 Pac. 900 (1904).

49. Silverman, Bennett and Lechliter, *Control by Licensing Over Entry Into the Market*, 8 LAW & CONTEMP. PROBS. 234, 236 (1941). This survey constituted a lead article in a symposium on governmental marketing barriers covering all facets of the topic.
Some illustrations of monopolistic licensing can be "mined" from Hanft and Hamrick, *Haphazard Regimentation Under Licensing Statutes*, 17 N.C.L. Rev. 1 (1938) (with special reference to North Carolina); Kirby, *Expansive Judicial Review of Economic Regulation Under State Constitutions*, 48 TENN. L. REV. 241 (1981) (reproduced with supplementation in DEVELOPMENTS IN STATE CONSTITUTIONAL LAW chap. 4 (1985).) Hanft and Hamrick contrasted Territory v. Kraft, 33 Haw. 397 (1937), invalidating licensing of photographers, with State v. Lawrence, 213 N.C. 674, 197 S.E. 586 (1938), sustaining such a law.

indicate the continued growth of trade restrictions as time passed; the trend skyrocketed in the field day for anti-competitive measures under the Industrial Codes of the National Industrial Recovery Act.

Of this rising tide of state and local licensing laws, few were litigated beyond lower courts. One exception was an ordinance of the City of Cincinnati forbidding the licensing of aliens for the conduct of pool and billiard establishments. Challenged by a subject of Great Britain, it was upheld in the Ohio courts with affirmance in the Supreme Court of the United States. The decision in *Clarke v. Deckebach*[50] was unanimous, unusual for an economic determination in the *Lochner* era. Justice Stone deemed it necessary only to assert that whereas the discrimination against aliens in *Yick Wo* had been "plainly irrational," the choice here was "not shown to be irrational." On faith, the evil influence of pool halls and billiard rooms was taken to be as great as Professor Harold Hall would depict them in Meredith Willson's classic musical *The Music Man*—but only when operated by foreigners! Neither counsel for Clarke urged, nor did any Justice sense, the ugly hand of local monopoly, possibly because such an occupation was hardly a trade or business anyway.

The outstanding decision of the Supreme Court, *New State Ice Co. v. Liebmann*,[51] came near the close of the *Lochner* period. Struck down was an Oklahoma law requiring a license for entry into the business of manufacturing, selling, and distributing artificial ice. Licensing procedure was modelled after that in vogue for public utilities; any applicant must procure from the state corporation commission a certificate of public convenience and necessity, which could be denied on a showing that existing facilities were sufficient to meet the public needs. "Common knowledge" told the majority of the Court that home production of ice by the use of natural gas or electricity had become suffi-

---

Their criticism of *Lawrence, id.* at 16-17, is thought to have led the supreme court of North Carolina to hold unconstitutional the State's attempt to force licensing of dry cleaners in State v. Harris, 216 N.C. 746, 6 S.E. 2d 854 (1940). In Professor Kirby's random survey one finds, *id.* at 267, n. 143, citation to three state decisions invalidating legislation requiring undertakers to be licensed embalmers. Two of these were quite early, Wyeth v. Board of Health, 200 Mass. 474, 86 N.E. 925 (1909); People v. Ringe, 197 N.Y. 143, 90 N.E. 451 (1910), while State ex rel. v. Whyte, 177 Wis. 541, 188 N.W. 607 (1922), appeared about the middle of the period. The Wisconsin law included a grandfather clause, which further tipped the legislature's hand.

50. 274 U.S. 392 (1927). Although the Arizona Initiative Measure invalidated in Truax v. Raich 239 U.S. 33 (1915), was technically not a licensing law it had similar effect by virtue of its prohibition in any employment of over 20 per centum of non-citizens of the United States. There the Court had seen the ugly hand of monopoly. Declared Justice Hughes for all save Justice McReynolds, dissenting on the ground the suit offended the Eleventh Amendment, "The discrimination is against aliens as such in competition with citizens in the described range of enterprises and in our opinion it clearly falls under the condemnation of the fundamental law." *Id.* at 43.

51. 285 U.S. 262 (1932).

ciently established to prevent classification of the business of ice-making as a natural monopoly justifying regulatory control for the protection of consumers. To the contrary, "the practical tendency of the restriction, as the trial court suggested in the present case," is to shut out new enterprises and thus create and foster monopoly in the hands of existing establishments, against, rather than in aid of, the interest of the consuming public."[52]

> The control here asserted does not protect against monopoly, but tends to foster it. The aim is not to encourage competition, but to prevent it; not to regulate the business, but to preclude persons from engaging in it.[53]

In a thirty-page dissent, Justice Brandeis took an entirely opposite direction. Clearly influenced by the economic upheaval already apparent in the Great Depression he reasoned from the postulate that an economy of scarcity had been supplanted by one of overabundance. From this fundamental alteration there emerged a new set of economic forces. Unregulated entry into occupations would bring destructive competition through excess of capacity over demand, warranting state intervention to stabilize the market. Where the product of business is a public necessity, as in the case of ice, "it is one which lends itself peculiarly to monopoly."[54] Substantive due process is not offended; rather, there is reconciliation with its anti-monopoly thrust! This new, startling creed is articulated in the following passage:

> It is no objection to the validity of the statute here assailed that it fosters monopoly. That, indeed, is its design. The certificate of public convenience and invention is a device—a recent social-economic invention—through which the monopoly is kept under effective control by vesting in a commission the power to terminate it whenever that course is required in the public interest. To grant any monopoly to any person as a favor is forbidden even if terminable. But where, as here, there is reasonable ground for the legislative conclusion that in order to secure a necessary service at reasonable rates, it may be necessary to curtail the right to enter the calling, it is, in my opinion, consistent with the due process clause to do so, whatever the nature of the business. The existence of such power in the legislature seems indispensable in our ever-changing society.
>
> It is settled by unanimous decisions of this Court, that the due process clause does not prevent a State or city from engaging in the business of supplying its inhabitants with articles in general use, when it is believed that they cannot be secured at reasonable prices from the private dealers. [Herein of the decisions considered in an opening paragraph of this chapter.] As States may engage in a business, because it is a public purpose to assure to their inhabitants an adequate supply of necessary articles, may they not achieve this public purpose, as Oklahoma has done, by exercising the lesser power of preventing single individuals from wantonly engaging in the business and thereby making impossible a dependable

---

52. *Id.* at 278.
53. *Id.* at 279.
54. *Id.* at 291.

private source of supply? As a State so entering upon a business may exert the taxing power all individual dealers may be driven from the calling by the unequal competition. If States are denied the power to prevent the harmful entry of a few individuals into a business, they may thus, in effect, close it altogether to private enterprise.[55]

Justice Stone alone joined the Brandeis dissent. Justice Holmes had left the Court; his replacement, Justice Cardozo, had taken his seat on the Bench only one week before and accordingly "took no part in the consideration or decision of this case." Chief Justice Hughes and Justice Roberts were aligned with the hard core Justices who were coming to be known as "the gang of four." There seemed to be no reason to believe the dissent would soon take the Court. Yet in two years, in an opinion by none other than Justice Roberts, *Nebbia v. New York*[56] had by bare majority vote installed the new reasoning in embracive language extending beyond original compass.

The public policy with respect to free competition has engendered state and federal statutes prohibiting monopolies, which have been upheld. On the other hand, where the policy of the state dictated that a monopoly should be granted, statutes having that effect have been held inoffensive to the constitutional guarantees.[57]

Footnotes 33 and 34 of the Roberts opinion supporting these respective assertions provide a striking comparison. Cited for "statutes prohibiting monopolies" are six decisions sustaining state laws and four upholding federal laws.[58] For statutes of opposite thrust three decisions are cited, all of them weak reeds.[59] This was indeed mighty slim basis on which to peg a revolution in constitutional law if such was the intended purpose.

55. *Id.* at 304–05.
56. 291 U.S. 502 (1934). This fateful decision is also considered elsewhere in this study, necessarily so in view of its great significance.
57. *Id.* at 529.
58. These decisions are with one exception among those reviewed in chap. 9, *infra*, pp. 265-269, text from note 17 through note 39.
59. To rely upon the majority opinion in *Slaughter-House Cases* is to beg the question respecting the anti-monopoly content to be found in substantive due process. Conway v. Taylor's Executor, 1 Bl. 603 (1861), concerned a conflict in ferry rights across the Ohio River at Cincinnati. The Taylor grant dated from 1794. When the city of Newport commenced operation of a rival boat, on the basis of a ferry grant of 1850, Taylor's executor sought to enjoin the competition. The decree of the Kentucky court of appeals favoring complainant was affirmed by the Supreme Court on the understanding that it was limited to protection of plaintiff's ferry rights on the esplanade of the Kentucky bank of the river at Newport. Plaintiff's ferry franchise "is as much property as a rent or any other incorporeal hereditament, or chattels, or realty." *Id.* at 632. "Those rights give them no monopoly, under 'all circumstances,' of all commercial transportation from the Kentucky shore. They have no right to exclude or restrain those there prosecuting the business of commerce in good faith, without the regularity or purposes of ferry trips, and seeking in no wise to interfere with the enjoyment of their franchise." *Id.* at 633. Equitable protec-

Sustainment of the basic framework of the New York Milk Control Act was followed by litigation over classifications made in the statute as amended. A major dispute arose over the one cent per quart differentiation in minimum price at retail between distributors with well-established trade names and those not well known in the market. The advantage accorded the latter, which the State urged preserved competitive opportunities and prevented monopoly, was upheld by a divided Court.[60] Justice Roberts wrote the majority opinion; the four who had dissented in *Nebbia* were again in disagreement. But the tables were turned with respect to another provision that required marketers entering the business after a date certain to sell at the higher figure.[61] The redoubtable Justice Roberts once again wrote for the majority in a decision of the same date; now the dissenting Justices were Cardozo, Brandeis, and Stone.

A decade later Equal Protection was unequal to the task of invalidating a clear instance of legislative restriction on market entry. Louisiana law required, for the piloting of ships to and from New Orleans through the Mississippi River, pilots appointed by the governor from a list of names certified by a board of pilots. Only those with six months apprenticeship under an incumbent pilot were eligible for certification, and the board certified only relatives and friends of the incumbents. A bare majority of the Court in an opinion by Justice Black doubletalked this scandalous monopolistic arrangement past the protective screen of Equal Protection.[62] Fellow Justices with whom he ordinarily agreed disagreed vigorously.

New Orleans was again in the judicial picture a generation later. As amended an ordinance forbade pushcart food vendors in the French Quarter but by a grandfather clause exempted those who had been in operation for eight or more years. There were two of the latter, one a vendor of hot dogs and the other of ice cream, thus giving monopoly position to each. On challenge in

---

tion of the Taylor ferry franchise with respect to a landing area on the Kentucky side, based on riparian ownership, hardly established a general state power to create monopolies.

Crawley v. Christensen, 137 U.S. 86 (1890), is even less relevant. A retail liquor dealer in San Francisco had been denied an extension of his license by the police commissioners. Continuing in business, he was arrested. On habeas corpus he challenged his detention on the ground that the controlling ordinance left decision on license applications first in the discretion of police commissioners and, on their refusal, in the hands of adjacent owners of real estate. The federal circuit court "held that the ordinance made the business of the petitioner depend upon the arbitrary will of others, and in that respect denied to him the equal protection of the laws, and accordingly ordered his discharge." *Id.* at 89. This decision was thought supported by *Yick Wo v. Hopkins*, considered in chap. 3 of this study. The Supreme Court reversed in an opinion of Justice Field who distinguished *Yick Wo* as "a business harmless in itself and useful to the community" whereas the liquor business "may be entirely prohibited or subjected to such restrictions as the governing authority may prescribe." *Id.* at 94.

60. Borden's Farm Products Co. v. Ten Eyck, 297 U.S. 251 (1936).
61. Mayflower Farms, Inc. v. Ten Eyck, 297 U.S. 2 (1936). Note the monopoly thrust.
62. Kotch v. Board of River Port Pilot Commissioners, 330 U.S. 552 (1947).

federal court by the hot dog vendor, Nancy Dukes, the ordinance was initially sustained but held invalid by a panel of the Fifth Circuit court of appeals that included Judge John Minor Wisdom.[63] That court saw the result of the amendment for what it was, creation of a "legislative monopoly."

The Supreme Court, however, reversed *per curiam* in an opinion that bears the imprint of Justice Douglas. *New Orleans v. Dukes.*[64] The short explanation for reversal is significant on two counts. In text and footnote there is conspicuous by its absence any recognition that monopoly by public action precipitates a constitutional issue; "in the local economic sphere, it is only the invidious discrimination, the wholly arbitrary act, which cannot stand consistently with the Fourteenth Amendment."[65] Secondly, the same passage sounds as much in terms of due process as of equal protection. The statement just quoted is followed by citation of *Ferguson v. Scrupa*;[66] *Williamson v. Lee Optical Co.*[67] is cited both earlier and later; and *Morey v. Doud*,[68] on which the court of appeals had relied as controlling, is cited only to be overruled. All three of these cases involved state laws restrictive of market entry:[69] *Ferguson* was decided primarily on due process, *Lee Optical* on both due process and equal protection but largely the former, and *Morey* wholly on equal protection.

Emergence of unorthodox methods of distribution, challenging traditional ways of doing business, added a further dimension to entrepreneurial rivalry. Threatened by this new kind of commodity competition, those fearing disaster in the marketplace turned to legislative halls for redress.[70] Responsive lawmakers invoked on their behalf both police and taxing powers of government. An early instance of regulation was the Pennsylvania law that forbade corpo-

---

63. Dukes v. City of New Orleans, 501 F. 2d 706 (C.C.A. 5th, 1974).

64. 427 U.S. 297 (1976).

65. *Id.* at 303-04.

66. 372 U.S. 726 (1963). The larger significance of this decision has been noted in chap. 6, p. 109, *supra.*

67. 348 U.S. 483 (1955).

68. 354 U.S. 457 (1957).

69. *Ferguson* concerned a Kansas statute restricting debt adjustment to lawyers; the Oklahoma law in *Lee Optical* sought by four provisions to stop the competition opticians were giving optometrists and ophthalmologists; and the Illinois statute in *Morey* gave a competitive advantage to American Express over other businesses operating currency exchanges.

70. My recollection of an instance of this political phenomenon remains vivid fifty years later. I was witness to the orchestrated descent upon the State Capitol of Iowa's independent retail druggists. Their message to the state legislators was clear; "we remain in Des Moines until you enact a resale price maintenance law that gives teeth to enforcement by inclusion of a non-signer clause." They did not have to remain long; the political process was quick to "correct" the perceived economic imbalance. The owner of the small Iowa City drug store whom I patronized gave me upon his return a blow-by-blow account of the highly successful mission accomplished!

rate ownership of pharmacies unless all stockholders were pharmacists. In essence an anti-chain store enactment, it was invalidated by a split Court in *Liggett Co. v. Baldridge*.[71] The major legislative response took the forms of heavy license taxation of chain stores, graduated on the basis of total units in the chain, and enactment of resale price maintenance laws binding non-signers as well as signers of contracts to adhere to manufacturers' stipulated prices. The taxing acts were directed especially at grocery chains, fair trade statutes in large part at drug store chains.

The latter type of law was sustained by the old Court in *Old Dearborn Distributing Co. v. Seagram-Distributors Corp.*,[72] the former in *Great Atlantic & Pacific Tea Co. v. Grosjean*.[73] In neither instance was there any recognition that such legislation created barriers to vigorous competition among rival sellers;[74] quite the contrary, the Court viewed these laws as designed "to promote fair competitive conditions and to equalize economic advantages"[75] and as such not inconsistent with Equal Protection. Their anti-competitive thrust was left to state courts to weigh; decisions there ran two to one for invalidation of the fair-trade type as violative of substantive due process.[76] Indeed, in a recent examination of state decisions Professor Kirby found that "[t]he most active subject for state judicial intervention against anti-competitive measures has been in the area of fair trade laws . . . where accumulated experience under such fair trade laws had revealed their true purpose as 'designed primarily to destroy competition at the retail level.' "[77] Repeal of federal law that underwrote application to non-signers[78] and altered legislative attitudes have resulted in the substantial disappearance of resale price maintenance laws.[79]

Legislation favoring butter over oleomargarine appears to have been the earliest instance of market exclusion of competition between rival products. The Court's sustainment in *Powell v. Pennsylvania*[80] of complete prohibition of the manufacture and sale of oleo made it possible for butter to enjoy a monopoly

---

71. 278 U.S. 105 (1928), earlier considered chap. 6, *supra*, pp. 101-02, text at notes 42-48.

72. 299 U.S. 183 (1936).

73. 301 U.S. 412 (1937).

74. A *Symposium on Governmental Marketing Barriers*, 8 LAW & CONTEMP. PROBS. 207-414 (1941), contains several accounts of the conflict between old and new methods of distribution.

75. Great Atlantic & Pacific Tea Co. v. Grosjean, 301 U.S. at 426.

76. 2 C.C.H. TRADE REG. REP. par. 6041 (collecting the cases as of 1979).

77. Kirby, *supra* note 49, at 252-53.

78. 89 STAT. 801 (1975).

79. 4 C.C.H. TRADE REG. REP. pars. 35,001-35,009 (data for 1984). There remain a few fair trade laws for designated businesses.

80. 127 U.S. 628 (1888), cited *supra* note 19, where reference is made to thorough consideration *supra* chap. 5.

of the breadspread market during the early decades of the present century wherever such prohibitory measures could gain legislative approval. This complete grip was removed in some States by statutory repeal or invalidation by judicial decision.[81] Yet prohibition of production and sale of colored oleomargarine remained common,[82] fully supported on judicial review.[83] Senior citizens will recall the experience of having to purchase uncolored oleo and achieving resemblance to yellow butter[84] by mixing into it coloring matter supplied with the package of margarine. What brought the "butter monopoly" to an end was the tremendous demand for the article in order to meet the needs of this country and its allies in World War II.[85] From 1939 to 1950 thirteen States rescinded their bans on colored oleo[86] and the federal taxes were repealed at the end of this period.[87] In another four years thirteen additional States had abolished restrictions, leaving only Minnesota and Wisconsin forbidding the sale of colored oleo.[88] Minnesota backed off ten years later,[89] leaving only Wisconsin which finally followed suit.[90]

---

81. *E.g.*, State v. Hanson, 118 Minn. 85, 136 N.W. 412 (1912) (invalidating statute construed to forbid oleo where resemblance to yellow butter achieved without use of artificial coloring); John F. Jelke Co. v. Emery, 193 Wis. 311, 214 N.W. 369 (1927) (statute, forbidding production and sale of oleo, openly supported by defendant counsel "in order to protect the Wisconsin dairy industry from unfair competition," held unconstitutional). The *Jelke* opinion noted that the Pennsylvania law upheld in *Powell* had been repealed and that the court knew of no other State having a statute prohibiting the manufacture and sale of uncolored oleomargarine.

82. "Thirty-two states have, at some time, passed laws prohibiting the sale of colored margarine." Wis. Leg. Ref. Bureau, *Developments in Wisconsin's Oleomargarine Legislation* 1 (1965).

83. Consult notes 21 and 22, *supra*; John F. Jelke Co. v. Emery, *supra* note 81, 193 Wis. at 320-321, 214 N.W. at 372, noting that Wisconsin had a separate statute, "the validity of which has been sustained, which prohibits the sale of oleomargarine colored to resemble butter. Section 352.57. Essex v. State, 170 Wis. 512, 175 N.W. 795."; A. Magnano Co. v. Hamilton, 292 U.S. 40 (1934), upholding an excise tax of fifteen cents per pound on all butter substitutes in challenge by producers of Nucoa, which the Court noted was a "nutritious and pure article of food" and conceded "that the tax is so excessive that it may or will result in destroying the intrastate business of appellant." *Id.* at 45.

84. Users of butter have long realized that butter varies in hue. For instance, "January butter" is a lighter yellow than is "June butter."

85. The study cited *supra* note 82, at 2, ascribes the "great shift in sentiments concerning oleomargarine" primarily to improvement in the production of oleo, making it more nutritious, but recognizing World War II as a "major factor." Doubtless the war demand made easier the turn to oleo because of its improvement. By this time vegetable oils had largely replaced animal fats in oleo production.

86. *Developments in Wisconsin's Oleomargarine Legislation, supra* note 82, at 2.

87. 64 STAT. Part I, 20 (1950). Repeal was replaced by provisions subjecting oleo production to controls against adulteration, misbranding, and unfitness.

88. *Developments, supra* note 86.

89. Minn. Laws 1963, chap. 832. Substituted was an excise tax of ten cents per pound

Agitation over the butter-oleo conflict lasted in this country for nearly a century. The degree of legislative attention to this type of product competition is highlighted by data disclosing that for a long period nearly every session of the Wisconsin legislature involved itself in the problem.[91] A recent decision of the Court of Justice of the European Economic Community reveals the persistence of this conflict in a new form. A West German manufacturer of vegetable margarine had contracted with a Belgian distributor for the sale of 15,000 kilograms of its product, Deli, packed in 500 gram tubs. A term of the contract provided that the goods should be accepted and paid for only if they could be marketed in Belgium in tubs having the shape of a truncated cone. At the time the contract was concluded a Belgium law of 1935 required that oleo be marketed in cube-shaped blocks. In late 1980 this provision was replaced by a Royal Decree to similar effect but fixing the prohibitory limits to the range between 50 grams and 2 kilograms. After inquiry of the Belgium Ministry of Health, which replied that restrictions continued to forbid sale except in cube-shape, defendant notified the West German company that it no longer wished to accept the goods. Plaintiff then brought suit in Hamburg Regional Court for performance of the contract, from which the dispute was referred to the Court of Justice of the EEC for provisional ruling. In *Ran v. De Smedt*[92] that Court ruled for plaintiff, finding that the Belgium requirement of the cuboid form of packaging violated Article 30 of the EEC Treaty because the equivalent of a quantitative restriction forbidden on imports among Members of the Community.[93]

The dairy industry's losing battle with oleomargarine was somewhat ameliorated by substantial success in ousting from the market filled milk as a competitor of condensed or evaporated natural milk. To express the result in a nutshell, cream lost but milk won. Legislative assault against filled milk, a product resulting from removal of butterfat from whole milk and substituting therefor a percentum of coconut or other oil, appeared in the early 1920s and culminated in litigation in the next two decades. The opinion in *United States v. Carolene Products Co.*,[94] which in 1938 sustained the Federal Act of 1923

---

concluded that "while spokesmen for the Minnesota dairy industry still contend that they have been hurt by competition from oleo, they have difficulty in finding suitable statistics to prove their contentions. (See Tables IV and V.)" These Tables are found in *id.* at 6.

90. WIS. STAT. ANN. §139.60. Like Minnesota, Wisconsin substituted an "occupation tax" but surprisingly at only 5.25 cents per pound.

91. *Developments, supra* note 82, at 7-12, lists Bills, other than Tax Bills, in the Wisconsin Legislature 1881-1965; *id.* at 13-17 are listed the Tax Bills for 1927-1965.

92. [1982] ECR 3961. There remained unresolved the question whether this was a "made case" beyond the Court's jurisdiction because the equivalent of an advisory opinion.

93. The Advocate General had reached the same conclusion in his opinion, Case 261/81.

94. 304 U.S. 144 (1938).

on demurrer to an indictment,[95] records in footnote 3[96] that when the federal act was passed "eleven states had rigidly controlled the exploitation of filled milk, or forbidden it altogether. H.R. 365, 67th Cong., 1st Sess." This statement is followed by the further observation that "[s]ome thirty-five states have now adopted laws which in terms, or by their operation, prohibit the sale of filled milk."[97] Carolene Products defended on grounds of violation of the Commerce, Equal Protection (Fifth Amendment), and Due Process Clauses. But with respect to the last defense, the assertion of unconstitutionality was couched in terms either of unspecified denial of due process or of deprivation of its property without due process of law;[98] allegations of monopoly objective were unrelated to the due process contentions.[99] As a consequence the resort to due process contention was rejected by the Court in reliance upon handy precedent[100] and upon "affirmative evidence" in the Senate and House hearings on the proposed legislation which it summarized in Footnote 2.[101] Part *Third* of the opinion, where famous Footnote 4 is found, concerned the weight of the "presumption of constitutionality" in economic issues elsewhere treated in this study.[102]

Considerations other than concern for public health were behind the pressure for enactment of legislation forbidding the manufacture and sale of filled milk. The Record in *Carolene I* more than hints at this fact. Appellee asserted that "[s]killfully directed agitation from 1921 to 1923, the year of the federal

---

95. Litigation respecting the Federal Act commenced with United States v. Carolene Products Co., 7 F. Supp. 500 (D. Ill. 1934), wherein the statute was held unconstitutional yet the adverse decisions could not be appealed by the United States because of technical limitation in the Criminal Appeals Act. On later indictment of Carolene Products the District Court again invalidated on the authority of the earlier decision. Direct appeal by the United States from sustainment of the demurrer to the indictment was possible under the Criminal Appeals Act and the Supreme Court reversed. Meantime, a federal court of appeals had upheld the law in Carolene Products Co. v. Evaporated Milk Association, 93 F. 2d 202 (C.A. 7th, 1937).

96. United States v. Carolene Products Co., 304 U.S. at 150, n. 3, ¶2.

97. *Ibid.*

98. United States v. Carolene Products Co., 304 U.S. 144, Record, Microfiche, card 4, at 3.

99. *Id.* at 3 & 31. At 31 of appellee's argument there was quoted from New State Ice Co. v. Liebmann, 285 U.S. 262, 279 (1932), the conclusion of the majority that "[t]he control here asserted does not protect against monopoly, but tends *to foster* it." Earlier, at 3, appellee asserted "the statute was passed by powerful majorities to eliminate competition, and not for preservation of the health, safety, or comfort of the public."

100. Hebe Co. v. Shaw, 248 U.S. 297 (1919), in which the Court had sustained against Fourteenth Amendment attack an Ohio law of broader import. Charles Evans Hughes was leading counsel for Hebe Co. Justice Holmes wrote the Court's opinion; Justice Brandeis was one of three dissenters on the issue of the interpretation of the statute.

101. United States v. Carolene Products Co., 304 U.S. at 149, n. 2.

102. This aspect of *Carolene Products* is considered in chap. 6, *supra*, text at note 66.

enactment, brought about passage of this law and similar ones in many states."[103] As with the advent of oleomargarine, the dairy industry was fearful of the substitute product. Sensitivity to this economic aspect is reflected in the quip of Dr. McCullom of Johns Hopkins University, a vigorous proponent of the federal law, that "to bring the American cow into competition with a co-conut grove is an injustice."[104] In the course of debate in the House of Representatives on the proposed Bill, May 24, 1922,[105] opposing congressmen were outspoken in denunciation of the measure as clearly designed to deal a "death blow" to a nutritious and wholesome product. "When the powers of the Government can be used to settle the question of competition in commercial life, the act becomes tyranny."[106] That it was a case of the dairy industry "wanting to destroy the competition of filled milk" was the conviction of others.[107]

On the other hand, there was ample testimony to support the prohibition as a health measure. Much of this represented a sincere concern for the public interest, although when offered by representatives of dairy organizations there were intimations of self-interest masquerading as general concern. Admittedly, filled milk was deficient in vitamins found in butterfat. Yet in appearance, taste, and packaging it was indistinguishable from condensed or evaporated whole milk and thus easily confused therewith; even careful labeling was inadequate to differentiate the two compounds because of ignorance among some consumers and the practice of bulk sales to large dealers with the consequence of absence of any marking when filled milk reached the consumer; and some dealers were found to have purposely marketed the substitute as the "same" as that from whole milk. In this view, filled milk was an inferior product requiring elimination from the marketplace for the public safety.

On the basis of evidentiary conflict, the Court having reversed sustainment of demurrer to the indictment, Carolene Products Co. was tried and convicted of violation of the Filled Milk Act and that conviction affirmed.[108] However, in the interval the Company had perfected a "vitamin fortification process" which completely eliminated the vitamin deficiency, formerly present in its product, that had figured so prominently in denunciation of filled milk. Thus legally fortified, the persistent Company sought and secured certiorari review in the Supreme Court. It contended in the alternative that (1) its improved product, now unquestionably nutritious and wholesome, was not within the intendment of the prohibitory Act or (2) if found to be so, the Act was unconstitutional under Fifth Amendment Due Process. On the issue of statutory

---

103. United States v. Carolene Products Co., 304 U.S. 144, Record, Microfiche, card 4, at 32.

104. *Id.* card 2, at 37.

105. 62 CONG. RECORD, Pt. 7, pp. 3580-3597, 3611.

106. *Id.* at 3596.

107. *E.g., id.* at 3611.

108. Carolene Products Co. v. United States, 140 F. 2d 61 (C.C.A. 4th, 1944).

interpretation Carolene counsel relied upon *Church of the Holy Trinity v. United States*,[109] a celebrated decision in which the Court had construed the Church's contract to employ an Englishman as rector to be without a federal law prohibiting "the importation or migration of foreigners and aliens under contract or agreement to perform labor in the United States. . . . "The constitutional assertion, (2), was grounded on deprivation of property without due process of law, citing for close relevancy *Weaver v. Palmer Brothers Co.*[110] the "shoddy case" from 1926 that has been considered in an earlier chapter of this study.[111]

The Supreme Court rejected both contentions in *Carolene Products Co. v. United States*,[112] known to constitutional commentators as *Carolene II*. Much of the opinion by Justice Reed was given over to the issue of statutory interpretation. *Church of the Holy Trinity* was relevant with respect to public health contentions now that the vitamin deficiency had been removed. However, while "the vitamin deficiency was an efficient cause in bringing about the enactment of the Filled Milk Act, it was not the sole reason for its passage. A second reason was that the compounds lent themselves readily to substitution for or confusion with milk products."[113] These considerations other than nutritional deficiencies "furnish an adequate basis, other than unwholesomeness, for the action of Congress."[114] *Weaver* was distinguishable. "It was pointed out in the course of the opinion, p. 413, that where the possibility of evil was not negatived, legislation prohibiting the sale of a wholesome article would not be invalidated. *Powell v. Pennsylvania*, 127 U.S. 678."[115] Reference to *Powell* was fatal to Carolene Products' contention of deprivation of property without due process of law.[116] "On the point of the constitutionality in relation to due process of the prohibition of trade in articles which are not in themselves dangerous but which make other evils more difficult to control, such as confusion in the filled milk legislation, the *Powell* case is authority for the validity of congressional action in the Filled Milk Act."[117]

Carolene Products Co. received small satisfaction from a closing paragraph of explanation for the Court's holding against it.

---

109. 143 U.S. 457 (1892). That there was strength in the statutory claim is suggested by the fact this question troubled Justice Brandeis in the *Hebe Co.* litigation involving an Ohio law equivalent to the Federal Act. He had there dissented from the Holmes opinion for the Court. Refer to note 100, *supra*.

110. 270 U.S. 402 (1926).

111. Chap. 6, *supra*, at notes 36 and 37.

112. 323 U.S. 18 (1944).

113. *Id*. at 22-23.

114. *Id*. at 29.

115. *Ibid*.

116. This seminal decision has been fully considered earlier, both in chap. 5, *supra*, and this chapter.

117. Carolene II, 323 U.S. at 29-30.

In the action of Congress on filled milk there is no prohibition of the shipment of an article of commerce merely because it competes with another such article which it resembles. Such would be the prohibition of the shipment of cotton or silk textiles to protect rayon or nylon or of anthracite to aid the consumption of bituminous coal or of cottonseed oil to aid the soybean industry. Here a milk product, skimmed milk, from which a valuable element—butterfat—has been removed is artificially enriched with cheaper fats and vitamins so that it is indistinguishable in the eyes of the average purchaser from whole milk products. The result is that the compound is confused with and passed off as the whole milk product in spite of proper labeling.[118]

At first blush this reasoning may be acceptable enough. The Court recognizes that among the economic facts of life there is the phenomenon of product competition in which governmental favoritism of one product over a competitor suggests an over-reaching of constitutional limitation. Yet the Court completely disregards the implications flowing from government's taking the side of dairy milk when confusion may obtain between two products equal in nutritional value. With reconstituted filled milk as healthful as whole milk through vitamin fortification, where is the justification for favoring the evaporated/condensed product over its rival? Why should filled milk be charged with consumer confusion any more than its counterpart? In view of the price differential in favor of filled milk who is to say that the consumer is to be protected in the "right" to pay more? Contentions of confusion do not justify favoritism once quality is equalized. The Court's reasoning fails on analysis.

There is a limit, albeit ill defined, beyond which government may not destroy one industry to the advantage of a competing industry. The limit must lie in the Due Process Clauses.[119] The Court opinion gives no hint of whether this springs from the anti-expropriation or the anti-monopoly core of due process. It would appear to be the former, for want of any suggestion of the latter. In public favoring of one business over a competitor to the point of destruction the situation can be viewed as the taking of property from A for the benefit of B. But much more compelling is analysis in terms of promotion of monopoly by public favoritism among competitors, for intense opposition to which there is the core of hostility to monopoly long resident in the substance of historic due process. Fault for disregard of this alternative defense to economic rape through forms of law must be shared by Courts, counsel, and commentators of the twentieth century. Or possibly the blame can be placed at the door of the favorite whipping boy, the *Lochner* Court, which draws attention away from the constitutional history of England of the seventeenth and eighteenth

118. *Id.* at 31.

119. Equal Protection, although at one time seemingly pregnant with similar constitutional limitation, *e.g.*, Justice Bradley concurring in *Butchers' Union v. Crescent City Livestock Co; Yick Wo v. Hopkins*, now appears to lack such content. Sage Stores Co. v. Kansas, 323 U.S. 32 (1944); the container cases next in analysis.

centuries and of the nineteenth century in the United States toward the false doctrine of freedom of contract. Whoever should properly bear the onus, there is no excuse for this continuing insult to constitutional scholarship.

Governmental favoritism among competing products, like that among rival sellers of the same product, has many illustrations. Appeals to legislatures for succor are especially strong in times of market stagnancy. The hardships of the Great Depression spawned major recourse to law-making assemblies. An effort was made in the aftermath of the Depression years to identify instances of governmental intervention in product competition.[120] The appeal from marketplace to legislative assembly continues, followed often by resort from enactment to the judiciary in an effort on the part of the loser to undue in the name of constitutional limitation the "correction" made at the legislative level.

At the state judicial level, appeal from anti-competitive laws in the economic area has been quite successful. This is the finding of an able commentator after an extensive survey.[121]

> Of the decisions surveyed, many invalidations of economic measures on due process grounds could have been based solely upon a determination of illegitimacy of legislative purpose; that is, the end prong of the *Nebbia* test has not been satisfied. Of these cases, nearly all rest upon a judicial determination that the legislation in question has the impermissible purpose of unreasonably preventing competition in the economic market place.[122]

Most of the cases in the survey concerned state legislative efforts to constrict commodity competition; however, some classify as attempts to hamper or destroy product (substituted) competition. The surveyor, like the courts, accords

---

120. *Note on Governmental Product Favoritism*, 8 LAW & CONTEMP. PROBS. 264 (1941). The entire issue of this journal in which the Note appears was devoted to examination of "marketing barriers that are the consequence of governmental, rather than private, action." *Foreword, id.* at 207. It was my privilege to serve as Visiting Editor for this issue.

121. Kirby, *supra* note 49. Supplementation of the original survey includes further cases of invalidation of governmental favoritism between rival entrepreneurs and products.

The emphasis on state constitutional interpretation is the subject of *Symposium: The Emergence of State Constitutional Law*, 63 TEX. L. REV. 959 (1985).

122. Kirby, *supra* note 49, at 252. The due process decisions from outside Tennessee are reviewed *id.* at 252-261; those from Tennessee *id.* at 269-272. In conversation with Professor Kirby in 1984 during the Williamsburg Conference on Developments in State Constitutional Law he capsuled his findings with the observation that conspicuous in the many invalidations he had unearthed was state court resort to substantive due process in protection of market competition. He is not completely symnpathetic with this pronounced trend. While "some substantive containment of legislatures is basic to our concept of limited government," yet at times "the courts are making economic judgments that are more appropriate for legislative determination and essentially are formulating antitrust policy which might be appropriate in the absence of legislation but hardly is appropriate in opposition to it." *Id.* at 257. I do not share this hesitancy for the reason that the anti-monopoly core of historic due process amply warrants constitutional review of all legislative marketing barriers that seriously impair economic efficiency.

no significance to differentiation between the two categories. Beyond the butter-oleo and filled milk–whole milk conflicts the Supreme Court has dealt with
the second type only as regards the container industry. The first of these cases
antedated *Carolene I*, the other has been quite recent.

Pacific States Box & Basket Co. v. White,[123] decided in late 1935, sustained
an administrative order, grounded on legislative authorization, that mandated
the hallock type of container for use in Oregon in the packaging of raspberries
and strawberries. "A hallock is a type of rectangular till box with perpendicular sides and a raised bottom. It is usually made of rotary cut veneer, taken
directly from spruce logs; but is sometimes made of paper or other material."[124] Justice Brandeis, writing for a unanimous Court, so described the
type of container exclusively permitted in the State after a short period for disposition of alternatives. Pacific States, a California corporation, there manufactured for sale in and out of California a type of container known as tin-top
or metal rim. "It differs from the hallock both in shape and construction,"
explained the Justice. "In shape, it is more like a cup; its sides slope outward;
and it has not the raised bottom. This cup is made from two thin strips of
wood crossing each other to form the bottom of the container and then bent
upward to form the sides, reinforced with a narrow metal strip to insure protection of the cup and its contents, as well as to insure uniformity of cubic
measure."[125]

Pacific States sought injunctive relief against the order in federal court, invoking both diversity and federal question as jurisdictional grounds. That
court denied the injunction and dismissed the bill. Justice Brandeis, in a variance from the Assignments of Error stated in the Record,[126] summarized the
Company's claims of invalidity thusly:

   (a) Under the due process clause of the Fourteenth Amendment, because the order
       is arbitrary, capricious, and not reasonably necessary for the accomplishment
       of any legitimate purpose of the police power;
   (b) Under the equal protection clause of the Amendment, because the order grants
       a monopoly to manufacturers of hallocks;
   (c) Under the commerce clause. . . .[127]

First disposed of was the due process claim, which "is directed solely to the
fixing of the dimensions and the form of the container." Because there are said
to be "34 other styles or shapes of berry basket in use somewhere in the United
States," retail buyers are less likely to be deceived as to condition and quantity
if packaging is limited to the familiar hallock form; a shallow container with

---

123. 296 U.S. 176 (1935).
124. *Id.* at 179.
125. *Id.* at 180.
126. *Id.*, Record, Microfiche, card 1, at 38.
127. Pacific States Box & Basket Co. v. White, 296 U.S. at 180.

perpendicular sides may "conceivably better preserve these fruits"; and, because containers are shipped in crates of 24 boxes, "the berries may conceivably be better stowed where the fruit basket has the bottom set-up peculiar to the hallock, than if it had the flat bottom of the plaintiff's metal-rim cup."[128] These are mighty flimsy justifications for support of a governmental decree entrenching the hallock to the exclusion of other types of container. At other times and places the false-bottom box has been viewed as the essence of deception. To sustain speculations regarding the superiority of the hallock in berry preservation and packaging requires heavy reliance upon a presumption of constitutionality that operates to uphold legislative action "if any state of facts reasonably can be conceived that would sustain it." This is exactly the extreme to which the Court went,[129] thus anticipating the use made of it in *Carolene I*.

The Company's charge that the administrative order constituted a monopoly by public grant was ineffectively presented in its Brief; again, counsel failed to relate the monopoly contention to due process, arguing rather that the order deprived plaintiff of property without due process of law.[130] Assigning the monopoly claim to Equal Protection, the Court disposed of it in the following paragraph:

> The charge that the order is void because it grants a monopoly to manufacturers of hallocks is unfounded. The plaintiff, and all others, are free to engage in the business, which, so far as appears, is not protected by patent or trademark and does not rest upon trade secrets. The business is not closely controlled; nor is it peculiar to Oregon. In 1933, at least 25 concerns were engaged in the United States in manufacturing hallocks. Less than one-fourth of them were located in Oregon and Washington. Plaintiff asserts that the order excludes it from the Oregon trade since its plant cannot be equipped to manufacture hallocks except at a prohibitive cost; and that the spruce logs, the veneer of which is customarily used in making hallocks, are not obtainable except in the Pacific Northwest. Obviously these allegations afford no support to the charge of monopoly; among other reasons, because the order does not prescribe the material from which hallocks may be made. They are in fact made, to some extent, from material other than spruce veneer. Moreover, the grant of a monopoly, if otherwise an appropriate exercise of the police power, is not void as denying equal protection of the law. Compare Slaughter-House Cases, 16 Wall. 36; Nebbia v. New York, 291 U.S. 502, 529.[131]

This paragraph, if allowed to stand as the Court's position, would be ominous as respects any constitutional protection against monopoly by public

---

128. *Id*. at 181-82.

129. *Id*. at 185.

130. The Assignments of Error filed by Pacific States in its appeal to the Supreme Court show no explicit resort to the monopoly contention. Record, Microfiche, card 1, at 38-42. The contention that the Company was deprived of its property in violation of the due process guarantee was argued, *id*. card 2, at 14-20. Citation to the invalidations of the 1920s was conspicuous.

131. Pacific States Box & Basket Co. v. White, 296 U.S. at 183-84.

grant. Certainly protection from governmental favoritism in product competition is washed out, if ever it had any toehold whatsoever. When Justice Brandeis, whose grasp of economics exceeded that of any other member of the Supreme Court, could view the facts of this case as presenting only an issue of
commodity competition there is no basis for expectation that the Court would
see monopoly in public interference with substituted competition. "[B]ecause
the order does not prescribe the material from which hallocks may be made,"
does not answer the charge of monopoly in product competition; Pacific States
still cannot market its type of container in Oregon. I cannot understand how
Brandeis could write such a sentence out of economic ignorance; his purpose
must have been to eliminate this form of competition from constitutional consideration. But even monopoly resulting from legislative intervention in commodity competition, to the disadvantage of the many for the benefit of the few,
is said not to be unconstitutional. Cited in support of this assertion are the
Slaughter-House Cases majority ruling and the statement of Justice Roberts in
Nebbia of legislative freedom to opt for monopoly policy. This constitutes reliance on a mighty slender reed, as earlier contended[132] and hereinafter more
fully developed. The only hope that this paragraph will not stand as the
Court's final position on this issue is the fact it is a judgment based on Equal
Protection rather than on Due Process which historically houses the core
theme of anti-monopoly.

In the food industry generally, packaging for buyer consumption has long
found the glass bottle and the tin can in active competition. For retail distribution of fluid milk the glass bottle originally occupied the field. By the middle
of the present century the non-refillable paperboard carton came to predomi-
nate over the refillable glass container because of sanitation, safety, and cost
factors. The law reports record an appeal from the marketplace of a trade war
between glass and paper milk bottles. American Can Co. and Ex-Cell-O
Corp. each provided milk distributors in the Chicago area with the newer paper container; the former by direct sale of its manufactured product, the latter
by leasing its patented machines. They sought a declaratory judgment "that
the milk ordinance of the City of Chicago does not prohibit the use of paper
milk containers or if it does that it is invalid." Their suit did not even reach the
merits, both the federal trial and appellate courts dismissing for lack of standing to sue.[133] In the 1960s nonreturnable plastic containers began to appear
as a rival to the nonrefillable paperboards; the plastic containers were less
awkward in handling, were free of leakage, and provided resealable caps.[134]

---

132. Refer to textual note 59, *supra*.

133. Ex-Cell-O Corp. v. City of Chicago, 115 F. 2d 627 (C.C.A. 7th, 1940).

134. The history of these developments is sketched by the trial judge and by an amicus
brief in the litigation arising from Minnesota legislation outlawing the plastic container.
Minnesota v. Clover Leaf Creamery Co., *infra* note 136, Microfiche, card 1, at 5-6; card
4, at 3.

Inevitably, competition developed between the two newer types of container, inviting legislative intervention at this point.[135] The likelihood became reality, producing litigation that culminated in the Supreme Court as *Minnesota v. Clover Leaf Creamery Co.*[136]

In novel legislation the Minnesota legislature at its 1977 session "enacted a statute banning the retail sale of milk in plastic nonreturnable, nonrefillable containers, but permitting such sale in other nonreturnable, nonrefillable containers, such as paperboard milk cartons."[137] The purpose of the law, declared the law-making body, was to discourage use of nonreturnable, nonrefillable containers and encourage that of returnable and reusable packaging, in the interest of reduction of solid waste, of preservation of energy sources, and of prevention of depletion in natural resources. Clover Leaf and others who opposed the legislation, after losing the battle in the legislature, filed suit in state district court to enjoin enforcement of the enactment. That court conducted extensive hearings, to find "in sharp conflict" evidence as to the law's probable consequences. However, concluding the State had not demonstrated that the challenged law would achieve the purported legislative objective of conservation, it was held violative of the due process clauses of both the Federal and the Minnesota constitutions and, as well, of the federal equal protection clause.[138]

The State appealed to the supreme court of Minnesota,[139] but with no success. "We affirm the trial court's judgment and hold that the Act violates the equal protection clause of the Fourteenth Amendment to the United States Constitution, because it establishes a classification which is not rationally related to a legitimate state interest."[140] The appellate court, with one dissent, read the conflicting evidence as had the trial court. In none of the three respects assigned by the legislature in justification of its enactment were nonrefillable plastic containers a greater threat to conservation than were paperboards. "Because paper containers are not environmentally superior to plastic nonrefillables, any asserted environmental benefit in preventing plastic nonrefillables from being widely used in Minnesota is illusory."[141]

Surely the Minnesota supreme court realized the certainty of reversal by the Supreme Court of the United States were the State to carry its case there, as it

---

135. The MEMORANDUM prepared by the trial judge in the *Clover Leaf* litigation to be discussed, and by him made a part of his Findings of Fact and Conclusions of Law, referred to Society of Plastic Industries v. New York City, 3 ERC 1370 (1971), invalidating an ordinance forbidding use of plastic milk containers. *Id.*, Record, Microfiche, card 1, at A-30.

136. 449 U.S. 456 (1981).

137. *Id.* at 458.

138. *Id.*, Record, Conclusions of Law of the District Court, Microfiche, card 1, at A-28.

139. Clover Leaf Creamery Co. v. State, 289 N.W. 2d 79 (Minn. 1979) (one dissent).

140. *Id.* at 80-81.

141. *Id.* at 86.

did through certiorari. True, it employed for Equal Protection the High Court's mandated test of rational basis but rationality is a concept of many colors.[142] Explained Justice Brennan writing for the Court:

> Whether *in fact* the Act will promote more environmentally desirable milk packaging is not the question: the Equal Protection Clause is satisfied by our conclusion that the Minnesota Legislature *could rationally have decided* that its ban on plastic nonreturnable milk jugs might foster greater use of environmentally desirable alternatives.[143]

Such a measure of rationality can be satisfied by any law enacted by a legislature not wholly bereft of its senses! The Court's judgment was inevitably one of reversal, only Justice Stevens dissenting.

Although there is no equal protection clause as such in the Minnesota constitution that instrument does include a due process clause on which the trial judge predicated his judgment along with the Due Process and Equal Protection Clauses of the Federal Constitution. The Minnesota supreme court, however, saw no reason to rely upon due process because "under substantive due process analysis, the means chosen by the challenged legislation similarly must bear a rational relationship to the public purpose sought to be served."[144] This was correct for federal due process but need not be the interpretation placed on state due process. The trial court had concluded from the relevant history of the statute that "the real basis for it was to serve certain economic interests (paper, pulpwood, and some dairies) at the expense of other competing economic groups (plastic and certain dairies) by prohibiting the plastic milk bottle."[145]

The Minnesota supreme court saw fit to pass over this finding and thus disregarded basis for invalidity on the anti-monopoly content that many state courts have found in the due process clauses of their state constitutions. This would have insulated the decision under the adequate and independent state ground rule. Once again the hard lesson was learned that Equal Protection is no protector against monopoly legislation. Again one may wonder what the explanation is for failure at the state level to cast attacks on grounds of constitutional opposition to legislative attempts at monopolization through stifling of competitive forces present in the marketplace. Such attacks require two steps: first, invocation of due process as the relevant constitutional provision; second, specific reference to this guaranty as the fountainhead of anti-

---

142. Leedes, *The Rationality Requirement of the Equal Protection Clause*, 42 Ohio St. L. J. 639 (1981).

143. Minnesota v. Clover Leaf Creamery Co., 449 U.S. at 466 (italics in the original).

144. Clover Leaf Creamery Co. v. State, 289 N.W. 2d at 87, n. 20.

145. MEMORANDUM of Judge Marsden, Record, *Clover Leaf*, Microfiche, card 1, at A-30. This and other portions of the Memorandum A-29 to A-33 were by him made a part of his Findings of Fact and Conclusions of Law. The same conclusion, somewhat differently expressed, constituted Finding of Fact #23, *id.* card 1, at A-27.

monopoly protection. In the present case, for instance, the trial court first assigned invalidity under due process but then added violation of equal protection; worse, with respect to each provision the assertion of unconstitutionality was expressed as a deprivation,[146] thus suggesting a taking of property conflicting with the other core concept of property expropriation. This despite the trial court's finding that as a matter of fact the actual purpose of the Minnesota law was to accord a monopoly position to paperboard containers.

Profession versus Purpose in Constitutional Adjudication. The fourth and final distinction between the germinative cases of *Dobbins* and *McCray* concerns the Court's posture on what a commentator has well described as "one of the most muddled areas of our constitutional jurisprudence."[147] In *McCray* the Court declined to look behind the face of a congressional enactment laying an excise tax on oleomargarine, a look that all the surrounding circumstances would reveal was not to raise revenue but to destroy butter's competition. In *Dobbins*, on the contrary, there was no effort at shamming; the City admitted by demurrer the plaintiff's assertion that the ordinance was designed to protect the rival utility "in the enjoyment of its monopoly." In the years since this early dichotomy the Court's record has been one of indecision. Chief Justice Warren attempted in *United States v. O'Brien*[148] to satisfy everyone that the Court had been consistent in following *McCray* but precedents would not support him.[149] And neither later Justices nor awakened commentators accepted the flawed attempt. Rejection by the Court was signalled by the decision in *Washington v. Davis.*[150] Professor Brest credits Dean Ely with breaking the "academic tradition of superficial treatment" of "the problem of

---

146. *Id.*, Conclusions of Law, card 1, at A-28.

147. Brest, *Palmer v. Thompson: An Approach to the Problem of Unconstitutional Legislative Motive*, 1971 SUP. CT. REV. 95, 99.

148. 391 U.S. 367, Part III (1968). Palmer v. Thompson, 403 U.S. 217 (1971), took the same tack as did *O'Brien.*

149. Brest, *supra* note 147, at 100, cites to three decisions of the 1960s where the Court inquired into "motivation." One, Epperson v. Arkansas, 393 U.S. 97 (1968), was contemporaneous with *O'Brien.* Note, 83 HARV. L. REV. 1887 (1970), cites to the same effect earlier and contemporaneous cases. *Contra*: A Magnano Co. v. Hamilton, 292 U.S. 40 (1934), earlier considered in this chapter.

150. 426 U.S. 229, at 244, n. 11 (1976).

In Hunt v. Washington Apple Advertising Comm., 432 U.S. 333, 352 (1977), the Court showed no hesitancy in taking note of a "most glaring" instance of intended byproduct of the North Carolina statute under challenge, although finding it unnecessary to "ascribe an economic protection motive to the North Carolina Legislature to resolve this case," invalidating the law as discriminatory against interstate commerce in Washington apples. The Court had spotted in the Appendix of the papers before it the passing statement of the Commissioner of Agriculture of North Carolina that it was the apple producers of his State who "were mainly responsible for this legislation being passed." Microfiche, card 1, at 21 (Exhibit "C").

Later Court decisions to similar effect are canvassed by Raveson, *infra* note 152.

judicial review of motivation."[151] "Motive has come a long way since *Palmer v. Thompson* and *United States v. O'Brien* revived the notion that legislative motive is not a basis for invalidating official enactments. Recently, writers seem to agree that motive should play some role in constitutional adjudication."[152]

The issue continues to be plagued with definitional difficulties because of the varying meaning given to the term "motive" or "motivation." It is agreed that judicial psychoanalysis of legislators is improper,[153] a futile quest.[154] Why a legislature did what it did is beyond the pale as requiring wholly subjective inquiry. But this leaves open the question whether what it did is to be judicially judged from the legislative profession contained in the statutory preamble or discovered from objective inquiry into the actual purpose lying behind the enactment, whether the same or different. Search for "motive" in this sense of

---

151. Brest, *supra* note 147, at 102, citing Ely, *Legislative and Administrative Motivation in Constitutional Law*, 79 YALE L. J. 1205 (1970).

152. Eisenberg, *Reflections on a Unified Theory of Motive*, 15 SAN DIEGO L. REV. 1147 (1978). Cited are the Brest and Ely analyses, his own observations, and the two major articles of the symposium to which he contributes the short comment on *Reflections*.

In an exhaustive inquiry into decisionmaker motive a commentator has now (1985) taken the unequivocal position that unconstitutional motivation/purpose is to be considered in constitutional adjudication. Raveson, *Unmasking the Motives of Government Decisionmakers: A Subpoena for Your Thoughts?* 63 N.C.L. REV. 879 (1985). The editorial summation at the commencement of the lengthy inquiry identifies the coverage of the article. By weighing numerous factors, it is there said, "courts can accommodate their obligation to examine legislative intent with a healthy degree of legislative freedom." This accommodation, the author asserts throughout his analysis, is required by the Court's "understanding of the separation of powers. . . . " *Id.* at 880. This assertion is correct enough as a matter of general principle in relations between branches of government; but it is not a mandate of the Constitution as he appears to assume. It is a common error of judges and commentators to associate judicial power to determine constitutionality with separation of powers. The origins of constitutional review make this error clear. Strong, *Bicentennial Benchmark: Two Centuries of Evolution of Constitutional Processes*, 55 N.C.L. REV. 1 (1976), tracing the evolution of judicial power to declare on constitutionality which developed quite independently of Montesquieu's principle against blending of governmental powers. Judicial power to determine constitutionality places courts in a relationship with the legislative and executive branches entirely contrary to that premised by the principle of separation of powers. Judicial inquiry into legislative motivation/purpose faces no impediment from constitutionalized separation of powers; rather, it must be accepted as a necessary tool in the full exercise of the adopted function of constitutional review.

153. A. BICKEL, THE LEAST DANGEROUS BRANCH 208 (1962).

154. Miller, *If "The Devil Himself Knows Not the Mind of Man," How Possibly Can Judges Know the Motivation of Legislators?* 15 SAN DIEGO L. REV. 1167, 1171 (1978). On the opening page of this query the author poses the contrary statements of Chief Justices Chase and Taft as "the polar opposites in the question whether it is appropriate for the Court to inquire into the legislature's motives." But here "motive" appears to mean "purpose" as used in the text of this paragraph.

purpose is a different matter.[155] It can be viewed as an investigation of "motivation" yet avoidance of confusion is gained by employing the term "purpose" to identify a judicial look at just what was the prime objective of the legislative act. While some critics insist that "motive" can be reasoned as "purpose" and vice versa, a sufficient distinction can be made pragmatically, between the two underlying concepts, to support further analysis.[156]

With legislative motive put to one side as an improper basis for judicial inquiry, there yet remains the justification for resort to purpose as properly perceived rather than acceptance solely of legislative profession. Here is the real rub, the issue on which judicial and lay opinions sharply differ. The Harvard Law Review notator previously cited[157] reached the conclusion

> that consideration of legislative purpose can help courts to understand the effects of legislation in various substantive areas of constitutional law, but that the reasons for considering purpose must be subjected to principled articulation by the courts to ensure that proper use is made of the concept.[158]

The proferred premise offers a constructive basis on which to resolve the conflict in viewpoint. The positions taken by major recent commentators are of this import although employing the term motivation in the sense of purpose.

Two decisions cited as precedent for Court declination to go behind profession to purpose are wide of the mark. *Veasie Bank v. Fenno*[159] sustained a federal tax of ten percentum on the circulating notes of state incorporated banks. A contention in the challenge to the tax, which two dissenters accepted, was that its purpose was to encourage national banks. The majority paid the claim no heed; not only did Congress have the power to tax but also to establish a national monetary policy. Futility would therefore have attended inquiry into hidden purpose because it would only have disclosed an alternate constitutional basis for the taxing act. *Mugler v. Kansas*[160] presented the opposite situation. Although the New York court of appeals by holding and the Supreme Court by dictum had earlier found a property right in liquor in existence at the date of enactment of state prohibition,[161] by the time of *Mugler* it was crystal clear that no property interest was judicially cognizable with respect to the

---

155. A. BICKEL, *op. cit. supra* note 153, at 209.

156. The Harvard Law Review Note cited *supra* note 149 provides, *id.* 1887, n. 1, an incisive consideration of "motive" and "purpose." At the end of this verbal tussle "motive" is put aside for attention to "purpose." *Cf.* Howell, *Legislative Motive and Legislative Purpose in the Invalidation of a Civil Rights Statute*, 47 VA. L. REV. 439 (1961).

157. Notes 149 and 156, *supra.*

158. Note, 83 HARV. L. REV. 1887, at 1889 (1970).

159. 8 Wall. 533 (1869).

160. 123 U.S. 623 (1887).

161. Wynehamer v. People, 13 N.Y. 378 (1856); Bartemeyer v. Iowa, 18 Wall. 129, at 133 (1873), both first considered chap. 2, *supra*, pp. 39-41, text at notes 55-60.

twin curses of society: alcohol and prostitution. Again, futility would attend search behind legislative profession by reason of the postulated absence of any constitutional right were devious purpose lurking in the background. Only of significance is the intermediate pattern where legislative profession always speaks to constitutionality while purpose will in some circumstances uncover conflict with constitutional limitation, direct or indirect.[162]

Chief Justice Warren was quite correct in *United States v. O'Brien* in recognizing that where a statute is challenged as a bill of attainder "the very nature of the constitutional question requires an inquiry into legislative purpose."[163] But he was entirely incorrect in insisting that bill of attainder and *ex post facto* litigation[164] constitute exceptions to the "familiar principle of constitutional law that this Court will not strike down an otherwise constitutional statute on the basis of an illicit legislative motive."[165] Neither is the principle of adherence to legislative profession "familiar" in the sense of constancy in application, nor can the two instances be properly viewed as unique.

A bill of attainder is violative of the constitutional design of separation of powers because it constitutes legislative usurpation of the very essence of the judicial function; the law-making department not only promulgates a general policy but adjudicates thereunder its specific applicability. An *ex post facto* law lacks due process because it renders criminal what when done was lawful; criminal legislation to be tolerable must be prospective. Similarly, official censorship of speech or press, imposition of religious establishment, denial of religious liberty, or abridgement of peaceable assembly violates the First or Fourteenth Amendment because of impingement upon substantive rights reserved to the People by the fundamental law of the nation. On the same rationale, "too great" legislative expropriation of private property or destruction of economic freedom by monopoly grant offends the Fifth or Fourteenth Amendment by reason of substantive due process restrictions on governmental power articulated in the Constitution. In these last two instances no less than in the first four, let alone the two identified by Chief Justice Warren, the Court must be informed as to legislative objective if its vaunted claim to untrammelled exercise of constitutional review is to be factual rather than fictional.

I continue in this conviction not alone by deduction from what to me is the clear teaching of the American constitutional design but as well from the Court's own historic deduction implicit in its persistent adherence to the doctrine of constitutional fact. My contention is that this tenet derives from the

---

162. I suggest that Alexander Bickel showed this insight, though perhaps dimly. A. BICKEL, *op. cit. supra* note 153, at 209. For this suggestion reliance is placed upon the central portion of the paragraph commencing on 209 and carrying over on 210.

163. United States v. O'Brien, 391 U.S. at 383, n. 30.

164. In his opinion in Trop. v. Dulles, 356 U.S. 86, at 95-96 (1958), the Chief Justice had linked *ex post facto* with bill of attainder, and *Trop* is cited in footnote 30 of *O'Brien*.

165. United States v. O'Brien, 391 U.S. at 383.

Court's realization that its insistence on being the ultimately exclusive interpreter of the Constitution requires that it have the final say with respect to controverted facts decisive of result in constitutional litigation. It matters not whether the initial determination has been made by administrator, administrative tribunal, judge, jury, legislature, or legislative delegate, the Court must make its own independent judgment if it is to play the role it has claimed for itself in our constitutional system. Finality belongs to the Court where constitutional issues are to be resolved.[166]

An able constitutional scholar does not view the independent judgment requirement as mandatorily grounded in the Constitution. In an informed analysis prompted by the Court's latest invocation of the tenet, *Bose Corp. v. Consumers Union of United States, Inc.,*[167] Professor Monaghan, as do the dissenting Justices, regards the doctrine as one of empowerment but not of duty.[168] On this major premise he treats the matter as one of judicial discretion; the question becomes that of determining the circumstances under which Rule 52(a) of the Federal Rules of Civil Procedure governs and those where an independent judgment is to be made. In conclusion he is not even persuaded that this latter category should include First Amendment cases, to which he reads the majority in *Bose* as limiting the stricter standard.

Although greatly respecting Professor Monaghan's constitutional scholarship, I differ with him also on this minor premise. I do not so read the footnote of the Stevens opinion on which he relies.[169] Although the first case cited for the obligation of the Court to make an independent constitutional judgment of the facts where challenges arise under the guarantees of the First and Fourteenth Amendments, *Jacabellis*, involved freedom of expression, the opinion of Justice Brennan for himself and Justice Goldberg did not restrict the requirement to First Amendment protections[170] nor did concurring Justices intimate such. It is to me convincing that in *Bose*, as in *Jacabellis* and elsewhere, the Court has meant only to stress the requirement "particularly" with respect to constitutional guarantees of aspects of freedom of expression.[171]

---

166. My major investigation into this judicial insight is found in Strong, *The Persistent Doctrine of Constitutional Fact*, 46 N.C.L. REV. 223 (1968). Supplementation appears in Strong, *Dilemmic Aspects of the Doctrine of "Constitutional Fact,"* 47 N.C.L. REV. 311 (1969). My insistence that the doctrine was properly invoked in instances of economic due process originally drew ridicule from Professor Kenneth Davis. K. C. DAVIS, ADMINISTRATIVE LAW TREATISE §§ 29.08, 29.09 (1970 Supp.). His attitude is now much more moderate. K. C. DAVIS, ADMINISTRATIVE LAW TREATISE §§ 28.3 and 29.23 (2d ed. 1984).

167. 466 U.S. 485 (1984) (White, Rehnquist and O'Connor, J. J. dissenting). The significance of *Bose* for libel actions is the subject of Abrams, *The Supreme Court Turns a New Page in Libel*, 70 A.B.A.J. 89 (1984).

168. Monaghan, *Constitutional Fact Review*, 85 COL. L. REV. 229 (1985).

169. Bose Corp. v. Consumers Union, 466 U.S. at 508, n. 27.

170. Jacabellis v. Ohio, 378 U.S. 184, at 189 (1964).

171. One must recognize the added burden on the Court of a requirement of independent

Lessons in constitutionalism teach that purpose in constitutional resolution is not to be compared with the function of purpose in statutory rendition. With the latter there are instances where by accepted principles of interpretation either of two different constructions may properly be adopted by a court. *Federal Trade Commission v. Bunte Bros.*[172] provides an excellent illustration. In controversy was the scope of Section 5(a) of the Federal Trade Commission Act which made unlawful "[u]nfair methods of competition in commerce . . . " and empowered the Commission to prevent their use. Bunte Brothers was an Illinois candy manufacturer that sold in that State what the trade called "break and take" packages. Candy manufacturers marketing interstate were barred by the Commission from selling such packages; it was ruled an unfair method of competition to offer a product where the amount received by the purchaser depended on chance. The Commission attempted to extend its prohibition to the Bunte Company, which countered that it was not within the intendment of the statute. With Justices Black, Douglas, and Reed dissenting, Justice Frankfurter for the Court sustained the defense. Referring to *United States v. Darby*[173] wherein two weeks earlier the Court had upheld the constitutionality of the Fair Labor Standards Act, he explained the difference in the two situations:

> We had there to consider the full scope of the power of Congress under the Commerce Clause in relation to the subject matter of [that Act]. This case presents the narrow question of what Congress did, not what it could do.[174]

Only where the more inclusive of two possible constructions of a statute raises questions of constitutionality does statutory interpretation present a situation analogous to the special considerations inherent in constitutional interpretation. Here the Court practice, recognized by Justice Brandeis in his celebrated listing of conditions for avoiding determination of validity on the merits,[175] is to adopt the narrower interpretation, a procedure Edward S. Corwin dubbed covert review of constitutionality.[176] *South Utah Mines & Smelt-*

---

fact judgment. However, that to me does not warrant its dilution into discretionary empowerment. I have offered a solution to the problem of the Court's workload based upon a distinction between ordinary judicial review and constitutional judicial review. Inasmuch as the basic distinction has enjoyed little attention, the proposed solution has experienced the same fate accorded other suggested patterns for relief. Strong, *The Time Has Come to Talk of Major Curtailment in the Supreme Court's Jurisdiction*, 48 N.C.L. REV. 1 (1969).

172. 312 U.S. 349 (1941).

173. 312 U.S. 100 (1941).

174. Federal Trade Comm. v. Bunte Bros., 312 U.S. at 355.

175. Ashwander v. T.V.A., 297 U.S. 288 at 346-48 (1936) (Rules 4 and 7).

176. Corwin, *Judicial Review*, 8 ENCYC. SOC. SCI. 457, 461 (1932). Professor Corwin employed the then accepted terminology *"judicial* review," which fuller understanding of the Court's role in the constitutional system should translate to *"constitutional* review."

ers v. Beaver County[177] is illustrative. Utah imposed upon metalliferous mines a property tax determined by a multiple of net annual proceeds. Beaver County taxing authorities, in assessing South Utah, included in their calculations proceeds from tailings deposits recovered from an abandoned mine. The resulting tax was paid under protest and suit brought in federal district court for recovery of the amount. South Utah Mines claimed the assessment was invalid under the Utah constitution and the Fourteenth Amendment. Judgment went for the County but was reversed by the Supreme Court which held that on the facts disclosed the tailings were not included within the terms of the taxing act. "The court should have so construed the statute and rendered judgment for the plaintiff. [Citations omitted.] This disposition of the case makes it unnecessary to adjudicate the questions under the Fourteenth Amendment."[178]

Clearly, the constitutional hazard must be one of substance. In *Chase Securities Corp. v. Donaldson*,[179] concerning attempted recovery on an illegal sale of securities, Minnesota had so amended its blue sky law as in effect "to lift the bar of the statute of limitations in a pending litigation, which [defendant] contends amounts to taking its property without due process of law."[180] Defendant lost in the Minnesota trial court and again on appeal, the Minnesota supreme court relying on *Campbell v. Holt*[181] and thereby declining to treat the amended statute of limitations as inapplicable. In *Holt* the Supreme Court had held that

> where lapse of time has not invested a party with title to real or personal property, a state legislature, consistently with the Fourteenth Amendment, may repeal or extend a statute of limitations, even after right of action is barred thereby, restore to the plaintiff his remedy, and divest the defendant of the statutory bar.[182]

The Court on appeal from Minnesota's high court now refused to reconsider and overrule *Holt*, reaffirming rather its "working hypothesis, as a matter of constitutional law, . . . that statutes of limitation go to matters of remedy, not to destruction of fundamental rights."[183]

The opinion in *Chase Securities* also disposed of defendant's contention, raised late on petition for rehearing in the Minnesota supreme court, that it "was denied due process of law because it had no opportunity to submit tes-

---

177. 262 U.S. 325 (1923).
178. *Id*. at 333.
179. 325 U.S. 304 (1945).
180. *Id*. at 305.
181. 115 U.S. 620 (1885).
182. Chase Securities Corp. v. Donaldson, 325 U.S. at 311-12, summarizing the earlier holding.
183. *Id*. at 314.

timony of legislators as to legislative intent.... " The Court labeled the claim frivolous.

> The state court has seen fit to draw inferences as to the intent of an act from its timing and from its provisions and from background facts of public notoriety. But that does not mean that the judgment must be set aside to afford a party the opportunity to call legislators to prove that the court's inferences as to intent were wrong. Statutes ordinarily bespeak their own intention, and when their meaning is obscure or dubious a state court may determine for itself what sources of extrastatutory enlightenment it will consult. Our custom of going back of an act to explore legislative history does not obligate state courts to do so, and there is nothing in the Constitution which by the widest stretch of the imagination could be held to require taking testimony from a few or a majority of the legislators to prove legislative "intent."[184]

It seems highly significant that forty years ago the Court would volunteer reference to its own "custom of going back of an act to explore legislative history.... " The reference is made with respect to statutory interpretation—but statutory interpretation in the context of covert constitutional interpretation with no caveat that this custom is not followed in outright interpretation of the Constitution. There can be little doubt from what through time the Court has said and done that Chief Justice Warren in O'Brien was careless with judicial history in his zeal to save the questionable amendment to the Selective Service Act. What is called for by impartial inquiry is an attempt to identify the circumstances in which the Court will go behind the asserted profession of public interest in a statute's preamble when underlying purpose points in the direction of a constitutionally impermissible objective.

Quong Wing v. Kirkendall[185] early placed the burden on counsel challenging legislation to present evidence that ulterior purpose underlay profession of concern for the public interest. Montana had imposed a license fee on hand laundries owned by males but exempting steam laundries.[186] Sustainment by the Montana supreme court was followed by affirmance in the Supreme Court, only Justice Lamar dissenting. However, the opinion for the Court by Justice Holmes closed with a telling paragraph.

> Another difficulty suggested by the statute is that it is impossible not to ask whether it is not aimed at the Chinese; which would be a discrimination that the Constitution does not allow. *Yick Wo v. Hopkins,* 118 U.S. 356. It is a matter of common observation that hand laundry work is a widespread occupation of Chinamen in this country while on the other hand it is so rare to see men of our race engaged in it that many of us would be unable to say that they ever had observed a case. But this ground of objection was not urged and rather was disclaimed when it was mentioned from the Bench at the argument. It may or may not be that if

---

184. *Id.* at 309, n. 5 (2).
185. 223 U.S. 59 (1912).
186. Refer to note 39, *supra.*

the facts were called to our attention in a proper way the objection would prove to be real.... It rests with counsel to take the proper steps, and if they deliberately omit them, we do not feel called upon to institute inquiries on our own account. Laws frequently are enforced which the court recognizes as possibly or probably invalid if attacked by a different interest or in a different way. Therefore without prejudice to the question that we have suggested, when it shall be raised, we must conclude that so far as the present case is concerned the judgment must be affirmed.[187]

Possibly word got around rapidly that the Court would not *sua sponte* take cognizance of evidence of actual legislative purpose at variance with purported profession as to intended objective. Or perhaps it was mere happenstance. In any event counsel did meet the procedural hurdle in litigation that followed hard upon that in *Quong Wing*. The instance was the little known case of *Smith v. Texas*,[188] decided by the Court two years later. Save for a grandfather clause and other exceptions, none relevant to the facts of this case, a Texas statute of 1909 forbade any person to act as conductor on a railroad train without having previously served for two years as conductor or brakeman on a freight train. For 21 years W. W. Smith had been a fireman or engineer on freight or passenger trains of the Texas & Gulf Railway, but he had never been a brakeman or conductor. On the day of July 22, 1910, however, he acted as a conductor of a freight train, for which he was prosecuted, convicted in a jury trial, and fined $25 with costs. On review, the Texas court of criminal appeals affirmed, to be reversed on further appeal by the United States Supreme Court.

Smith's lawyers acted in the nick of time. The Record discloses that in both the trial court and the state appellate court constitutional defense was rested on generalized claims of freedom of contract and obligation of contracts.[189] It was only in the Reply Brief for Smith in the Supreme Court that the claim of monopoly was advanced and then on the justification that the State, having "gone outside the record" to explain in its Brief the system of seniority among trainmen (from fireman to conductor) established by the railroads of Texas themselves,

> we beg to suggest that this statute was not passed at the instance of railroad companies; actually the railroads are frequently forced to adopt certain rules or regulations upon demand of trainmen's unions and it is safe to say that the Texas statute was passed to subserve the interests of brakemen's and firemen's associations and to give their associations a monopoly, as that is the obvious and natural result.[190]

The continuing contention by the State in defense of the validity of the law was that it was an exercise of the police power in protection of the safety of

---

187. *Id.* at 63-64.
188. 233 U.S. 630 (1914).
189. Record, Smith v. Texas, 233 U.S. 630, Microfiche, card 1, at 3-4, 29-34.
190. *Id.* card 2, at 5-6.

passengers, fellow employees, and property by guaranteeing the competence of those engaged in train operation, whether freight or passenger. However, the Court was not persuaded.

> There is no claim in the brief for the State that [Mr. Smith] was not competent to perform the duties of that position. On the contrary it affirmatively and without contradiction appeared that the plaintiff in error, like other locomotive engineers, was familiar with the duties of that position and was competent to discharge them with skill and efficiency.[191]
>
> . . . .
>
> The liberty of contract is, of course, not unlimited; but there is no reason or authority for the proposition that conditions may be imposed by statute which will admit some who are competent and arbitrarily exclude others who are equally competent to labor on terms mutually satisfactory to employer and employee. None of the cases sustains the proposition that under the power to secure the public safety, a privileged class can be created and be then given a monopoly of the right to work in a special or favored position.[192]

In reversing on the basis of an amalgam of due process and equal protection the Court may have been further influenced by an undercover factor. Unionization of labor first developed in the railroad industry. Counsel's reference to the fact that railroads were sometimes forced to accept unwanted union regulations reveals the early power of the Brotherhoods. Undisputed also is the fact that discrimination against non-whites was practiced by the Brotherhoods.[193] Add to this the curious fact that it was not the Texas & Gulf Railway but the employee who was prosecuted for violation of the statute and the suspicion arises that Mr. Smith may well have been a black. *Yick Wo v. Hopkins* was cited by Smith's counsel along with other decisional support yet beyond that analogy there is no hint that the monopoly argued and found was enmeshed in racial discrimination.[194]

There was one dissent in *Smith v. Texas* and that by none other than Justice Holmes! Because he dissented without opinion it is left to commentators to speculate what prompted him in this surprising action. Could there have been some personal pique between him and Justice Lamar? The latter had in *Quong Wing* dissented from Holmes' opinion for the Court; now Holmes dissents

---

191. Smith v. Texas, 233 U.S. at 635.

192. *Id.* at 638.

193. Steele v. Louisville & Nashville R. R. Co., 323 U.S. 192 (1944), disclosed Brotherhood continuation of discrimination against blacks thirty years later. There it appeared that Negro firemen were excluded from the Brotherhood of Locomotive Firemen and Enginemen but as a minority were under the Railway Labor Act required to accept the Brotherhood as their representative of the craft. The Court's intervention prevented an effort by the union in exercise of its power to achieve total exclusion of Negro firemen from service in the employ of the Railroad.

194. *Yick Wo v. Hopkins* is considered in chap. 3, *supra*, pp. 63-66, commencing at note 81.

from Justice Lamar's opinion in *Smith*. Or did Holmes feel that Lamar had undercut *Quong Wing* by adding the Court's own inquiry behind legislative profession to counsel's demonstration of hidden purpose? Noting the custom of the railroads to have the freight engineer act as conductor "in the event the regular conductor is disabled en route," Justice Lamar had stated:

> If we cannot take judicial knowledge of these facts the record contains affirmative proof on the subject. For, according to the testimony of the State's witness "acting as engineer on a freight train will better acquaint one with a knowledge of how to operate a freight train than acting as brakeman."[195]

Neither explanation seems plausible, and if Smith was indeed a Negro, Holmes' behavior defies understanding. The most charitable explanation for the dissent is offered later.

The disappointment with Holmes aside, *Quong Wing* and *Smith* foretold the hurdles that would beset efforts to persuade the Court to peer behind legislative profession, always cast in terms of deep concern for the public interest, for evidence of actual purpose to achieve an invalid objective. Success in that persuasion would necessitate (1) convincing demonstration of (2) an unconstitutional end. Analysis will be clarified by treating each of these requisites in turn. Determination of the first properly requires the Court to scrutinize every facet of the legislative action in question. Legislative history is of course relevant to the extent it can be found. Rare indeed will be the candor of those supporting constitutionality who testify to the presence of actual purpose. One such rarity is found in the Michigan law reports.[196] Not uncommonly, on the other hand, the internal history of a statute will disclose that participating

---

195. Smith v. Texas, 233 U.S. at 640-41. The testimony is set forth at length in footnote 1 on the first of these pages.

196. S. S. Kresge Co. v. Mayor of Detroit, 290 Mich. 185, 287 N.W. 427 (1939). A Depression ordinance of Detroit provided for "the regulation and licensing of florists," purportedly for the protection of customers against "fraudulent practices on the part of irresponsible merchants." The supreme court of Michigan invalidated the ordinance on the strength of testimony of two witnesses *for the defendant* in an action brought by the Kresge Co.

> The purpose of the ordinance may be gleaned from the testimony of defendants' witness Brown: "We were protecting our business by getting rid of these people who sold in the streets.... That is why the Florists Association lobbied this ordinance through.
>
> "It is true that these second-hand flowers were sold at second-hand prices. They sold roses at twenty-five cents a dozen. I sold them for a dollar and a dollar and a half. They were selling second-hand roses and I was selling first-hand roses. It is true that that was just a depression condition. People would not buy dollar dozen roses during the depression as much as when times were good."
>
> And the witness Lutey who testified: "There is nothing wrong with selling those imperfect roses as bull-heads at reduced prices. The object of this ordinance lobbied by my florist committee was to get rid of those merchants that sold that type of flower and old flowers. They were underselling our association of florists."

290 Mich. at 191, 287 N.W. at 430.

legislators will have pointed to deviance between the law's profession and its purpose. Thus in the draft card burning case Chief Justice Warren observed "[i]t is principally on the basis of the statements by these three Congressmen that O'Brien makes his congressional-'purpose' argument."[197] This argument he rejected:

> We decline to void essentially on the ground that it is unwise legislation which Congress had the undoubted power to enact and which could be reenacted in its exact form if the same or another legislator made a "wiser" speech about it.[198]

The fault line in this futility thesis, which to my disappointment Professor Ely embraced in an "admittedly somewhat hasty" consideration,[199] is its myopic quality. Legislative history is but one facet of a full investigation of circumstances surrounding enactment of law. Recall the Court's footnote in *Chase Securities* where it was observed that the Minnesota court "had seen fit to draw inferences as to the intent of an act from its timing and from its provisions and from background facts of public notoriety."[200] Thorough inquiry into these and other aspects of the making of a statute is a distinctive characteristic of those decisions where the Court has gone behind legislative profession. Reenactment of a questionable statute might enable a legislator to make a "wiser" statement about it but this would alter not a whit evidence from beyond legislative history.

In *O'Brien* the Chief Justice was concerned with the difficulty of ascertaining the intendment of an entire legislative assembly. "Inquiries into congressional motives or purposes are a hazardous matter."[201] While no one would deny the point, the observation makes no contribution to resolution of the issue of choice between legislative profession and purpose. Much of the administration of law, consensual and non-consensual, requires analogous determination of intent. The Chief Justice sought to distinguish the situation in

---

197. United States v. O'Brien, 391 U.S. at 385. *O'Brien* has been earlier considered in the text commencing at note 163. A check of the references to the Congressional Record discloses only two comments, one by Congressman Rivers the other by Senator Thurmond (both South Carolinians). In their remarks each more than hinted that the objective sought by amendment of the Universal Military Training and Service Act was to criminalize knowing mutilation or destruction of draft cards. To Congressman Rivers the intentional violator "can be sent to prison, where he belongs." 111 CONG. REC. (Part 15) 19871 (1965). Senator Thurmond declared that "[s]uch conduct as public burnings of draft cards and public pleas for persons to refuse to register should not and must not be tolerated...." *Id.* (Part 15) 20433 (1965). Even the House vote, recorded at *id.* 19872, of 393 to 1, with 40 not voting belied the Government's assertion that the statutory alteration was made in the interest of "the smooth and efficient functioning of the Selective Service System."
198. United States v. O'Brien, 391 U.S. at 384.
199. Ely, *supra* note 151, at 1214-15 (incl. note 31).
200. Refer to textual quotation, *supra*, p. 244, note 184.
201. United States v. O'Brien, 391 U.S. at 383.

constitutional interpretation from that in statutory by asserting that in the former the stakes are higher. Professor Ely's response perforated the attempt.

> But the height of the stakes argues both ways: the fact that a man's constitutional rights are in the balance may be the very reason a difficult inquiry must be undertaken. Of course, courts should "eschew guesswork" in constitutional adjudication, as elsewhere. That resolution argues, however, for non-intervention when the proof of motivation is less than clear and not necessarily for a total rejection of its relevance.[202]

Choice must be made on the basis of weight of the total evidence. Reasonable minds can differ on the degree of cogency that should obtain before profession is put aside for purpose. In the scales there should be an element of deference toward a coordinate branch of government; at the same time, however, there must be sensitivity to the judicial responsibility for protection of constitutional design. It is paradoxical that a Court at times so bent on enforcement of constitutional limitation is nevertheless on other occasions so timid in the quest.

However, no amount of evidence provocative of conviction that a legislature's profession of beneficial objective is but a cover for less laudable design will avail in a challenge to validity if there exists no constitutional impediment to the intended objective. This is the lesson taught by *Veasie Bank* and *Mugler*, as earlier learned.[203] More than Equity declines to engage in vain endeavors. Only if the contrived end is constitutionally impermissible can success attend persuading the Court to "lift the veil." Historically, monopoly by public grant has constituted forbidden fruit in the legislative domain of policy making because substantive due process embraced an anti-monopoly core. In constitutional litigation the missing link has not been lack of precedent but lack of economic understanding.

Despite valiant efforts from time to time in a few law schools to interrelate law with the (other?) social sciences, legal training has not been conducive to an understanding of economics. Witness the fiasco in interpretation of the antitrust laws where even the ablest of judges could not comprehend how "reasonable" concentrations of economic power could bring about monopolistic structure in industry by destruction of effective market competition. Preced-

---

202. Ely, *supra* note 151, at 1212. Two paragraphs later, however, this commentator terms "apt" the Chief Justice's characterization of judicial choice in the *O'Brien* circumstances as "guesswork." *Id.* at 1214. With due respect I find only intellectual circularity in Professor Ely's acceptance of Chief Justice Warren's justification for refusal to consider ulterior purpose on the ground of "disutility." "Judges are not to act on the basis of their own political preferences, but must instead for purposes of constitutional adjudication presume to be 'good laws' those which were enacted by the politically responsible departments and meet the Constitution's various tests of legitimacy." *Id.* at 1215-16. The crux of the matter is whether the legislative product *does* square with the Constitution.

203. If intervening analysis has dimmed recollection refer to text accompanying notes 159 and 160, *supra*, p. 239, this chapter.

ing analysis of Supreme Court litigation in which economic factors were intimately involved forces realization of the general ineptitude of both advocate and judge.[204] Time and again the relevance of the hostility to monopoly of substantive due process was missed by counsel because of failure to appreciate economic reality. Often they failed at clear articulation of even the other core dimension of substantive due process, that of opposition to expropriation of private property. Perhaps surprisingly, of the Justices of the Supreme Court Justice Reed showed more than usual sensitivity to competitive realities in *Carolene II*. Justice Brandeis' failure in *Pacific States Box & Basket* to see product monopoly in the exclusion of producers of tin-rim berry boxes because of wide competition among manufacturers of hallocks is difficult to understand.[205] However, it accords with the near universal absence of appreciation of the monopoly thrust of legislative inroads on substituted competition and therefore of the relevance of constitutional limitation grounded in the anti-monopoly core of substantive due process of law. There is no occasion to look behind legislative profession if "hidden" purpose would suggest no constitutional barrier.

Litigation culminating in *Daniel v. Family Security Life Insurance Co.*[206] presented unusual features with respect to each of the two considerations just examined. Involved was the validity of a South Carolina law that if enforced would outlaw operation of a business specializing in "funeral insurance." The relief sought by plaintiff company was the customary one of injunction, the basis of complaint violation of the Due Process and Equal Protection Clauses of the Fourteenth Amendment. At the hearing before a federal statutory court plaintiff exhibited an affidavit sworn to by one Charles Honig in which this knowledgeable undertaker recited the history of burial financing among the poor of South Carolina.[207] Expenses were met by "burial clubs" to which members contributed as they could from their meager incomes. Assessments followed no pattern; practices were not sound actuarially. Established life in-

---

204. Majoring in Economics in college and instructing in the subject for two years at the university level before attending law school admittedly has greatly influenced me in my views on Constitutional Law. Compare the effect on another law trained one-time teacher, self-taught in Economics. R. POSNER, ECONOMIC ANALYSIS OF LAW (2d ed. 1977).

205. For refreshment of recollection of the Justice's statement, refer to the quotation at note 131, *supra*. The Justice's last sentence, asserting state power to grant monopoly, is baffling. At one fell blow it repudiates a mass of constitutional history. For support of the pronouncement the astonished reader is to "compare" the majority opinion in *Slaughter-House Cases* and Justice Roberts' equally surprising aside to the same effect in *Nebbia*. Earlier the fragility of this supposed support is demonstrated. Refer to note 59, *supra*. No attention to this revolutionary view, anywise comparable to its significance, has emerged. Any heed paid it would surely have stirred great reaction among the commentators.

206. 336 U.S. 220 (1949).

207. Daniel v. Family Security Life Insurance Co., 336 U.S. 220, Microfiche, card 1, at 51-60.

surance companies priced their policies out of this market; the alternative to crude mutual insurance was individual self-help. In these circumstances several enterprising morticians saw an opportunity to meet a socio-economic need. They judged the situation aright; in three months after organization and licensing of Family Security Life $838,000 in insurance had been written and further demand loomed great.[208]

The opinion of the trial court continued the account from this point.

> As the business of the plaintiff company increased rapidly its competitors became active. At meetings of agents of the competing insurance companies, pressure for legislation to destroy plaintiff company and to proscribe its agents was agreed upon. Division developed, too, among the morticians themselves and some of them joined with the competing insurance companies in promoting special legislation intended to destroy plaintiff company and its business. It seems obvious from the record that this legislation had its genesis in the desire of the existing insurance companies to eliminate the plaintiff company as a competitor. As a result of this pressure, the Legislature of South Carolina enacted, and the Governor approved on April 14, 1948, the challenged statute.[209]

The Act, reproduced in full in Appendix A, the court summarized as making it unlawful (1) for any insurance company to own a mortuary or to permit its officers or employees to operate a mortuary, and (2) for any funeral director or employee of a mortuary to be licensed as an insurance agent."[210] The legislative aim hit the mark inasmuch as the Company marketed its policies through undertakers and their employees acting as insurance salesmen.

The State's attorney general, defending the law's validity, did not dispute plaintiff's contention respecting actual statutory purpose; rather, it was deemed to be of no pertinency. "The defendants do not have information as to motive or intent of this regulation but aver that legislative intent in enacting a statute is irrelevant here."[211] By inference Circuit Judge Dobie, who dissented from the judgment of invalidity reached by the two District Judges of the panel, took the same position. On appeal by the State this treatment of "motivation" won approval. In an opinion reversing the lower court Justice Murphy declared:

> It is said that the "insurance lobby" obtained this statute from the South Carolina legislature. But a judiciary must judge by results, not the varied factors which may have determined legislators' votes. We cannot undertake a search for motive in testing constitutionality. See *Hammer v. Dagenhart*, 247 U.S. 251, overruled in *United States v. Darby*, 312 U.S. 100.[212]

---

208. *Ibid.*
209. Family Security Life Ins. Co. v. Daniel, 79 F. Supp. 62, 64-65 (E.D.S.C. 1948).
210. *Id.* at 62-63.
211. Paragraph 9 of the Answer. Daniel v. Family Security Life Insurance Co., 336 U.S. 220, Microfiche, card 1, at 21.
212. Daniel v. Family Security Life Insurance Co., 336 U.S. at 224. The paragraph in

With its mind set on legislative profession the Supreme Court speculated that:

> The South Carolina legislature might well have concluded that funeral insurance, although paid in cash, carries the same evils that are present in policies payable in merchandise or services: the beneficiary's tendency to deliver the policy proceeds to the agent-undertaker for whatever funeral the money will buy, whether or not an expensive ceremony is consistent with the needs of the survivors. Considerations which might have been influential include the likelihood of overreach on the part of insurance companies, and the possibilities of monopoly control detailed in affidavits introduced in the court below.[213]

The first sentence in this passage was surely intended to answer the Question put in plaintiff's appellate brief.

> Does this statute offend the due process and equal protection clauses of the 14th Amendment... (a) Because [directed] with premeditated precision to the destruction of the plaintiff Life Insurance Co., with no reasonable relationship [between objective and evil to be prevented].[214]

As in so many other instances counsel challenging legislative favoritism in competition of entrepreneurs or products failed to rest constitutional contention on the anti-monopoly facet of substantive due process, depending rather on the concept's opposition to publicly fostered expropriation of private property.

The "possibilities of monopoly control" recognized by Justice Murphy in the second sentence of the above passage had not been pressed by the plaintiff; the context makes it clear this is a reference to monopoly control *by* Family Security Life and not at the instigation of the competing insurance companies! The affidavits of which the Justice is speaking are those introduced at the trial level *by the State*. That of Thomas McAfee, an undertaker, stated that in conversation with Gordon Floyd, one of the principal organizers of the new enterprise, the latter in urging the former to become an agent had stressed that "the effect of going into his insurance plan would be to freeze the undertakers' business and would monopolize and perpetuate the business for the existing morticians."[215] The affidavit of Harold Sale was to similar effect, adding the explanation that the plan would "keep out returning veterans who were in such numbers that established undertakers could not absorb them."[216]

---

which this rejection of purpose appears is concluded by two further comparisons of Court holdings, in each of which earlier inquiry behind legislative profession was not countenanced in later decision.

213. *Id.* at 222-23.

214. Daniel v. Family Security Life Insurance Co., 336 U.S. 220, Microfiche card 6, at 3.

215. *Id.* Microcard, Exhibit D to Answer, card 1, at 27.

216. *Id.* Microcard, Exhibit E to Answer, card 1, at 28.

There is indeed irony for Family Security Life Insurance Co. in the outcome of this litigation. The argument of public monopoly it had at hand but bungled is displaced by the State's contention of private monopoly possibly arising from aggressive conduct of the business of funeral insurance.[217] The Company is hoisted on its own petard, and contemplated victory is swallowed up in defeat for want of resort to the pertinent constitutional limitation.

A case decided during the 1984 Term again well illustrates a pattern of dual considerations impelling Court resort to purpose over profession. *Hunter v. Underwood*[218] concerned the constitutionality of a section of the Alabama Constitution of 1901 which disenfranchised persons convicted of, among other offenses, "any crime involving moral turpitude." Pursuant to this provision Underwood, a white, and Edwards, a black, had been denied the vote because each had been convicted of passing a worthless check. The Court affirmed decision by a federal court of appeals, which had reversed a district court finding of no violation of equal protection. That finding was rested upon reasoning from *Palmer v. Thompson* that although disenfranchisement of blacks was a major purpose in the constitutional revision, based on belief that blacks were more likely to commit the crimes included in the expanded section, this fact did not warrant invalidation in the face of the permissible motive of "governing exercise of the franchise by those convicted of crimes." It is significant that the Court rejected this reasoning as well as the contention on behalf of the registrars that a permissible motive of disenfranchisement of poor whites "trumps any proof of a parallel impermissible motive."

Here the factor of an unconstitutional end clearly protrudes; the Constitution has no more specific prohibition than that that the franchise shall not be abridged on account of race or color. That attainment of that forbidden objective was the purpose of the amendment was equally manifest. Chief Justice Warren's concerns were neatly overcome; "the sort of difficulties of which the Court spoke in *O'Brien* do not obtain in this case."[219]

> Although understandably no "eye witnesses" to the 1901 proceedings testified, testimony and opinions of historians were offered and received without objection. These showed that the Alabama Constitutional Convention of 1901 was part of a movement that swept the post-Reconstruction South to disenfranchise blacks.... The delegates to the all-white convention were not secretive about their purpose.... Indeed, neither the District Court nor appellants seriously dispute the claim that this zeal for white supremacy ran rampant at the convention.[220]

Standing alone, the unanimous decision in *Hunter* might be argued to be reconcilable with Chief Justice Warren's assertion that only with claims of vi-

---

217. The relation between private monopoly and substantive due process of law is the subject of chap. 9, *infra*.
218. 105 Sup. Ct. 1916 (1985).
219. *Id.* at 1920.
220. *Id.* at 1920-21.

olation of the Bill of Attainder or Ex Post Facto guaranties is the Court to look behind legislative profession. Perhaps with the Fifteenth Amendment as well, he would say that "the very nature of the constitutional question requires an inquiry into legislative purpose."[221] But the Warren theory cannot withstand vigilant analysis[222] and is notably disregarded in *Wallace v. Jaffree*,[223] a later decision of the 1984 Term. At issue was the validity of an Alabama statute challenged as violative of the Establishment Clause as absorbed into the Fourteenth Amendment. That law authorized teachers in the State's public schools to announce at commencement of the first class of each day that "a period of silence not to exceed one minute in duration shall be observed for meditation or voluntary prayer.... "An earlier statutory provision differed only in being limited to elementary grades and to meditation.

The relation of the later enactment to its predecessor, together with post-enactment testimony of the prime sponsor of the legislative supplementation that it constituted "an effort to return voluntary prayer to our public schools ...," satisfied two-thirds of the Court that the Establishment Clause was improperly impacted. From this conclusion the Chief Justice vigorously dissented. "The notion that the Alabama statute is a step toward creating an established church borders on, if it does not trespass into, the ridiculous."[224] "The mountains have labored and brought forth a mouse."[225] Justice Rehnquist launched a powerful dissent, which Justice White "appreciated," predicated on thorough examination of the history of the religion clauses of the First Amendment. Most significant for present purposes is the fact that in not one of the opinions in *Jaffree* is there any challenge to Court indulgence in inquiry into the actual purpose of contested legislation.[226]

There was more convincing evidence of "hidden" monopoly purpose in *Daniel v. Family Security Life Insurance Co.*[227] than of intended breach of the wall of separation in *Jaffree*. The relative ease with which the current majority passed over legislative profession, invoking the satirical comments of Chief Justice Burger, makes nonsense of Justice Murphy's supercilious pronouncement in *Daniel* that "[w]e cannot undertake a search for motive in testing constitutionality."[228] Only the "Berlin Wall" of a double standard in constitutional determination blocks consistent judicial behavior. And this wall is no

---

221. Earlier quoted in the text at note 163, *supra*.

222. Refer to text at pp. 240-41, *supra*.

223. 105 Sup. Ct. 2479 (1985).

224. *Id*. at 2507.

225. *Id*. at 2508.

226. "In applying the purpose test, it is appropriate to ask 'whether the government's actual purpose is to endorse or disapprove of religion.' In this case, the answer to that question is dispositive." Justice Stevens for the majority, *id*. at 2490.

227. Cited *supra* note 206 and textually discussed at notes 207-16.

228. This appears in the quotation in the text at note 212, *supra*.

more justified than that between East and West when the reach of substantive due process of law, properly understood in its historically explicit meanings, is no more uncertain than is that of the First Amendment the vaunted specificity of which has disappeared after half a century of confused and conflicting judicial embroidery.

What Price the Voidance of Anti-Monopoly Due Process?

With respect to governmental takings the Reconstructed Court has avoided expropriative due process, yet in instances of extreme attempts at A to B transfers it has accorded protection to property rights through manipulation of the Contract and Taking Clauses. But the historic opposition of due process of law to monopoly attained through governmental favoritism has lost all potency; even side appeals to Equal Protection, where the legislative play to favorites has been blatant, have proved fruitless. The Court's justification has been twofold: (1) the challenged governmental action pronounces the will of the sovereign (2) whose "motives" cannot be inquired into by nonelected judges. Neither of those predicates can withstand analysis. While the legislative grants of market monopoly in form represent the public wish, in actuality this naive assumption often belies the known circumstance of the legislative process. Professor Walter Gellhorn, in whose unbiased judgment all have had implicit confidence, has stated with respect to occupational licensing

> That restricting access is the real purpose, and not merely a side effect, of many if not most successful campaigns to institute licensing can scarcely be doubted.[229]

After setting forth concrete instances of abuse of licensing by state and local authorities,[230] he repeated his conclusion.

> Only the credulous can conclude that licensure is in the main intended to protect the public rather than those who have been licensed or, perhaps in some instances, those who do the licensing.[231]

The contention that the Court must remain blind to episodic takeovers of legislatures by special interests is nothing but a red herring. No one seriously contends for fruitless investigation of explanations as to why a legislative body does the things it does. The issue is whether the objective professed in the statutory preamble is an honest one of public concern or but a cover up for a dis-

---

229. Gellhorn, *Abuse of Occupational Licensing*, 44 U. OF CHI. L. REV. 6, at 11 (1976). The assertion had been made earlier by Hanft and Hamrick, *Haphazard Regimentation Under Licensing Statutes*, 17 N.C.L. REV. 1 (1938).

230. *Gellhorn, supra* note 229, at 11-18.

231. *Id.* at 25. That the many forms which market restriction can take are the product of legislative favoritism, is manifest in a symposium on *Marketing Barriers*, 8 LAW & CONTEMP. PROBS. 207-414 (1941).

tinctly unpublic purpose that raises questions of constitutionality. With an occasional exception such as the case of draft card destruction the Court is not blind to ulterior purpose in civil liberty contexts. Those decisions of recent decades where chaff has been judicially separated from wheat disclose that the process harbors potential for error. Yet the Court does not shrink from the task; the alternative is fundamentally at odds with its self-asserted high office of exclusive interpreter of the Constitution. If anything, fact determination in economic affairs is less hazardous than in the counterpart. The double standard of constitutional interpretation, which rationalizes a legislature's economic actions yet distrusts the political and social enactments of that same legislature, just does not make sense.

Although one influential constitutionalist exhumed determinations of the *Lochner* era only to rebury them, he nevertheless conceded the telling point that "the scattered individuals who are denied access to an occupation by state-enforced barriers are about as impotent a minority as can be imagined."[232] It was error for the Court to allow the famous footnote of *Carolene I* to accord to the political process theory the weight it was subsequently assumed to give; freedom from direct restraint in the marketplace of ideas is no guarantee of equal effectiveness for all economic interests in legislative deliberations.[233]

A newcomer to constitutional debate is to be commended for insistence that "*Lochner* paranoia" must be replaced by a more balanced approach to constitutional adjudication. Viewing that infamous decision as impacting on monopoly rather than expropriation, Professor Wonnell declares that monopoly legislation should be invalidated absent strong justification in the public interest.[234] He concludes:

> If decisions such as *Lochner* stalled societal progress, it is useful to remember that other cases from that era, such as *New State Ice Co. v. Liebmann*, helped prevent a regression toward a medieval economy of privileged merchants and guilds. One can feel quite comfortable with the demise of the *Lochner* constitutional

---

232. McCloskey, *Economic Due Process and the Supreme Court: An Exhumation and Reburial,* 1962 SUP. CT. REV. 34, 50.

233. Wonnell, *Economic Due Process and the Preservation of Competition,* 11 HASTINGS CONST. L. Q. 91, at 109 (1983).

> *Carolene Products* thus poses an empirical question about the reliability of the political process to insure repeal of particular types of statutes that prove to be undesirable. The model analyzed in the previous sections suggests that the political process sometimes can be quite unreliable even where a statute does not directly restrict the operation of the process itself.

> The problem is most striking at the state level. Occupational licensing statutes can fail completely to carry out their stated purpose of consumer protection and still remain on the books. Even if the licensing statutes were in fact passed to protect the consumer, the concentrated-beneficiaries-and-diffuse-victims phenomenon tends to block their repeal if they prove to be ineffective or counterproductive.

234. *Id. passim.*

doctrine, and yet sense the unreality of the judicial rhetoric in cases such as *Williamson v. Lee Optical, Inc.* and *Ferguson v. Skrupa*. Prevailing jurisprudence is beginning to provide doctrinal support for the theory that monopoly legislation, except where deliberately engineered to combat other concentrations of bargaining power, is an abuse of the power to regulate economic activity. The ghost of *Lochner* thus far has prevented the Court from openly recognizing that position under the Due Process Clause.[235]

However, this commentator undercuts his thesis by allowing public interest to justify monopoly legislation in order "to protect the reliance interest created by pre-existing monopoly laws."[236] He resists the temptation of wholesale invalidation "because of the thousands of monopoly laws already on the statute books" which "might create powerful opposition to heightened judicial scrutiny of monopoly laws, and thereby jeopardize the prospective declaration of an anti-monopoly principle."[237] The exception comes close to swallowing up the rule; one would think that the very multiplicity of existing monopoly provisions would dictate forthwith declaration of unconstitutionality. The Court showed no such timidity in its repudiation of *Lochner* and its progeny. The historic presence of the due process core of anti-monopoly demolishes the concept of "reliance" as a constitutional impediment.[238]

Thurman Arnold taught that to achieve a viable legal system there must be a rule for guidance, an exception to the rule to prevent woodenness in its application, but an exception to the exception to prevent the latter from engulfing the rule. His insight should be helpful in the present context. The rule is the conception of competition as the central pattern of economic organiza-

---

235. *Id.* at 133-34. *New State Ice* has been cited and considered textually *supra* this chapter, pp. 219-21, at notes 51-55; *Ferguson* and *Lee Optical* are cited *id.*, p. 223, notes 66 and 67, and their facts and holdings stated at note 69.

236. *Id.* at 130. Professor Wonnell also excepts laws that "correct defects in bargaining power" from his "general rule that protection of the producers constitutes an insufficient state interest to justify monopoly legislation. . . ." *Ibid.* He conceives of private concentrations of economic power in monopolistic terms, justifying resort to public monopoly as an offset. This view is akin to the concept of due process as one of a sword available to government against private monopoly, the subject of analysis in chap. 9, *infra*. However, rectification of imbalances in bargaining power among factors of production can involve major flows of wealth from *A*s to *B*s, suggesting property expropriation. The problem can better be analyzed in these terms, as has been done in chap 7, *supra*. Redistribution of income by governmental decree collides with the Constitution's commitment to the institution of private property, requiring an accommodation of conflicting values. In the context that concerns Professor Wonnell that is achieved by postulating that the transfers from *A*s to *B*s are not unconstitutional expropriations from *A*s but compensations owing *B*s in a balancing of socio-economic accounts.

237. *Id.* at 131.

238. Great Northern Ry. Co. v. Sunburst Oil & Refining Co., 287 U.S. 358 (1932), holds that prospectivity in judicial decision is not constitutionally mandated. Noted 42 YALE L. J. 779 (1933). The Court's employment of prospectivity in some constitutional decisions in criminal procedure, on which Professor Wonnell places his reliance, is not to the contrary. Indeed, I do not find these decisions to be apposite.

tion,[239] dominant in the West with the demise of mercantilism.[240] The exception to the rule is monopoly, the ultimate in rejection of a policy of open competition.[241] Under Coke English constitutional law took sides against monopoly when in the form of grants by the sovereign to favored individuals; monopoly grants were held to be contrary to the due process guarantee of Magna Carta. Reception of English law in the New World included this heritage, only to be lost by the Supreme Court (although not by many state courts) in the initial perversion of substantive due process at the end of the nineteenth century. By contrast resort to monopoly by government itself, whether in supplantation or supplementation of competition, presented no conflict with the due process concept. However, exception to further toleration of monopoly would be necessary to protect the rule of competition from disintegration.

The decision in *Smith v. Texas*[242] was responsive to this consideration. A state statute that had given the force of law to discrimination by a railroad union was stricken as violative of the Fourteenth Amendment. The prohibition against advancement to the rank of train conductor except after two years of service as brakeman or conductor on a freight train was seen by all Justices but one for what it was, an attempt to confer a monopoly "of the right to work" on a favored class. The decision would have been unnoteworthy had the lone dissenter not been Justice Holmes. Because he gave no reasons for his disagreement, one can only speculate as to what they were. No explanation being adequate, the most charitable of several possibilities[243] could be that he felt this presumably isolated instance of legislative curtailment of market entry did not justify judicial nullification. Holmes had shown himself not to be overly alarmed at the spectre of monopoly.[244] The threat that the Texas law held for a regime of competition was arguably *de minimis*. Had Holmes lived to sit in deliberations on the two Louisiana statutes challenged in *Dukes* and *Kotch* he might well have concurred in the judgments of sustainment; these instances of narrow, rather isolated monopolistic pockets could have no observable impact on the general economy. Yet *Kotch*, involving a more substantial business op-

---

239. Stigler, *Competition*, 3 INTER. ENCYC. SOC. SCI. 181 (1968).

240. Read, *Mercantilism: The Old English Pattern of a Controlled Economy*, in C. READ, THE CONSTITUTION RECONSIDERED 63 (1938, 1968).

241. Clark, *Monopoly*, 10 ENCYC. SOC. SCI. 623 (1933).

242. 233 U.S. 630 (1914), earlier considered in the text, *supra* this chapter, pp. 245-46, following citation at note 188.

243. Refer to text *supra* this chapter, pp. 246-47, at notes 193-95.

244. For instance, Holmes is said to have "considered the Sherman Act 'a humbug, based on ignorance and incompetence.' " C. BOWEN, YANKEE FROM OLYMPUS 382 (1944). Early in his career Holmes had written that "it is pretty certain that meanings undreamed of by the framers of *Magna Carta* have been imported into it." HOLMES' BOOK NOTICES AND UNCOLLECTED LETTERS AND PAPERS 100 (Shriver ed. 1936), reproducing a Book Notice of 1871 on Cooley's multi-volume TREATISE ON CONSTITUTIONAL LIMITATIONS. Holmes may have been of the opinion that one "importation" was Coke's association of the Great Charter with hostility to monopoly grants by the Crown.

eration than that in *Dukes,* was borderline as suggested by the 5 to 4 vote on the issue of Equal Protection.[245] Measured by degree of impact *Liggett, New State Ice, Morey, Grosjean, Old Dearborn, Lee Optical, Daniel,* and *Ferguson* all presented entry restraints of magnitude sufficient to affect adversely the dynamics of competition. Of the first three listed one has been impliedly and the other two expressly overruled;[246] in the other five, barriers received judicial blessing. There remains the teasing question of why Justice Douglas was in the majority in *Morey v. Doud,* rather than with Justices Black, Frankfurter, and Harlan in dissent. Did he, in this one instance, entertain doubts concerning the Court's determined disregard of the anti-monopoly teaching of substantive due process? Reasonable regard for that historic teaching would have produced opposite results in most of those eight decisions; the three repudiated would have been allowed to stand, while three of the remaining five would have been decided differently. The two possible exceptions would have been *Old Dearborn* and *Ferguson;* in the early years of resale price maintenance laws their basically monopolistic thrust was not fully realized, and limitation of debt adjusting to lawyers had some justification in truly public interest.

Where buyer demand for an item of merchandise is widespread, governmental outlawry of product competition cannot but impose monopolistic barnacles on the market mechanism. Legislative protestations of concern for public health or safety must be critically examined lest they be but a masquerade for private interest that for the moment has captured the lawmaking process through "cultivation" of politically sensitive legislators. The prohibition of oleomargarine as a substitute for butter or of filled milk for dairy milk immediately becomes suspect. Even when produced from animal fats, oleo could be manufactured without hazard to consumers. *Powell v. Pennsylvania* was wrongly decided, as the highly respected Professor Ernst Freund declared in his seminal treatise on *The Police Power.*[247] Certainly with the substitution of vegetable fats for animal fats, the dairy lobby should never have been allowed to maintain its monopoly on breadspread to the middle of the present century. With the introduction in filled milk of vitamin fortification after the initial decision in *Carolene I,* the Court should not have resustained prohibition of this competing product in *Carolene II.* To the extent the contentions of deception in marketing were more than rationalization after the challenge to health had been refuted, they justified only differential packaging required as much of evaporated/condensed milk as of reconstituted filled milk. *Powell* should not have controlled decision in *Carolene II;* at last the Court recognized the

---

245. McCloskey, *supra* note 232, although after review of the new Court's economic decisions to date was disposed to rebury them in their "uneasy grave," took exception to the bare majority decision in *Kotch.*

246. *Liggett,* by North Dakota Board of Pharmacy v. Snyder's Drug Stores, 414 U.S. 156 (1973); *Morey,* by New Orleans v. Dukes, 427 U.S. 497 (1976).

247. E. FREUND, THE POLICE POWER, §§ 62, 541, 547 (1904).

constitutional issue in substituted competition yet resorted to an end run around it. *Carolene II*, like *Powell*, was incorrectly decided.

Because the demand for fluid milk is great throughout the country, there is a major market in containers for retail distribution. The original container, the glass milk bottle, was replaced by paper containers possessing distinct advantages; the abortive *Ex-Cell-O* case suggests there was some, but ineffective, effort on the part of glass manufacturers to discourage resort to the newer type of container through adoption or interpretation of local ordinances favoring the glass bottle. More recently, the clash between producers of paperboard and of plastic milk containers reached the Supreme Court in *Clover Leaf Creamery* through circumstances that have earlier been detailed. These played into the hands of the Court which sustained the Minnesota law by reliance upon its flimsy interpretation of the rational nexus test for Equal Protection. The Minnesota trial court had recognized the anti-competitive nature of the legislation, and the impact on the significant milk container industry of this monopolistic restraint was far too considerable to justify disregard under a rule of *de minimis*. Critiquing this litigation with proper regard for the hostility due process should show to monopoly that markedly shackles competition in a major retail market, judgment comes easily. The Minnesota supreme court should have affirmed the trial court on its independent interpretation of the State's due process clause, thus invalidating the statute as clearly a monopoly grant to favored manufacturers and protecting that holding from certain reversal by the Supreme Court through invocation of the adequate and independent state ground rule.

By contrast, judgment does not come easily with respect to the Court's disposition of *Pacific States Box & Basket Co.* in which was sustained the Oregon administrative order forbidding use by Oregon growers of the tin-top type of berry container. Because Oregon was then, as it continues to be, a major producer of berries and fruits, governmental favoritism in product competition seriously impacted the marketing mechanism. Only one of the three justifications that Justice Brandeis gave for limitation of berry containers to the hallock type carries much conviction; that was that the hallock stowed better for shipping. The contention of better preservation of the berries the Justice himself conceded to be only "conceivable." That the hallock involved less danger of deception is contrary to long standing judgment that its false bottom was purposely deceptive.

Most difficult to accept is the Brandeis analysis that the facts before him presented no evidence of monopoly because there existed many manufacturers of hallocks. This oversight of the essence of the situation as one of product, not commodity, competition is impossible to reconcile with the understanding of economic principles that Justice Brandeis seemingly had. Furthermore, it would appear quite contrary to Brandeisian philosophy to reach a decision that in effect fostered state economic protectionism. True, the State concerned was Oregon which thirty years earlier had engaged the brilliant young graduate of Harvard Law School to defend its hour and wage legislation against certain challenge from *Lochner v. New York*. But the principles by which the Justice lived would never permit that association to result in litigant favoritism. Perhaps explanation may lie unarticulated in the Justice's well-known advocacy of viewing the States as political "laboratories" for economic and social experimentation.

That the result of *Pacific States* fostered economic protectionism is clear from factual analysis. In the Kansas City marketing area, to my personal knowledge, hallock containers came from manufacturers "knocked down"; they were assembled in the berry fields of local truck farmers. On the contrary, metal-rim containers were so constructed that they could be shipped to destination in final form ready for immediate use. The practice must have been the same elsewhere. With Oregon one of the major growers of raspberries and strawberries, and less than one-fourth of producers of hallocks located in Oregon and Washington, the added employment for local workers would be considerable. At the same time the decision was advantageous to the Oregon timber industry. Although the administrative order did not specify the material to be used in manufacture of hallock containers, veneer from spruce logs was the standard vehicle. Other materials came later. As the Pacific States company contended, spruce logs were obtainable only in the Pacific Northwest. The advantages to the Oregon economy from the marketing barrier interjected by state authority were thus not insignificant, especially in the years of the Great Depression.

The asserted absence of monopoly was but one leg of the Brandeis decision of constitutionality. There was another basis in the alternative. Even if monopoly be conceded, the decisional result would not differ. For support in precedent for this assertion the Justice offered only "comparison" with *Slaughter-House Cases* and the passage in *Nebbia v. New York* wherein Justice Roberts had relied on *Slaughter-House Cases* and two highly inapposite decisions for the propositions that government was empowered to adopt monopoly policy. Careful analysis discloses that Roberts outdid Brandeis' thesis in the latter's dissent in *New State Ice*. That thesis, while upending in comparison with earlier constitutional doctrine, was not open ended. In the first of the two paragraphs reproduced earlier from that dissent,[248] monopoly grants to private entities are justified in the context of public utility regulation; "[t]o grant any monopoly to any person as a favor is forbidden even if terminable." Impliedly at least, the following paragraph further qualified the extent to which monopoly grants are constitutionally permissible by invoking the "well settled" principle, noted in the opening discussion of this chapter, that due process offers no obstacle to publicly-owned monopoly enterprise.

But in *Pacific States* Justice Brandeis approaches acceptance of the broader assertion of *Nebbia* that whenever public policy dictates "that a monopoly

---

248. Refer to textual quotation at note 55, *supra* , pp. 220-21 of this chapter.

should be granted, statutes having that effect have been held inoffensive to the constitutional guarantees."[249] The only distinction in their positions — and this can be significant—is that whereas Justice Roberts in using the plural in referring to constitutional limitations must have intended inclusion of Due Process as well as Equal Protection, Justice Brandeis declared only that "the grant of a monopoly, if otherwise an appropriate exercise of the police power, is not void as denying equal protection of the law."[250] This circumspect language does leave latent the anti-monopoly core of substantive due process of law. Yet to depend today on this latency would be highly questionable in light of *Pike v. Bruce Church, Inc.*[251] Disposition of an attack on an administrative order of an Arizona official, requiring that all cantaloupes grown in that State be placed in closed containers of specified compactness, went far to establish that the only restraint on state preferment of its economic interests lies in Commerce Clause limitations. Justice Stewart for the full Court, stating that the "purpose and design" of the Arizona regulation "are simply to protect and enhance the reputation of [local] growers," observed:

> These are surely legitimate state interests. *Sligh v. Kirkwood,* 237 U.S. 52, 61. We have upheld a State's power to require that produce packaged in the State be packaged in a particular kind of receptacle, *Pacific States Box & Basket Co. v. White,* 296 U.S. 176. And we have recognized the legitimate interest of a State in maximizing the financial return to an industry within it. *Parker v. Brown,* 317 U.S. 341. Therefore, as applied to Arizona growers who package their produce in Arizona, we may assume the constitutional validity of the Act.[252]

Without doubt a high price has been paid for the Court's refusal to invoke the anti-monopoly core of substantive due process in challenges to serious legislative and administrative impedimenta to open commodity and substituted competition. Experience is replete with instances of economic loss by reason of presence in the market of monopolistic blockage. Those blockages are as detrimental to the business marketplace as are governmental obstructions in the marketplace of ideas. The Court's continued insistence on a double standard in constitutional adjudication is unadulterated nonsense!

---

249. Nebbia v. New York, 291 U.S. at 529.
250. Quoted note 131, *supra*, p. 233 of this chapter.
251. 397 U.S. 137 (1970).
252. *Id.* at 143.

9. Private Monopoly and Substantive Due Process

Munn v. Illinois,[1] decided in 1877, is one of the most misunderstood decisions of the Supreme Court of the United States. Commentators have hardly known how to square it with contemporaneous decisions expanding judicial review with attendant invalidation of state laws through resort to the new Due Process Clause of the Fourteenth Amendment.[2] In *Nebbia v. New York*[3] Justice Roberts had to twist it out of shape in order to make it fit his demonstration that states had the constitutional power to fix minimum prices for fluid milk.[4] These difficulties of Court and commentator lie in failure to differentiate between substantive due process as shield and as sword. Their minds have been tuned to the familiar view of due process as understood from Coke in English constitutional law; that view provided a guarantee against intrusion by the sovereign upon the property of the subject. In the determinative case of *Mitchel v. Reynolds.*[5] Lord Macclesfield had been unequivocal on the point that freedom from monopoly through voluntary private restraints could not

---

1. 94 U.S. 113 (1877).
2. L. Tribe, American Constitutional Law 433 (1978) accords it a sentence of text, the thrust of which is that, although upholding Illinois' regulation of grain elevator charges, *Munn* was a warning of likely increase in invalidating Court review under Due Process. Kitch and Bowler, *The Facts of Munn v. Illinois*, 1978 Sup. Ct. Rev. 313, allude to the monopolistic behavior of the strategically-placed warehousemen, but only in conclusion, by quoting from J. Commons, Legal Foundations of Capitalism 33 (1924), do they exhibit any awareness of the significance for constitutional decision of the fact of private monopoly. G. Gunther, Constitutional Law 508 (10th ed. 1980), gives *Munn* a paragraph of description; because "the business owners . . . had a near monopoly on grain storage, regulation of their rates was similar to traditional price regulation of utilities and monopolies." But lacking is appreciation that Due Process is here used to *validate* antimonopoly legislation directed at private effort to circumvent competition.
3. 291 U.S. 502 (1934), considered earlier in chap. 8, *supra*, and *infra* this chapter.
4. *Id.* at 531-33. The passage is quoted in the text, *infra* at note 152, and criticized in the text following.
5. 1 P. Wms. 181, 24 Eng. Rep. 347 (1711).

look to Magna Carta for support.[6] But although this watershed judgment was handed down from Chancery in 1711, postdating by several decades Lord Hale's Tracts entitled, respectively, *De Jure Maris* and *De Portibus Maris*,[7] it discloses no recognition of Hale's thesis that reasonable charges are required of private individuals enjoying a virtual monopoly by reason of the unique characteristics of their businesses.

Proven Power of Substantive Due Process as Sword

Two major decisions at the very beginning of the nineteenth century gave formal footing to this principle in English law but unrelated to Due Process.[8] Early American law was also hostile to private monopoly, again without reference to Due Process.[9] But in *Munn* the novel connection is made by Chief Justice Waite on the suggestion, it has been hazarded, of Justice Bradley.[10] In its new posture, the anti-monopoly core of substantive due process operates not as a shield against governmental action but as a sword undergirding its affirmative power of action. No wonder counsel for Munn and Scott were astonished at the turn of the events. Due process had been confidently cited as forbidding governmental regulation of maximum rates. Was it not clear that monopoly "has its origin . . . in grant from the State"; the Court was standing the Constitution on its head! Reaffirmance of *Munn* in *Spring Valley Water Works v. Schottler*[11] made it clear that the surprising decision was no fluke. Repeating quotation from earlier analysis,

> That it is within the power of the government to regulate the prices at which water shall be sold by one who enjoys a virtual monopoly of the sale, we do not doubt. That question is settled by what was decided on full consideration in *Munn* v. *Illinois*. . . . As was said in that case, such regulations do not deprive a person of his property without due process of law.[12]

Munn survived frontal attack in *Budd v. New York*,[13] where counsel for the grain warehousemen of Brooklyn and Buffalo challenged New York legislation

---

6. *Id.* at 188, 24 Eng. Rep. at 350. *Mitchel v. Reynolds* is fully considered *supra* chap. 1, pp. 19-21, text at notes 91-98.

7. Found in F. HARGRAVE'S LAW TRACTS, *Pars Prima and Pars Secunda* (1787). The pertinent passages are quoted in chap. 1, *supra*, pp. 23-24, text at notes 109 and 110.

8. The two decisions are cited and considered chap. 1, *supra*, text at notes 111, 113.

9. Refer to chap. 3, *supra*, pp. 47-50, text at notes 1-18.

10. Fairman, *The So-called Granger Cases, Lord Hale, and Justice Bradley*, 5 STAN. L. REV. 587, at 588-92 (1953).

11. 110 U.S. 347 (1884).

12. *Id.* at 354. Fuller consideration of *Munn* and *Schottler* appears in chap. 4, *supra*, pp. 70-73, text at notes 11-28.

13. 143 U.S. 517 (1892).

regulative of maximum rates for elevating and related operations. Again attack was based upon substantive due process as a limitation on state power, only to result in effect in majority reliance on that constitutional provision as a "guarantee" of state authority to legislate for the public interest in the presence of conditions approximating monopoly. Sustainment, however, was not without the dissent of three Justices, that number climbing to four in *Brass v. North Dakota ex rel. Stoeser*.[14] Doubt whether Brass had any monopoly power led to the view among the dissenters and commentators[15] that the majority in sustaining the legislation had abandoned the *Munn* principle of state power grounded in anti-monopoly to open the gates to pervasive public authority in maximum price fixation. That uncertainty persisted into the present century.

Against Business Monopoly

Meantime, the movement toward monopoly through both loose-knit and close-knit combinations had led to enactment of state antitrust laws and, in 1890, to the Sherman Act.[16] Section 1 of the latter made illegal "[e]very contract, combination in the form of trust or otherwise, or conspiracy, in restraint of trade or commerce among the several States...." In the first case to raise the question of proper interpretation of this prohibition a bare majority of the Supreme Court adopted a literal construction of the Section.[17] The consequence was the illegality of a rate-fixing agreement among Western railroads regardless of the reasonableness of charges. Shortly thereafter an essentially identical agreement among Eastern roads met the same fate.[18] It had been strenuously contended in this second litigation that such literal interpretation surely placed the Act in conflict with the Fifth Amendment Due Process Clause. The government's successful answer was that the *Munn* principle was applicable.[19] Consternation enveloped the business world. In its immediate application *Munn* left the monopolist free to continue in business subject to the requirement that his charges be reasonable. But sustainment of literal interpretation of the Sherman Act would mean congressional power (and presumably state power in its federalistic sphere via Fourteenth Amendment Due Process) to destroy all private arrangements tainted with marks of monopoly. At century's close, due process and anti-monopoly were legal twins; legislative

---

14. 153 U.S. 391 (1894). *Budd* and *Brass* are considered *supra*, chaps. 4 and 5, respectively.

15. *E.g.*, 1 R. CALLMANN, UNFAIR COMPETITION, TRADEMARK AND MONOPOLIES § 3.18 (rev. ed. 1981).

16. 15 U.S.C. §§ 1-7.

17. United States v. Trans-Missouri Freight Association, 166 U.S. 290 (1897).

18. United States v. Joint Traffic Association, 171 U.S. 505 (1898).

19. Fuller treatment of the antitrust cases to 1900 is found *supra* chap. 5, pp. 83-85.

strikes at private monopoly could not possibly violate substantive due process of law which had in this context metamorphosed into a sword of empowerment.[20]

The Justices were not of one view in this matter of interpreting the Sherman Act. The issue carried over to adjudication of the application of the Act to an instance of close-knit combination, the consolidation by use of the new holding company device of the Great Northern and the Northern Pacific railroads. *Northern Securities Co. v. United States*[21] held the combination unlawful and ordered dissolution. The decision was 5 to 4, with the Yankee from Olympus[22] one of the latter. President Theodore Roosevelt had been certain that his new appointee was safely in the fold for this major thrust at trust busting. He was outraged at Holmes' vote against him, and the incipient friendship between them never flowered as it surely would have otherwise.[23] The Holmes dissent, in which the other three "lost sheep" joined,[24] concluded on a note of satisfaction with his unbending conviction that Congress did not intend to enact a statute at odds with substantive due process as a shield against extremism in atomization of the rising industrial complex.

> In view of my interpretation of the statute I do not go further into the question of the power of Congress. That has been dealt with by my brother White and I concur in the main with his views. I am happy to know that only a minority of my brethren adopt an interpretation of the law which in my opinion would make eternal the *bellum omnium contra omnes* and disintegrate society so far as it could into individual atoms. If that were its intent I should regard calling such a law a regulation of commerce as a mere pretense. It would be an attempt to reconstruct society. I am not concerned with the wisdom of such an attempt, but I believe that

---

20. Constitutional literature abounds with failure to recognize substantive due process in its role of antagonism to private monopoly, so concentrated has been attention to its operation in other roles. In seeking to outlaw private aggregations of capital bent on monopolistic control of segments of the economy Congress was intervening in, not withdrawing from, economic regulation of market forces. In so doing it faced several obstacles, interpretational and constitutional. One of the latter was the doubt of its constitutionality under due process if literally interpreted. The Sherman Act of 1890, far from giving expression to the doctrine of *laissez-faire*, aligned with numerous state statutes in expressing opposition to monopoly. 1 C.C.H. Trade Regulation Rep. § 860. Substantive due process shared, not blocked, that hostility. *Cf.* the number of constitutional expressions of opposition to monopoly among the original state constitutions. See note 3, chap. 3, *supra.*

21. 193 U.S. 197 (1904).

22. This was the title chosen by Catherine Drinker Bowen for her outstanding biography of Holmes, cited note 23, *infra.*

23. C. Bowen, Yankee from Olympus 370-71 (1944).

24. In turn Holmes joined in the dissent of Justice White, which also had the support of the Chief Justice and Justice Peckham. Thus rejection of the majority opinion was "solid." On the other hand, Justice Brewer's concurrence was essential to the creation of a majority for the government.

Congress was not entrusted by the Constitution with the power to make it and I am deeply persuaded that it has not tried.[25]

The Rooseveltian victory in the Supreme Court was to prove a Pyrrhic one. In less than a decade the Sherman Act was judicially amended to incorporate within it a "rule of reason." This profound dilution was officially explained as required by correct interpretation of the common law from which the Act took its cue; that source was said to condemn, not all combinations but only those that were in unreasonable restraint of trade. It is true that the later common law knew of a rule of reason; in contracts ancillary to realization of legitimate objectives in the ordinary course of commercial dealings within a basically competitive framework, covenants not to compete were enforced if in space and time the restriction was reasonable when tested against the justifiable protection of the coventees. However, contracts incorporating covenants between the contracting parties not to compete, unancillary to legitimate objectives but designed wholly and nakedly for suppression of competition were, with few exceptions, not tolerated by American state courts.

There was no analytical or historical justification for introducing the "rule of reason" into agreements of the latter type that supplied the foundation for the combination movements in this country.[26] The decisions in *Standard Oil*[27] and *American Tobacco*,[28] which turned the trick, were either unmerited exercises in judicial legislation or reactions to continuing uncertainty regarding the constitutionality of the Sherman Act if construed literally to apply to all industrial combinations.[29] No less an accepted constitutional authority than Edward S. Corwin entertained the view that the "rule of reason" was essential to unquestioned validity of Sherman and its analogues against contentions of conflict with due process, understood as protective of private interests through the doctrine of freedom of contract.[30]

---

25. Northern Securities Co. v. United States, 193 U.S. at 411 (italics in original). Because of Brewer's concurrence, Holmes was able to refer to "a minority of my brethren."

26. An economist of the same period as John R. Commons and Walton Hale Hamilton was contemptuous of the "rule of reason" for its economic nonsense. F. FETTER, THE MASQUERADE OF MONOPOLY 347-49 (1931). The entire volume, as the title indicates, constitutes a biting attack on Supreme Court ineptness in the earlier antitrust decisions. Part I is critical of the *Oil* decision.

27. Standard Oil Co. v. United States, 221 U.S. 1 (1911).

28. United States v. American Tobacco Co., 221 U.S. 106 (1911).

29. A succinct statement of the background and adoption of the "rule of reason" is provided by M. Handler, *A Study of Construction and Enforcement of the Federal Antitrust Laws*, TNEC Monograph No. 38, at 3-9 (1941). Add the incisive analysis by Bork, *The Rule of Reason and the Per Se Concept: Price Fixing and Market Division*, 74 YALE L. J. 775, at 801-14 (1965), which varies from that advanced in the text.

30. Corwin, *The Antitrust Acts and the Constitution* 18 VA. L. REV. 355, at 368, 370, 372 (1932). Throughout his career, Professor Corwin never sensed anything amiss in the

Only Justice Harlan, who had written the majority opinion in *Northern Securities*, dissented from the Court's adoption of the rule of reason.[31] Holmes, now the great "liberal" for his dissent in *Lochner* one year after his dissent in *Northern Securities*, was a member of the majority in the fateful decisions of 1911. Before one joins the hallelujah chorus over his celebrated opinion in *Lochner*, his position in the antitrust cases warrants attention. In them Holmes missed the relevance of substantive due process as an anti-monopoly sword, thinking of the concept only in its function as a shield against deprivation of property interests either by expropriation or by monopoly grant. Apparent absence in the bakeshop case of either of these deprivations did enable him to recognize as spurious the majority's resort to substantive due process for *Lochner's* decision of invalidity.[32] But is it enough that Olympians bat 500?

Justice Holmes had opportunity to redeem himself, and redemption would have overcome the 1911 decisions. In *United States v. United Shoe Machinery Co.*,[33] decided in 1918, and *United States v. United States Steel Corp.*,[34] decided two years later, the rule of reason saved the two combinations from dissolution.[35] The array of the Justices was exactly the same in the two cases; Justice McKenna wrote the opinions for the plurality consisting of him, Holmes, Van Devanter, and White; Day, Clarke, and Pitney dissented; Brandeis and McReynolds abstained. What critic Fetter said of *Steel* was equally true of *Shoe*: It was "A Close Call," a "Thrilling Escape."[36] "The Corporation was declared to be a good trust, or at least a reformed sinner. . . ."[37] In *Oil* and *Tobacco*, dissolution had been decreed because of *un*reasonable monopolistic conduct; but now with dissolution twice foiled it was clear enough that the thrust of antitrust was badly blunted by introduction of the test of

---

engrafting onto substantive due process of the alien doctrine of *laissez-faire*. But neither did any other vaunted constitutional scholar. If indeed the revised version of the Sherman Act was the consequence of constitutional concerns, the Court's action should be understood as acceptance of substantive due process as shield, as against substantive due process as sword. But how can *reduction* in anti-monopoly be supported on the basis of reliance on substantive due process as shield against monopoly? Clearly, it cannot, and the introduction of the "rule of reason" was a miscarriage!

31. Harlan's summary of his position appears in *Standard Oil* at 106 of 221 U.S., in *American Tobacco* at 193 of the same volume.

32. For consideration of *Lochner* refer to chap. 6, *supra*, pp. 95-97, text at notes 2-19.

33. 247 U.S. 32 (1918).

34. 251 U.S. 417 (1920).

35. F. FETTER, *op. cit. supra* note 26, at 62, observed, with respect to the "trust issue" in the presidential campaign of 1912: "The Oil dissolution decree lent new plausibility and hope to that method, but the 'rule of reason' had raised new doubts and fears in many minds."

36. Part II of F. FETTER, *id.*, is entitled "Steel Makes Its Thrilling Escape." "A Close Call" is the subheading in FETTER under which appears the quotation that follows.

37. *Id.* at 63.

reasonableness. "As in 1920, so today, 'mere size is no offense.' "[38] The outcome could have been otherwise; employed as a sword, substantive due process would have provided constitutional support for unequivocal proscription of all private business monopoly.

Introduction of the rule of reason in federal antitrust law is the more unjustified, at least on constitutional grounds, when attention is directed to a series of Court decisions lying before and after 1911. These were decisions concerning the validity of state antitrust statutes challenged on direct appeal from state courts. The interpretation of these state laws was for the lower courts to determine, and in none of the cases is there indication of modification of the strictures against monopoly through the intervention of a rule of reason similar to the federal. Sustainment of the statutes by the Supreme Court was the result in every instance.[39] A paragraph in the unanimous opinion in the first of these cases is most revealing:

> Undoubtedly there is a certain freedom of contract which cannot be destroyed by legislative enactment. In pursuance of that freedom parties may seek to further their business interests, and it may not be always easy to draw the line between those which are beyond the reach of the police power and those which are subject to prohibition or restraint. But a secret arrangement, by which, under penalties, an apparently existing competition among all the dealers in a community in one of the necessaries of life is substantially destroyed, without any merging of interests through partnership or incorporation, is one to which the police power extends. That is as far as we need to go in sustaining the judgment in this case. That is as far as the Supreme Court of the State went. If other transactions are presented, in which there is an absolute freedom of contract beyond the power of the legislature to restrain, which come within the letter of any of the clauses of this statute, the courts will undoubtedly exclude them from its operation.[40]

Smiley, decided just shortly before *Lochner v. New York*, should have put constitutionalists on notice that the bastard doctrine of freedom of contract was not going to render impotent antitrust laws directed at prevention or elimination of private monopoly. Properly understood, hostility toward monopoly expresses a tenet of substantive due process as it evolved in England and would have flowered in the United States had it not been for the misholding in *Powell*

---

38. C. KAYSEN AND D. TURNER, ANTITRUST POLICY 106 (1965).

39. Smiley v. Kansas, 196 U.S. 447 (1905); National Cotton Oil Co. v. Texas, 197 U.S. 115 (1905); Waters-Pierce Oil Co. v. Texas, 212 U.S. 86 (1909); Hammond Packing Co. v. Arkansas, 212 U.S. 322 1909); Granada Lumber Co. v. Mississippi, 217 U.S. 433 (1910); Central Lumber Co. v. South Dakota, 226 U.S. 157 (1912) (unanimous opinion by Holmes!); International Harvester Co. v. Missouri, 234 U.S. 199 (1914). All of these cases involved price fixing by loose-knit combinations. Later the Court took price-fixing out of the "rule of reason" in federal antitrust cases. United States v. Socony-Vacuum Oil Co., 310 U.S. 150 (1940).

40. Smiley v. Kansas, 196 U.S. at 456-57 (1905).

v. Pennsylvania[41] and the colossal blunder of the Court in converting freedom of trade into freedom of contract. But antitrust laws aimed at monopoly by private action escaped this latter trap; because of their hostility to monopoly, substantive due process operates to undergird them rather than to invalidate them as destructive of private economic interest.[42]

Fairmont Creamery Co. v. Minnesota,[43] decided in 1927, is not in fundamentals at odds with *Smiley* and the other earlier cases. The Court there reversed a state court conviction on the ground that the state law forbidding price variations in purchasing at different geographical locales in Minnesota omitted to specify statutory intent to forbid discrimination only when done with the objective of creating monopoly. The Court was on track on the constitutional level; it was only derailed in its judgment on the facts. The statute was a revision of earlier enactments that did include such a specification. The Attorney General of the State and his Assistant had explained in argument that omission was the consequence of "the almost impossibility of proving by competent evidence that price discrimination between localities was for the purpose of creating a monopoly."[44] This explanation should have been sufficient to sustain the amended statutory language; such must have been the feeling of Justices Holmes, Brandeis and Stone although they dissented without opinion. The result in *Fairmont* should have been to the contrary on any reasonable conclusion regarding the intendment of the statute, especially when the Court itself recognized the legislative objective might have been prevention of "things which may tend to monopoly."[45]

---

41. Criticism of Powell v. Pennsylvania, 127 U.S. 678 (1888), first appears in chap. 5, *supra*, pp. 86-89, following citation at note 29.

42. Two decisions of the 1940s assist in understanding the less familiar aspect of substantive due process as sword in contrast with its operation as shield. Railway Mail Association v. Corsi, 326 U.S. 88 (1945), sustained, against attack as violative of Due Process, a section of the New York Civil Rights Law forbidding a union to deny membership on the basis of race, color, or creed. Concurring, Justice Frankfurter observed that "a State may choose to put its authority behind one of the cherished aims of American feeling by forbidding indulgence in racial or religious prejudice to another's hurt. To use the Fourteenth Amendment as a sword against such State power would stultify that Amendment." *Id.* at 98.

Giboney v. Empire Storage & Ice Co., 336 U.S. 490 (1949), was a suit to enjoin an AFL affiliate from picketing its premises in violation of Missouri Antitrust Law. Picketing of Empire was for the avowed purpose of forcing it to comply. Empire's business had been reduced 85% by its refusal. The Court's reaction is apropos. "Missouri has by statute regulated trade one way. The appellate union members have adopted a program to regulate it another way.... We hold that the state's power to govern in this field is paramount, and that nothing in the constitutional guaranties of speech or press compels a state to apply or not to apply its anti-trade-restraint law to groups of workers, businessmen or others." *Id.* at 504.

43. 274 U.S. 1 (1927).

44. *Id.* at 3.

45. *Id.* at 9.

Nor was the Court out of line in a decision handed down in the month following *Fairmont*. Invalidity was again the verdict in *Cline v. Frink Dairy Co.*[46] but under the doctrine of void for vagueness. The Colorado Anti-Trust Law was unusual because of a proviso that prohibited acts were exempt from penalty in those situations where products could not be sold at reasonable profit levels in the absence of market restraint otherwise unlawful. The term "profit" was not a dirty word, but it was full of ambiguity. "Such an exception in the statute leaves the whole statute without a fixed standard of guilt in an adjudication affecting the liberty of the one accused."[47] Yet a unanimous Court was not troubled by the absence from the state law of any expression to the effect the objective was the curbing of monopoly. It was sufficient that the law "denounces conspiracies and combinations" in the seven particulars which the Court lists;[48] after all, was not the Colorado statute an antitrust law?

Three decades after *Fairmont* and *Cline* the supreme court of Wisconsin was faced with a statute of that jurisdiction reading exactly as had the Minnesota law.[49] Two justices were of the opinion that, since *Fairmont* had never been overruled, it controlled. The majority, however, reversed the trial court that had been of the same opinion in consequence of which it had held the statute invalid and enjoined its enforcement against plaintiff. Although necessarily conceding that *Fairmont* remained unsullied in technical fact, the majority viewed its doctrine as repudiated by Supreme Court decisions beginning with *Nebbia*.[50] The court therefore concluded that because of all that had intervened between 1927 and 1960, § 100.22 "should be re-examined, and the questioned validity of sec. 100.22, freshly resolved upon a record which presents the pertinent facts."[51] But this time the state legislature acted before the judiciary managed reconsideration. The long existing § 100.22 was amended[52] by insertion into the price discrimination prohibition of the italicized clause "*where the effect may be to lessen substantially competition or to tend to create a monopoly or to injure, destroy or prevent competition*." The proviso remains today, cured of the likelihood of invalidity.[53]

The period intervening between *Fairmont* and *White House* was one of major legislative and judicial activity. Section 2 of the Clayton Act was expansively amended by the Robinson-Patman Act of 1936.[54] Section 2(a) continued

---

46. 274 U.S. 445 (1927).

47. *Id.* at 457.

48. *Id.* at 455.

49. White House Milk Co. v. Reynolds, 12 Wis. (2d) 143, 106 N.W. (2d) 441 (1960), reviewing WIS. STAT. ANN. § 100.22.

50. Nebbia v. New York, 291 U.S. 502 (1934), analyzed *supra* chaps. 6 and 8, and *infra* this chapter.

51. White House Milk Co. v. Reynolds, *supra* note 49, at 150, 106 N.W. (2d) at 445.

52. Wis. Laws 1961, c. 386, §1.

53. WIS. STAT. ANN. §100.22

54. 15 U.S.C. §13.

the Clayton restriction that illegalized discriminations must have had as their objective anti-competitive behavior of the forms described in the Wisconsin statutory revision. Indeed, the Wisconsin wording may well have been basically adapted from Section 2(a). The repugnancy of monopoly to substantive due process as sword underscores the validity of such statutory provisions, clearly antitrust in their thrust.

The times were marked by much state legislation presumably directed against "unfair competition" as the concept had expanded in the Codes of the NIRA. Most relevant for present purposes were the laws against selling below cost and engaging in price discrimination. One current source gives 30 as the number of States having laws of the first type;[55] another gives the same figure for price discrimination laws.[56] Within each type have been variations: some general in application, others limited to specific products especially from the dairy; about half restricted to intent or effort to bring about monopoly, others with no such statutorily expressed limit in purpose.[57]

State judicial decisions on these statutes have varied. Constitutionality was sustained in three challenges of sale-below-cost-laws although in one[58] there was no restriction to provocation of monopoly whereas in the two others[59] the challenged statutes were expressly confined to instances of purpose to create monopoly. A Montana law forbidding price discrimination in petroleum products whatever the objective was early invalidated,[60] whereas the equally unrestricted general price discrimination provision of Arkansas' Unfair Practices Act[61] was upheld on the strength of the implied limitation from the State's constitutional prohibition of monopoly.[62] Unless constitutionally jeopardized

55. 1A R. CALLMANN, UNFAIR COMPETITION, TRADEMARKS AND MONOPOLIES § 702 (rev. ed. 1981).

56. 1 C.C.H. TRADE REGULATION REPORTER § 3510.

57. Idaho has three categories of statutory provision condemnatory of price discrimination. §§ 37-1001 and 37-1002 apply to dairy products and carry no restriction respecting monopoly (but cf. § 37-1003b[e]). § 22-1601, relating to farm products, and § 48-202, which is of general application, both incorporate the proviso that illegality attends price discrimination undertaken to destroy competition or to create a monopoly. Not uncommon is it for a state to have prohibitions against both sales below cost and price discrimination.

58. State v. Sangley, 53 Wyo. 332, 84 P. 2d 767 (1938).

59. People v. Pay Less Drug Store, 25 Ca. 2d 108, 153 P. 2d 9 (1974); Schwegmann Brothers Giant Super Markets v. McCrory, 237 La. 768, 112 So. 606 (1959), app. dism. 361 U.S. 114 (1959).

60. Clark Co. v. P. S. C. of Montana, 94 Mt. 488, 22 P. 2d 1056 (1933).

61. ARK STATS. ANN.. § 70-301. A neighboring state has a constitutional provision that looks both ways with respect to the policy available to the state legislature on price discrimination legislation. "Unless otherwise provided by law, no person...shall, for the purpose of creating a monopoly or destroying competition in trade, discriminate...." OKLA. CONST. Art. 9, § 45.

62. Concrete, Inc. v. Arkhola Sand & Gravel Co., 230 Ark. 315, 322 S.W. 2d 452 (1959).

by over-vagueness or excessive delegation of legislative power, statutes containing the proviso signaling antitrust purpose seemed less likely to be overturned than was true of statutory counterparts lacking the proviso.

Explanation lies in the fact that before the *Nebbia*[63] reformation the latter form of statute was challengeable for violation of genuine or spurious substantive due process conceived in its role as protector to private interest. This would account for the difference in result between the Montana and Arkansas cases. On the other hand, in the wake of *Nebbia*'s tolerance of legislative latitude, sale-below-cost and price discrimination statutes of later enactment or challenge, although omitting the antitrust proviso, became defensible constitutionally on the ground that a different legitimate objective partially underlay these enactments—that of protection of traditional methods of merchandising threatened with extinction by chain stores, mail-order houses, and other new types of powerful merchandizers despite absence of evidence of monopoly thrust.[64]

Against Monopoly Pricing

No complete survey of case and statute of this area of the law is necessary to conclude that in the immediate background for judge and legislator was the Supreme Court's range of decisions on direct fixation of price maxima from the time of *Munn* on. "Modern trade regulation had its genesis with *Munn v. Illinois*."[65] Reviewing the cases through *Nebbia* author Callmann insists that in *Brass v. Stoeser*, the last one before 1900, the Court "discarded the monopoly test in a five-to-four decision."[66] This reading I have earlier questioned[67] to such an extent as to leave in doubt what stance the Court would take after the turn of the century. Later developments proved Callmann mistaken, as ensuing text demonstrates, but with no retraction on his part.

German Alliance Insurance Co. v. Kansas[68] was the first case of the twentieth century to present the issue.[69] It concerned state regulation of fire insur-

---

63. Cited *supra* note 50, where references to analysis of this case are found.

64. C. EDWARDS, THE PRICE DISCRIMINATION LAW 5-14 (1959).

65. 1 R. CALLMANN, *op. cit. supra* note 15.

66. *Id.* note 9 of § 3.18.

67. Text accompanying notes 5-10, chap. 5, *supra*, pp. 80-82.

68. 233 U.S. 389 (1914).

69. Cotting v. Kansas City Stock Yards Co., 183 U.S. 79 (1901), a stockholders' derivative suit challenging a Kansas statute setting maximum rates for driving, yarding, watering, and weighing of cattle, hogs, and sheep in Kansas stockyards, would have been the first relevant litigation in the new century had the Court not avoided the issue by finding the law invalid on grounds of unconstitutional discrimination because applicable only to the Kansas City Stock Yards. At that period there were other stockyards in the State but none fell within the strictures of the statute which applied only to any stockyards that for the preceding year "had an average daily receipt of not less than one hundred head of cat-

ance companies, most basically with respect to maximum rates to be charged insureds. Relief sought was restraint of enforcement on the ground of violation of the Fourteenth Amendment, largely because of deprivation of property without due process of law. Thus the Constitution was looked to for protection of private right, not for power to govern. Yet the decisional conclusion was sustainment of the challenged statute. True, the result came hard. *Munn* and *Budd* were unquestioned, but *Brass* had "extended the principle of the other two cases and denuded it of the limiting element which was supposed to beset it—that to justify regulation of a business the business must have a monopolistic character."[70] Nevertheless, as the Court majority pondered the significance of fire insurance its uniqueness to the conduct of modern business set it apart from other types of enterprise. A sentence hints of analogy to *Munn* and even back to Lord Hale in terms of public dependence upon the "product" although an insurance policy is but a contract of indemnity as the dissent insisted.[71] The point was sufficiently telling to lead the dissent to counter with the assertion that when one adds up the instances where power to regulate prices has been sustained, "they appear to be grouped around the common carrier as the typical public business...."[72]

In closing its analysis under Due Process the *German Alliance* majority combined the analogy with doubts that insurance rates are in reality fixed in open, vigorous competition; the pattern looks more like common agreement on rates among oligopolists. The paragraph is reassuring that the Court has not abandoned something akin to the "monopoly test" in crossing the century line. Indeed, *German Alliance* is less uncertain than was *Brass v. Stoeser*.

> We may venture to observe that the price of insurance is not fixed over the counters of the companies by what Adam Smith calls the higgling of the market, but formed in the councils of the underwriters, promulgated in schedules of practically controlling constancy which the applicant for insurance is powerless to oppose and which, therefore, has led to the assertion that the business of insurance is of monopolistic character and that "it is illusory to speak of a liberty of contract." It is in the alternative presented of accepting the rates of the companies or refraining from insurance, business necessity impelling if not compelling it, that we may discover the inducement of the Kansas statute, and the problem presented is whether the legislature could regard it of as much moment to the public that they who seek insurance should no more be constrained by arbitrary terms than they who seek transportation by railroads, steam or street, or by coaches whose itinerary may be

---

tle, or three hundred head of hogs, or three hundred head of sheep." The constitutional issue of maximum price fixation of stock-yard functionaries did finally arise and was favorably resolved in Tagg Bros. v. United States, 280 U.S. 420 (1930), considered *infra*.

70. German Alliance Insurance Co. v. Kansas, 233 U.S. at 410.

71. *Id*. at 416. "If we are brought to a comparison of [regulations of the business of insurance], in relation to the power of government, how can it be said that fixing the price of insurance is beyond that power and the other instances of regulation are not?"

72. *Id*. at 427.

only a few city blocks, or who seek the use of grain elevators, or be secured in a night's accommodation at a wayside inn, or in the weight of a five-cent loaf of bread. We do not say this to belittle such rights or to exaggerate the effect of insurance, but to exhibit the principle which exists in all and brings all under the same governmental power.[73]

Upon the heels of *German Alliance* came two decisions of relevance in Court reaction to the relationship between private monopoly and substantive due process. Although seldom noted in this context, they bear attention, the more for the fact the opinions were written by Justices Holmes and Brandeis respectively. Holmes' position in the antitrust cases was one of insensitivity to the concept of substantive due process as sword. Brandeis, controversial for his opposition to private monopoly power, was writing one of his earliest opinions after the bitter battle over his confirmation following nomination by President Wilson. The results in each case were significant for future litigation.

The Terminal Taxicab Co. of Washington, D.C., did three kinds of business. With the Washington Terminal Co., owner of Washington Union Station, it had a lease giving it the exclusive right to solicit livery and taxicab business at the Station; with unnamed hotels it enjoyed the exclusive right to solicit hotel guests; and it furnished taxi service out of its central garage, generally on orders by telephone. About one-third of its total business was of the first type; one-fourth, of the second; and the remainder of the last. The Taxicab Co. sued to restrain the public utilities commission of the District of Columbia from exercising jurisdiction over it by virtue of a Congressional Appropriations Act of 1913 for the District, which incorporated a comprehensive enactment granting the public utilities commission the full powers common to such legislation.[74] By Par. 24 every public utility within its jurisdiction must file a schedule of rates and tolls, to deviate from which was declared unlawful. As a matter of statutory interpretation the Supreme Court, modifying the lower district court, held the Taxicab Co. to be within the commission's jurisdiction as to types one and two of its total business, but not type three. *Terminal Taxicab*

---

73. *Id.* at 416-17.
Careful readers will be surprised at the last illustration given by the Court of businesses subject to special regulation. Citation to governmental power to fix "the weight of a five-cent loaf of bread" is hardly reconcilable with the decision a decade later in which the Court invalidated a Nebraska law prohibiting sale of loaves of bread of weights other than those legislatively prescribed. Jay Burns Baking Co. v. Bryan, 264 U.S. 504 (1924), considered chap. 6, *supra*, p. 100, text at notes 33-34. The Court in *German Alliance* must have been thinking of the then recently decided case of Schmidinger v. Chicago, 226 U.S. 78 (1913), that had sustained a Chicago ordinance prohibiting sales of bread save at weights prescribed. *Burns Baking* can be factually distinguished on the basis of its restrictions on excess as well as on short weights, yet its contrary conclusion on validity is unsupportable as Justices Brandeis and Holmes insisted in their dissent. Moreover, there was in this context no shred of evidence of monopoly.

74. 37 STAT. Part I, chap. 150. § 8.

Co., Inc. v. District of Columbia.[75] Implicit in the unanimous decision by Holmes was acceptance of rate fixation, primarily maxima under the circumstances, for a business possessing the characteristics of monopoly. For type one, analogy was found in *Munn v. Illinois*; for type two, in *German Alliance Ins. Co. v. Kansas.*

Van Dyke v. Geary[76] was a suit to enjoin enforcement of an order of the Arizona corporation commission, entered after hearing, reducing water rates for much of the town of Miami. Federal jurisdiction was based upon the familiar assertion that the rates so ordered were confiscatory and consequently in violation of the Fourteenth Amendment. Plaintiffs were a wife and husband who, having purchased a tract of land with the objective of establishing a town thereon, developed a water system on their property for supplying commercial and domestic users settling in the town they had created. Lot purchasers bought with the understanding that water could be had from the Van Dykes at rates fixed by the supplier. For the Court, with only the dissent of Justice McReynolds, the new Justice Brandeis sustained the commission's jurisdiction in this unusual situation, ruled the business public, and found not confiscatory the lower rates set by the Commission. The pertinent passage in the affirmance of the lower federal court reads as follows:

> The Van Dyke system appears to be the only water supply of the inhabitants of the original town of Miami (not including the "additions"). The number of water takers is not shown. But it appears that the large consumers who used meters numbered, at the time of the commission's investigation, 675, yielding a revenue of $11,378.10; and that the number of small takers must have been much larger, since the revenue derived from the flat rates was $14,517.35. "Property does become clothed with a public interest when used in a manner to make it of public consequence, and affect the community at large." *Munn v. Illinois*, 94 U.S. 113, 126. The property here in question was devoted by its owners to supplying a large community with a prime necessity of life.[77]

The decision in *Van Dyke* was announced just one month after that in *Bunting v. Oregon*,[78] where Brandeis recused himself because author, with the aid of Felix Frankfurter, of the Brief for the State of Oregon.[79] In *Bunting* the more familiar issue was the reach of substantive due process as a shield of property interests, not that of the impact of substantive due process as sword in the presence of private monopoly.[80] Does *Van Dyke* demonstrate that from the first Brandeis understood the difference in constitutional theory?

---

75. 241 U.S. 252 (1916).
76. 244 U.S. 39 (1917).
77. *Id.* at 47.
78. 243 U.S. 426 (1917).
79. This period in the life of Louis Brandeis is recalled early in the segment of chapter 7 entitled *Employer-Employee Relationships.*
80. The *Bunting* decision is considered in the context of employer-employee relations

In the wake of World War I critical housing shortages occurred in New York City and in Washington, D.C. Responding to the crises Congress in 1919 and the New York Legislature in 1920 enacted rent control laws that in effect set maximum prices for the duration of the emergency. Renters were allowed to remain after term in premises rented before the effective dates of the legislation, at rentals theretofore existing. In the inevitable attack on the rent control laws[81] the nature of the restrictions suggested challenge on the ground of expropriation of property rights as well as on that of virtual monopoly. A passage in Holmes' opinion in *Hirsch* appears responsive to each.

> The main point against the law is that tenants are allowed to remain in possession at the same rent that they have been paying, unless modified by the Commission established by the act, and that thus the use of the land and the right of the owner to do what he will with his own and to make what contracts he pleases are cut down. But if the public interest be established the regulation of rates is one of the first forms in which it is asserted, and the validity of such regulation has been settled since *Munn v. Illinois*, 94 U.S. 113. It is said that a grain elevator may go out of business whereas here the use is fastened upon the land. The power to go out of business, when it exists, is an illusory answer to gas companies and waterworks, but we need not stop at that. The regulation is put and justified only as a temporary measure. See *Wilson v. New*, 243 U.S. 332, 345, 356. *Fort Smith & Western R.R. Co. v. Mills*, 253 U.S. 206. A limit in time, to tide over a passing trouble, well may justify a law that could not be upheld as a permanent change.[82]

The statutes were sustained with the aid of the temporary feature.

The Court of Industrial Relations Act of Kansas was invalidated on a number of grounds in a unanimous opinion by Chief Justice Taft, former President of the United States. The explanation, making *Wolff Packing Co. v. Court of Industrial Relations*[83] a difficult case for analysis, lies in the fact the opinion is not a model of the art of judicial exposition. However, measured by percentage of the opinion and number of citations devoted to the validity of price control, *Wolff* is properly characterized as one of the adjudications in the line of decisions under consideration. Admittedly, there are difficulties in this disposition of the case. It involved wage, not price, control, but are not wages the price of labor? More obstructive is the fact the statute did not "fit" the category of monopoly by private contract. Yet neither did it fall within the definitional limits of monopoly by public grant or of expropriation through governmental alienation. It concerned a compulsory arbitration act, restrictive of the contractual rights of both employer and employee. One might think the restriction on

---

involving alleged taking from "*A* for the benefit of *B*." Bunting v. Oregon, 243 U.S. 426, *supra*, text at notes 64-68 of chap. 7, pp. 129-30.

81. Block v. Hirsch, 256 U.S. 135 (1921); Marcus Brown Holding Co. v. Feldman, 256 U.S. 170 (1921). Four members of the Court dissented in each case.

82. Block v. Hirsch, *supra* note 81, at 157.

83. 262 U.S. 522 (1923).

the latter was the greater, but the decision was ultimately rested on the deprivation of Wolff's "property and liberty of contract without due process of law."

In any event the core of the opinion was concerned with the question whether the facts brought the case within the rule of *Munn* and its progeny through *Block v. Hirsch*. The answer was clear.

> There is no monopoly in the preparation of foods. The prices charged by [Wolff, a small packing house] are it is conceded, fixed by competition throughout the country at large. Food is now produced in greater volume and variety than ever before. Given uninterrupted interstate commerce, the sources of the food supply in Kansas are countrywide, a short supply is not likely, and the danger from local monopolistic control is less than ever.[84]
>
> . . . .
>
> The regulation of rates to avoid monopoly is one thing. The regulation of wages is another. A business may be of such character that only the first is permissible, while another may involve such a possible danger of monopoly on the one hand, and such disaster from stoppage on the other, that both come within the public concern and power of regulation.[85]

During the second half of the 1920s, in successive years, governmental setting of maximum prices was invalidated in split decisions. The first of these cases was *Tyson & Brother v. Banton*.[86] New York had sought to restrict the prices at which brokers of theater tickets in Manhattan could sell over the box office price. A bare majority, treating the issue as one concerning prices charged by some sixty first-class theaters, reversed the lower federal court on the case precedents and its understanding of Lord Hale's "rule."

> A theatre or other place of entertainment does not meet this conception of Lord Hale's aphorism or fall within the reasons of the decisions of this court based upon it. A theatre is a private enterprise, which, in its relation to the public, differs obviously and widely, both in character and degree, from a grain elevator, standing at the gateway of commerce and exacting toll, amounting to a common charge, for every bushel of grain which passes on its way among the states; or stock yards, standing in like relation to the commerce in live stock; or an insurance company, engaged, as a sort of common agency, in collecting and holding a guaranty fund in which definite and substantial rights are enjoyed by a considerable portion of the public sustaining interdependent relations in respect of their interests in the fund. Sales of theatre tickets bear no relation to the commerce of the country. And, certainly, a place of entertainment is in no legal sense a public utility; and, quite

---

84. *Id.* at 538. In his three-fold categorization of "[b]usinesses said to be clothed with a public interest" Chief Justice Taft cites both *Terminal Taxicab* and *Van Dyke*, the former in category (2) and the latter in (3). *Id.* at 535, 536.

85. *Id.* at 539.

86. 273 U.S. 418 (1927).

as certainly, its activities are not such that their enjoyment can be regarded under any conditions from the point of view of an emergency.[87]

Justice Brandeis concurred in a typically short dissent penned by Holmes, who thought "that theatres are as much devoted to public use as anything well can be."[88]

It took Justice Stone to get the facts straight; the challenged law involved price fixing by ticket brokers, not by the theaters at the box offices. The Record disclosed that the practice of the brokers was to subscribe in advance for the most desirable seats for the first eight weeks. "A virtual monopoly of the best seats, usually the first fifteen rows, is thus acquired and the brokers are enabled to demand extortionate prices of theatre goers."[89] Given these facts the pertinent precedents were those decisions in which statutory regulation of price had been sustained. "That should be the result here."[90] Stone had mastered the *Munn* rule of substantive due process as sword. But had Holmes and Brandeis forgotten the basis of their opinions of a decade earlier?

Ribnik v. McBride[91] followed the next year. This time the majority pronounced invalidity upon a New Jersey law limiting the fees charged by private employment agencies. Dissenting at length Justice Stone determined, upon the basis of demonstrated evils of such agencies and the resulting mass of state legislation directed against them, that there "is a marked difference between the character of this business" of employment brokerage and that of other types of brokers; especially so of ticket brokers involved in *Tyson v. Banton*, where an attempt had been made to limit enhancement of ticket prices by brokers, "an expedient adopted to break up their monopolistic control of a luxury, not a necessity."[92] The case was a puzzler; there was no monopoly here,[93] and yet present was an equivalency of evils. The essence of Justice Stone's conclusion is caught in the following paragraph:

> Examination of the various reports of public bodies and the legislation referred to can, I think, leave no doubt that the practices of the private agencies with respect

---

87. *Id.* at 439-40.

88. *Id.* at 447.

89. *Id.* at 450.

90. *Id.* at 452. Justice Sanford regretted he too must dissent. "My own view is more nearly that expressed by Mr. Justice Stone." *Id.* at 454.

91. 277 U.S. 350 (1928).

92. *Id.* at 362.

93. Uncontradicted by counsel for New Jersey was the assertion of Ribnik's lawyers that "there is no monopoly, or danger of monopoly, in the operation of employment agencies. ... Nineteen States have established competitive free state employment agencies, and in at least seven others there are municipal agencies. An organization has been established called the 'American Association of Public Employment Offices' which is seeking to put private agencies out of business." Argument for Plaintiff in Error, 277 U.S. at 351. Counsel noted that these facts were taken from the dissenting opinion of Justice Brandeis in *Adams v. Tanner*, 244 U.S. 590 (1917).

to their fees presented a problem for legislative consideration different from any other that this Court has passed on in ruling on the power to regulate prices, but certainly more akin to that in *Munn v. Illinois, supra,* and *German Alliance Insurance Co. v. Kansas, supra,* than to that in *Tyson v. Banton, supra,* and, unless we are to establish once and for all the rule that only public utilities may be regulated as to price, the validity of the statute at hand would seem to me to be beyond doubt. Certainly it would be difficult to show a greater necessity for price regulation.[94]

The last of the trio was *Williams v. Standard Oil Co.*[95] in which the Standard Oil Co. and the Texas Co. successfully challenged in a three-judge federal district court a Tennessee act of 1927 empowering a state agency to fix the prices at which gasoline could be sold within the state. On appeal the lower court was affirmed. According to the State's Brief the background facts were that in late 1925 Standard Oil, then selling nearly fifty per cent of the gasoline marketed in Tennessee, and other "large companies" initiated a price war designed to crush competition from the smaller companies. Aroused, the Governor addressed the General Assembly, urging legislative regulation of gasoline sales. "The message stated that this commodity to all effects and purposes is now controlled by a monopoly. . . . "[96] The stated objective of the enactment that followed was "to prevent the destruction of competition and to prevent extortionate prices."[97] The means of regulation, placed in the state agency, was a permit system restricting entry into gasoline business to those agreeing to "reasonable" profits, nondiscrimination and no rebating.

Passages in the State's Brief assert two bases in support of the statute, antitrust law and the *Munn* rule.[98] Antitrust cases are cited, yet ouster under the state act is "no answer" because Standard, regarded as the chief offender, would return in the form of another corporate entity.[99] Primary dependence was on *Munn*; "The Munn case is the guidepost—the chart."[100] In the Brief and repeated in the summary thereof in the official Report are cited *Munn* and the primary *Munn* progeny sustaining constitutionality of maximum price fixing in the presence of monopoly or its likeness.[101] The Standard Oil Brief is by

---

94. *Id.* at 372-73. Holmes and Brandeis joined in this dissent rather than writing separately as they had in *Tyson.*

95. 278 U.S. 235 (1929).

96. Williams v. Standard Oil Co., 278 U.S. 235, Record, Brief of Appellant, Microfiche, card 3, at 4.

97. Tenn. Laws 1927, chap. 22, §1.

98. Summary of the State's Brief in the official Report, 278 U.S. at 236-37, reflects the two-fold attack.

99. Brief of Appellant, Williams v. Standard Oil Co., 278 U.S. 235, *supra* note 96, card 3, at 38-40.

100. *Id.* at 42.

101. *Id.* at 36-42; 278 U.S. at 236. Note the inclusion of *Brass v. North Dakota* but the absence of *Terminal Taxicab* and *Van Dyke.*

John W. Davis, who had successfully challenged Pennsylvania's Kohler Act. He makes little reference to the antitrust aspects of the case, despite his involvement in federal antitrust litigation. Indeed, the only reference appears to be inferential. "The act can not be sustained on the theory that it is necessary to prevent a monopoly and to protect competition. It does not protect but destroys competition and, assuming for argument only that a monopoly is threatened, price regulation is not the constitutional remedy."[102]

Like the State's, Davis' concentration is on the pertinency of *Munn*. He first cites the Court decisions that had struck down state price regulation in absence of monopoly: *Fairmont, Wolff, Tyson, Ribnik*.[103] Much space is then devoted to "explaining" *Munn* and those decisions that stood or fell on the reasoning of *Munn*. In the course of this exchange on the precedents, opposing counsel tangled over the English case of *Allnutt v. Inglis*.[104] The State Attorney General had included *Allnutt* in his citations supporting the Tennessee Act,[105] declaring later that it held that the "right of the state to regulate charges applies not only to monopolies arising out of a grant from the sovereign, *but also to conditions where there is in fact a monopoly*,"[106] and that *Allnutt* had been approved in *Munn*. Davis challenged this claim on fundamental grounds, alternatively expressed. First, in *Allnutt* there was "a *legal* monopoly on landing goods in a public port"; secondly, inasmuch as Parliament is omnipotent, neither the court in *Allnutt* nor Lord Hale could "have been considering constitutional limitations . . . [nor] Mr. Chief Justice Waite when, in the Munn, opinion, he was discussing these authorities."[107] In light of the background supplied by the briefs, judicial disposition of the appeal to the Supreme Court is highly significant on several counts. The percentage of the market in gasoline sales in Tennessee controlled by Standard Oil and Texas clearly created a duopoly, presenting hazards to the public interest similar to those resulting from monopoly. However, judicial understanding of the economics of market shares did not exist at the date of *Williams*, even in antitrust analysis where it finally appeared later. Hence to the majority,

> There is nothing in the point that the act in question may be justified on the ground that the sale of gasoline in Tennessee is monopolized by appellees, or by

---

102. Williams v. Standard Oil Co., 278 U.S. 235, Record, Brief of Appellees, Microfiche, card 4, at 10.

103. *Id.* at 8.

104. 2 East 527, 104 Eng. Rep. 206 (K.B. 1810). *Allnutt* is first considered in the context of note 113, p. 25 of chap. 1, *supra*, and later that of note 19 of chap. 4, p. 72.

105. Williams v. Standard Oil Co., 278 U.S. 235, Record, Brief of Appellant, Microfiche, card 2, at 25, 38-39.

106. *Id.* at 38. It is noteworthy that the emphasis by use of italics is that of the Attorney General.

107. Williams v. Standard Oil Co., 278 U.S. 235, Record, Brief of Appellee, Microfiche, card 4, at 27-28. Italic supplied by me.

either of them, because, objections to the materiality of the contention aside, an inspection of the pleadings and of the affidavits submitted to the lower court discloses an utter failure to show the existence of such monopoly.[108]

Moreover, as Davis had argued, the case somehow did not look like one for price regulation. It smacked more of a case for antitrust action. Holmes's dissent was therefore perhaps unsurprising but not so the concurrence in the result on the part of Brandeis and Stone. Having "come over" to the view of monopoly as the key to governmental empowerment under substantive due process, they agreed in principle with the majority's edict of "no monopoly, no constitutionality" in price fixing cases under *Munn*.[109] But significantly, they had not taken the bait held out by Davis to challenge the very foundation of *Munn* that Waite had developed on the basis of the Hale tracts. This contention of Davis, certainly one of the brilliant that made him the great advocate he was, seemingly went unnoticed by the concurrers. The foundations of *Munn* were weak, a clear rejection of Lord Macclesfield's pronouncement in *Mitchel v. Reynolds* that opposition to private monopoly could not be grounded on the reach of Chapter 29 of Magna Carta.[110] The passage from the opinion of the majority just quoted, "objections to the materiality of the contention aside," may have been a deft reference to the Davis challenge but one the majority did not need to face because of its holding that no monopoly was involved. That Brandeis and Stone did not see fit to take the cue suggests satisfaction with the operation of the *Munn* doctrine.

In the string of Court decisions cited for constitutionality by the Brief for Tennessee was *Stafford v. Wallace*,[111] that in 1922 had sustained the Packers and Stockyards Act of the previous year. At first thought, the inclusion seems out of place; *Stafford* is familiar for its expansion of congressional power vis-à-vis the states. However, in the course of his opinion for the Court by Chief Justice Taft there appeared these lines at the opening of a long paragraph following a graphic description of the business involved:

> The act, therefore, treats the various stockyards of the country as great national public utilities to promote the flow of commerce from the ranges and farms of the West to the consumers in the East. It assumes that they conduct a business affected by a public use of a national character and subject to national regulation. That it is a business within the power of regulation by legislative action needs no discussion. That has been settled since the case of *Munn v. Illinois*, 94 U.S. 113.[112]

---

108. Williams v. Standard Oil Co., 278 U.S. at 240.

109. Here the use of quotation marks is mine, designed as a short-cut paraphrase of the *Munn* rule.

110. Refer to quotation at start of note 95, p. 20, and text following in chap. 1, *supra*.

111. 258 U.S. 495 (1922).

112. *Id*. at 516.

Tagg Bros. v. United States[113] was decided the very day that Charles Evans Hughes took his seat as Chief Justice of the United States, succeeding Taft. There was no further changing of the guard from the year of *Williams*. Again under challenge was the constitutionality of the Packers and Stockyards Act, this time with specific respect to the power delegated to the Secretary of Agriculture to fix the commissions, maximum and minimum, of market agencies operating in the major stockyards of the country. Upon a hearing after notice as specified by the statute

> [t]he Secretary found that monopolistic power was exercised by the plaintiffs without the usually attendant economy of minimizing expenditures for business getting, that the operating costs of the several agencies for the performance of similar services varied widely; that some of the expenses were wasteful and unnecessary; that the profit yielded by Tariff No. 2, on the basis of the estimated reasonable cost of conducting the business, allowing for reasonable salary expenses, advertising costs, overhead, Exchange assessments and dues and interest at the rate of 7 per cent. on the invested capital, was unreasonable. . . .[114]

The Secretary also found complainants' Tariff No. 2 "unduly complicated and confusing," and unjust in other important particulars. He therefore concluded that for these several reasons

> . . . the operation of Tariff No. 2 should be suspended and there should be substituted the schedule drawn by the Secretary which prescribed generally lower charges, eliminated the several unjust discriminations and yielded a reasonable return to the plaintiffs above the legitimate cost of their service.[115]

But the challenge to the statute failed not alone with respect to the Secretary's findings and order; the underlying power of Congress to direct the fixing of commission rates was sustained.

> Plaintiffs perform an indispensable service in the interstate commerce in live stock. They enjoy a substantial monopoly at the Omaha Stock Yards. They had eliminated rate competition and had substituted therefor rates fixed by agreement among themselves, without consulting the shippers and others who pay the rates. They had bound themselves to maintain uniform charges regardless of the differences in experience, skill and industry. The purpose of the regulation attacked is to prevent their service from thus becoming an undue burden upon, and obstruction of, that commerce.[116]

---

113. 280 U.S. 420 (1930).

114. *Id.* at 440.

115. *Id.* at 441.

116. *Id.* at 439. It was with consideration of *Tagg Bros.* that Walton Hamilton closed his *Affectation With Public Interest*, 39 YALE L. J. 1089 (1930). Rather buried, *id.* at 1096, is the only recognition I have found, in the literature of substantive due process, of its positive role of power rather than of limitation. Quite correctly the paragraph attributes the "find" to Chief Justice Waite. Even "Hamie" did not see the analogy of Section 5 of the Fourteenth Amendment.

The opinion for the entire Court was written by Mr. Justice Brandeis.

The case for constitutionality seemed clear enough in *O'Gorman & Young v. Hartford Insurance Co.*[117] The issue was validity of a New Jersey statute limiting the commissions that insurance companies could pay their local agents. *German Alliance* had earlier sustained state power to regulate insurance rates, and now *Tagg Bros.* had validated maximum price fixation of commissions in a business found to possess monopolistic characteristics. In full conversion to the constitutional principle of substantive due process in service to anti-monopoly, Mr. Justice Brandeis wrote briefly for the Court. Judged by established precedent, the law passed muster. Consistency remained, but unanimity was absent. What today's critics call the "gang of four" separated themselves from their colleagues, among whom was Owen Roberts in place of Edward Sanford. This time, they insisted, the Court had gone over the brink. "Rates constitute the matter of public concern, not the compensation of employees or representatives, which is after all, only an item of expense. And so far as we can see, this legislation will afford no protection to those who wish to insure."[118]

The central issue in *New State Ice Co. v. Liebmann*[119] was not price fixing but control of market entry. The case has been considered with other holdings in the immediately preceding chapter.[120] However, the debate between Justice Sutherland for the majority and Justices Brandeis and Stone dissenting is pertinent to the line of cases under present consideration. The date of the *New State Ice* litigation fell at the time of emergence of mechanical refrigeration by electricity or gas. To the majority "whatever may have been the fact in the past" it was now true that one or the other energy source was to be had "in practically every part of the country," thus making it possible for every citizen to "manufacture ice for himself."[121]

> Under such circumstances it hardly will do to say that people generally are at the mercy of the manufacturer, seller and distributor of ice for ordinary needs. Moreover, the practical tendency of the restriction [on entry], as the trial court suggested in the present case, is to shut out new enterprises, and thus create and foster monopoly in the hands of existing establishments, against, rather than in aid of, the interest of the consuming public."[122]

Amassing factual data typical of the Brandeis Brief, the dissenters held a conflicting view.

---

117. 282 U.S. 251 (1931). Decided with it was O'Gorman & Young v. Phoenix Assurance Co., Ltd.

118. *Id.* at 270.

119. 285 U.S. 262 (1932).

120. Chap. 8, *supra*, pp. 219-21, text at notes 51-55.

121. New State Ice Co. v. Liebmann, 285 U.S. at 278.

122. *Ibid.*

In 1925 domestic mechanical refrigeration had scarcely emerged from the experimental stage. Since that time, the production and consumption of ice manufactured for sale, far from diminishing, has steadily increased. In Oklahoma the mechanical household refrigerator is still an article of luxury.[123]

. . . .

The business of supplying ice is not only a necessity, like that of supplying food or clothing or shelter, but the legislature could also consider that it is one which lends itself peculiarly to monopoly.[124]

The economics of the ice business, that accounts for this disposition toward monopoly, is then succinctly explained.

That these forces were operative in Oklahoma prior to the passage of the Act under review, is apparent from the record. Thus, it was testified that in only six or seven localities in the State containing, in the aggregate, not more than 235,000 of the total population of approximately 2,000,000, was there "a semblance of competition"; and that even in those localities the prices of ice were ordinarily uniform. The balance of the population was, and still is, served by companies enjoying complete monopoly. Compare *Munn* v. *Illinois*, 94 U.S. 113, 131, 132; *Sinking Fund Cases*, 99 U.S. 700, 747; *Wabash, St. L. & P. Ry. Co.* v. *Illinois*, 118 U.S. 557, 569; *Spring Valley Water Works* v. *Schottler*, 110 U.S. 347, 354; *Budd v. New York*, 143 U.S. 517, 545; *Wolff Co.* v. *Industrial Court*, 262 U.S. 522, 528.[125]

Whatever the merits in this economic debate, the significant fact is that *all* the Justices had now committed themselves unreservedly to the monopoly test for adjudication of cases raising the constitutional issue of government power to legislate maxima in instances of private pricing.

New State Ice served to resolve the question of governmental pricing power with respect to the ginning of cotton. To the contention that ice production was a business "affected with a public interest" on analogy to cotton ginning, the majority of the Court inquired "with some particularity" into the characteristics of the business of cotton ginning "in order to put them in contrast with the completely unlike circumstances which attend the business of manufacturing, selling and distributing ice."[126] In stating in its own words, in contrasting paragraphs, the differences in the two situations[127] much reliance was placed upon the seriatim opinions of three circuit judges in the recently decided case of *Chickasha Cotton Oil Co.* v. *Cotton County Gin Co.*[128]

---

123. *Id.* at 289-90.
124. *Id.* at 291.
125. *Id.* at 293. Note the list of cases to be "compared." Save for *Wolff*, they are the earlier decisions in which substantive due process operates as a sword against private monopoly, beginning with *Munn*. Omission of *Brass v. Stoeser* suggests that Brandeis and Stone now regarded it as a "black sheep."
126. *Id.* at 277.
127. *Id.* at 276-77.
128. 40 F. 2d 846 (C.C.A. 10th, 1930).

While the three lower court judges were agreed that cotton ginning was so in the public interest as to support legislation of the same type as that challenged in *New State Ice*,[129] their reasoning to this result varied. It was Judge Phillips who summarized the Record that disclosed facts strikingly like those in *Brass v. Stoeser*[130] although that decision was not cited.[131] In Eastern Oklahoma "the farmers do not have convenient access to more than one gin." In the Western part of the State gins were more numerous, farmers employed trucks for haulage, transport for greater distances gave them access to more than one gin. Yet as of the date of enactment of the regulatory law, cotton farmers as a class could not afford their own gins, "a large proportion of the cotton communities had convenient access to only one gin," and "there was very little competition in price."[132] From these facts Judge Phillips concluded:

> I think it plainly appears that a cotton gin operator renders an indispensable service and, in the average cotton growing community, enjoys a practical monopoly, and that regulation of prices and service are [sic] necessary in order to afford cotton farmers good ginning at fair prices.
>
> It follows then that the business of cotton ginning falls within that class of businesses which render a necessary and indispensable public service, which must enjoy a practical monopoly, absent regulation, in order to operate without economic waste, and which must be regulated in order to protect the patrons against exorbitant prices for poor and inadequate service.[133]

In the momentous year of 1937, indeed during the 168 days that the Roosevelt Court Bill was before Congress and the Nation, the Supreme Court had before it once again, in *Townsend v. Yeomans*,[134] the validity of state fixation of maximum rates for a product of private enterprise. Functionally, the fact pattern was akin to that in *Tagg Bros.* Undisputed findings of the three-judge federal district court were to the effect that the tobacco warehousemen of Georgia were organized as The Tobacco Warehousemen's Association, and that "through the Warehousemen's Association and their 'common agreement' as to charges the complainants 'maintain and enjoy a virtual monopoly in the field covered by their operations'. . . . "[135] Of the three items composing warehouse charges, the state law reduced two from the levels obtaining prior to governmental intervention. The lower court dismissed complainants' bill to

---

129. Both cases involved Oklahoma legislation.

130. 153 U.S. 391 (1894), first considered in the text at notes 5-10, chap. 5, *supra*, pp. 80-82. Note also references to *Brass* earlier in the present chapter.

131. Possibly the omission was the consequence of the decision's unsteady history; *cf.* note 125, *supra*. Yet it was included in the string of *Munn*-controlled cases in *Townsend*, *infra* note 134.

132. Chickasha Cotton Oil Co. v. Cotton County Gin Co., *supra* note 128, at 850.

133. *Ibid.*

134. 301 U.S. 441 (1937).

135. *Id.* at 448.

restrain enforcement of the statute. The Supreme Court unanimously affirmed in record time—20 days from argument to decision.

The pith of the reasoning was that:

> [O]ur rulings are decisive in support of the state action. *Munn* v. *Illinois*, 94 U.S. 113; *Budd* v. *New York*, 143 U.S. 517; *Brass* v. *Stoeser*, 153 U.S. 391; *German Alliance Insurance Co.* v. *Lewis*, 233 U.S. 389; *O'Gorman & Young* v. *Hartford Insurance Co.*, 282 U.S. 251; *Nebbia* v. *New York*, 291 U.S. 502.
>
> Confiscation is not shown. The presumption of reasonableness has not been overthrown. *O'Gorman & Young* v. *Hartford Insurance Co.*, *supra*. It is apparent that the return to the warehousemen will largely be governed by the volume and value of the tobacco crop. The evidence relates chiefly to the years of the great depression and affords no appropriate criterion for a more normal period. Moreover, we find no sufficient ground for disturbing the finding of the District Court that the evidence did not satisfactorily establish what any warehouseman, individual or corporate, lost by reason of the prescribed scale of charge in contradistinction to its effect upon the warehousemen as a group. See *Aetna Insurance Co.* v. *Hyde*, 275 U.S. 440, 447, 448. The burden resting upon appellants to make a convincing showing that the statutory rates would operate so severely as to deprive them, respectively, of their property without due process of law, was not sustained.[136]

This passage in the unanimous opinion by Chief Justice Hughes is of unusual significance. The first portion of the quotation has a familiar ring to it up to the final citation. In the second portion the Court's concern is the defensive one of whether private property has been taken in violation of Due Process as shield. Absence of a showing of confiscation establishes that there has occurred no invalid deprivation of private property. Expropriation as a denial of due process has been considered earlier in this study; the paragraph is included at this point for contrast with the Court's continued resort to the concept of Due Process as sword. For the affirmative base sustaining the Georgia statute is the *Munn* rule. The intervening decision in *Nebbia*,[137] upholding state minimum price fixing for fluid milk, is tacked onto the string of citations to four of the applications of *Munn*, including *Brass v. Stoeser* but curiously omitting *Tagg Bros*.

Citing several of the Court's decisions invalidating maximum price fixing for lack of satisfying evidence of monopolistic conditions, counsel for Nebbia had boldly asserted in his Brief: "The Statute and Order in question cannot be upheld unless the Federal Constitution has undergone profound changes since

---

136. *Id.* at 450-51. Paragraphs following in the opinion dispose of the contention regarded by the Court as the major one, that the Georgia statute conflicted with congressional authority under the Commerce Clause.

137. Nebbia v. New York, 291 U.S. 502 (1934), earlier cited note 50, p. 271, and its impact stressed in chap. 6, *supra*, pp. 103-04. The Supreme Court affirmed the New York court of appeals by a vote of five to four. The dissent, again of the "gang of four," is considered in chap. 7, *supra*, p. 160.

[those decisions]."[138] *Williams v. Standard Oil Co.* was singled out as "[a]lmost identical on its facts."[139] Granting that New York State faced a serious imbalance between supply and demand in fluid milk, aggravated by the Great Depression, counsel insisted that *Wolff* had rejected the thesis that emergency could be a source of state power.[140] The earlier emergency housing laws sustained in *Block* and *Brown* were explained as barely within constitutional limits. Those decisions

> ...undoubtedly went to the very limit of the police power. They were based upon a shortage of houses and a multitude of persons anxious for housing, which allowed a grasping landlord to victimize the tenant for his own profit. The statutes which penalize forestalling, engrossing, usury, and combining to restrain trade express the same policy.[141]
>
> At the opposite extreme is the statute now before the Court. With the State of New York flooded with wholesome milk, the Legislature and Milk Control Board purport to fine and jail anyone who sells it to the public below the price set by order. There is a certain grammatical symmetry in the statement that if a Legislature can provide for fixing a maximum price for houses it can provide for fixing a minimum price for milk; but the resemblance between the two is purely verbal.[142]

The Brief for Nebbia reflected an assurance that reversal of the adverse judgment below would occur.

Faced with the strong Brief supporting Nebbia's challenge of the Milk Control Act and the Order of the Milk Control Board thereunder, counsel for the State pitched much of defense under the umbrella of the public utility analogy. Early in the State's Brief appear statements that the milk distribution business shows monopolistic tendencies.[143] For these, reference is made to the Pitcher Report resulting from inquiry by a legislatively-authorized investigative committee named for its chairman. Point II of the Brief asserts in bold type "The distribution of milk is a business of such nature as to justify the application to it of some of the forms of regulation ordinarily applied to a public utility."[144] Under this heading *Fairmont*, *Williams*, and *New State Ice*, on which Nebbia's Brief relied, are distinguished as having less of the characteristics of the public utility concept.[145] Although noting that "[t]he public utility concept in this

---

138. 27 P. KURLAND and G. CASPER, BRIEFS AND ARGUMENTS OF THE SUPREME COURT OF THE UNITED STATES: CONSTITUTIONAL LAW 674 (1975).

139. *Id.* at 676.

140. *Id.* at 691-93.

141. Note the insightful reference to "forestalling" and "engrossing" and to "combining to restrain trade." It was out of these concepts that American courts built the constitutional principle of monopoly by private contract as impugned by substantive due process, for consideration of which refer to chap. 4, *supra*.

142. Brief for Nebbia, Nebbia v. New York, 291 U.S. at 509.

143. 27 P. KURLAND and G. CASPER, *op. cit. supra* note 138, at 713, 714, 715.

144. *Id.* at 735.

145. *Id.* at 737-38.

country traces back to *Munn* v. *Illinois*...,"[146] a disregard of the different constitutional bases for maximum and minimum public pricing enabled counsel to cite in support of the latter the then recent decision of *Public Service Comm. v. Great Northern Utilities Co.*[147] wherein the Montana commission was sustained in setting a specific minimum rate to resolve a price-cutting war between two local public utilities.

At the end of the Brief is still another suggestion that the milk business can in certain circumstances behave monopolistically.[148] Incorporated into the Brief as an Appendix is an analysis of the "Constitutionality of Regulating Milk as a Public Utility" by Henry Manley,[149] counsel to the Milk Control Board, ultimately published in the Cornell Law Quarterly.[150] In the analysis appears this passage in further support of the analogy of the New York law fixing minimum prices for fluid milk to monopolistic conditions that are always a feature of the public utility.

> The milk business operates in such a way as to attain its greatest efficiency as a monopoly, and has the tendency to become one. This is not to say that it is now being monopolized in New York State; on the contrary the milk business appears to be engaged in one of those expensive and destructive struggles by which monopoly comes into being. In other states the tendency of the milk busines to monopoly has been observed. The dairy companies of Colorado successfully challenged the anti-trust law of that state, because it was too vague in terms. [Citation] Minnesota faiied in its attempt to regulate unfair competition in cream buying because it did not, or could not, put into the record evidence as to how the competition operated and how its statute would curb it. [Citation] In New York State in the past the milk business has shown its monopolistic tendencies more obviously than at the present time, and it should be possible for the Legislature to act upon that experience, in reasonable anticipation of evils to come, without exposing the citizens of this State to a complete repetition of them.[151]

The Supreme Court was badly split in *Nebbia v. New York*. The prevailing opinion, sustaining the legislative cure for the existing predicament, was written by Justice Roberts, a relative newcomer to the Court who therefore had

---

146. *Id.* at 741.

147. 289 U.S. 130 (1933).

148. 27 P. KURLAND and G. CASPER, *op. cit. supra* note 138, at 747.

149. *Id.* at 749-62.

150. Manley, *Constitutionality of Regulating Milk as a Public Utility*, 18 CORN. L. Q. 410 (1933).

151. 27 P. KURLAND and G. CASPER *op. cit. supra* note 138, at 759-60. The two citations within the quoted passage, not here renumbered are

   [18]Cline v. Frink Dairy Co., 274 U.S. 445, 47 Sup. Ct. 681 (1927).

   [19]Fairmount Creamery Co. v. Minn., 274 U.S. 1, 47 Sup. Ct. 506 (1927); cf. State v. Central Lumber Co., 226 U.S. 157, 33 Sup. Ct. 66 (1912) and O'Gorman & Young v. Hartford F. Ins. Co., 282 U.S. 251, 51 Sup. Ct. 130 (1931).

The identical passage appears in Manley, *supra* note 150, at 416-17.

had little exposure to the issue of legislative power with respect to price regulation. This minimum familiarity is disclosed in the lengthy paragraph that keys the decision.

We may as well say at once that the dairy industry is not, in the accepted sense of the phrase, a public utility. We think the appellant is also right in asserting that there is in this case no suggestion of any monopoly or monopolistic practice.... The thought seems nevertheless to have persisted that there is something peculiarly sacrosanct about the price one may charge for what he makes or sells, and that, however able to regulate other elements of manufacture or trade, with incidental effect upon price, the state is incapable of directly controlling the price itself. This view was negatived many years ago. *Munn v. Illinois*, 94 U.S. 113. The appellant's claim is, however, that this court, in there sustaining a statutory prescription of charges for storage by the proprietors of a grain elevator, limited permissible legislation of that type to businesses affected with a public interest, and he says no business is so affected except it have one or more of the characteristics he enumerates. But this is a misconception. Munn and Scott held no franchise from the state. They owned the property upon which their elevator was situated and conducted their business as private citizens. No doubt they felt at liberty to deal with whom they pleased and on such terms as they might deem just to themselves. Their enterprise could not fairly be called a monopoly, although it was referred to in the decision as a "virtual monopoly." This meant only that their elevator was strategically situated and that a large portion of the public found it highly inconvenient to deal with others. This court concluded the circumstances justified the legislation as an exercise of the governmental right to control the business in the public interest; that is, as an exercise of the police power. It is true that the court cited a statement from Lord Hale's *De Portibus Maris*, to the effect that when private property is "affected with a public interest, it ceases to be *juris privati* only"; but the court proceeded at once to define what it understood by the expression, saying: "Property does become clothed with a public interest when used in a manner to make it of public consequence, and affect the community at large" (p. 126). Thus understood, "affected with a public interest" is the equivalent of "subject to the exercise of the police power"; and it is plain that nothing more was intended by the expression.[152]

In this paragraph are some mighty peculiar statements of law or fact. Those on the Brief for the State, who struggled so valiantly to disclose monopolistic elements in the fluid milk business, must have been surprised at the second statement of the passage. So also of the later assertion that the factual situation found in *Munn* "could not fairly be called a monopoly, although it was referred to in the decision as a 'virtual monopoly.' " Most astonishing is the reading of Lord Hale and the interpretation of the holding in *Munn*. True, James Carter in his Brief in *Smythe v. Ames* had suggested such reasoning[153] but it is clear from the subsequent judicial history of *Munn* that the Court had

---

152. Nebbia v. New York, 291 U.S. at 531-33.
153. For the Carter proposed reading, refer back to the text accompanying note 12, chap. 5, *supra*, p. 82.

never paid it heed. If that was what Chief Justice Waite meant by the expression, a distinguished line of later Justices wasted endless time determining the presence or absence of monopoly from *Budd* through *Townsend*. Justice Roberts completely mistook the contemporary thrust of *Munn v. Illinois*; in his defense it can only be said that he has had plenty of scholarly company in this error. To understand correctly that major decision in light of the decisional trail it blazed, he should have realized that the matter of monopoly was irrelevant to the issue of governmental power to set minimum prices; whether monopoly obtained in a given factual pattern was relevant only to maximum price fixation, as Brandeis, Stone, and even other Justices had come to appreciate.

What the *Nebbia* litigation required for adequate resolution of the issue before the Court was identification of an analogical principle for those situations in which monopoly's extreme opposite is present. Such situations would include those where competition is not operating constructively, where demand and supply are out of stable equilibrium and economic forces are proving unequal to the task of correcting the impasse. In short, where there was too much competition, as contrasted with too little. *Public Service Comm. v. Great Northern Utilities Co.*,[154] the unanimous decision by Justice Butler surely still fresh in the judicial mind, furnished a building block. *Stephenson v. Binford*,[155] which at the close of his opinion Justice Roberts links with *Public Service* as providing precedent for state "fixing of minimum prices" is only tangentially supportive but might command a "Cf."[156]

The explanation must be that the majority in *Nebbia* were after "bigger game" than that of establishing as firm a constitutional base for legislative regulation of minimum prices as had long obtained for maximum price fixation by government. It has been a truism with constitutional commentators, I included,[157] that *Nebbia v. New York* dealt *Lochner v. New York* a mortal blow. Care must be taken, however, to appreciate what *Nebbia* technically did to *Lochner*, in order to differentiate its impact from later denunciations of *Lochner* and its progeny. *Nebbia* removed from constitutional law the reading of freedom of contract into substantive due process of law, replacing this miscon-

---

154. 289 U.S. 130 (1933), cited *supra* note 147.

155. 287 U.S. 251 (1932).

156. These two decisions did have their limitations for use as building blocks. Both involved minimum prices for public utilities, traditionally subject to greater governmental regulation than the independent category of the common run of private corporations. In the law a "public utility" has always been regarded as a hybrid—half private, half public. Secondly, the central issue in *Stephenson* was whether it could be distinguished from Frost Trucking Co. v. Railroad Comm., 271 U.S. 583 (1926), that had invalidated a California Act which as construed by the supreme court of the State transformed contract motor carriers into common carriers by legislative fiat. The cases constitute a special sub-category within the general class of legislative expropriations.

157. Strong, *The Economic Philosophy of Lochner*, 15 ARIZ. L. REV. 419, 435 (1973).

struction with the litmus test of nexus that had served to sustain, in *Holden v. Hardy*,[158] the Utah reduction of hours in smelting and underground mining. This new test was no more derivative from historic substantive due process than was liberty of contract; but in degree of perversion, if gradations may be made in extent of error, it was far more palatable.[159]

The new test of "reasonable relation to a proper legislative purpose" provided affirmative basis for sustainment of governmental fixing of minimum prices. For maximum price regulation the litmus test of nexus was not inconsistent with the previous monopoly test, as *Townsend* attests. Moreover, the overrulings by *Olsen v. Nebraska*[160] and *Gold v. DiCarlo*[161] were more corrections in application of the rule of *Munn* than outright rejections. *Olsen* in effect substituted for the majority opinion in *Ribnik v. McBride* the dissenting opinion of Justice Stone. Even though by 1941 there was competition from public employment agencies, evidence continued of some of the abuses formerly found with private agencies. The *Tyson* ruling that maximum price fixation of ticket brokers was invalid went on the shelf when in *Gold* the Court affirmed the lower federal court *per curiam*.[162] Yet what transpired was but another substitution of Stone dissenting that time from a majority opinion based on mistaken facts. In *Gold* as in *Tyson* the question was the constitutionality of maximum pricing with respect to ticket brokers vending theater tickets for plays on Broadway and off. The lower court had found that the abuses of the late 20s had not disappeared in the early 60s.[163] As with the rumor of Mark Twain's death, any report of the demise of the rule of *Munn* would be highly exaggerated. At most it has but been absorbed into the more embracive nexus test.

Against Union Monopoly

Indeed, the predicate of *Munn*, that private monopoly is offensive to substantive due process and therefore cannot withstand legislative attack employing due process as sword, reappeared in the very decision that reconfirmed *Nebbia* by repudiating *Lochner* and its progeny by name. This decision was

---

158. 169 U.S. 366 (1899), considered textually at notes 1-4 in chap. 5, *supra*, pp. 79-80.

159. The role of *Nebbia* in the "reform" of *Lochner* is described earlier in text accompanying notes 56-62, chap. 6, *supra*, pp. 103-05.

160. 313 U.S. 236 (1941).

161. 380 U.S. 520 (1965).

162. *Id.*, affirming Gold v. DiCarlo, 235 F. Supp. 817, at 820 (S.D.N.Y. 1964). Note two important changes in the restatement. *Rational* relationship is substituted for *reasonable*; "permissible objective" is preceded by the adverb "constitutionally." Comment on these changes is made in chap. 6, *supra*, pp. 105-06.

163. Gold v. DiCarlo, 235 F. Supp. at 820-21.

Lincoln Federal Labor Union v. Northwestern Iron & Metal Co.,[164] decided after *Olsen* but prior to *DiCarlo*. Litigated was the constitutionality of the right-to-work laws of Nebraska and North Carolina; the fate of this type of legislation depended upon a determination of legislative power to outlaw the closed shop as a device for union security. The underlying issue was again that of the constitutional status of private monopoly power, for the closed shop means union monopoly in the labor market. Unembarrassed by invoking the previously detested *Adair* and *Coppage* decisions,[165] the union now relied upon them as precedent for invalidation under substantive due process of state (and therefore federal) legislation allowing industrial workers freedom to choose between unionism and disassociation.

The unanimous response of the Court, in a crisp opinion by Justice Black, was unequivocal:

> This court beginning at least as early as 1934, when the *Nebbia* case was decided, has steadily rejected the due process philosophy enunciated in the *Adair-Coppage* line of cases....
>
> Appellants now ask us to return, at least in part, to the due process philosophy that has been deliberately discarded. Claiming that the Federal Constitution itself affords protection for union members against discrimination, they nevertheless assert that the same Constitution forbids a state from providing the same protection for non-union members. Just as we have held that the due process clause erects no obstacle to block legislative protection of union members, we now hold that legislative protection can be afforded non-union workers.[166]

Lincoln Federal is a watershed in labor law. Rejected are the decisions of the *Lochner* era that had given irrevocable sanctity to employer imposition of the open shop by setting the Constitution against unionization. Rejected at the same time is the contention that the Constitution enshrines the closed shop in a protective mantle impervious to legislative alteration. The resulting fact of great economic significance is that legislative choice of policy is present in labor-management relations. This condition obtains because private monopoly in the labor market, whether sought by Capital or by Labor, is hostage to substantive due process of law as sword.

Compulsory unionism continues to be a hotly contested issue in labor-management relations,[167] not only in the United States but elsewhere.[168] Right-to-

---

164. 335 U.S. 525 (1949).

165. Considered in chap. 6, *supra*, p. 97, text at notes 16-21.

166. Lincoln Federal Labor Union v. Northwestern Iron & Metal Co., 335 U.S. at 536-37. On the basis of *Lincoln Federal* the Court simultaneously sustained an amendment to the constitution of Arizona constituting a right-to-work enactment. American Federation of Labor v. American Sash & Door Co., 335 U.S. 538 (1949).

167. An extensive examination of the contest over compulsory unionism of forty years ago, condensed from a master's thesis prepared under the supervision of Dr. Harry Wolf, Professor of Labor Law, and Judge Warren Madden, former Chairman of the NLRB, Uni-

work laws have been vigorously denounced[169] and strongly justified.[170] Louis Brandeis, implacable foe of monopoly that he was, opposed the closed shop; "the American people should not, and will not, accept unionism if it involves the closed shop. They will not consent to the exchange of the tyranny of the employee."[171] Yet his sympathy for trade unionism led him to endorse the preferential shop[172] which it has been observed could amount to a closed shop were the hiring hall to be partial to union members in recommendations made to employers.[173] For Frank Porter Graham, liberal though he was, a union shop was unacceptable because it constituted a "private monopoly."[174]

Under the Wagner Act closed shops were legal and quite prevalent. By implication from § 8(a) (3), Taft-Hartley nullified that ideal of union security. On the other hand, the subsection tolerated the union shop, by which employers may hire nonunion workers but continued employment after a grace period is conditioned upon union membership. However, the Supreme Court's interpretation in *NLRB v. General Motors Corp.*[175] of the term "membership" as "whittled down to its financial core" contemplates only an agency shop unless a union in negotiating a collective bargaining agreement has the clout to force upon the employer a greater degree of union security. In the agency shop the employees' only obligation is to contribute in money payments an amount equal to the cost of full union membership.

Adding insult to injury in Labor's view, § 14(b) of Taft-Hartley authorizes states to enact right-to-work laws that permit prohibition of even "the initiation fees and dues obligations of agency shops," thus enabling nonunion members to be "free riders" while enjoying representation by the union. *Retail*

versity of North Carolina, is found in Hammond, *The Closed Shop in World War II*, 21 N.C.L.REV. 127 (1945).

168. C. HANSON, S. JACKSON, and D. MILLER, THE CLOSED SHOP (1981) (Great Britain, United States, West Germany).

169. Pollitt, *Right to Work Law Issues; An Evidentiary Approach*, 37 N.C.L. REV. 233 (1959).

170. W. HARRISON, THE TRUTH ABOUT RIGHT-TO-WORK LAWS (1959). Greater objectivity is found in Eissinger, *The Right-to-Work Imbroglio*, 51 N.D.L. REV. 571 (1975). C. HANSON, S. JACKSON, and D. MILLER, *op. cit. supra* note 168, Part III, provides a considerable bibliography of U.S. references. Contentions pro and con are set out by P. Hunt, *Right to Work: An Overview*, Major Studies of the Cong. Res. Serv., Microfilm, Reel 1 (1975).

171. Frankfurter, J., in concurrence in A.F. of L. v. American Sash & Door Co., 335 U.S. at 551, quoting from a letter by Brandeis to Lincoln Steffens.

172. L. BRANDEIS, THE CURSE OF BIGNESS 94-95 (Fraenkel ed. 1965).

173. C. HANSON, S. JACKSON, and D. MILLER, *op. cit. supra* note 168, at 122.

174. P. SULTAN, RIGHT-TO-WORK LAWS 45 (1958). The similar views of Charles Wyzanski and Franklin Roosevelt are noted *id.* at 45, 46. Opponents of unionism were wont to attack it as "a vicious monopoly." *Id.* at 62.

175. 373 U.S. 734 (1963).

Clerks v. Schermerhorn.[176] In effect § 14(b) shelters the right-to-work laws of the states that have enacted them. Despite vigorous union effort, this legislative pattern so offensive to organized labor has not been altered. State right-to-work provisions remain in most of the jurisdictions where once adopted, for a total of nineteen jurisdictions or near forty per cent of the country; and *Lincoln Federal* stands intact.

One investigation concludes that in generality right-to-work laws have not made much difference.[177] On the other hand, there are specific instances where presence or absence has had economic or political implications. John Bricker of Ohio accounted for his loss of a seat in the United States Senate by reason of his support (unsuccessful) for a right-to-work law in that State. In the Kansas City area the boundary line between Kansas and Missouri runs due south from the point where the Kansas River flows into the Missouri. In the open countryside southward beyond present full urbanization much greater commercial and industrial development is occurring on the Kansas side. It is said thereabouts that in part this is because Kansas has a right-to-work law whereas Missouri does not.[178]

Lincoln Federal surfaced in *Exxon Corp. v. Governor of Maryland*[179] as a citation supporting the validity of the Maryland statute forbidding a producer or refiner of petroleum products to operate a company service station within the State. However, the reference appears in a paragraph of the opinion in which Exxon's reliance on substantive due process as shield is rejected on the authority of *Ferguson v. Skrupa.*[180] It is said the contention that divestiture "will frustrate rather than further the State's desired goal of enhancing competition" speaks to the wisdom of the statute "and cannot override the State's authority 'to legislate against what are found to be injurious practices in their internal commercial and business affairs. . . .' *Lincoln Federal Labor Union v. Northwestern Iron & Metal Co.*, 335 U.S. 525, 536." Continuing in this vein the paragraph ends with the statement that whatever "the ultimate economic efficacy of the statute, we have no hesitancy in concluding that it bears a reasonable relation to the State's legitimate purpose in controlling the gasoline retail market, and we therefore reject appellants' due process claim."[181]

This mode of resolution of constitutional challenge is typical of resort to the nexus test into which substantive due process was transformed by *Nebbia* and its sequel.[182] Such usage of *Lincoln Federal* misses its central teaching that the

---

176. 373 U.S. 746 (1963).
177. C. HANSON, S. JACKSON, and D. MILLER, *op. cit. supra* note 168, at 172-75.
178. Tarpy, *Home to Kansas*, 168 NAT. GEOGRAPHIC 352, at 365 (1985).
179. 437 U.S. 117 (1978).
180. 372 U.S. 726 (1963), in which the Court presided at the attempted burial of substantive due process as shield. The "funeral" is depicted in chap. 6, *supra*, p. 109.
181. Exxon Corp. v. Governor of Maryland, 437 U.S. at 124-25.
182. Examined in chap. 6, *supra*, text commencing note 56, p. 103.

Constitution enshrines no right of monopoly, which is to say that substantive due process is intolerant of monopolistic grip whatever the private claimant. Justice Stevens who wrote the *Exxon* opinion may have had some intimation of this in appending to the citation of *Lincoln Federal* a footnote declaring it is

> worth noting that divestiture is by no means a novel method of economic regulation, and is found in both federal and state statutes. To date, the courts have had little difficulty sustaining such statutes against a substantive due process attack. See, e.g., *Paramount Pictures, Inc. v. Langer*, 23 F. Supp. 890 (N.D. 1938), dismissed as moot, 306 U.S. 619; see generally, Comment, Gasoline Marketing Practices and "Meeting Competition" under the Robinson-Patman Act, 37 Md. L. Rev. 323, 329 n. 44 (1977).[183]

True, the second sentence makes it clear that the Justice is thinking of substantive due process in its familiar role as shield against deprivation of private property interests. It is also true that the attack on the North Dakota prohibition of ownership of exhibiting theaters by motion picture producers and distributors was similarly couched. However, the federal district court of three judges that sustained the North Dakota law in *Paramount Pictures* felt disposition of the challenge compelled it to look to what Court decisions there were on the constitutionality of divestiture statutes.

One such case was *Crescent Oil Co. v. Mississippi*.[184] The Anti-Gin Act of the State, forbidding corporate producers of cottonseed oil from owning cotton gins, was enacted assumedly "in aid of the Anti-Trust laws of the State," "to prevent a practice conceived to be promotive of monopoly with its attendant evils."[185] It was unsuccessfully challenged only on Commerce and Equal Protection grounds; conspicuous by its absence was attack under due process. Account was also taken of *United States v. Swift & Co.*[186] in which the Court had refused to allow modification of the celebrated consent decree originally approved in *Swift & Co. v. United States*[187] whereunder the Sherman Act was construed to require the Big Five meat packers to divest themselves of trading in the wholesaling or retailing of groceries. While under the decree the packers did not confess violation of any federal law, the fact remained that monopoly through vertical integration was lawfully destroyed without any hindrance from substantive due process of law.

---

183. Exxon Corp. v. Governor of Maryland, 437 U.S. at 124-25, n. 13. The Comment in the Maryland Law Review refers to other instances of vertical divestiture. Cited for fuller treatment could have been Cook, *Legislative Restrictions on Marketing Integration*, 8 LAW & CONTEMP. PROBS. 273 (1941); Note, 28 VAND. L. REV. 1277, 1292-98 (1975).
184. 257 U.S. 129 (1921).
185. *Id.* at 133, 137.
186. 286 U.S. 106 (1932).
187. 276 U.S. 311 (1928).

The court of appeals of Maryland, whose sustainment of the state divestiture law against assertion of violation of Due Process,[188] was affirmed in *Exxon Corp.*, was nearer on point for observing that "[e]xclusion of producers and refiners may conceivably be a reasonable means of preserving competition and preventing monopolistic control of gasoline marketing by a few large oil companies."[189] Admittedly, there is nowhere an affirmative recognition of substantive due process as sword, and the slender reed of a possibly insightful footnote[190] receives no support from the context in which *Lincoln Federal* is cited in *New Motor Vehicle Board v. Orrin W. Fox Co.*[191] The Court is too wrapped up in its continuing determination to deflate substantive due process as a shield of property rights to accord currency to the precedent of *Munn v. Illinois* and its modern counterpart of *Lincoln Federal Labor Union v. Northwestern Iron & Metal Co.*

Potentiality for Land Reform of Affirmative Due Process in Challenges to Resource Monopolization

Experience of substantive due process as sword in applications to Capital and Labor combinations suggests a potency sharply contrasting with the distain for substantive due process in its traditional hostility toward governmental taking and governmental monopoly. Judicial sustainment of the forced breakup of Ma Bell demonstrates the continuing vitality of Court decisions implementing opposition to private aggregations of concentrated power in the marketplace, by whomever achieved. Implications of this stance for land reform are readily apparent. For numerous nations around the world the major blockage to economic development lies in maldistribution of land ownership, essentially a condition of monopoly with respect to the most basic factor of production. Fortunately, the continental United States is not burdened with this economic bondage, although there are critics who see in current trends evidence of drift toward such a condition.[192] Nevertheless, this bondage does obtain close to home, in one of the fifty States and in a nearby country possessing unique ties with the American Union.

---

188. Governor of Maryland v. Exxon Corp., 279 Md. 410, 370 A. 2d 1102 (1977).

189. *Id.* at 427, 370 A. 2d at 1112.

190. Refer back to note 183. Appeal of the lower court decisions in *Paramount Pictures* was dismissed as moot by the Supreme Court because meantime the North Dakota law had been repealed by N. D. Laws 1939, chap. 202. One can wonder whether the Court, had the merits been open, would have treated substantive due process as sword in view of the fact that the date of appeal came only two years after *Townsend v. Yeomans*, the last of the price fixing cases rested on *Munn v. Illinois*.

191. 439 U.S. 96, 107 (1978).

192. *Cf.* P. BARNES, THE PEOPLE'S LAND INTRO. (1975).

The issue of constitutionality of agrarian reform first reached American courts from Puerto Rico. Some forty-five years ago the legislative branch of the Puerto Rican government enacted a Land Law authorizing a far-reaching program of revision of landholdings, looking to the atomization of large estates with transfer of small parcels to the landless. Proceedings were instituted to condemn land on the Island of Vieques held by Eastern Sugar Associates, producers of sugar cane. Associates resisted, relying upon the Organic Act of Puerto Rico which contained limitations of due process and eminent domain paralleling the prohibitions of the Fifth Amendment. The issue was decided by the court of appeals of the first circuit, with certiorari denied by the Supreme Court.[193] The intermediate appellate court found that the social and economic conditions on the Island justified the condemnation as one for a definitely public purpose under eminent domain. Due process was cited for the general rule forbidding the taking of property for transfer to another, but the purpose of the reference was to stress the necessity of satisfying the test of "publicness" for taking consistent with constitutional limitation.

Recently the High Court has addressed the constitutional question in full opinion. Under attack was Hawaii's Land Reform Act of 1967. The enactment envisaged agrarian reform to free land ownership from the feudal land tenure system introduced by the original Polynesian immigrants to the Islands, a system strikingly akin to the European Feudalism of the Middle Ages. The court of appeals for the ninth circuit had viewed that Act as "a naked attempt on the part of Hawaii to take the private property of A and transfer it to B solely for B's private use and benefit."[194] Reversing,[195] the unanimous Court had this to say through Justice O'Connor.

> Regulating oligopoly and evils associated with it is a classic exercise of a State's police powers. See *Exxon Corp. v. Governor of Maryland* . . . ; *Block v. Hirsh* . . . ; see also *People of Puerto Rico v. Eastern Sugar Associates.* . . .[196]

In neither the Puerto Rican nor the Hawaiian decision was there any hint of reliance on substantive due process as sword. Justice O'Connor is as concerned as was Judge Woodbury that the land transfers constituted a *public* purpose, thus conforming to the requirement for exertion of the power of eminent domain. Yet three times in the course of her opinion the Justice spoke of the "land oligopoly" problem that the Hawaii legislature sought to resolve. This is exactly the type of situation for governmental invocation of substantive due process as sword. Eminent domain is a general grant of power of government to take private property on two conditions; the objective must be genu-

---

193. People of Puerto Rico v. Eastern Sugar Associates, 156 F. 2d 316 (C.C.A. 1st, 1946), *cert. den.* 329 U.S. 772 (1946).

194. Midriff v. Tom, 702 F. 2d 788, at 798 (C.C.A. 9th, 1983).

195. Hawaii Housing Authority v. Midriff, 467 U.S. 229 (1984).

196. *Id.* at 242.

inely public and just compensation must be paid. Substantive due process as sword provides a specific authority to destroy monopoly with less, uncertain protections afforded those dislodged from their positions of advantage. Destruction of monopoly is by definition an exercise in substantive due process of law from which there is no shield!

Understandably, land reform has been thought of in terms of breakup of large landed estates, as illustrated in the instances from Hawaii and Puerto Rico. Yet with the twentieth century phenomenon of mass movement of population from countryside into the cities and environs, a different dimension of land scarcity is unfolding. Monopolistic-like patterns are emerging in land control at the county and municipal levels. A product largely of zoning, these appear on the surface as instances of public grants of exclusivity. However, the moving force in many is private jockeying for strategic position within or adjacent to a city's boundaries; zoning authorities are pressured to provide the instrumentation for privately engineered quasi-monopolistic configurations, much as was true of community zoning against blacks before *Buchanan v. Worley*[197] and *Shelley v. Kraemer*.[198]

In retrospect, *Moore v. City of East Cleveland*[199] may have been a reaction to this condition although unfortunately articulated through the *Roe* medium of noninterpretivism. The supreme court of New Jersey has moved closer to a view of substantive due process as underwriting an affirmative exercise of power. In the second *Mt. Laurel* decision[200] it restated in clear terms "the *Mount Laurel* doctrine" from its first encounter with exclusionary urban zoning.[201]

> Municipal land use regulations that conflict with the general welfare [broadly][202] defined abuse the police power and are unconstitutional. In particular, those regulations that do not provide the requisite opportunity for a fair share of the region's need for low and moderate income housing conflict with the general welfare and violate the state constitutional requirements of substantive due process and equal protection.[203]

---

197. 245 U.S. 60 (1917).

198. 334 U.S. 1 (1948).

199. 431 U.S. 494 (1977).

200. Mount Laurel II, 92 N.J. 158, 456 A. 2d 390 (1983).

201. Mount Laurel I, 67 N.J. 151, 336 A. 2d 713 (1975).

202. *I.e.*, defined to encompass not only citizens of a municipality but as well those residing outside the city within "the region that contributes to the housing demand" therein.

203. Mount Laurel II, 92 N.J. at 208-09, 456 A. 2d at 415.

About the Author

Frank Ransom Strong is an honor graduate (1929) of Yale College (Phi Beta Kappa) and the Yale Law School (The Order of the Coif). Between college and law school he was Instructor in Economics at the University of Delaware. Admitted to the Bars of Iowa and Ohio, he has spent his professional career in legal education and administration. His specialization in the study, research, and teaching of American Constitutional Law has covered fifty years and involved him in varied scholarly associations. These include law faculty appointments at Iowa, Ohio State, and North Carolina; visiting professorships at Duke, Cornell, Hastings, and Kansas; summer teaching at a number of other American law schools; faculty participation in the Salzburg Seminar in American Studies and the AALS Orientation Program in American Law; creative casebook editing and extensive writing in legal publications; and occasional consulting within the legal profession on issues of constitutional law. He holds the honorary degree of Doctor of Laws from two universities, N.C. Central and Ohio State, and continues association with the Ohio State University as Dean and Professor of Law, Emeritus; and with the University of North Carolina at Chapel Hill as Cary C. Boshamer University Distinguished Professor, Emeritus.

Index

(Cases indexed are those critically considered in text or footnote)